Lecture Notes in Computer Science 13700

More information about this series at https://link.springer.com/bookseries/558

Hans P. Reiser · Marcel Kyas (Eds.)

Secure IT Systems

27th Nordic Conference, NordSec 2022
Reykjavic, Iceland, November 30–December 2, 2022
Proceedings

Editors
Hans P. Reiser 🆔
Reykjavik University
Reykjavik, Iceland

Marcel Kyas 🆔
Reykjavik University
Reykjavik, Iceland

ISSN 0302-9743   ISSN 1611-3349 (electronic)
Lecture Notes in Computer Science
ISBN 978-3-031-22294-8   ISBN 978-3-031-22295-5 (eBook)
https://doi.org/10.1007/978-3-031-22295-5

This Springer imprint is published by the registered company Springer Nature Switzerland AG
The registered company address is: Gewerbestrasse 11, 6330 Cham, Switzerland

Preface

This volume contains the papers presented at the 27th Nordic Conference on Secure IT Systems (NordSec 2022). The conference was held from November 30 to December 2, 2022, in Reykjavik, Iceland.

The NordSec conference series started in 1996 with the aim of bringing together researchers and practitioners in computer security in the Nordic countries, thereby establishing a forum for discussion and cooperation between universities, industry, and computer societies. The NordSec conference series addresses a broad range of topics within IT security and privacy, and over the years it has developed into an international conference that takes place in the Nordic countries. NordSec is currently a key meeting venue for Nordic university teachers and students with research interests in information security and privacy.

NordSec 2022 received a record number of 89 submissions, of which 85 were considered valid submissions and were double-blind reviewed each by three members of the Program Committee (PC). After the reviewing phase, 20 papers were accepted for publication and included in the proceedings (an acceptance rate of 24%). Additionally, a poster session was organized to encourage further discussion, brainstorming, and networking on interesting topics of IT security.

We were honored to have two brilliant invited keynote speakers: Véronique Cortier from Loria, France, and Sigurður Emil Pálsson from the NATO Cooperative Cyber Defence Centre of Excellence.

We sincerely thank everyone involved in making this year's conference a success, including, but not limited to, the authors who submitted their papers, the presenters who contributed to the NordSec 2022 program, the PC members and additional reviewers for their thorough and constructive reviews, and EasyChair for their platform.

November 2022

Hans P. Reiser
Marcel Kyas

Organization

General Chair

Marcel Kyas   Reykjavik University, Iceland

Program Committee Chairs

Hans P. Reiser   Reykjavik University, Iceland
Marcel Kyas   Reykjavik University, Iceland

Website Chair

Stewart Sentanoe   University of Passau, Germany

Steering Committee

Mikael Asplund   Linköping University, Sweden
Aslan Askarov   Aarhus University, Denmark
Tuomas Aura   Aalto University, Finland
Karin Bernsmed   SINTEF ICT and Norwegian University of
                                Science and Technology, Norway
Billy Bob Brumley   Tampere University, Finland
Sonja Buchegger   KTH Royal Institute of Technology, Sweden
Mads Dam   KTH Royal Institute of Technology, Sweden
Bengt Carlsson   Blekinge Institute of Technology, Sweden
Simone Fischer-Huebner   Karlstad University, Sweden
Dieter Gollmann   Hamburg University of Technology, Germany
Nils Gruschka   University of Oslo, Norway
René Rydhof Hansen   Aalborg University, Denmark
Audun Jøsang   University of Oslo, Norway
Marcel Kyas   Reykjavik University, Iceland
Helger Lipmaa   University of Tartu, Estonia
Antonios Michalas   Tampere University, Finland
Katerina Mitrokotsa   Chalmers University of Technology, Sweden
Simin Nadjm-Tehrani   Linköping University, Sweden
Hanne Riis Nielson   Technical University of Denmark, Denmark
Hans P. Reiser   Reykjavik University, Iceland
Juha Röning   University of Oulu, Finland

Program Committee

Magnus Almgren	Chalmers University of Technology, Sweden
Mikael Asplund	Linköping University, Sweden
Stefan Axelsson	Stockholm University, Sweden
Musard Balliu	KTH Royal Institute of Technology, Sweden
Felipe Boeira	Linköping University, Sweden
Hai-Van Dang	Plymouth University, UK
Tassos Dimitriou	Computer Technology Institute, Greece, and Kuwait University, Kuwait
Nicola Dragoni	Technical University of Denmark, Denmark
Ulrik Franke	RISE, Sweden
Kristian Gjøsteen	Norwegian University of Science and Technology, Norway
Dieter Gollmann	Hamburg University of Technology, Germany
Nils Gruschka	University of Oslo, Norway
Mohammad Hamad	Technical University of Munich, Germany
Rene Rydhof Hansen	Aalborg University, Denmark
Martin Gilje Jaatun	SINTEF Digital, Norway
Meiko Jensen	Karlstad University, Sweden
Thomas Johansson	Lund University, Sweden
Ulf Kargén Linköping	University, Sweden
Ville Leppänen	University of Turku, Finland
Stefan Lindskog	SINTEF Digital and Karlstad University, Sweden
Olaf Maennel	Tallinn University of Technology, Estonia
Raimundas Matulevicius	University of Tartu, Estonia
Per Håkon Meland	SINTEF ICT, Norway
Antonis Michalas	Tampere University, Finland
Simin Nadjm-Tehrani	Linköping University, Sweden
Nils Nordbotten	Thales Norway and University of Oslo, Norway
Tomas Olovsson	Chalmers University of Technology, Sweden
Nicolae Paladi	CanaryBit AB and Lund University, Sweden
Arnis Paršovs	University of Tartu, Estonia
Shahid Raza	RISE SICS, Sweden
Einar Snekkenes	Norwegian University of Science and Technology, Norway
Nikola Tuveri	Tampere University, Finland
Emmanouil Vasilomanolakis	Technical University of Denmark, Denmark
Øyvind Ytrehus	University of Bergen, Norway

Additional Reviewers

Abasi-Amefon Affia
Amir M. Ahmadian
Alexandros Bakas
Mariia Bakhtina
Carlos Barreto
Christian Berger
Guillaume Bour
Gaurav Choudhary
Jacob Dexe
Edlira Dushku
Philipp Eichhammer
Eugene Frimpong
Dimitrios Georgoulia
Bjorn Greve
Gudmund Grov
Kaspar Hageman
Fredrik Heiding
Mubashar Iqbal

Håkon Jacobsen
Felix Klement
Antti Kolehmainen
Johannes Köstler
Chunlei Li
Ameer Mohammed
Danielle Morgan
Karl Norrman
Johannes Olegård
Danny Bøgsted Poulsen
Emanuel Regnath
Mari Seeba
Stewart Sentanoe
Madhusudan Singh
Andrea Skytterholm
Matvey Soloviev
Shreyas Srinivasa
Martin Strand

Additional Reviewers

Contents

Forensics

Privacy

On the Effectiveness of Intersection Attacks in Anonymous Microblogging

Sarah Abdelwahab Gaballah$^{(\boxtimes)}$ ⓘ, Lamya Abdullahⓘ, Minh Tung Tranⓘ,
Ephraim Zimmerⓘ, and Max Mühlhäuserⓘ

Telecooperation Lab (TK), Technical University of Darmstadt, Darmstadt, Germany
{gaballah,abdullah,max}@tk.tu-darmstadt.de,
minhtung.tran@stud.tu-darmstadt.de, zimmer@privacy-trust.tu-darmstadt.de

Abstract. Intersection attacks, which are popular traffic analysis attacks, have been extensively studied in anonymous point-to-point communication scenarios. These attacks are also known to be challenging threats to anonymous group communication, e.g., microblogging. However, it remains unclear how powerful these attacks can be, especially when considering realistic user communication behavior. In this paper, we study the effectiveness of intersection attacks on anonymous microblogging systems utilizing Twitter and Reddit datasets. Our findings show that the attacks are effective regardless of whether users post their messages under pseudonyms or publish them to topics without attaching identifiers. Additionally, we observed that attacks are feasible under certain settings despite increasing userbase size, communication rounds' length, cover traffic, or traffic delays.

Keywords: Anonymous communication · Traffic analysis · Intersection attacks · Microblogging

1 Introduction

Microblogging is one of the most popular forms of online social networking that attracts millions of users. Twitter, for example, is one of the leading microblogging services. It had approximately 290.5 million active users worldwide, monthly, in 2019, with a projected increase to over 340 million users by 2024 [9]. All the known microblogging services are based on a centralized architecture, that enables those systems to know everything about users' messages and interests [28]. These services may collect data about their users and sell or reveal this information to third parties such as governments. In fact, many services already do this, for example, Facebook said that it has produced data for 88% of the U.S. government requests [24]. This type of data disclosure could endanger many users, including political dissidents, human rights activists, and people who want to share sensitive information (e.g., about health problems, or sexual harassment experience, etc.). Therefore, many Anonymous Communication Systems (ACSs) have been proposed over recent years in order to conceal

H. P. Reiser and M. Kyas (Eds.): NordSec 2022, LNCS 13700, pp. 3–19, 2022.
https://doi.org/10.1007/978-3-031-22295-5_1

user's interests from the microblogging service providers, other users, and even a global adversary (e.g., an internet service provider, a government authority, or an intelligence agency) who can monitor the network communication, by means of hiding their metadata (e.g., who is communicating with whom, when, and how frequently they communicate). Some of these systems are specifically focused and designed towards social networking scenarios such as microblogging [1,4,8,10,15,16,20].

The vast majority of the existing ACSs are vulnerable to traffic analysis attacks [6]. Intersection attacks are one of the most common and powerful types of traffic analysis attacks [27]. This type of attack takes advantage of the change in the set of users participating in the system over time. An ACS initially might ensure that a user is not identifiable within a set of other users, which is called an anonymity set [21]. However, changes in the communication behaviors of users (e.g., online and offline time of participating users) will evolve and add up to further information for the adversary in order to reduce the anonymity set or even single out (i.e., de-anonymize) specific users. A potentially large anonymity set can be reduced over time just by monitoring, storing, and repeatedly intersecting the online status of participating users when new messages are exchanged. To deduce with absolute certainty that two users are communicating, the adversary usually needs to launch the attack for a long time [2]. While intersection attacks are deterministic, there is a probabilistic version. It is called statistical disclosure attacks, which enables an adversary to estimate the likelihood that a targeted sender was communicating with a specific recipient [12].

Intersection attacks are commonly used to link sender and recipient in anonymous point-to-point communication settings. These attacks, however, can also be applied to anonymous group communication scenarios, such as anonymous microblogging [27]. Because user messages are publicly published in the microblogging scenario, an adversary can leverage the use of the intersection attacks to link users to their published messages or topics of interest.

The existing literature has studied intersection attacks, statistical disclosure attacks, and suitable mitigation approaches to those attacks in ACSs extensively [2,7,12,14,23,25,27]. However, we identified several pitfalls that render those works incomplete under realistic communication scenarios. First, user communication behavior often is assumed to follow a Poisson distribution [17]. On the contrary, by utilizing real-world data collection, it has already been shown that realistic communication behavior does, in fact, not follow such a distribution [17]. The communication behavior, however, has a huge impact on the effectiveness of intersection attacks as well as on mitigation measures, as will be shown in the remainder of this paper. Which is why common assumptions about the user communication behavior must be reconsidered. Second, proposals of ACSs, such as [1,3,10], consider constant user participation, i.e., the requirement of users to be always online and sending messages to the system, as the only way to protect against intersection attacks. Another approach proposed in [12,27] is grouping users into anonymity sets and only allows all users to join the system at the same time and having the same sending rate. Yet, constant user participation, homogeneous user joining and message sending does not reflect realistic user communication behavior either, and enforcing it would significantly reduce the practicability of ACSs. Third, common mitigation techniques proposed against intersection attacks suggest either an increase in the size of the userbase as the anonymity set, a random delay of sending messages to the communication system, or utilizing cover traffic to hide real message sending. However, it has been demonstrated that those mitigation measures cannot provide long-term protection against intersection attacks [2,11]. Still, a detailed investigation of these mitigation effects and their usefulness in realistic communication settings and especially in microblogging scenarios are missing.

To the best of our knowledge, no previous work has provided a *practical investigation* which answers the following questions:

- How effective are the intersection attacks on different anonymous microblogging scenarios? Especially,when realistic communication settings are considered.
- What impact does realistic user communication behavior (e.g., sending rates) have on these attacks?
- To what extent can common mitigation measures against intersection attacks, more specifically the increasing in cover traffic, delay, and userbase, facilitate the attack mitigation under realistic microblogging scenarios?

We believe that answering these questions is critical to understand how and under what conditions intersection attacks are powerful. Additionally, this understanding can facilitate and enhance the development of effective mitigation measures to protect against intersection attacks in practical ACSs. In this paper, we address the aforementioned questions by investigating intersection attacks on two different messaging patterns: pseudonym-based and topic-based messaging of anonymous microblogging. We use real-world datasets from Twitter and Reddit to simulate realistic user communication behavior. We launch the attack to reveal the identity of the publishing user (i.e., de-anonymize the user), hence the posts and messages can be linked to the sending user. Using an intersection attack for the other direction, i.e., to discover which topic a user subscribed to is beyond our scope[1].

This paper is organized as follows: The assumptions, anonymous microblogging messaging patterns, and threat model are all introduced in Sect. 2. Then, in Sect. 3, we present our intersection attack for each messaging pattern. Following that, in Sect. 4, we discuss the evaluation results of our experiments. Finally, Sect. 5 concludes the paper and presents some points for future work.

---

[1] It is noteworthy that a solution for this intersection attack direction has been addressed already by utilising *broadcasting* of published messages, i.e., sending every published message to all users, as seen in [1,4,5]. Nonetheless, broadcasting imposes a high communication overhead on users, which makes it an inefficient solution. Thus, more research in this area is clearly needed.

2   Design and Assumptions

In this work, we consider an anonymous microblogging system that has a set of users $U = \{u_1, u_2, ...u_n\}$. Each user, $u_i \in U$, can independently decide how many messages to send, and when to send them. Thus, there are no agreements on communication behavior between users, which is closest to commonly used existing non-anonymous microblogging systems. All messages transmitted between users and the system are encrypted and padded to the same length i.e., they appear indistinguishable to any external observer. The users do not include any personally identifiable information (e.g., real names or addresses) in their messages, as the messages are published publicly on the system. The communication in the system is assumed to proceed in rounds, $R = \{r_1, r_2, ...r_w\}$, and u_i is *online* in a round $r_x \in R$ when she sends messages during this round. The system publishes all messages at the end of the round. It also can support special anonymity features like cover traffic and the delay of messages.

2.1   Messaging Patterns

To investigate the effectiveness of intersection attacks on different anonymous microblogging scenarios, we consider two major microblogging messaging patterns which differ based on how users publish their messages.

Pseudonym-Based Messaging Pattern. Every u_i uses a *pseudonym* (i.e., a fictitious username), $p' \in P = \{p_1, p_2, ...p_m\}$, in order to publish her messages in the system, see Fig. 1(a). The pseudonyms must not contain any personal information about the users. The system is responsible for ensuring *unlinkability* between u_i and p'. Any user of the system can read the content published under every pseudonym but cannot realize the real identity of the pseudonym's owner. In this pattern, we assume a one-to-one relationship between the sets of users U and pseudonyms P, which means that each user $u_i \in U$ has only one pseudonym $p' \in P$ and vice versa. The pseudonym is considered *online* during round r_x only when messages are published under this pseudonym during r_x.

Topic-Based Messaging Pattern. Users follow the *topic-based publish/subscribe* (pub/sub) paradigm. In this pattern, the users publish their messages to topics i.e., a user u_i who posts a message to a topic $t' \in T = \{t_1, t_2, ...t_q\}$ is called a publisher, see Fig. 1(b). As the topics are the focus, publishers do not need to have any kind of identity (e.g., pseudonyms) on the anonymous microblogging system. Ensuring unlinkability between u_i and t' is assumed to be assured by the system. Any user of the system can read every message published to every topic but cannot know anything about who publishes these messages. In this pattern, the users U and Topics T have a many-to-many relationship, which means that t' can have many publishers and u_i can publish to multiple topics. Additionally, we assume a topic to be *active* during round r_x when it receives new messages in r_x. Furthermore, any user can send messages to multiple topics in the same round.

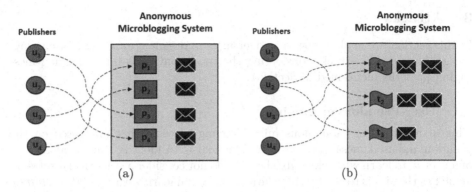

Fig. 1. The publishing process in (a) Pseudonym-based messaging pattern and (b) Topic-based messaging pattern.

2.2 Threat Model

We assume a global passive adversary $\mathcal{A}$ who monitors the whole communication during the set of rounds R and can learn who participates in each round and how many messages each participant sends. $\mathcal{A}$ does not have any means to interrupt the traffic by dropping or altering data packets, nor does $\mathcal{A}$ gain intelligence about the actual content of the encrypted messages during transmission. It cannot collude with the anonymous system, but it can corrupt an arbitrary number of users. Moreover, it can read all published messages every round.

2.3 Delay

The messages can be arbitrarily delayed on the system for a number of rounds ($\leq d$ rounds) to prevent $\mathcal{A}$ from correlating the incoming messages—sent by the users to the system—with the published ones. $\mathcal{A}$ can realize the maximum allowed delay (d), but it cannot learn the exact number of rounds for which a message will be delayed. To deal with this issue, when a message is sent in r_x, $\mathcal{A}$ shall observe the published content during $r_x, r_{x+1}, \cdots, r_{x+d-1}$ as the message must be published in one of these rounds. Therefore, $\mathcal{A}$ will treat these consecutive rounds as one joint big round.

2.4 Cover Traffic

Users can produce cover traffic (also referred to as *dummy messages*) to prevent $\mathcal{A}$ from discovering when and how many real messages are sent. Since the system does not publish cover messages, $\mathcal{A}$ can detect the presence of cover traffic if the total number of sent messages by users is larger than the total number of eventually published messages. Nonetheless, it is not possible to determine the exact number of real messages sent by each user. $\mathcal{A}$ can only be certain that the user's real messages are less than or equal to the number of messages sent by her.

3   Attacks

In this section, we explain how the adversary can de-anonymize users by employing an intersection attack, considering the two anonymous microblogging messaging patterns mentioned in Sect. 2.1.

3.1   User-Pseudonym Linking

This attack targets anonymous microblogging systems that are based on the pseudonym-based messaging pattern. The goal is to identify the pseudonym p' of a user u_i to learn what she publishes. We do not consider a statistical disclosure attack as the aim is to study what the adversary can learn with *absolute certainty*. Thus, we consider $\mathcal{A}$ as being *successful* only when it can narrow down the u_i's list of potential pseudonyms to only p'.

The *naive approach* for launching the attack (i.e., link u_i to p') is described as follows: When u_i is *online* for the first time in round r_x, $\mathcal{A}$ creates the set of potential pseudonyms, P_{u_i}, which constitutes the anonymity set of u_i at this point. P_{u_i} contains every *online* pseudonym p_j in r_x that meets the following two requirements:

- p_j is *online* for the first time, i.e., messages are published under this pseudonym for the first time.
- $M_{p_j} = M_{u_i}$, where M_{p_j} is the number of messages published under p_j, and M_{u_i} is the number of messages sent by u_i.

In every subsequent round $(r_{x+1}, r_{x+2}, \cdots)$, if u_i sends a message, any pseudonym $p_l \in P_{u_i}$ that does not publish new messages, shall be removed from P_{u_i}. When the size of P_{u_i} drops to only one, it means that the pseudonym p' of u_i is identified. However, this naive approach does not consider the following issues:

- u_i may send only dummy messages either in her first round (r_x) or in subsequent rounds. In this case, u_i will be *online* but her pseudonym p' will not be *online* as the dummy messages are not published on the system.
- u_i may send both real and dummy messages either in r_x or in subsequent rounds. In this case, p' will have published fewer messages than what u_i has sent (i.e., $M_{p'} < M_{u_i}$).

To overcome these issues and perform a more powerful intersection attack for linking a user to her pseudonym, we consider the following approach for our investigations. It is based on the observation that the attack can be more efficient if $\mathcal{A}$ does not only consider the *online* rounds of u_i but also her *offline* rounds. In other words, $\mathcal{A}$ can track pseudonyms in P_{u_i} which are *online* while u_i is *offline* and excludes them from P_{u_i} which might lead to faster convergence:

Step 1. Creating the initial anonymity set.

Let P_{u_i} be the set of potential pseudonyms for u_i (anonymity set). Initially, it includes every p_j that publish messages in r_x for the first time while at the same time u_i is online for the first time as well. Additionally, p_j has published the same or a fewer amount of messages compared to the number of messages sent by u_i, i.e., $M_{p_j} \leq M_{u_i}$.

Step 2. Verifying whether p' is in P_{u_i}.

$\mathcal{A}$ compares the total number of *online* users to the total number of *online* pseudonyms during r_x. If they are equal, it means all online users published real messages, so P_{u_i} definitely includes p'. In such a case, a flag f is set to *true*, which indicates that no new pseudonyms can be added to P_{u_i}.

Step 3. Updating P_{u_i} during every subsequent round.

(a) Every p_l that fulfills one of the following conditions will be removed from P_{u_i}:
  – it is *online* while u_i is *offline*.
  – $M_{p_l} > M_{u_i}$.
  – it is *offline* while u_i is *online* and the number of online users is the same as the number of *online* pseudonyms, i.e., p' is definitely *online* in this particular round. (When this happens, the flag f must be set to *true*.)
(b) If u_i is *online* and f is *false*, $\mathcal{A}$ adds to P_{u_i} every pseudonym p_j that is online for the first time, and $M_{p_j} \leq M_{u_i}$.

Step 4. Repeat Step 3 until: the flag f is *true* and P_{u_i} contains only one pseudonym (p').

Figure 2 shows a simple example of the proposed method. In this example, we assume a group of four users $U = \{u_1, u_2, u_3, u_4\}$ publishing during four rounds $R = \{r_1, r_2, r_3, r_4\}$, and the goal is to determine each user's pseudonym. $\mathcal{A}$ can learn the following over each round:

○ r_1: $P_{u_1} = \{p_2, p_3\}$, $P_{u_2} = \{p_2, p_3\}$, $P_{u_3} = \{p_2, p_3\}$
○ r_2: $P_{u_1} = \{p_1, p_3, p_4\}$, $P_{u_2} = \{p_2\}$, $P_{u_3} = \{p_1, p_3, p_4\}$, $P_{u_4} = \{p_1, p_4\}$
○ r_3: $P_{u_1} = \{p_1, p_3, p_4\}$, $P_{u_2} = \{p_2\}$, $P_{u_3} = \{p_1, p_3\}$, $P_{u_4} = \{p_1, p_4\}$
○ r_4: $P_{u_1} = \{p_1\}$, $P_{u_2} = \{p_2\}$, $P_{u_3} = \{p_3\}$, $P_{u_4} = \{p_4\}$

Intuitively, the more rounds that are observed, the more information is gathered; thus, the likelihood of a pseudonym being exposed increases. As we discussed in Sect. 2.2, $\mathcal{A}$ does not know the actual content of the messages sent, so it cannot distinguish between the cover messages and the real ones.

3.2 User-Topic Linking

This attack targets anonymous microblogging systems that use a topic-based messaging pattern. The adversary's goal is to identify the topic(s) on which u_i is publishing extensively. In this attack, a ranking-based approach [18] is utilized for our investigations, where $\mathcal{A}$ keeps a list of potential interest topics for user u_i, let's call it T_{u_i}. Each topic $t_k \in T_{u_i}$ is assigned a score (initially zero). The topic(s) with the highest score is most likely to be the one with the most posts by the user. This attack is especially effective when the user has been immersed in a specific topic for a long time. The scores of topics can be calculated by $\mathcal{A}$ using the methods outlined below.

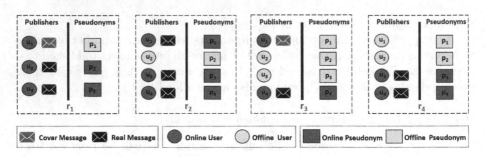

Fig. 2. Example of the User-Pseudonym Linking Attack

Method 1: In every round r_x in which u_i is *online*, $\mathcal{A}$ adds to T_{u_i} any topic that is *active* for the first time. Then, it updates the scores of topics that are in T_{u_i} by taking the following actions:

– increasing the score of each $t_k \in T_{u_i}$ by a number a if it is *active* in r_x.
– decreasing the score of each $t_k \in T_{u_i}$ by a number b if it is *inactive* in r_x.

$\mathcal{A}$ cannot realize the topic(s) on which u_i publishes messages. Therefore, it considers every *active* topic if u_i is *online* as a potential interest and it increases the score of this topic. To expand the score gap between interesting topics and not-interesting ones, $\mathcal{A}$ decreases the score of topics that are *inactive* when u_i is *online*. It does not exclude these topics, as u_i may post messages on them during subsequent rounds.

To maintain high scores for the topics that are in fact interesting to u_i, but that are not posted to by u_i in every round, i.e., they are sometimes *inactive* even though u_i is *online*, the increasing number a should be greater than the decreasing number b.

Figure 3 shows a simple example for using Method 1 to update the scores of the topics over rounds, assuming u_i is *online* during the rounds $R = \{r_1, r_2, r_3, r_4\}$. In this example, at the end of the four rounds, t_4 is assumed to be the most likely interesting topic for u_i because it has the highest score. For simplicity, a and b have been set to one, so the increasing and decreasing of each topic's score is done by one. Later, in the evaluation, we discuss further the increasing and decreasing numbers.

Method 2: Some topics are so popular that they are *active* throughout the majority of the rounds. By just observing rounds in which u_i is *online*, these topics will get high scores in T_{u_i} even if they are not of any interest to the user. To tackle this issue, in addition to updating the topics' scores during rounds in which u_i is *online* (similar to Method 1), $\mathcal{A}$ can do the following:

– for every round in which u_i is *offline*, $\mathcal{A}$ adds to T_{u_i} any topic that is *active* for the first time, and decreases the score of each $t_k \in T_{u_i}$ by a number b if it is *active*.

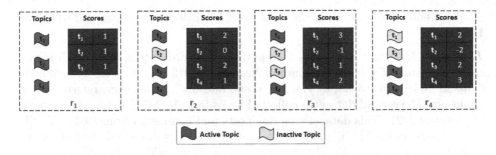

Fig. 3. Example of the User-Topic Linking Attack

That enables excluding irrelevant highly *active* topics while retaining relevant highly *active* topics as top-ranked topics in T_{u_i}.

Method 3: u_i may be interested in several topics that are not widely popular. Since u_i may not publish on all of these topics every time she goes *online*, some of them may be *inactive* when she is *online*. Reducing the scores of these topics every time u_i is *online* can result in a significant drop in their scores. Thus, in order to keep high scores for these topics, in this method, $\mathcal{A}$ does not reduce the score of every *inactive* $t_k \in T_{u_i}$ in the rounds in which u_i is *online*. The steps of this method, executed every round regardless whether u_i is *online* or not, are as follows:

- adding to T_{u_i} any topic that is *active* for the first time.
- increasing the score of each $t_k \in T_{u_i}$ by a number a if it is *active* when u_i is *online*.
- decreasing the score of each $t_k \in T_{u_i}$ by a number b if it is *active* when u_i is *offline*.

4   Evaluation

In this section, we measure the effectiveness of the presented intersection attacks for linking a user to a pseudonym and/or topic on anonymous microblogging. The communication is simulated using two real-world datasets collected from two popular microblogging platforms, Twitter and Reddit. Users' messages are assigned to communication rounds based on their timestamps in the datasets. All rounds have the same length of time. We tested three round length values: 30 min (1,800 s), 1 h (3,600 s), and 2 h (7,200 s), where an increase in the round length usually means an increase in the number of users participating in the round, i.e., anonymity set size. To simulate the adversary $\mathcal{A}$, a *logger* was implemented to record all traffic generated by users and all messages posted on the anonymous microblogging system during rounds. The data gathered by the *logger* serves as input for an *analyzer*, which executes the attacks. Our simulation prototype is implemented using Java and Python. We conducted the experiments on a machine equipped with a 16-core Intel Xeon E5-2640 v2 processor and 64 GB of RAM.

Datasets. The first dataset is a collection of records extracted from Twitter over the course of the entire month of November 2012 [13, 19]. This dataset contains 22, 534, 846 tweets, 6, 914, 561 users, and 3,379,976 topics, referred to as hashtags. The second dataset is collected by us from Reddit for the entire month of October 2021. This dataset contains posts and comments from 1,638,157 different users and 3,403 different topics, referred to as subreddits. Both datasets include a timestamp, user id, and topic (hashtag/subreddit) at each record.

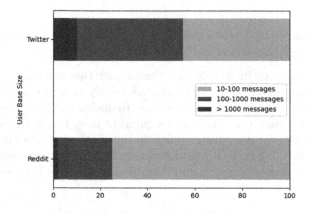

Fig. 4. The distribution of users based on sending rates (userbase size = 1 million)

Users. To investigate the impact of the number of users on the performance of the intersection attacks, in our experiments, we tested userbases of different sizes: 10,000, 100,000, and 1,000,000. Each userbase is created by choosing users randomly and independently from the datasets. To study the influence of user communication behavior on the attacks, we looked into the relationship between how many messages a user sends (user's sending rates) and the vulnerability to the attack. For that, we focused on three groups of sending rates in particular: $(10 - 100)$ messages, $(100 - 1,000)$ messages, and $(> 1,000)$ messages. Figure 4 shows the percentage of users who belong to each group in the userbase of one million users. The shown distribution was found to be nearly the same in 10,000 and 100,000 userbases. As illustrated in Fig. 4, most Reddit users sent between 10 and 100 messages during the observed month, which is different from the Twitter dataset. The difference in sending rates between users on Twitter and Reddit is expected, given that the two platforms have different service models.

Cover Traffic and Delay. To study the implications of using cover traffic on the effectiveness of the intersection attacks, each user generates a fixed number of dummy messages to hide every single real message (this is the same cover traffic generation approach used in [22]). The generated dummy messages are sent in random rounds to create noise in the user's sending rate. We tested three different cover-to-real message ratios: 1:1, 5:1, and 10:1. Similarly, to study the effectiveness of the delay on the intersection attacks, we evaluated three values for the maximum delay d in terms of number of rounds: one round, three rounds, and five rounds. Messages are delayed arbitrary rounds up to at most d rounds.

4.1 User-Pseudonym Linking

To evaluate the effectiveness of the user-pseudonym linking attack, we computed the maximum amount of time required to link a user to her pseudonym (de-anonymization), as shown in Fig. 5(a) and Fig. 5(b). For instance, $\mathcal{A}$ needs a maximum of 200 rounds to learn the pseudonym of any user—regardless of the sending rate—when the userbase size is 100,000 users and the round length is 3,600 seconds, see Fig. 5(a). While as illustrated in Fig. 5(b), when the system has one million users and the round length is 7,200 seconds, then $\mathcal{A}$ needs a maximum of 210 rounds to learn the pseudonym of any user who has sent more than 1,000 messages. As depicted in Fig. 5(a) and Fig. 5(b), the time needed for the de-anonymization increases when the round length, the number of users, or the sending rates increase. Nonetheless, having a large round length or a large user base still does not provide long-term protection, especially for users with high sending rates.

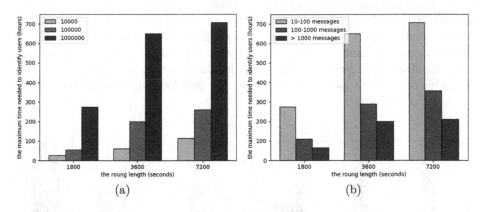

Fig. 5. The maximum time needed to de-anonymize users in the Twitter dataset. (a) studying the impact of various userbase sizes, where the userbase includes users of different sending rates, (b) studying the impact of sending rates (userbase size = 1 million).

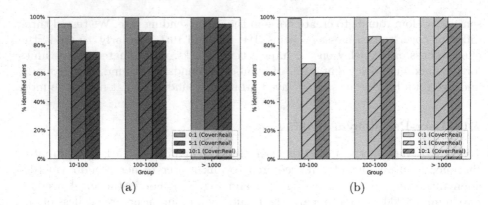

Fig. 6. The impact of cover traffic on the number of de-anonymized users (userbase size = 1 million, round length = 1 h). (a) Twitter, (b) Reddit.

In Fig. 6(a) and Fig. 6(b), we show the impact of using cover traffic on the number of identified users in the Twitter and Reddit datasets, respectively. According to our findings, sending random cover traffic increases the number of required observed rounds. However, it can only slightly reduce the number of de-anonymized users by the end of the observation period. For example, if users randomly send 10 dummy messages for every real message (i.e., ratio 10:1)—that definitely leads to high bandwidth overhead—, the adversary still can identify pseudonyms of over 70%, 80%, and 90% of users who send $(10-100)$, $(100-1,000)$, and $(> 1,000)$ messages, respectively, see Fig. 6(a). We think that the main reason behind the ineffectiveness of cover traffic in protecting the users is the randomness in generating and sending the dummy messages, which seems incapable of creating anonymity sets that can provide long-term protection for the users' pseudonyms.

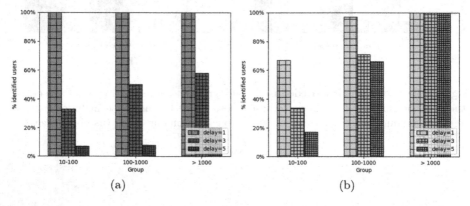

Fig. 7. The impact of delay on the number of de-anonymized users (userbase size = 1 million, and round length = 1 h). (a) Twitter, (b) Reddit.

In Fig. 7(a) and Fig. 7(b), we illustrate how delaying messages can help in degrading the effectiveness of the user-pseudonym linking attack. Since the adversary cannot learn the exact number of rounds for which a message has been delayed, it treats every message as if it has been postponed by d rounds. That results in very large anonymity sets, hence, it reduces the attack performance. Using the delay is more powerful on Twitter than on Reddit, especially for users with sending rate of more than 100 messages. That is because nearly 60% of users in the Twitter dataset post more than 100 messages, whereas there are only about 25% of users in the Reddit dataset who have similar sending rates, see Fig. 4. In the Reddit dataset, for example, there are only five users who have sent more than 1,000 messages. The communication behaviors of these five users are also noticeably different, making it difficult to conceal each one's behavior using delay. Nonetheless, it appears that cover traffic is more effective in protecting these users as shown in Fig. 6(b).

4.2   User-Topic Linking

The increasing and decreasing numbers (a and b), described in Sect. 3.2, were tested using several values. We found that in the Twitter dataset, the best results can be produced for all userbases when $a = 5$ and $b = 1$. While in the Reddit dataset, the best values are $a = 7$ and $b = 1$.

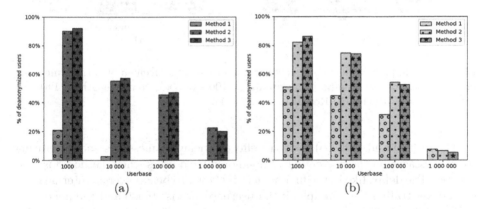

Fig. 8. The impact of increasing the userbase size on the effectiveness of three methods in linking users to topics (sending rate group is $(100 - 1,000)$, and round length $= 1$ h). (a) Twitter ($a = 5$, $b = 1$), (b) Reddit ($a = 7$, $b = 1$).

In Fig. 8(a) and Fig. 8(b), the effectiveness of the user-topic linking attack is studied using each of the three methods of computing topic scores, described in Sect. 3.2. As demonstrated in both figures, any increase in the userbase leads to a significant decrease in the number of de-anonymized users. Furthermore, predictably, the attack is greatly influenced by the users' sending rates, i.e., users posting more messages are much more vulnerable to the attack. In the figures, we show only the results of users who sent $(100-1,000)$ messages.

The second and third methods produce significantly better results than the first method, see Fig. 8(a) and Fig. 8(b). Since the irrelevant topics are filtered out in the second and third methods by decreasing the scores of topics that are *active* when the user is *offline*. The third method appears to behave similarly to the second, implying that lowering the scores of *inactive* topics when the user is *online* has little effect on the results.

The first method seems to be far more effective on Reddit than on Twitter, implying that updating the scores of topics during users' *offline* rounds has less impact on Reddit than on Twitter. That is due to differences in the two datasets; e.g., Reddit has a smaller number of high popular topics compared to Twitter.

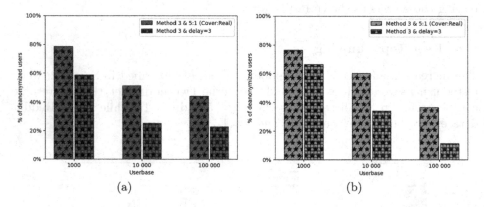

(a)   (b)

Fig. 9. The impact of delay and cover traffic on the effectiveness of various methods in user-topic linking (sending rate group is $(100-1,000)$, round length $= 1\,\mathrm{h}$). (a) Twitter ($a = 5$, $b = 1$), (b) Reddit ($a = 7$, $b = 1$).

Figure 9(a) and Fig. 9(b) show the effect of delaying messages and generating cover messages on the percentage of de-anonymized users when method 3 is considered. The delay, like in the first attack, is shown to be a better countermeasure than cover traffic. For example, if the userbase size is 10,000 and the maximum delay is 3 hours, the percentage of the de-anonymized users is reduced from 57% to 25%. While using five cover messages for each real message (i.e., 5:1) can only decrease the percentage of de-anonymized users to 51%, see Fig. 9(a).

Overall, the user-pseudonym linking attack is far more effective than the user-topic linking attack. That is mainly for two reasons. First, it is due to the many-to-many relationship between users and topics, whereas users and pseudonyms have a one-to-one relationship. The user may publish on various topics every round, and each topic can get messages from different users over rounds. The second reason is that some of the topics can be *active* for the majority of the time. Thus, it is difficult to distinguish whether the user publishes on that topic or on another one.

5   Related Work

Anonymous Microblogging. Several systems have been proposed to support anonymous microblogging scenarios. The methods used to achieve sender anonymity differ between these systems. The commonly used methods are *mixnets* (Atom [16] and Riffle [15]), *DCnets* (Dissent [5]), *private information retrieval* (Blinder [1], Riposte [4], 2PPS [10], and Spectrum [20]), and *random forwarding* (AnonPubSub [8]). For receiver anonymity, systems like Dissent, Riposte, Blinder, Atom, and Spectrum depend on the concept of broadcasting messages to all users. While systems like AnonPubSub, 2PPS, and Riffle have addressed this goal by proposing anonymous multicast communication mechanisms.

Intersection Attacks. Many studies on intersection attacks and statistical disclosure attacks have been conducted. In [7,14,25], researchers demonstrated the efficacy of statistical disclosure attacks against mixnets-based systems, especially when the systems support full bidirectional communications [7]. Statistical disclosure attacks have been proven to be effective in attacking the Signal application's sealed sender mechanism in order to deduce the relationship between the sender and the recipient of an end-to-end encrypted message stream [18]. Intersection attacks combined with social network analysis were shown in [26] to be capable of determining the social relationships of a targeted social network user. A variant of statistical disclosure attacks based on an Expectation-Maximization algorithm has also been demonstrated to be feasible on anonymous email networks [23].

6   Conclusion and Future Work

In this paper, we conducted intersection attacks in anonymous microblogging against pseudonym-based and topic-based messaging patterns. The findings demonstrate that the attacks are effective and practical in de-anonymizing users, particularly when they post messages under pseudonyms. In the user-topic linking attack, increasing the user base has proven to be a far more effective mitigation solution than in the user-pseudonym linking attack. The users with high sending rates are found to be more vulnerable to the attacks, especially when the number of these users is small. We evaluated the impact of using delay and cover traffic, which are common mitigation techniques against intersection attacks. According to our results, delaying messages for several hours can reduce the performance of intersection attacks better than cover traffic. However, both delay and cover traffic do not completely prevent intersection attacks because they only extend the time at which users lose their anonymity. Furthermore, they introduce significant latency and bandwidth overhead, making them less convenient for all scenarios.

In the future, we would like to investigate even more improved and sophisticated intersection attacks in the topic-based messaging pattern. Additionally, we will work on developing suitable mitigation approaches which can create stable, long-lived anonymity sets without imposing high latency or bandwidth overhead on users while considering realistic user communication behavior, such as users' ability to join the anonymity system at any time and have various sending rates.

Acknowledgements. This work was partially supported by funding from the German Research Foundation (DFG), research grant 317688284. We thank Tim Grube for his insightful comments on an earlier draft of the manuscript. We would also like to thank the anonymous NordSec reviewers for their feedback.

References

1. Abraham, I., Pinkas, B., Yanai, A.: Blinder-scalable, robust anonymous committed broadcast. In: Proceedings of the 2020 ACM SIGSAC Conference on Computer and Communications Security, pp. 1233–1252 (2020)
2. Berthold, O., Langos, H.: Dummy traffic against long term intersection attacks. In: Dingledine, R., Syverson, P. (eds.) PET 2002. LNCS, vol. 2482, pp. 110–128. Springer, Heidelberg (2003). https://doi.org/10.1007/3-540-36467-6_9
3. Cheng, R., et al.: Talek: private group messaging with hidden access patterns. In: Annual Computer Security Applications Conference, pp. 84–99 (2020)
4. Corrigan-Gibbs, H., et al.: Riposte: an anonymous messaging system handling millions of users. In: 2015 IEEE Symposium on Security and Privacy, pp. 321–338. IEEE (2015)
5. Corrigan-Gibbs, H., Ford, B.: Dissent: accountable anonymous group messaging. In: Proceedings of the 17th ACM Conference on Computer and Communications Security, pp. 340–350 (2010)
6. Danezis, G., Serjantov, A.: Statistical disclosure or intersection attacks on anonymity systems. In: Fridrich, J. (ed.) IH 2004. LNCS, vol. 3200, pp. 293–308. Springer, Heidelberg (2004). https://doi.org/10.1007/978-3-540-30114-1_21
7. Danezis, G., Diaz, C., Troncoso, C.: Two-sided statistical disclosure attack. In: Borisov, N., Golle, P. (eds.) PET 2007. LNCS, vol. 4776, pp. 30–44. Springer, Heidelberg (2007). https://doi.org/10.1007/978-3-540-75551-7_3
8. Daubert, J., et al.: Anonpubsub: anonymous publish-subscribe overlays. Comput. Commun. **76**, 42–53 (2016)
9. Dixon, S.: Number of twitter users worldwide from 2019 to 2024. https://www.statista.com/statistics/303681/twitter-users-worldwide/ (2022)
10. Gaballah, S.A., et al.: 2PPS-publish/subscribe with provable privacy. In: 2021 40th International Symposium on Reliable Distributed Systems (SRDS), pp. 198–209. IEEE (2021)
11. Grube, T., Thummerer, M., Daubert, J., Mühlhäuser, M.: Cover traffic: a trade of anonymity and efficiency. In: Livraga, G., Mitchell, C. (eds.) STM 2017. LNCS, vol. 10547, pp. 213–223. Springer, Cham (2017). https://doi.org/10.1007/978-3-319-68063-7_15
12. Hayes, J., Troncoso, C., Danezis, G.: TASP: towards anonymity sets that persist. In: Proceedings of the 2016 ACM on Workshop on Privacy in the Electronic Society, pp. 177–180 (2016)
13. Karissa, M., et al.: Truthy: enabling the study of online social networks. In: Proceedings 16th ACM Conference on Computer Supported Cooperative Work and Social Computing Companion (CSCW) (2013)

14. Kedogan, D., Agrawal, D., Penz, S.: Limits of anonymity in open environments. In: Petitcolas, F.A.P. (ed.) IH 2002. LNCS, vol. 2578, pp. 53–69. Springer, Heidelberg (2003). https://doi.org/10.1007/3-540-36415-3_4
15. Kwon, A., et al.: Riffle: an efficient communication system with strong anonymity. Proc. Priv. Enhancing Technol. **2016**(2), 115–134 (2016)
16. Kwon, A., et al.: Atom: horizontally scaling strong anonymity. In: Proceedings of the 26th Symposium on Operating Systems Principles, pp. 406–422 (2017)
17. Madani, S.: Improving security and efficiency of mix-based anonymous communication systems. PhD thesis, RMIT University (2015)
18. Martiny, I., et al.: Improving signal's sealed sender. In: The Internet Society, NDSS (2021)
19. McKelvey, K., et al.: Design and prototyping of a social media observatory. In: Proceedings of the 22nd International Conference on World Wide Web Companion, WWW 2013 Companion, pp. 1351–1358 (2013)
20. Newman, Z., et al.: Spectrum: high-bandwidth anonymous broadcast with malicious security. Cryptol. ePrint Arch. (2021)
21. Pfitzmann, A., Hansen, M.: A terminology for talking about privacy by data minimization: anonymity, unlinkability, undetectability, unobservability, pseudonymity, and identity management (2010)
22. Piotrowska, A.M.: Studying the anonymity trilemma with a discrete-event mix network simulator. In: Proceedings of the 20th Workshop on Workshop on Privacy in the Electronic Society, pp. 39–44 (2021)
23. Portela, J., et al.: Disclosing user relationships in email networks. J. Supercomput. **72**(10), 3787–3800 (2016)
24. Thorbecke, C.: Facebook says government requests for user data have reached all-time high. https://abcnews.go.com/Business/facebook-government-requests-user-data-reached-time-high/story?id=66981424 (2019)
25. Troncoso, C., Gierlichs, B., Preneel, B., Verbauwhede, I.: Perfect matching disclosure attacks. In: Borisov, N., Goldberg, I. (eds.) PETS 2008. LNCS, vol. 5134, pp. 2–23. Springer, Heidelberg (2008). https://doi.org/10.1007/978-3-540-70630-4_2
26. Trujillo, A.G.S., Orozco, A.L.S., Villalba, L.J.G., Kim, T.-H.: A traffic analysis attack to compute social network measures. Multimed. Tools Appl. **78**(21), 29731–29745 (2019)
27. Wolinsky, D., et al.: Hang with your buddies to resist intersection attacks. In: Proceedings of the 2013 ACM SIGSAC Conference on Computer & Communications Security, pp. 1153–1166 (2013)
28. Xu, T., Chen, Y., Fu, X., Hui, P.: Twittering by cuckoo: decentralized and socio-aware online microblogging services. In: Proceedings of the ACM SIGCOMM 2010 Conference, pp. 473–474 (2010)

Data Privacy in Ride-Sharing Services: From an Analysis of Common Practices to Improvement of User Awareness

Carsten Hesselmann[1]([⊠]), Delphine Reinhardt[2], Jan Gertheiss[3],
and Jörg P. Müller[1]

[1] Clausthal University of Technology, Adolph-Roemer-Straße 2A,
38678 Clausthal-Zellerfeld, Germany
{carsten.hesselmann,joerg.mueller}@tu-clausthal.de

[2] Georg August University Göttingen, Wilhelmsplatz 1, 37073 Göttingen, Germany
reinhardt@cs.uni-goettingen.de

[3] Helmut Schmidt University, Holstenhofweg 85, 22043 Hamburg, Germany
jan.gertheiss@hsu-hh.de

Abstract. Individuals are frequently confronted with privacy-related decisions under uncertainty especially in online contexts. The resulting privacy concerns are a decisive factor for individuals to (not) use online services. In order to support individuals to make more informed decisions, we assess the current state of practice of certain online services. This analysis is focused on ride-sharing and includes popular services in Germany, Austria, and Switzerland and we investigate how they handle user data. The results show that services include a wide-ranging set of personal data and lack standardization. Furthermore, they offer limited privacy-related features. Based on this analysis, we developed a Transparency Enhancing Technology in the form of a browser extension that informs users about data practices of the services at the time of data disclosure. In addition to this, we conducted a scenario-based online experiment with a representative sample to evaluate the usability of our tool and its effect on users' concerns and behavior. Results show significant improvements in awareness and decision reflection with limited decrease in disclosure rates of personal data.

Keywords: Data privacy · Disclosure behavior · Sharing economy · Transparency enhancing technology

1 Introduction

Privacy has been a topic of expanding interest for researchers, economists, and regulators alike [37]. This is a distinct indicator that the recent developments in data collection and processing are problematic as privacy regulations and privacy research are reactive areas [7]. More specifically, individuals – also referred to as users in this work – frequently make privacy-related decisions under uncertainty as a consequence of incomplete information and information asymmetry [3]. This, in turn, results in a lack of transparency and control over personal data while increasing individuals' anxiety and concern [6]. This is substantiated by examples such as the misuse of web browsers' device battery API by companies to increase prices [29] and the growing market for online personal data which stays obscure and out of reach for the individual [4]. Tools and technologies that try to aid individuals in their privacy choices exist in physical (shutter for privacy webcams [24]) and in digital form (tools that help with privacy choices [12]) but are scarce in numbers.

Digital data collection is substantially easier and more broadly applied compared to the physical world. In addition, concerns about digital privacy are similar to concerns in the physical world [48]. Therefore, they have to be taken into consideration from the stakeholders of any data collection and processing. Moreover, the research on how the privacy practices of companies affect individuals is limited [6] and needs to be extended on.

This applies especially well to the sharing economy – a term summarizing Peer-to-Peer (P2P) markets for the temporary share or rental of goods – as sharing blends borders between the online and offline [33] as well as the private and the economic spheres [39]; in this work we focus on services for sharing rides. Markets in the sharing economy are partly based on reputation systems which enable consumers to evaluate other (unknown) participants in the market based on crowd-sourced information [36]. In addition to that, the quality of interactions in P2P markets can vary greatly depending on each individual and the market is regulated by reciprocity [31]. For these reasons, user retention and loyalty are of major importance and any barriers and impediments should be reduced. One of the dominant factors that prevent participation and transaction execution in e-commerce and the sharing economy are privacy concerns [1, 16, 44].

The topic of data collection and disclosure in sharing services is complex and equivocal. The disclosure of personal information required to gain access to (ride-sharing) services is applied in a ask-on-first-use principle – typically used in mobile applications – which is insufficient to match individuals' preferences [20, 49] and, furthermore, occurs at an early stage of digital interaction, making the individual feel hopeless about their data [21]. Supporting an individual's assessment of privacy choices is a needed area of research [12] as users are willing to rethink their decision when provided with a plausible reason [23].

In this paper, we present the results of our ongoing research on privacy concerns and disclosure behavior in the sharing economy. Our goal is to make data practices of ride-sharing services more transparent for the user. Therefore, we decided to design and implement a TET in the form of a browser extension that adds relevant information to the sign-up process and later data disclosures — its functionality is depicted with a simplified example in Fig. 1 and further detailed in Sect. 4. There are multiple reasons for our decision to create a TET. Firstly, personal preferences surrounding privacy are highly subjective [38]. Secondly, recent research has shown that individuals not only have differing preferences

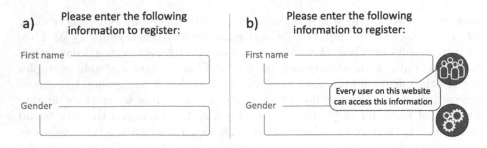

Fig. 1. Simplified registration form without a) and with b) the proposed TET

about partly giving up control but prefer to remain in control of their decisions [11,21,23,26]. Thirdly, incomplete information hinders privacy decisions [2] especially due to the disconnect between data collection and its usage. This disconnect is felt on the users side as lack of awareness about the data usage [49]. Lastly, transparency positively affects individuals' reaction and a lack of it could result in future backlash [6] as lack of awareness is one of the key components of privacy concerns [34]. In consequence of this, we chose the Internet Users' Information Privacy Concern (IUIPC) metric [25] to evaluate the effects of our tool on users' privacy concerns. It is designed specifically to fit privacy research in an online context. In addition to that, the IUIPC statements used to assess an individual's privacy concerns are divided into the three dimensions *control*, *collection*, and *awareness* which fit the aforementioned issues surrounding the control over the data, the online data disclosure, and the lack of transparency.

The contributions of this paper are threefold. After reviewing related research in Sect. 2, we analyze the state of practice of popular ride-sharing services in Sect. 3 and identify differences in data practices and privacy-related features, addressing the following Research Questions (RQs):

RQ 1: *What personal data are commonly included in ride-sharing services?*
RQ 2: *How much of the personal information is exposed to other individuals?*
RQ 3: *What privacy-related features do services for ride-sharing offer?*

Our analysis shows that privacy-related features are rare. In addition, most services' transparency about data practices could be improved, as opt-out options are commonly difficult to access [13]. A preliminary study [17] based on this analysis showed that the differences in data practices affect users' privacy concerns and their disclosure behavior. However, the data was attained in a self-reporting manner which usually correlates less with actual behavior.

Therefore, we implemented a tool which integrates privacy-related information into the websites of ride-sharing services via an icon-based approach, as described in Sect. 4. The tool is a browser extension that works with all common browsers. The goal of this is to empower individuals to make a more informed decision when deciding about disclosing personal information. We formulated the following RQs for the development of our tool:

RQ 4: *How much personalization and automation is applicable?*
RQ 5: *Which technical approach is applicable for the described goal?*
RQ 6: *Which design approach is suitable?*
RQ 7: *How can long-term usefulness be ensured and data set kept up-to-date?*

Subsequently, as a first evaluation of our tool, we conducted a scenario-based experiment with a fictional ride-sharing service *MyCarPool* and asked participants to create a personal profile during the experiment, as discussed in Sect. 5. The sample ($n = 1093$) was representative of the German online population. Our goal was to answer the following RQs:

RQ 8: *Do the icons change the participant's privacy concerns?*
RQ 9: *Do the icons change the participant's decision about data disclosure?*
RQ 10: *Do the participants perceive and understand the icons?*
RQ 11: *Are the participants aware of how much data they actively disclosed?*
RQ 12: *Do the participants use or perceive the available profile settings?*
RQ 13: *What is the most helpful information for the participants?*

We used the IUIPC metric with its dimensions control, collection, and awareness to assess participants' privacy concerns and observed the disclosure of personal information. We compared the results of the control and test group with logistic regression models for effect size and significance, as discussed in Sect. 6. The results indicate significant effects on users' awareness and (partly) collection. Furthermore, the disclosure rates are affected for certain combinations of icon and personal data.

2   Related Work

Privacy research is multifaceted. We start by mentioning a set of notable works which include similar approaches based on visual cues, data disclosure, and transparency improvements. Similar to [22], we analyze the disclosure behavior during a sign-up process and aim to improve the transparency of underlying data practices for the individual based on visual cues. A key difference from their work is that we do not analyze affection in our experiment and therefore do not include framing in our visual cues. Instead, the visual and textual cues in our experiment are designed and formulated neutrally. Furthermore, our experiment is adjusted to the sharing economy and includes common practices based on a prior analysis of services. Therefore, it contributes specifically to this field of research.

The process of signing up for digital services is similar to the installation process of mobile applications at least as far as the disclosure of information is concerned. It is mandatory to disclose a set of personal information to complete a sign-up process. Equally, the installation of a mobile application demands the granting of permissions, which in turn leads to the disclosure of a variety of data. [18] study individuals' disclosure behavior during the installation process of mobile applications by adding visual cues hinting at potentially dangerous permissions. In consequence, the authors use the Mobile Users' Information Privacy Concern (MUIPC) metric instead of IUIPC which is used in our work. Additionally, our work does not include a three-color approach which typically conveys implicit information – for example, by using green, yellow, and red visual cues – as we firstly wanted to evaluate the effects of visual cues without framing. Furthermore, we do not include individuals' general privacy concerns as a separate set of questions in order to compare their decisions with their self-stated attitudes because we compare the results from the test and control group. In addition to that, the IUIPC metric includes broad privacy statements and the visual cues used in our work include the most imminent consequences of potential data disclosure by highlighting the data practices of the service and paying emphasis specifically to other individuals' access to the personal information.

Similarly to the installation of mobile applications, [20] investigate users' knowledge about browser extensions and their preferences for installation notifications. This directly relates to our proposed tool as it is a browser extension and we have incorporated minimal permission requests and limit the extension's activity to relevant websites of ride-sharing services. Furthermore, [20] found that users prefer more extensive dialogues with examples of what data is potentially accessed. We integrate this finding in our implementation and offer a summary function that includes all relevant data which are otherwise communicated via individual icons across the website and its sub-pages. [13] measure how risk-based icons (icons that convey the result of a risk analysis) can lead to a more informed consent of individuals. Our approach shows similarity to the work of [13] as both aim at providing means of comparability between different services and policies respectively. However, in contrast to [13], our work focuses on data disclosure instead of privacy policies.

Furthermore, [9] evaluate how different explanations affect users' satisfaction with an algorithmic decision. Similarly, [8] compare different explanation styles to evaluate users' perceived justice of a given algorithmic decision. While both works are related to our work in terms of improving transparency, the goal is different. The aforementioned works focus on explaining decisions made on already collected data while the work presented in this paper focuses on transparency of data practices before a disclosure decision is made. In summary, our work contributes to the privacy research specifically for the sharing economy by evaluating the disclosure behavior of individuals during a sign-up process in a scenario-based experiment without decision-nudging or framing.

3 Analysis of Ride-Sharing Services

To assess the current state of practice of ride-sharing services and how transparent they present their practices to the user for RQs 1–3, we analyzed the websites of the most popular ride-sharing services in Germany, Austria and Switzerland, according to various ratings [14, 41–43]. The results cover 11 ride-sharing services and 39 data attributes in total (after merging similar attributes, as summarized in Table 1). Our analysis shows which data attributes are included in a service

Table 1. Merged data attributes

Contact information	Cellphone number, landline number, fax number
Social media	Facebook, YouTube, personal website
Personal description	Personal characteristics, self description, things I like
Interests	Sport, hobby, movie
Job	Job description, job industry
Address	Country, city, zip code, street

and are exposed to other users, as discussed in Sect. 3.1. In addition, available privacy settings and the validation of information are reviewed in Sect. 3.2.

This analysis was limited to shared rides. Therefore, if cargo transport or the like is offered, it is not included. In addition, this analysis was limited to those areas and features of the websites which are accessible to users, e.g., the privacy policies. The analysis only includes information that is directly linked to the individual, their preferences, or information about their vehicle. Information relating solely to a ride offer, e.g., locations and routes, is not included in this analysis as it is an extensive research area on its own.

The following steps were carried out during the analysis: (i) register an account, (ii) complete the profile, (iii) check for profile settings, (iv) review profile pages, (v) review ride offers, (vi) create ride offers, and (vii) book ride offers.

3.1 Collection and Exposure of Personal Information

Our results show that there is a great variety of user data which is included in the services, as depicted in Table 2. The set of collected data attributes ranges

Table 2. Details of collection and exposure of personal data

	bessermitfahren	Blablacar	Clickapoint	E-carpooling	Fahrgemeinschaft	Foahstmit	Greendrive	Mifaz	Mitfahrportal	Pendlerportal	Twogo
Collected data	9	23	12	16	14	5	6	16	29	21	14
Mandatory	3	14	3	9	5	4	2	2	4	12	10
Optional	6	9	9	7	9	1	4	14	25	9	4
Exposed data	9	12	10	11	11	5	4	15	17	11	10
Profile page	0	2	0	1	3	0	0	0	5	0	2
Ride offer	9	4	5	5	3	5	4	7	10	11	8
Both	0	6	5	5	5	0	0	8	2	0	0

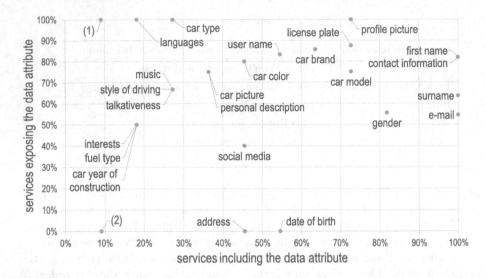

Fig. 2. Services that collect (x-axis) and expose (y-axis) data attributes. Abbreviations: (1) COVID test results and/or vaccination status, job, membership automobile club, phone owner, phone provider (2) marital status, bank account, PayPal account, air-condition, car mileage, country of car registration, fuel consumption

between 5 and 29, and the set of exposed data attributes varies between 4 and 17. In addition, Fig. 2 displays the full set of included data attributes across all analyzed services. The data points are widely spread as the data entries on both axes range from below 10% to 100%. This indicates the diversity in included personal information and a lack of standardization in this regard. The fact that each data attribute is on average included in 36% of ride-sharing services confirms this lack of standardization and concludes RQ 1.

To assess the exposure of personal information for RQ 2, we investigated whether disclosed personal information is accessible for other users. Information about smoking behavior, the vehicle and profile picture are shared most often. On average, services show 75% of the disclosed personal information to other users. This means one quarter of the disclosed personal information is not part of any user-to-user interaction and remains only with the service provider. Some services are close to the 50% margin, which emphasizes how different the data practices depend on the choice of service. This raises the question as to why the user should disclose their personal information to the service provider if not even half of it is accessible to the other users, especially in the context of sharing rides, where – by design – the interaction with other users is arguably the main reason for an individual to use such a service. This question is further aggravated by the fact that explanations to the user on why this information should be disclosed are lacking in almost all instances as the privacy policies provide basic legal terminology. Only a limited number of services mention privacy settings (e.g., change exposure of information towards other users) in the privacy policies.

Table 3. Validation of authenticity (V) and privacy settings (S) offered by ride-sharing services

	Email		Phone number		First name		Last name		License plate		Vehicle model		Driver's license		Automobile club	
	S	V	S	V	S	V	S	V	S	V	S	V	S	V	S	V
Bessermitfahren	X		X													
Blablacar		X		X												
Clickapoint	X	X	X													
E-carpooling														X		
Fahrgemeinschaft	X	X	X				X		X		X					X
Foahstmit																
Greendrive	X															
Mifaz			X		X		X									
Mitfahrportal	X		X													
Pendlerportal									X							
Twogo				X												

The analysis also includes the type of disclosure of personal information which can be either *mandatory* or *optional*. On average, 29% of the considered 39 data attributes is mandatory. The rest is optional, which advocates a tendency towards a user-friendly type of collection at a first glance. However, only in few cases is the optional disclosure made transparent, enticing users to disclose more information due to the over-disclose phenomenon [30].

Furthermore, the exposure of each attribute towards other users is either not exposed or exposed on the *profile page* and/or together with the *ride offer*. Certain information is exposed in a reduced fashion; for instance, if the date of birth is disclosed, only the age (in years) is made accessible to other users. Ten data attributes are never displayed for other users, which makes the collection of this information questionable from a user perspective.

3.2   Privacy-Related Features

An analysis of the privacy-related features for RQ 3 shows that only a limited number of shared mobility services offer these features. Moreover, the range and type of these features vary greatly. Some services offer or require the user to complete a process to validate the authenticity of personal information while other services offer privacy settings to change the exposure of certain data. Those can affect the communication with other users, matchmaking among groups, and whether specific information (e.g., email address or phone number) is accessible for others (as shown in Table 3). In almost all instances, the availability of profile settings is not communicated to the user at the time of disclosure.

4   Proposed Transparency Enhancing Technology

In order to address the differences in data practices and the improvable degree of transparency, we implemented a tool and tested its functionality with the services

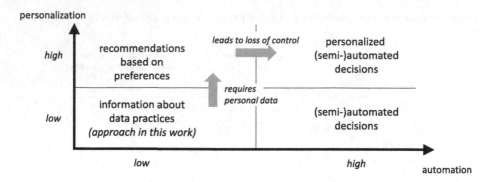

Fig. 3. Degree of personalization and automation of privacy tools

included in the prior analysis. We first decided on the degree of personalization and automation (as stated in RQ 4) to be included in the implementation, as referred to in Fig. 3. The fact that we choose *low* for both has a number of reasons. On the one hand, a higher degree of personalization is considerate of the subjective and contextual nature of privacy. However, the loss of privacy accumulates with every disclosure of information [28] and the additional collection and processing of personal preferences pose a risk of (future) privacy infringements. Moreover, the protection of privacy based on collection of personal data is contradictory. On the other hand, a higher degree of automation promises a reduced cognitive burden for the individual but is difficult to achieve especially due to the mentioned subjective nature of privacy, the conception of privacy, and the subsequent decisions. Furthermore, recent research has made apparent that individuals do prefer to remain in control over their privacy-related decisions [11,21,23,26]. In this context, the transparency gained by our approach can be sufficient for individuals to make informed decisions. We achieve this by displaying the imminent consequences of the underlying data practices, since individuals tend to devalue and underestimate decisions and consequences due to psychological distance [5]. With that in mind, we chose to design a TET focused on the underlying data practices of the respective ride-sharing service and aimed at increasing the awareness on the side of the individuals. This enables individuals to take more informed decisions and react accordingly if needed, e.g., by not disclosing or purposefully falsifying information.

In order to make the data practices of service providers transparent to individuals, we then decided on the technical approach (formulated as RQ 5). It is important to reduce barriers on the side of the user as far as possible as adoption is difficult to achieve [38]. For that reason, we committed to the premise to focus on a technology that could integrate additional information directly into the website of the ride-sharing service. The corresponding mobile applications of ride-sharing services are closed systems and a third-party app based on the service's API (if available) would have contradicted our premise. Therefore, we

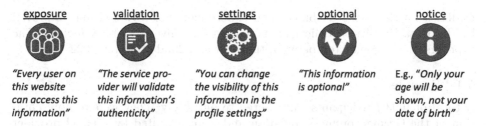

exposure	validation	settings	optional	notice
"Every user on this website can access this information"	*"The service provider will validate this information's authenticity"*	*"You can change the visibility of this information in the profile settings"*	*"This information is optional"*	E.g., *"Only your age will be shown, not your date of birth"*

Fig. 4. Current set of icons included in the proposed TET and their respective tool-tip

chose to implement our idea as a browser extension. This also incorporates the well-established notion that privacy is contextual [2,27].

Subsequently, we chose an icon-based approach for the design of our tool and the integration of information (for RQ 6), as depicted in Fig. 1. Icons have multiple advantages over text- or color-based designs. The memorization of icons works effortlessly as a results of picture superiority [10]. This is crucial, as individuals can only dedicate a limited time for privacy protection [38] and are at the same time confronted with a considerable number of privacy-related decisions [49]. Icons are free from linguistic barriers and if used as a standardized set across multiple instances can create comparability [13], in our case between different ride-sharing services. However, the set of icons needs to be small enough to not risk an information overload [13] similar to a notification fatigue which leads to inattentive permission granting since receiving too many notifications has the same effect as receiving no notifications at all [49].

Our tool covers most of the ride-sharing services included in the prior analysis. For each website, additional icons are displayed next to the input fields; a simplified example is depicted in Fig. 1. These icons indicate privacy-related information, e.g., whether the corresponding personal information is exposed to other registered users. In total, the current implementation features five different icons; *exposure*, *validation*, *settings*, *optional*, and *notice* (covering information that does not fit in the four prior categories), as shown in Fig. 4. Each icon has a tool-tip explaining its meaning, accessible via mouse-over/touch. The icons were chosen based on prior interviews in which multiple icon options were displayed and the participants interpreted their meaning.

The browser extension communicates with a server to receive the relevant data about websites and icons. In order to keep the data set up-to-date (for RQ 7), we have implemented feedback functionalities that report input fields to the server. This function only reports strings in the name or id attribute of certain website elements, e.g., surname, and does not include any personal information.

5   Scenario-Based Online Experiment

After implementing our tool, we conducted a scenario-based online experiment in order to receive a first evaluation of its impact on user behavior and gain feedback on the tool's usability. The experiment was reviewed and approved by the Data Protection Officer of the Clausthal University of Technology. The experiment was conducted between the 10th and 22nd of March 2022.

5.1 Sample

A total of 1093 participants contributed to our study. They were a representation of the German online population and were recruited by a panel provider (certified ISO 20252:2019). The average age of our sample is 44 years and gender distributions are 51% female and 49% male. The majority of participants with education levels 2 and 3 are 40 years or older while education levels 4 and 5 are predominantly young adults (30 years or younger). The full demographic information is presented in Table 7 in the Appendix.

5.2 Setup

In the experiment, we showed the participants a fictional ride-sharing service and asked them to create a personal profile and adjust it to their preferences. This includes disclosure of personal information and adjustment of privacy-related profile settings. To capture the disclosure behavior of participants, meta data (i.e., dirty fields) was stored during the experiment. Consequently the resulting data set does not include any personal information. After finishing the profile creation we investigated the participants' privacy concerns and asked further questions. Since privacy requires a proxy to be measured [37], we used the IUIPC metric with the dimensions *control* (cont.), *collection* (coll.), and *awareness* (awar.) as it is specifically designed for online contexts [25]. Control and collection have 3 statements respectively while awareness has 2 statements, as listed in Table 8 in the Appendix. We adapted the IUIPC metric to the context of our experiment and re-formulated the statements to match our fictional ride-sharing service *MyCarPool*.

To evaluate the effects of our privacy tool, we used a control ($n = 551$) and a test ($n = 542$) group. Both groups' demographics are representative of the German online population. The latter had access to additional visual cues at the time of data disclosure based on our proposed tool. The experiment included the icons indicating the *exposure* of personal data, the *validation* of authenticity, and the availability of user-specific *profile settings*, as shown in Fig. 1. An icon marking *optional* data disclosure is not included since existing research demonstrated its effectiveness [23] and we focused on the remaining icons. In addition to that, it is difficult to differentiate between a user's decision on to not disclose information for privacy reasons and the decision on to not disclose information because it is optional. Since the disclosure of *first name* and *email* was mandatory during the experiment, they are not listed in the results.

5.3 Methods

We use logistic additive regression models (ordinal/binary), fitted through R add-on package mgcv [32, 45–47], to compare the participants' answers to the

IUIPC statements and their disclosure behavior between control and test group. In addition to that, *group* and *gender* are being considered as binary factors, i.e., the value of *group* indicates the difference between the control and test group. For *age* and *education level* we allow for smooth, potentially nonlinear effects, with age-effects being modeled as (penalized) thin plate regression splines (mgcv default). For the ordinal education factor, a discrete, second-order smoothing penalty is used as proposed in [15,40].

6   Results

We used the IUIPC metric to measure participants' privacy concerns (RQ 8) and collected the disclosure rates of personal information via meta data (RQ 9). On top of that, we asked the participants further questions to answer RQs 10–13.

6.1   Privacy Concerns

The results show significant differences between the control and test group in the awareness dimension and significance in part of the collection dimension as displayed by the *group* variable in Table 4. The difference in awareness indicates a higher degree of users' certainty about the data practices of the service provider, since the respective statements refer directly to the service providers' transparency about their data practices. Additionally, coll.2 shows an increase in decision reflection. The gender variable displays additional, though smaller, increases in awareness (awar.1) and decision reflection (coll.2) for women, but also an increase in expressed discomfort (coll.1) and concern (coll.3), which aligns with prior literature [3,35]. Higher age is typically associated with stronger agreement to IUIPC statements, but effects vary in terms of size, shape, and significance — see Fig. 5. Agreement to general privacy statements (cont.1 & cont.2) shows a (rather) linear increase with age while awar.1 shows increases starting around age 40. Positive association between education level and IUIPC is observed for cont.1, cont.2 and coll.1, but with some statistical uncertainty as indicated by p-values and (pointwise) confidence intervals. For awar.1 and awar.2, the association seems to be negative, at least for higher education levels (where uncertainty is lower). For the remaining statements, no clear effects are observed.

Table 4. Ordinal/cumulative logistic regression coefficients for IUIPC metric responses for *group* (test) and *gender* (female) with usual significance codes *** (0.001), ** (0.01), * (0.05).

	cont.1	cont.2	cont.3	coll.1	coll.2	coll.3	awar.1	awar.2
Group	0.021	−0.024	0.109	0.085	0.480	0.153	0.628	0.550
P-value	0.846	0.825	0.310	0.430	0.000***	0.153	0.000***	0.000***
Gender	−0.062	0.354	0.017	0.318	0.480	0.311	0.245	0.036
P-value	0.573	0.002**	0.875	0.004**	0.000***	0.005**	0.026*	0.741

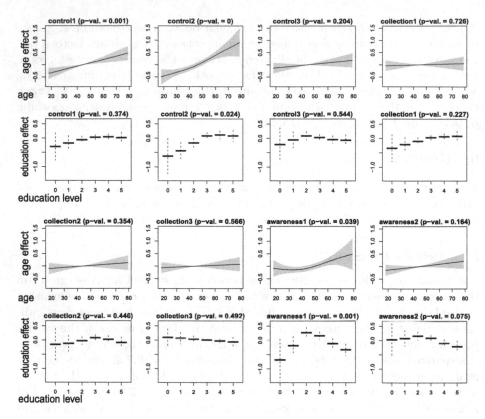

Fig. 5. Effect of *age* and *education level* on the IUIPC metric responses (note, for model identifiability, effects are centered around zero across the data observed [47]). Shaded regions and dashed lines indicate approximate, pointwise 95% confidence intervals.

6.2 Disclosure Rate

Applying the procedure from Sect. 6.1 to the disclosure rates leads to the results summarized in Table 5 and Fig. 6. Looking at the coefficient of the *group* variable (i.e., being in the test group) in Table 5, we can see some behavioral changes depending on data sensitivity and type of icon; particularly *date of birth* and *last name* show a decrease in disclosure rate when combined with the *exposure* icon. In contrast to that, the disclosure of *license plate* increases when it is presented in combination with the *profile settings* icon (which, however, does not apply for the disclosure of *sex*). Furthermore, gender differences show that men tend to disclose less information about themselves but more about their vehicle and vice versa for women. Except for *sex*, higher age is associated with increased disclosure rates, but with varying effect sizes — see Fig. 6. With respect to education, higher levels show lower disclosure rates of information about the individual. In contrast to this, participants with higher levels of education tend to disclose more information about their vehicles.

Table 5. Logistic regression coefficients for disclosure rate for *group* (test) and *gender* (female) with usual significance codes *** (0.001), ** (0.01), * (0.05). Attached icons for test group: 1 = *exposure*, 2 = *validation*, 3 = *settings*

	Address	Date of birth[1]	Driver's license[2]	Last name[1]	Sex[3]	Vehicle color[1]	License plate[3]	Vehicle model[2]
Group	−0.102	−0.352	−0.065	−0.507	0.065	−0.149	0.328	−0.073
P-value	0.500	0.016*	0.671	0.004**	0.668	0.379	0.010*	0.681
Gender	0.581	0.202	0.450	0.595	0.588	−0.341	−0.273	−0.465
P-value	0.000***	0.178	0.004**	0.001**	0.000***	0.053	0.037*	0.013*

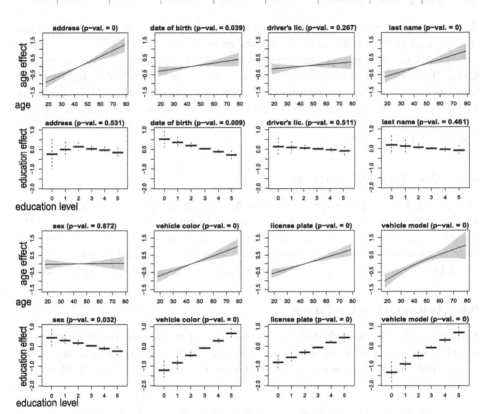

Fig. 6. Effect of *age* and *education level* on the disclosure rate (note, for model identifiability, effects are centered around zero across the data observed [47]). Shaded regions and dashed lines indicate approximate, pointwise 95% confidence intervals.

6.3 Icon Recognizability and Understandability

Next, for RQ 10, we evaluate the recognizability of the used icons. Therefore, we ask all participants in the test group to identify a given icon. In addition, we ask participants to recall who was able to access one piece of personal information they had disclosed during the profile creation. Our results show that more participants are able to correctly recall privacy-related information linked to one of their personal information; 28% of participants identified the given icon correctly and 37% correctly recalled who was able to access their personal information. Moreover, we ask participants to state how often the additional privacy-related information did influence their disclosure decision. In total, 55% stated it had an influence on their decision (combining the answers *sometimes*, *most of the time*, and *always*), with 14% being unsure and 31% stating *never*.

6.4   Data Disclosure

Then, additionally, the participants had to reflect on the amount of personal information they had disclosed during the experiment (for RQ 11). This question was raised to both groups and the answers indicate differences; in the control group 19% are able to correctly state how many attributes of personal information they had disclosed compared to 28% in the test group. This indicates improved – yet small – reminiscence and awareness. While these numbers remain relatively low they are higher than usually recorded in privacy research with failure rates of above 90% [19].

6.5   Use of Profile Settings

We note a similar difference in the data for RQ 12. As the icon set includes one icon specifically dedicated to the availability of profile settings, we evaluated the usage of these settings or (in case they were not adjusted by the participant) asked participants if they had perceived them. In the control group, 26% used or at least perceived the profile settings compared to 35% in the test group.

6.6   Information Usefulness

Finally, for RQ 13, we asked the participants to state the additional information which they regard most useful (or in case of the control group; which they would most liked to have), presenting them multiple options, as stated in Table 6. The

Table 6. Answers about most useful information (values rounded)

	Control group	Test group
If my data was exposed to others	44%	35%
If the service provider offered to validate my data	15%	11%
If profile settings for this information were available	10%	10%
If I should not provide a piece of information	17%	13%
I am not sure	15%	32%

results show interesting differences. While both groups state a piece of information's exposure as most useful, the test group shows noteworthy changes in the distribution of answers. The option for information exposure scores noticeably fewer answers in the test group while, at the same time, the number of uncertain answers more than doubles. This supports the theory that individuals are often unable to correctly evaluate their own privacy preferences as, once confronted with a given scenario, the individual's evaluation of helpful information shifts.

7   Limitations

Some shortcomings and limitations are worth mentioning. Firstly, the analysis of ride-sharing services is limited to the user perspective. That means that internal data processing and further data practices on side of the service provider are not included. To complement our analysis with the provider's side remains a task of our ongoing research. Secondly, the participants were notified twice before participating in the experiment that any disclosed personal data would not be stored. Though the term privacy was not mentioned explicitly to the participants, this possibly affected some participants in their disclosure decisions but was inevitable as this notification was required by the panel provider. Thirdly, our data indicate that participants with a higher level of education are more likely to disclose information about their vehicle. However, we did not ask participants about the possession of a vehicle, which could be a mediating factor. Lastly, the combinations of data attributes and icon type could be changed to examine whether different combinations of information and icon type yield insights about individuals' disclosure behavior.

8   Conclusion and Outlook

With this work, we contribute to the current state of privacy research in the sharing economy. Firstly, we analyzed the current practices of ride-sharing services to uncover part of their data practices. Secondly, we proposed and implemented a TET in the form of a browser extension that is capable of integrating additional information seamlessly into the services' websites and support individuals to make more informed decisions. Thirdly, we conducted a scenario-based online experiment with two representative samples for the test and control groups to evaluate our tool. For this experiment, we used a fictional ride-sharing service and asked participants to create a profile with their personal information. Based on our findings, we can confirm that a higher degree of transparency of data practices does not necessarily lead to less disclosed information. Consequently, we recommend service providers to offer profile settings for sensitive personal information and illustrate data practices which apply to their service and website more clearly. The direction of our future research includes the provider's perspective on the data practices and the overall affect data practices have on the individual's choice of service when they are able to compare services with the help of our tool. In addition to that, our prior analysis of ride-sharing services only covered the countries Germany, Austria, and Switzerland. Therefore, broader cultural differences and their effects on privacy concerns and disclosure behavior are not accounted for in this work.

Appendix

Table 7. Demographic data of respondents

%	Gender	%	Age	%	Education
51	Female	3	18–20	1	Not finished school (yet)
49	Male	20	21–30	6	Primary school certificate
		20	31–40	21	Primary school certificate & vocational training
		19	41–50	32	Secondary school certificate or equivalent
		23	51–60	19	Higher education entrance qualification
		15	>60	21	Higher education

Table 8. Context-specific formulations of IUIPC metric (answers were given as degree of agreement on a seven-point Likert scale)

Question	Statement
cont.1	My privacy is really a matter of my right to exercise control and autonomy over how MyCarPool collects, uses, and shares my information.
cont.2	The control of my personal information lies at the heart of my privacy.
cont.3	I believe that MyCarPool has taken or reduced my control over my data as a result of a marketing transaction.
coll.1	It bothered me when MyCarPool asked me for personal information.
coll.2	When MyCarPool asked me for personal information, I sometimes thought twice before providing it.
coll.3	I am concerned that MyCarPool collected too much personal information about me.
awar.1	MyCarPool did disclose the way my data are collected, processed, and used.
awar.2	I was aware and knowledgeable about how MyCarPool uses my personal information.

References

1. Acquisti, A., Grossklags, J.: Privacy attitudes and privacy behavior. In: Camp, L.J., Lewis, S. (eds.) Economics of Information Security, Advances in Information Security, vol. 12, pp. 165–178. Kluwer Academic Publishers, Boston (2004). https://doi.org/10.1007/1-4020-8090-5_13
2. Acquisti, A., Grossklags, J.: Privacy and rationality in individual decision making. IEEE Secur. Priv. **3**(1), 26–33 (2005). https://doi.org/10.1109/MSP.2005.22
3. Acquisti, A., John, L.K., Loewenstein, G.: The impact of relative standards on the propensity to disclose. J. Mark. Res. **49**(2), 160–174 (2012). https://doi.org/10.1509/jmr.09.0215
4. Agogo, D.: Invisible market for online personal data: an examination. Electron. Mark. **31**(4), 989–1010 (2020). https://doi.org/10.1007/s12525-020-00437-0
5. Bandara, R., Fernando, M., Akter, S.: Is the privacy paradox a matter of psychological distance? an exploratory study of the privacy paradox from a construal level theory perspective. In: Proceedings of the 51st Hawaii International Conference on System Sciences (2018). https://doi.org/10.24251/HICSS.2018.465
6. Beke, F.T., Eggers, F., Verhoef, P.C.: Consumer informational privacy: current knowledge and research directions. FNT Mark. Found. Trends Mark. **11**(1), 1–71 (2018). https://doi.org/10.1561/1700000057
7. Bélanger, F., Crossler, R.E.: Privacy in the digital age: a review of information privacy research in information systems. MIS Q. **35**(4), 1017 (2011). https://doi.org/10.2307/41409971
8. Binns, R., van Kleek, M., Veale, M., Lyngs, U., Zhao, J., Shadbolt, N.: It's reducing a human being to a percentage. In: Mandryk, R., Hancock, M., Perry, M., Cox, A. (eds.) Proceedings of the 2018 CHI Conference on Human Factors in Computing Systems, pp. 1–14. ACM, New York, NY, USA (2018). https://doi.org/10.1145/3173574.3173951
9. Bove, C., Aigrain, J., Lesot, M.J., Tijus, C., Detyniecki, M.: Contextualization and exploration of local feature importance explanations to improve understanding and satisfaction of non-expert users. In: 27th International Conference on Intelligent User Interfaces, pp. 807–819. ACM, New York, NY, USA (2022). https://doi.org/10.1145/3490099.3511139
10. Childers, T.L., Houston, M.J.: Conditions for a picture-superiority effect on consumer memory. J. Consu. Res. **11**(2), 643 (1984). https://doi.org/10.1086/209001
11. Colnago, J., et al.: Informing the design of a personalized privacy assistant for the internet of things. In: Proceedings of the 2020 CHI Conference on Human Factors in Computing Systems, pp. 1–13. Association for Computing Machinery, New York, NY, USA (2020). https://doi.org/10.1145/3313831.3376389
12. De, S.J., Le Metayer, D.: Privacy risk analysis to enable informed privacy settings. In: 2018 IEEE European Symposium on Security and Privacy Workshops (EuroS&PW), pp. 95–102. IEEE (2018). https://doi.org/10.1109/EuroSPW.2018.00019
13. Efroni, Z., Metzger, J., Mischau, L., Schirmbeck, M.: Privacy icons: a risk-based approach to visualisation of data processing. Eur. Data Prot. L. Rev. **5**(3), 352–366 (2019). https://doi.org/10.21552/edpl/2019/3/9
14. Entega Plus GmbH: Mitfahrgelegenheit und Co.: Fahrgemeinschaft 2.0. https://www.entega.de/blog/fahrgemeinschaft-die-wichtigsten-onlinemitfahrportale/
15. Gertheiss, J., Scheipl, F., Lauer, T., Ehrhardt, H.: Statistical inference for ordinal predictors in generalized additive models with application to bronchopulmonary

dysplasia. BMC. Res. Notes **15**(1), 112 (2022). https://doi.org/10.1186/s13104-022-05995-4

16. Hann, I.H., Hui, K.L., Lee, S.Y.T., Png, I.P.: Overcoming online information privacy concerns: an information-processing theory approach. J. Manag. Inf. Syst. **24**(2), 13–42 (2007). https://doi.org/10.2753/MIS0742-1222240202

17. Hesselmann, C., Gertheiss, J., Müller, J.P.: Ride sharing & data privacy: how data handling affects the willingness to disclose personal information. Findings (2021). https://doi.org/10.32866/001c.29863

18. Jackson, C.B., Wang, Y.: Addressing the privacy paradox through personalized privacy notifications. Proc. ACM Interact. Mobile Wearable Ubiquit. Technol. **2**(2), 1–25 (2018). https://doi.org/10.1145/3214271

19. Kamleitner, B., Sotoudeh, M.: Information sharing and privacy as a socio-technical phenomenon. TATuP - Zeitschrift für Technikfolgenabschätzung in Theorie und Praxis **29**(3), 68–71 (2019). https://doi.org/10.14512/tatup.28.3.68

20. Kariryaa, A., Savino, G.L., Stellmacher, C., Schöning, J.: Understanding users' knowledge about the privacy and security of browser extensions. In: 2021 Seventeenth Symposium on Usable Privacy and Security (SOUPS), pp. 99–118 (2021)

21. Kitkowska, A., Shulman, Y., Martucci, L.A., Wästlund, E.: Facilitating privacy attitudes and behaviors with affective visual design. In: Hölbl, M., Rannenberg, K., Welzer, T. (eds.) SEC 2020. IAICT, vol. 580, pp. 109–123. Springer, Cham (2020). https://doi.org/10.1007/978-3-030-58201-2_8

22. Kitkowska, A., Warner, M., Shulman, Y., Wästlund, E., Martucci, L.A.: Enhancing privacy through the visual design of privacy notices: exploring the interplay of curiosity, control and affect. In: Sixteenth Symposium on Usable Privacy and Security (SOUPS 2020), pp. 437–456. USENIX Association (2020)

23. Krol, K., Preibusch, S.: Control versus effort in privacy warnings for webforms. In: Proceedings of the 2016 ACM on Workshop on Privacy in the Electronic Society - WPES 2016, pp. 13–23. ACM Press, New York, New York, USA (2016). https://doi.org/10.1145/2994620.2994640

24. Machuletz, D., Laube, S., Böhme, R.: Webcam covering as planned behavior. In: Mandryk, R., Hancock, M., Perry, M., Cox, A. (eds.) Proceedings of the 2018 CHI Conference on Human Factors in Computing Systems, pp. 1–13. ACM, New York, NY, USA (2018). https://doi.org/10.1145/3173574.3173754

25. Malhotra, N.K., Kim, S.S., Agarwal, J.: Internet Users' Information Privacy Concerns (IUIPC): the construct, the scale, and a causal model. Inf. Syst. Res. **15**(4), 336–355 (2004). https://doi.org/10.1287/isre.1040.0032

26. Marsch, M., Grossklags, J., Patil, S.: Won't you think of others? interdependent privacy in smartphone app permissions. Proc. ACM Human Comput. Inter. **5**(CSCW2), 1–35 (2021). https://doi.org/10.1145/3479581

27. Nissenbaum, H.: Privacy in Context: Technology, Policy, and the Integrity of Social Life. Stanford University Press, Stanford, CA (2009). https://doi.org/10.1515/9780804772891

28. Nissim, K., Wood, A.: Is privacy privacy? Philos. Trans. Ser. A Math. Phys. Eng. Sci. **376**(2128), 20170358 (2018)

29. Olejnik, L., Englehardt, S., Narayanan, A.: Battery status not included: assessing privacy in web standards. CEUR Workshop Proc. **1873**, 17–24 (2017)

30. Preibusch, S., Krol, K., Beresford, A.R.: The privacy economics of voluntary over-disclosure in web forms. In: Böhme, R. (ed.) The Economics of Information Security and Privacy, pp. 183–209. Springer, Heidelberg (2013). https://doi.org/10.1007/978-3-642-39498-0_9

31. Proserpio, D., Xu, W., Zervas, G.: You get what you give: theory and evidence of reciprocity in the sharing economy. Quant. Mark. Econ. **16**(4), 371–407 (2018). https://doi.org/10.1007/s11129-018-9201-9
32. Team, R.C.: R: a language and environment for statistical computing. R Foundation for Statistical Computing, Vienna, Austria (2022). https://www.R-project.org/
33. Ranzini, G., Etter, M., Lutz, C., Vermeulen, I.E.: Privacy in the sharing economy. SSRN Electron. J. (2017). https://doi.org/10.2139/ssrn.2960942
34. Rath, D.K., Kumar, A.: Information privacy concern at individual, group, organization and societal level - a literature review. Vilakshan - XIMB J. Manag. **18**(2), 171–186 (2021). https://doi.org/10.1108/XJM-08-2020-0096
35. Reinhardt, D., Khurana, M., Hernández Acosta, L.: I still need my privacy: exploring the level of comfort and privacy preferences of German-speaking older adults in the case of mobile assistant robots. Pervasive Mob. Comput. **74**, 101397 (2021). https://doi.org/10.1016/j.pmcj.2021.101397
36. Schor, J., et al.: Debating the sharing economy. J. Self Gov. Manag. Econ. **4**(3), 7–22 (2014)
37. Smith, J.H., Dinev, T., Xu, H.: Information privacy research: an interdisciplinary review. MIS Q. **35**(4), 989 (2011). https://doi.org/10.2307/41409970
38. Story, P., et al.: Awareness, adoption, and misconceptions of web privacy tools. Proc. Priv. Enhancing Technol. **2021**(3), 308–333 (2021). https://doi.org/10.2478/popets-2021-0049
39. Teubner, T., Flath, C.M.: Privacy in the sharing economy. J. Assoc. Inf. Syst. **20**, 213–242 (2019). https://doi.org/10.17705/1jais.00534
40. Tutz, G., Gertheiss, J.: Regularized regression for categorical data. Stat. Model. **16**(3), 161–200 (2016). https://doi.org/10.1177/1471082X16642560
41. Utopia GmbH: Die besten Mitfahrgelegenheiten. https://utopia.de/ratgeber/mitfahrgelegenheiten/
42. VCS Verkehrs-Club der Schweiz: Carpooling. https://www.verkehrsclub.ch/ratgeber/auto/autoteilen/carpooling/
43. VGL Verlagsgesellschaft: Mitfahrzentralen im Vergleich. https://www.vergleich.org/mitfahrzentrale/
44. Wang, Yu., Wang, S., Wang, J., Wei, J., Wang, C.: An empirical study of consumers' intention to use ride-sharing services: using an extended technology acceptance model. Transportation **47**(1), 397–415 (2018). https://doi.org/10.1007/s11116-018-9893-4
45. Wood, S.N.: On p-values for smooth components of an extended generalized additive model. Biometrika **100**(1), 221–228 (2013). https://doi.org/10.1093/biomet/ass048
46. Wood, S.N.: Fast stable restricted maximum likelihood and marginal likelihood estimation of semiparametric generalized linear models. J. Roy. Stat. Soc. Ser. B (Stat. Methodol.) **73**(1), 3–36 (2011). https://doi.org/10.1111/j.1467-9868.2010.00749.x
47. Wood, S.N.: Generalized Additive Models. Chapman and Hall/CRC (2017). https://doi.org/10.1201/9781315370279
48. Yao, M.Z., Rice, R.E., Wallis, K.: Predicting user concerns about online privacy. J. Am. Soc. Inform. Sci. Technol. **58**(5), 710–722 (2007). https://doi.org/10.1002/asi.20530
49. Zhang, S., Feng, Y., Bauer, L., Cranor, L.F., Das, A., Sadeh, N.: Did you know this camera tracks your mood? Proc. Priv. Enhancing Technol. **2021**(2), 282–304 (2021). https://doi.org/10.2478/popets-2021-0028

Location Privacy, 5G AKA, and Enhancements

Mohamed Taoufiq Damir[✉] and Valtteri Niemi

Department of Computer Science, University of Helsinki, Helsinki, Finland
{mohamed.damir,valtteri.niemi}@helsinki.fi

Abstract. We introduce a linkability attack variant on 5G AKA that we call the *Replay In GUTI* (RIG) attack. Our attack investigates the case where the *temporary identifier* GUTI is used for identification. Recalling that the GUTI-based identification is the most frequently used case, the goal of the RIG attack is to check the presence of a target user in an attack area, that is by linking two *Authentication and Key Agreement* (AKA) sessions. We further explain how our attack works also against some enhancements of 5G AKA, in which the GUTI case is not covered. We focus on protocols where authentication requires a contribution from the *User Equipment* (UE). As an example of such enhancements, we discuss the works in [5,15,16], then we examine the protocol proposed in [2] in more detail. Moreover, we propose a USIM-compatible fix against our attack.

Keywords: 5G-AKA · Privacy · IMSI catchers

1 Introduction

Over the years, active attacks on mobile telephony networks became gradually a serious security and privacy threat. Such a type of attack was often ignored during the design of early mobile security protocols. For example, 2G networks have only a little protection against active attacks, or even against passive ones. The 2G networks suffered from the use of weak cryptography algorithms and the lack of mutual authentication between users and the networks. Despite the security improvements deployed in subsequent mobile network generations, various works introduced attacks on 3G, 4G, and even 5G [7–9]. Moreover, active attacks became more feasible in practice, which is due to the availability of the software and hardware that is needed to perform such attacks [10].

In the present work, we mainly focus on tracking and localising 5G users. More precisely, we are concerned with detecting the presence of a target user in an attack area. The detection is by intercepting the message flow in the 5G *Authentication and Key Agreement* protocol (5G AKA).

This work was supported by the Business Finland Consortium Project "Post-Quantum Cryptography" under Grant 754/31/2020.

H. P. Reiser and M. Kyas (Eds.): NordSec 2022, LNCS 13700, pp. 40–57, 2022.
https://doi.org/10.1007/978-3-031-22295-5_3

In mobile networks, every user is assigned a globally unique identifier called *International Mobile Subscriber Identity* (IMSI) in 4G and *Subscriber Permanent Identifier* (SUPI) in 5G. This identifier is used to identify the user during communication, but it is also used to locate and track the user. The tracking is required for billing and legal obligation purposes and also because, for incoming calls, the network has to find the user. In this setting, intercepting the SUPI/IMSI is a serious privacy threat.

To intercept communication between a user and a network, the attacker uses the so-called IMSI catcher[1]. An IMSI catcher works as a fake base station to obtain users' identities by impersonating the real network. Smartphones' baseband modem keeps selecting the base station with the best signal quality. Based on the fact that the modem does not distinguish between fake and legit base stations, the IMSI catcher is in theory able to attract most users in its attack area. Obtaining users' identities in an attack area can serve the attacker to detect the presence of a *Person of Interest* (PoI) with a known identifier, or to simply collect information about users visiting the attack zone.

To avoid IMSI catching in 4G/5G, the serving network assigns to the USIM a *Globally Unique Temporary Identity* (GUTI), which is a temporary and frequently changing identifier. Note that knowing a user's GUTI would not serve in distinguishing such a user from random users during the next communication if the GUTI has been changed. Unfortunately, in 4G, there are circumstances where the user is required to send the permanent identifier (IMSI) as plain text. For example, when the network is unable to derive the IMSI from the GUTI, or when the GUTI is not yet assigned, which might accrue during the first contact to a new network in the case of roaming.

Consequently, an active attacker can recover the IMSI by simply emulating one of the above scenarios. The technical specification for security architecture and procedures in 5G, 3GPP TS.33.501, improved in resisting IMSI catchers by imposing SUPI concealment. More precisely, in 5G, the permanent identifier SUPI is never sent as plain text. The concealed SUPI is called the *Subscription Concealed Identifier* (SUCI). Despite the adoption of encrypting the SUPI in 5G networks, various works, see Sect. 3, showed that it is still possible to track users based on investigating the user's behavior during the 5G AKA procedure. The most popular way of tracking is by the so-called *linkability* attacks.

Known linkability attacks against 5G are particular cases of replay attacks, where the attacker intercepts and replays messages between a user X and its service provider to link different 5G AKA sessions to the same user. Usually, the attacker replays recorded messages from a previous execution of the AKA protocol to users in an attack area, then observes answers from the users. A linkability attack is "successful" if the attacker is able (based on the received answers) to distinguish the user X from the other users in the attack area, that is even if the identity of X is encrypted or randomized, i.e., X used the SUCI or GUTI for identification. In this work, we introduce a linkability attack in the

---

[1] Conventionally called IMSI catchers also in the case of 5G although the permanent identifier is SUPI.

case of GUTI-based identification. We aim to further highlight the importance
of considering the GUTI case in 5G AKA enhancements. The GUTI-based identification is often ignored while designing enhancements for 5G AKA resisting
linkability attacks. Moreover, most 5G AKA enhancements use the fact that the
user is performing extra operations, such as generating randomness or encrypting SUPI, before sending its identifier to the network. However, this is not the
case for GUTI-based identification and the enhancements cannot be extended to
GUTI-based identification. For a complete exposition of our work, we will first
recall the 5G mobile network architecture, then we will describe our contributions in more detail.

2   Mobile Network Architecture

Mobile network architecture consists of three major entities.

- The *User Equipment* (UE) which includes the *Mobile Equipment* (ME) and
  the *Universal Subscriber Identity Module* (USIM). These two can be illustrated, respectively, as a phone and a SIM card.
- The *Home Network* (HN) is the core network that handles all management
  tasks for the user. For the present work, the HN is the entity responsible for
  authentication and key agreement. We denote the identity of the HN by ID_H.
- The *Serving Network* (SN) is the network the user is connected to. It is also
  responsible of forwarding messages between the UE and HN. We denote the
  identity of the SN by ID_S.

Communication between the UE and the SN is either initiated by the UE, e.g.,
for outgoing call, or by the SN, e.g., for incoming call. In both cases, the UE is
required to send its identity to the SN. In 5G networks, the HN assigns to every
UE a unique identifier called the *Subscription Permanent Identifier* (SUPI).

   As mentioned in the introduction, sending the SUPI as plaintext is a serious
privacy threat. A new feature in 3GPP TS 33.501, the 5G security specification,
is the use of public-key cryptography for SUPI encryption, i.e., ECIES algorithm, which results in the *Subscription Concealed Identifier* (SUCI). The SUPI
encryption (resp., decryption) is performed at the UE (resp., HN) using an HN
public key (resp. secret key) that we denote by pk_H (resp. sk_H).

   Whenever a SUCI is received by the SN, this last forwards it to the HN. Next,
the HN proceeds on generating an authentication challenge for the UE based on
a freshly generated random bitstring $RAND_H$ and the user's stored credentials.
The UE and the HN share a long-term key K, and a dynamic sequence number
SQN, where K is stored at the temper-resistant part of the USIM at the UE side,
while SQN is used to check synchronization and detect replay attacks. We denote
by SQN_H and SQN_U, the sequence numbers at the HN and UE, respectively.

   Once a mutual authentication and key agreement are established between
the UE and SN via the HN, the serving network assigns to the UE[2] a *Globally*

---

[2] The GUTI assignment is done over a secure channel established after authenticating
the UE by the SN via the HN.

Unique Temporary Identity (GUTI). The GUTI is an 80 bits string, where the first 48 bits carry some "predictable" information, e.g., the mobile country code, while the remaining 32 bits are the "unpredictable" part of the GUTI[3].

Compared to the SUCI, GUTI is the more frequent mean of identification. For the UE side, the use of GUTI does not require extra computations, i.e., encryption, while on the SN side, it is not necessary to ask for the HN's help to identify the UE, which is the case for getting decryption of the SUCI. For securing the communication between the SN and the UE, the SN can choose either to use the previously established keys with the UE or to start a new AKA procedure by first resolving the SUPI from GUTI, then sending the SUPI to the HN to trigger a new authentication, see Sect. 4 for a detailed exposition of 5G AKA.

We summarise the used notations in Table 1.

Table 1. Summary of notations

Notation	Meaning
HN	Home network
UE	User equipment
SN	Serving network
ID_H	HN identity
ID_S	SN identity
SUPI	Subscriber permanent identifier
pk_H/sk_H	HN public/private ECIES keys
K_D	The shared SUPI encryption key resulting from ECIES
SUCI	Subscriber Concealed Identifier (encrypted SUPI)
GUTI	Globally unique temporary identifier
K	Long term key shared between HN and UE
SQN_U	Sequence number at UE
SQN_H	Sequence number at HN
$RAND_H$	The HN random challenge

3 Contributions and Related Work

Various works considered and proposed solutions to resist active attackers in 5G and beyond, see for instance [5–9] and the references therein. Such proposals often require some contribution from the user. In fact, the user contribution is usually carried to the HN during the SUPI-based identification. Thus, such

---

[3] Typically it is just the unpredictable part of GUTI that needs to be explicitly included in messages between the network and the UE.

enhancements typically do not cover the GUTI case. In the present work, we propose a linkability attack against 5G AKA with user identification based on GUTI. Indeed, a similar attack against 5G AKA is proposed in [10] in the case where user is identified based on SUCI. In our work, we emphasize that our GUTI variant of the attack works also against the 5G AKA enhancement in [2], while this enhancement protects against the attack in [10]. In fact, linkability attacks were blocked in in [2] by re-using an ECIES shared key between the UE and the core network. The primary purpose of this shared key is to encrypt the SUPI. In the present work we explain how our attack works against the protocol proposed in [2] and its possible extensions to the GUTI case.

We further discuss the protocols in [5,15,16]. To block linkability attacks, these protocols (at least) require the UE to send both the SUPI and a freshly generated random bitstring in an encrypted message to the SN. In fact, such 5G AKA enhancements did not cover the GUTI-based identification, thus, we discuss the effect of our attack on their possible extensions to the GUTI case. Our aim behind discussing the protocols in [2,5,15,16] is to highlight the importance of considering the GUTI-based identification in future 5G AKA enhancements. Moreover, we argue that the enhancements using public key encryption during identification are usually not extendable to the GUTI case to protect against our attack, that is keeping in mind the purpose of using the GUTI. Finally, we propose a fix against our attack. The fix is USIM compatible.

In summary, our contributions consist of:

- An attack on 5G AKA and 5G AKA', the 5G AKA enhancement proposed in [2].
- We suggest a USIM compatible privacy preserving fix against this RIG attack.
- Emphasizing the importance of covering the GUTI based identification in AKA enhancements by further discussing the protocols in [5,15,16].

4   5G Authentication and Key Agreement Protocol (5G AKA)

Before proceeding with describing our attack, we will first give details of the 5G AKA protocol. The 5G system supports two protocols, namely, the 5G-*Authentication and Key Agreement* and a mobile network specific method for the *Extensible Authentication Protocol*, denoted 5G-AKA and EAP-AKA', respectively. The two protocols are similar in our context, thus, we will mainly focus on the 5G AKA. In 5G AKA, we distinguish two steps, the UE identification, which consists of the SUPI concealment and the UE's identification by the HN, and the authentication phase, which allows both the UE and the HN to securely authenticate each other and agree on shared secret keys.

4.1   The UE's Identification

The identification in 5G is either done by sending the GUTI from the UE or the SUCI. It is also possible that identification is triggered by request from the network side. The GUTI is a frequently changing identifier that appears as random[4]. Hence, a scenario where a malicious but passive entity intercepts it does not threaten the privacy of the user. This may be the underlying reason why most works on linkability attacks ignore the case of GUTI in their design. In our work, we will show why it is worth considering such case. For the sake of completeness, we will first describe the SUCI-based identification in 5G AKA and enhancements. In the rest of this section, we focus on the SUCI case.

For the SUPI concealment, the UE uses an *Elliptic Curve Integrated Encryption Scheme* (ECIES) algorithm, see 3GPP TS 33.501 Annex C, with the HN public key, pk_{HN}. This public key is stored at the USIM and it is used to to derive an ECIES key K_D, shared between the UE and the HN. The SUPI encryption can be performed by a next generation USIM [3GPP TS 31.102] or by the mobile equipment. The SUCI is then sent to the HN via the SN, together with a MAC tag, and pk_U, an ephemeral public-key generated at the UE.

Reflecting the UE side, the HN will use its secret key, sk_{HN}, to generate K_D using pk_U, check the MAC, and decrypt the SUCI. Then the UE data is retrieved from the HN database and the HN proceeds with an authentication procedure.

4.2 The Authentication and Key Agreement

As specified by 3GPP TS 33.501, the 5G-AKA uses a *Key Derivation Function* (KDF) and seven independent symmetric key algorithms denoted by $f_1, f_2, f_3, f_4, f_5, f_1^*$ and f_5^*. These functions are assumed to be one-way functions and they are used, e.g., to derive keys that protect integrity and confidentiality.

Authentication in 5G-AKA. The authentication procedure starts once the HN decrypts the SUCI. If the MAC check passes, then based on the SUPI, the HN retrieves the long term key K, and its related *sequence number*, denoted SQN_H, which is a 48 bits string used for the purpose of proving to the UE that the authentication data sent to it is fresh (and not something recorded and replayed by an attacker). The HN further generates a 128-bit random number $RAND_H$, then proceeds on computing an authentication vector (AV) by running the algorithm in Fig. 1 using K, SQN_H, $RAND_H$ and an Authentication Management Field (AMF) in which a specific separation bit equals 1. The AMF is a 16 bits string, where the first bit is called the "AMF separation bit". It is used for the purposes of differentiating between mobile generations, the last 8 bits can be used for proprietary purposes. As the next step, the HN sends ($RAND_H$, AUTN, HXRES*) to the SN, then this last forwards $RAND_H$ and AUTN to the UE.

At this point, we distinguish two types of operations at the UE, namely, those performed by the ME and those performed by the USIM. As depicted by Figs. 2 and 3, we put together the operations at the USIM (resp. ME) into a single algorithm that we denote by At-USIM (resp. At-ME).

---

[4] The unpredictable part appears as random.

AV(RAND, K, SQN_H, ID_{SN}, AMF)
1. Compute $Mac =$
   $f_1(K, RAND, \mathrm{SQN}_H, \mathrm{AMF})$.
2. $\mathrm{XRES} = f_2(K, RAND)$.
3. $CONC = f_5(K, RAND) \oplus \mathrm{SQN}_H$.
4. $\mathrm{AUTN} = \{CONC, \mathrm{AMF}, \mathrm{MAC}\}$.
5. $\mathrm{CK} = f_3(K, RAND)$, $\mathrm{IK} = f_4(K, RAND)$.
6. $\mathrm{XRES}^* =$
   $\mathrm{KDF}(\mathrm{CK}, \mathrm{IK}, RAND, \mathrm{XRES}, \mathrm{ID}_{SN})$.
7. $\mathrm{HXRES}^* = SHA256(RAND, \mathrm{XRES}^*)$.
8. $K_{ausf} = \mathrm{KDF}(\mathrm{CK}, \mathrm{IK}, RAND, CONC, \mathrm{ID}_{SN})$.
9. $K_{seaf} =$
   $\mathrm{KDF}(K_{ausf}, \mathrm{ID}_{SN})$.
10. **Return** (RAND, AUTN, HXRES^*,
    K_{ausf}, K_{seaf}).

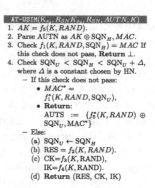

AT-USIM(K_s, $R_{SN}K_s$, R_{SN}, AUTN, K)
1. $AK = f_5(K, RAND)$.
2. Parse AUTN as $AK \oplus \mathrm{SQN}_H$, MAC.
3. Check $f_1(K, RAND, \mathrm{SQN}_H) = MAC$ If
   this check does not pass, **Return** $\perp$.
4. Check $\mathrm{SQN}_U < \mathrm{SQN}_H < \mathrm{SQN}_U + \Delta$,
   where Δ is a constant chosen by HN.
   - If this check does not pass:
     • $MAC^* =$
       $f_1^*(K, RAND, \mathrm{SQN}_U)$,
     • **Return**:
       $\mathrm{AUTS} := \{f_5^*(K, RAND) \oplus$
       $\mathrm{SQN}_U, \mathrm{MAC}^*\}$
   - Else:
     (a) $\mathrm{SQN}_U \leftarrow \mathrm{SQN}_H$
     (b) $\mathrm{RES} = f_2(K, RAND)$.
     (c) $\mathrm{CK} = f_3(K, RAND)$,
        $\mathrm{IK} = f_4(K, RAND)$.
     (d) **Return** (RES, CK, IK)

Fig. 1. Challenge and key material generation at HN

Fig. 2. Challenge response at the USIM

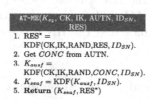

AT-ME(K_{s_2}, CK, IK, AUTN, ID_{SN}, RES)
1. $\mathrm{RES}^* =$
   $\mathrm{KDF}(\mathrm{CK}, \mathrm{IK}, RAND, \mathrm{RES}, \mathrm{ID}_{SN})$.
2. Get $CONC$ from AUTN.
3. $K_{ausf} =$
   $\mathrm{KDF}(\mathrm{CK}, \mathrm{IK}, RAND, CONC, \mathrm{ID}_{SN})$.
4. $K_{seaf} = \mathrm{KDF}(K_{ausf}, \mathrm{ID}_{SN})$.
5. **Return** (K_{seaf}, RES^*)

Fig. 3. Session key and RES^* generation at the ME.

In the case of a successful run of AT-USIM, the ME generates RES^* using AT-ME, then forwards it to the SN. The SN receives the value of RES^* from the UE and then compares $\mathrm{SHA256}(\mathrm{RAND}_H, \mathrm{RES}^*)$ with HXRES^*. If the two values are equal, then the SN forwards RES^* to the HN which verifies the equality $\mathrm{XRES}^* = \mathrm{RES}^*$. If this last check passes, then finally, the HN sends the SUPI and K_{seaf} to the SN.

Figure 4 (Appendix) summarizes the workflow in 5G AKA.

5   A New Attack: Replay in GUTI (RIG)

When the GUTI is sent in a connection request from UE to the SN, the SN resolves the SUPI from GUTI, then decides between either communicating using previously established keys or starting a new 5G AKA authentication procedure, very similar to the one described in the case of SUCI. For the purposes of the attack, we utilize the latter option where the SN chooses to authenticate the UE via the HN. More precisely, in our attack, we link two 5G AKA sessions, where a different GUTI is used as an identifier for each session.

5.1 The RIG Attack

We distinguish two steps in our attack, namely, a discovery phase and an attack phase.

The Discovery Phase. In the first phase of our attack, the attacker,

1. sniffs the network traffic for a GUTI-based 5G AKA protocol run related to a Person of Interest (PoI), denoted as U_{target}. Linking the 5G AKA session with the PoI can be done by other means e.g. surveillance cameras or with fine-grained location information.
2. records the authentication vector sent by the SN to the UE consisting of the target's AUTN and RAND that we denote by AV_{target}. The attacker also observes and records the identity of the local operator that serves the UE.

Please not that the attacker remains passive throughout the discovery phase, i.e., it just receives and records radio signals but does not have to transmit anything.

The Attack Phase. In the attack phase, we assume that U_{target} is using the GUTI for its next connection. Note that this GUTI is not typically the same one that has been seen by the attacker in the discovery phase. In order to localise U_{target} in an attack area, the attack goes as follows.

1. The attacker sets up a fake base station which pretends to belong to a local operator identified in the discovery phase.
2. Because the fake base station has a strong signal, some devices in the attack area try to create a radio connection to the attacker base station. Users that are registered to the claimed local operator, send their temporary identifier (unpredictable part of GUTI) if they have one [3GPP TS 38.331]. If the PoI U_{target} is in the attack area, then it will send (unpredictable part of) its GUTI that we denote by $GUTI_{\text{target}}$[5].
3. The attacker sends authentication request [3GPP TS 24.501] with the previously recorded authentication data AV_{target} to every connected user in the attack area.
4. The attacker receives the users' responses.
   The attacker is expected to receive two types of responses:
   - The non-targeted users in the attack area will reply with an authentication failure, that is because the MAC check in step 3 in Fig. 2 fails, which is due to the fact that AV_{target} is generated using the "wrong" key material.
   - If U_{target} is in the attack area, then the attacker will receive a response containing a MAC check pass and a synchronization failure message as depicted in step 4 in Fig. 2.

---

[5] At this stage $GUTI_{\text{target}}$ is unknown to the attacker and not linked yet to the PoI.

5. In the latter case the attacker learns that U_{target} is in the attack area and records $GUTI_{target}$.

Note that recording $GUTI_{target}$ might lead to further tracking of U_{target}, that is in case the same $GUTI_{target}$ was re-used for U_{target}. In fact, previous works on GUTI re-allocations shows that some operators fail to frequently renew their subscribers GUTIs after every communication, see for instance [11]. Anyways, after the GUTI has finally been re-allocated, the attack phase needs to be repeated in the same, extended or different attack area.

6   Feasibility of the RIG Attack

In this section, we discuss the practical setting of our attack.

6.1   IMSI-Catchers

Communication between the UE and SN is either initiated by the UE (*registration request*) or the SN (*identification request* or *paging*). In both cases, the UE sends the user identifier (SUCI or GUTI) to the SN. Such an identification is not authenticated, thus, an IMSI-catcher (fake base station) can either send an identification request to the UE or a registration request to the SN. Moreover, we assume that the IMSI-catcher can impersonate the real network and replay messages from both the SN and the UE. Various works showed that these assumptions are feasible in practice [12–14].

6.2   The Attack Area

The ME continuously monitors the signal strength in its surrounding area, then selects the cell with the strongest signal. Such a procedure is not authenticated, thus, the ME cannot distinguish between a legit SN and a fake base station. Consequently, in practice an IMSI catcher is assumed to attract the mobile devices in its range.

7   Attacking 5G AKA Enhancements

7.1   Applying the RIG Attack to 5G AKA'

In [2], and to bypass known linkability attacks, the authors showed that it is enough to use 5G AKA with the addition of hiding the $RAND_H$ used in AV from an attacker operating in the channel between the SN and the UE. For this end, the authors in [2], suggested encrypting $RAND_H$, the random number generated at the HN, by re-using the key that was primarily utilized to encrypt the SUPI, namely the key K_D in Sect. 4.1. More precisely, the authentication vector sent by the HN to the SN is the same as the one in Fig. 4, but with $Enc_{K_D}(RAND_H)$, an encrypted $RAND_H$, instead of plaintext $RAND_H$. Using the fact that K_D

is initially shared with the UE, this last obtains $RAND_H$ by decrypting the received message, then runs Algorithms 2 and 3 in a similar fashion than is done in "standard" 5G AKA. The protocol in [2] is denoted 5G AKA'. It is worth mentioning that the authors in [2] used Tamarin tool to formally verify the security of 5G AKA'.

The Attack on 5G AKA'. The case of GUTI is indeed not mentioned in [2]. In our context, in the case of GUTI, the SN first resolves the SUPI from GUTI, then starts an authentication phase by sending the SUPI (or a stored SUCI from the first identification) to the HN. For the authentication phase, there are two possible scenarios:

1. The HN uses the authentication procedure as in 5G AKA in the case of GUTI.
2. The HN uses the authentication procedure as in 5G AKA' in the case of GUTI, where the HN uses K_D, the ECIES shared key which is stored during the last SUCI based identification, that is to encrypt the RAND in the newly generated authentication vector.

The first scenario is vulnerable to the RIG attack as described in the beginning of the section. For the latter scenario to be possible, the ME has to store the key K_D after the previous SUCI based identification and HN keeps using the same key K_D for encrypting $RAND_H$ in every GUTI-based identification.

As described in the RIG attack, the attacker records AV_{target}, the target's authentication vector resulting from a first GUTI based identification, which in the 5G AKA' case consists of AUTN and $En_{K_D}(RAND_H)$, the symmetric encryption of $RAND_H$ using K_D. Hence, the attack on 5G AKA' is as follows:

1. The attacker records the target's authentication vector AV_{target} from the first connection.
2. The attacker waits for users in an attack area to request for radio connection.
3. For each connected user, the attacker replays the recorded AV_{target} containing $Enc_{K_D}(RAND_H)$ and AUTN in an authentication request.
4. The non-target users will reply with an authentication failure.
5. If the target user is in the attack area, then U_{target} will successfully decrypt $En_{K_D}(RAND_H)$ and the MAC check at the UE will pass, while the synchronization check will fail.
6. The attacker learns whether U_{target} is in the attack area and, in the positive case, records its GUTI.

Note that our attack is successful against 5G AKA' because of the re-use of the key K_D from the SUCI based identification. As this key is generated during the SUPI encryption, then renewing it will only accrue when a new SUCI based authentication was initiated.

Finally, with our attack we highlight two problems:

– Re-using the ECIES key[6] to block linkability attacks might still lead to other linkability attacks when the GUTI case is not covered.

---

[6] The key used for encrypting the SUPI.

- The case of GUTI must be considered in formal verification of AKA protocols in 5G and beyond.

7.2   Discussion on Further 5G AKA Enhancements

In the previous section, we examined the 5G AKA' which is a 5G AKA enhancement that is resistant to linkability attacks. In this section, we discuss two examples of 5G AKA enhancements that considered[7] further security properties, namely, the works in [5,15,16].

In [3], the authors conducted a 5G AKA formal verification using Tamarin. Among the security issues pointed out by the verifier is the lack of session key confirmation. In [5], the authors proposed a protocol with session key confirmation that is resistant to known linkability attacks. The work in [16], considered another security issue in 5G AKA, namely, the lack of perfect forward secrecy. In [15], both perfect forward secrecy and session key confirmation are investigated.

The key idea in [15] requires the UE to generate a random bitstring R_U, and R_U is encrypted with the SUPI and ID_{SN} using pk_H, while the protocols in [5,16], additionally require the SN to send a random R_S to the UE, then both R_S and R_U are encrypted with the SUPI and ID_{SN} using pk_H. In the three protocols, the encrypted message is sent to the HN via the SN. This idea does not directly carry over to the GUTI case because the SN does not have access to sk_H. Indeed, if GUTI would be encrypted in place of SUPI, the SN would need to consult HN for decryption. But this would completely undermine the purpose of GUTI which allows the SN to protect the identity privacy without bothering HN. Recall that SN has the option not to authenticate the GUTI but instead use the previously established shared keys with the UE. On the other hand, if SN decides to go for authentication in the GUTI case, then this needs to be done with "standard" 5G AKA, and it follows that the RIG attack would apply.

To extend the protocol in [15] to cover the GUTI case, we discuss next a modification where the identity (which is GUTI instead of SUPI) is sent in plaintext while the random R_U and ID_{SN} are still sent in encrypted form, using the public key of the HN. If the SN chooses the option of not authenticating the UE, the encrypted message is ignored by the SN. Later the UE will find out that authentication is not required, and the UE can delete the freshly generated R_U. On the other hand, if the SN wants to authenticate, then it forwards the encrypted R_U and ID_{SN} to the HN, together with the permanent identity, after resolving it from the GUTI. Note that the SN must have received such a permanent identity from HN when the UE was authenticated by the SN for the first time. Indeed, the SN cannot forward GUTI to the HN because the latter cannot resolve it.

To extend the protocols of [5,16] the above modification does not work as such because both protocols begin by the UE receiving a fresh random R_S, generated by the SN, which needs to be encrypted together with SUPI, R_U, and

---

[7] In addition to linkability attacks.

ID_{SN}. In the case of GUTI, and when SN wants to skip the authentication, the SN would not need to generate such a random at all. Therefore, there are (at least) two possible ways how to extend these two protocols to the GUTI case.

- The UE will first send just a GUTI. If the SN does not want to authenticate (but use session keys from previous connection) then the protocol is completely skipped. On the other hand, if SN wants to authenticate, the protocol is run from the beginning, similarly as in the SUPI/SUCI case (as proposed in [5,16]). It is clear that this solution is not optimal because SN already has the identity of the UE but this information is not utilized, and the message flow is increased by one message from the UE to the SN.
- The SN always begins by generating its random R_S, regardless of what follows. This random could then be encrypted together with R_U and ID_{SN}, using the public key of the HN, while GUTI is sent in plaintext (similarly as in the above modification to the [15]). If the SN does not want to authenticate then both randoms are wasted. On the other hand, if SN wants to authenticate, the protocol continues in the modified form, based on the same idea as above for [15]: the encryption of the R_S, R_U and ID_{SN} replaces the SUCI of [5,16] while the permanent identity is sent separately from the SN to the HN. This solution is also not fully satisfactory either because of all the wasted effort dealing with generating and encrypting random strings (in case SN decides that authentication is not needed).

In the next section, we will propose a more efficient enhancement of 5G AKA, which is non-vulnerable to known linkability attacks, and the newly proposed RIG attack. Our fix is also USIM compatible, which means that our proposal does not require changes at the USIM, hence, it is compatible with previous mobile generations.

8   Protecting Against the RIG Attack

Before proceeding on describing our fix, we first precise the used threat model.

8.1   Threat Model

Our threat model follows from the requirements specified in TS 33.501. In fact, our threat model assumptions were implicitly introduced in Sect. 6.

The Channel Between the UE and the SN. The 3GPP standard, TS 33.501, does not specify conditions on the channel between the UE and the SN. In our context, we assume the existence of an attacker (IMSI-catcher) with the ability of sending messages to users in its attacking range. Moreover, the attacker can intercept, manipulate and replay messages in the channel between the SN and the UE.

The Channel Between the SN and the HN. As specified in TS 33.501, the channel between the SN and the HN is a core network interconnection wired channel. We assume that such a channel is secured by means outside of the scope of this paper.

The Channel Between the USIM and ME. In our model, we consider the UE as a single entity. Therefore, for the purposes of this paper, the communication between the USIM and the ME is assumed secure.

8.2 A Privacy-Preserving GUTI Protocol

In our fix, we suggest that during the GUTI assignment, the SN additionally generates a random value $RAND_S$ and then sends it, together with the GUTI, over the established encrypted channel between the SN and the UE. More precisely, the shared $RAND_S$ is stored at both the UE and SN sides, preserving its association to the assigned GUTI. The $RAND_S$ is used during the authentication procedure following identification with the associated GUTI for masking/unmasking the RAND involved in generating the authentication vector and in running the AT-USIM algorithm.

More precisely, we distinguish two phases.

1. **The GUTI assignment phase:**
   – The SN generates a GUTI and $RAND_S$ then sends

$$c = \mathrm{Enc}_{K_s}(\mathrm{GUTI}, \mathrm{RAND}_S)$$

   where K_s is the previously established session key used to protect the channel between the UE and the SN.
   – The ME decrypts c and stores GUTI and $RAND_S$.
2. **The authentication phase:**
   (a) The UE sends the GUTI to the SN in the radio connection request.
   (b) The SN resolves the SUPI from GUTI and forwards the SUPI to the HN.
   (c) The HN generates the authentication vector and sends HXRES*, AUTN and $RAND_H$ to SN.
   (d) The SN computes $RAND_S' = RAND_S \oplus RAND_H$, and sends $RAND_S'$ and AUTN to the ME.
   (e) The ME computes $RAND_H = RAND_S \oplus RAND_S'$.
   (f) The UE runs $\mathrm{At-USIM}$ and $\mathrm{At-ME}$ using $RAND_H$, computes K_{seaf}, and sends RES* to the SN.
   (g) The SN computes $SHA512(RAND_H, RES^*)$ and compares it with HXRES.
   (h) If the two are equal, the SN sends RES* to the HN. Otherwise, the authentication ends in failure.
   (i) The HN receives RES* and compares it with XRES* .
   (j) If the previous check passes, then the HN sends K_{seaf} to the SN.

Please note that the above procedure is similar to 5G AKA except for steps (d) and (e), where the SN (resp., ME) masks (resp., unmasks) $RAND_H$.

8.3   Remarks on the Security of the Fixed Protocol

As described in Sect. 5.1, the main idea behind the RIG attack is to explore the
fact that a recorded authentication vector will pass the MAC check in Fig. 2.
Clearly, the whole authentication procedure will be aborted by detecting a synchronization failure anyways, but receiving a synchronization failure message by
the attacker is enough in our case to conclude that such a message is sent by the
target user. In fact, our fix is enforced by a mechanism to detect replayed authentication vectors. According to 3GPP standards, the GUTI should be changed
with each voice call. Adapting this requirement to our fix results in the ME storing a new random 128 bitstring $RAND_S$ with every GUTI assignment. Assuming
that an attacker is performing the RIG attack by recording an authentication
vector sent by the SN to the UE consisting of AUTN and

$$RAND'_S = RAND_S \oplus RAND_H.$$

Then for the next communication, the UE is supposed to obtain a new GUTI
and randomness $RAND''_S$ from the SN. Now assuming that the UE starts a new
communication with the SN, then the UE is expecting a new authentication
vector containing a bitstring of the form $RAND''_S \oplus RAND'_H$, where $RAND'_H$ is
a freshly generated randomness at the HN.

Finally, if the attacker replayed $RAND'_S$ to the target user, this last is supposed to first compute

$$R = RAND''_S \oplus RAND'_S = RAND''_S \oplus RAND_S \oplus RAND_H,$$

which is different from $RAND'_H$ (with a high probability). Next, the target user
will use R instead of $RAND'_H$ in the MAC check in Fig. 2, which will abort the
communication before the synchronization check.

The remaining case in this direction is when the same GUTI is used (at
least) twice to identify an UE. In that case, the same $RAND_S$ would be used (at
least twice) to mask different instances of $RAND_H$. From cryptographic point of
view, masking two different random challenges with the same key using an XOR
operation is clearly not a secure solution. But because the re-use of the same
GUTI would anyways allow linkability of different messages, this shortcoming
does not decrease security level of our solution. Please note that with our fix,
the user can detect any replayed authentication vector. In fact, known linkability
attacks [7–9] rely on observing the user's responses after receiving a replayed
authentication vector. The mentioned works are described in the SUCI case, but
we note that they can be also extended to our case, where the AKA protocol is
based on a GUTI identification. Consequently, our proposal is also secure against
such attacks.

8.4   Formal Verification

To further analyze the linkability attack resistance of our fix, we use the well-
known formal verification tool Tamarin [18]. Linkability attacks follow from an

attacker distinguishing two protocol executions, say by two users UE1 and UE2. In other words, we aim to prove that the attacker will not be able to conclude information about UE2, even if the attacker is observing/recording a protocol execution by UE1. Tamarin can be used to check tractability and distinguishability using the operator `diff`. The `diff` operator takes as input two arguments. In our case, such two arguments are given by two GUTIs representing UE1 and UE2. In the diff mode, also known as the *observational equivalence* mode, Tamarin generates two instances of the protocol referred to by a *Left Hand Side* (LHS) and *Right Hand Side* (RHS). Moreover, Tamarin automatically generates a lemma called `Observational_equivalence`, where proving such a lemma implies that an intruder cannot distinguish LHS from RHS. Consequently, that proves that an attacker cannot link two protocol executions.

For our formal verification, we consider a Dolev-Yao attacker [17] in the channel between the UE and SN, namely an attacker who can eavesdrop, modify, delete and inject messages. However, the attacker cannot break cryptographic primitives and can only use them via their legitimate interface. We further consider the SN and the HN to be one single entity. Thus, the protocol is seen as a two-party protocol between the UE and the SN/HN. Please note that such assumptions do not contradict our assumptions in Sect. 8.1 on the attacker's abilities and the secure channel between the HN and SN.

Our Tamarin code is based on the script in [3], where the authors evaluated the security of 5G AKA using Tamarin. In [3], the authors considered a SUCI-based identification. Hence, the difference between our script and the code in [3] consists of considering the GUTI case instead of SUCI. Additionally, we implement our fix by masking the RAND used in the 5G AKA authentication vector. The masking is done using a random bitstring $RAND_S$ generated and sent by the SN during the GUTI assignment.

Verification Results. As pointed out in [18], the observational equivalence mode requires extra precomputations compared to the trace mode[8]. The observational mode usually results in long proof times or even non-termination. In fact, we run the Tamarin privacy script of the standardized 5G AKA [3]. Tamarin found traces for different linkability attacks in approximately four hours. As argued in the previous section, Tamarin is not expected to find such counterexamples in our fix. Indeed, Tamarin did not find any attack against our fix in a running time of approximately 24 h, which helped us establish more confidence in the security of our protocol. Moreover, we tested the above mentioned traces of the linkability attacks found in the standardized 5G AKA against our fix. As a result, Tamarin showed that our protocol is non-vulnerable to those attacks.

---

[8] The trace mode is used to prove "usual" security properties, e.g., keys secrecy or authentication.

8.5   Efficiency and Backward Compatibility

Our fixed protocol is similar to 5G AKA with the minimal additions. In summary, compared to 5G AKA, the additional computational, communication and memory overheads are:

1. **Computational overhead:**
   - Generating a random bitstring, $RAND_S$, at the SN.
   - During authentication, the SN performs one extra XOR operation:

$$RAND'_S = RAND_S \oplus RAND_H.$$

   - At the UE, the ME performs one extra XOR operation:

$$RAND_H = RAND_S \oplus RAND'_S.$$

2. **Communication overhead:**
   - Additional encrypted $RAND_S$ sent during the GUTI assignment phase by the SN.
   - We emphasize that no extra bits are sent over the radio channel between the SN and the UE. We recall that in 5G AKA, $RAND_H$ is sent by the SN to UE during authentication. Thus, our fix does not affect the size of the parameters sent over the radio channel during authentication, as it only requires sending $RAND_S \oplus RAND_H$ instead of $RAND_H$.
3. **Memory overhead:**
   - Storing $RAND_S$ at the ME and SN.

Please note that our fix does not require any changes at the USIM, which enables our proposal to be implemented using previous USIMs.

9   Conclusion

In the present work, we introduced a new linkability attack on 5G AKA in the case where the temporary identity GUTI is used for identification. We further show that the attack works also against several proposed enhancements of 5G AKA. We discuss how the enhancements known in the literature could be further enhanced to protect against the new attack. Unfortunately, it seems there are no straightforward extensions that would be sufficiently efficient in the case of GUTI. Therefore, we propose our own fix as an USIM-compatible extension of 5G AKA that resists all known linkability attacks, including the new one. For future research, it is important to include the case of temporary identity when mobile system authentication is developed further, including in standardization. Another future work is to try out the new RIG attack and the protection against it in an experimental set-up.

APPENDIX

The Message Flow in 5G AKA

```
5G AKA
─────────────────────────────────────────────────────────────────────────
UE                              SN                      HN
(pk_H, K, SQN_E, SUPI, GUTI)    (ID_S)                  (sk_H, ID_H)

SUCI ← Enc(pk_H, SUPI)
or Send GUTI
                    (SUCI or GUTI)
                    ─────────────────►
                                        Resolve SUPI from GUTI
                                        SUCI or SUPI
                                        ─────────────────►
                                                                SUPI ← Dec(sk_H, SUCI)
                                                                or use SUPI
                                                                Recover K, SQN_H, AMF
                                                                Generate RAND_H
                                                                Run AV(RAND_H, SQN_H, K, , AMF, ID_SN)
                                                RAND_H
                                                AUTN, HXRES*
                                        ◄─────────────────
                    RAND_H, AUTN
                    ◄─────────────────
Run AT − USIM
Case 1:
AT − USIM Returns ⊥
                    Mac Failure
                    ─────────────────►

Case 2:
AT − USIM Returns AUTS
                    (Sync Failure, AUTS)
                    ─────────────────►
                                        AUTS, RAND_H, SUCI
                                        Sync Failure
                                        ─────────────────►
                                                                If Mac* = f_1*(K, SQN_U, RAND_H)
                                                                SQN_H ← SQN_U + 1
Case 3:
AT − ME Returns (RES*, K_seaf)
                    RES*
                    ─────────────────►
                                        If SHA(RAND_H, RES*) = HXRES*
                                        ( SUCI, RES*)
                                        ─────────────────►
                                                                If RES*=XRES, then
                                                                Return SUPI, K_seaf
                                        SUPI, K_seaf
                                        ◄─────────────────
```

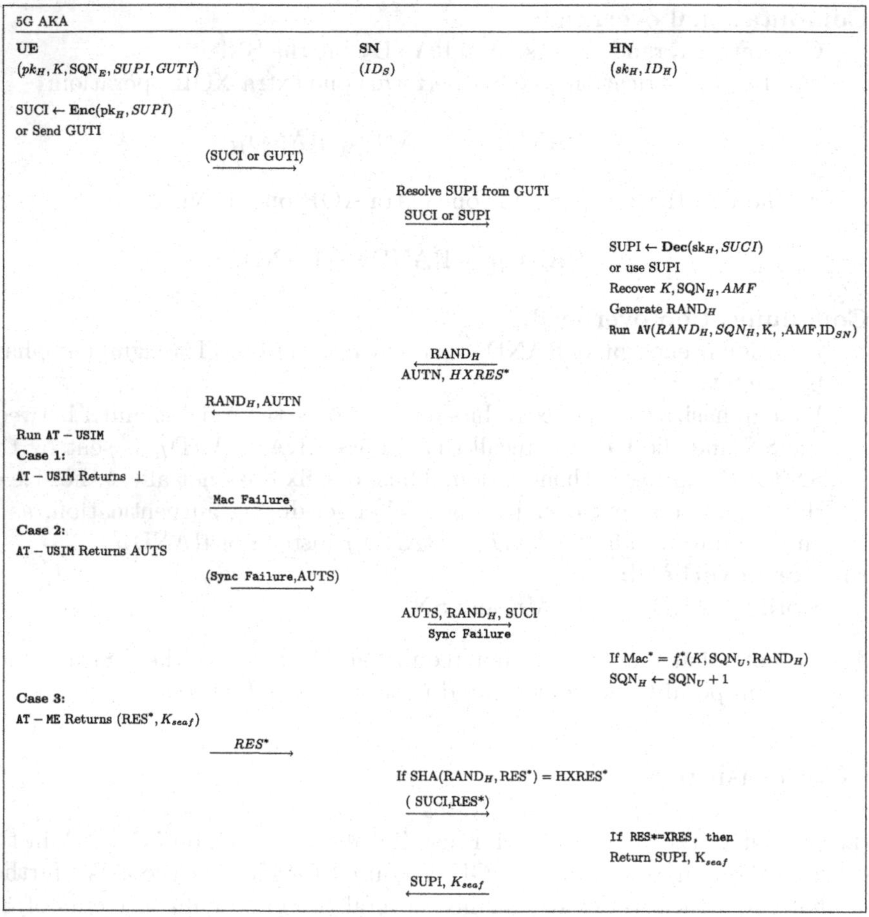

Fig. 4. The message flow in 5G AKA

References

1. Sikeridis, D., Kampanakis, P., Devetsikiotis, M.: Post-quantum authentication in TLS 1.3: a performance study. IACR Cryptol. Eprint Arch. 2020, pp. 71 (2020)
2. Wang, Y., Zhang, Z., Xie, Y.: Privacy-Preserving and Standard-CompatibleAKA Protocol for 5G. In: 30th USENIX Security Symposium (USENIX Security 21), pp. 3595–3612 (2021)

3. Basin, D., Dreier, J., Hirschi, L., Radomirovic, S., Sasse, R., Stettler, V.: A formal analysis of 5G authentication. In: Proceedings of the 2018 ACM SIGSAC Conference on Computer and Communications Security (CCS), pp. 1383–1396 (2018)
4. Meier, S., Schmidt, B., Cremers, C., Basin, D.: The TAMARIN prover for the symbolic analysis of security protocols. In: Sharygina, N., Veith, H. (eds.) CAV 2013. LNCS, vol. 8044, pp. 696–701. Springer, Heidelberg (2013). https://doi.org/10.1007/978-3-642-39799-8_48
5. Braeken, A., Liyanage, M., Kumar, P., Murphy, J.: Novel 5G authentication protocol to improve the resistance against active attacks and malicious serving networks. IEEE Access. **7**, 64040–64052 (2019)
6. Koutsos, A.: The 5G-AKA authentication protocol privacy. In: 2019 IEEE European Symposium On Security And Privacy (EuroS&P), pp. 464–479 (2019)
7. Arapinis, M., et al.: New privacy issues in mobile telephony: fix and verification. In: Proceedings of the 2012 ACM Conference on Computer and Communications Security (CCS), pp. 205–216 (2012)
8. Fouque, P., Onete, C., Richard, B.: Achieving better privacy for the 3GPP AKA protocol. Proc. Priv. Enhancing Technol. **2016**, 255–275 (2016)
9. Borgaonkar, R., Hirschi, L., Park, S., Shaik, A.: New privacy threat on 3G, 4G, and upcoming 5G AKA protocols. Proc. Privacy Enhancing Technol. **2019**, 108–127 (2019)
10. Chlosta, M., Rupprecht, D., Pöpper, C., Holz, T.: 5G SUCI-catchers: still catching them all?. In: Proceedings of the 14th ACM Conference on Security and Privacy in Wireless and Mobile Networks (WiSec), pp. 359–364 (2021)
11. Hong, B., Bae, S., Kim, Y.: GUTI reallocation demystified: cellular location tracking with changing temporary identifier. In: Network And Distributed Systems Security (NDSS) Symposium 2018 (2018)
12. Shaik, A., Borgaonkar, R., Seifert, JP., Asokan, N., Niemi, V.: Practical attacks against privacy and availability in 4G/LTE mobile communication systems. In: Symposium on Network and Distributed SystemSecurity Network And Distributed Systems Security (NDSS) Symposium 2016 (2016)
13. Chlosta, M., Rupprecht, D., Holz, T., Pöpper, C.: LTE security disabled: misconfiguration in commercial networks. In: Proceedings of the 12th Conference on Security and Privacy in Wireless and Mobile Networks (WiSec), pp. 261–266 (2019)
14. Hussain, S., Chowdhury, O., Mehnaz, S., Bertino, E.: LTEInspector: a systematic approach for adversarial testing of 4G LTE. In: Network And Distributed Systems Security (NDSS) Symposium 2018 (2018)
15. Liu, T., Wu, F., Li, X., Chen, C.: A new authentication and key agreement protocol for 5G wireless networks. Telecommun. Syst. **78**, 317–329 (2021)
16. Hojjati, M., Shafieinejad, A., Yanikomeroglu, H.: A blockchain-based authentication and key agreement (AKA) protocol for 5G networks. IEEE Access. **8**, 216461–216476 (2020)
17. Dolev, D., Yao, A.: On the security of public key products. Stanford University, Department of Computer Science (1981)
18. Tamarin Prover Manual (2022). https://tamarin-prover.github.io/manual/index.html. Accessed Oct 2022

Local Differential Privacy for Private Construction of Classification Algorithms

Mina Alishahi[✉], Daan Gast, and Sam Vermeiren

Department of Computer Science, Open Universiteit, Heerlen, The Netherlands
mina.sheikhalishahi@ou.nl, seg.vermeiren@studie.openuniversiteit.be

Abstract. In recent years, Local differential privacy (LDP), as a strong privacy preserving methodology, has been widely deployed in real world applications. It allows the users to perturb their data locally on their own devices before being sent out for analysis. In particular, LDP serves as an effective solution for the construction of privacy-preserving classifiers. While several approaches in the literature have been proposed to build classifiers over distributed locally differential private data, an understanding of the difference in the performance of these LDP-based classifiers is currently missing. In this study, we investigate the impact of using LDP on four well-known classifiers, *i.e.*, Naïve Bayes, Decision Tree, Random Forest, and Logistic Regression classifiers. We evaluate the impact of dataset's properties, LDP mechanisms, privacy budget, and classifiers' structure on LDP-based classifiers' performance.

Keywords: Classification · Local differential privacy · Privacy

1 Introduction

With the rapid development of information technology, the collection of users' data has dramatically increased. The amount of data created globally is growing exponentially, from 15 zettabytes in 2010 to 64 in 2020 and expected to reach to 168 in 2025[1].

To extract valuable information out of this massive amount of data, data-driven decision-making techniques should be used. Classification algorithms (or classifiers) have particularly served as effective tools in data analysis for making precise decisions in new situations using previous experiences. These algorithms are widely employed in our modern society, including but not limited to medical image analysis, natural language processing, biometric identification, Spam detection, and smart grid [18,28]. In general, the classification algorithms are accurately trained when they have access to a large amount of data. However, due to privacy concerns an access to this data is not possible as the data owners are unwilling to share their original data with third parties.

A large body of research has been devoted to the construction of a classifier, where the users' privacy is protected [4,5,12,17,28]. Existing solutions

---

[1] https://www.statista.com/.

© The Author(s), under exclusive license to Springer Nature Switzerland AG 2022
H. P. Reiser and M. Kyas (Eds.): NordSec 2022, LNCS 13700, pp. 58–79, 2022.
https://doi.org/10.1007/978-3-031-22295-5_4

for privacy-preserving classifiers' construction can be divided into three main categories. The first category employs cryptographic-based approaches, which mainly find the model's parameters over encrypted inputs. These approaches, however, are not scalable both in terms of execution runtime and bandwidth usage. The other category solves the problem at hand using data anonymization techniques, where the data under analysis is perturbed before being released, e.g., k-anonymity, ℓ-diversity, and t-closeness. These techniques are, however, criticized for not protecting the users' privacy properly. The last category comprises the application of Differential Privacy (DP) and Local Differential Privacy (LDP), which offers a rigorous privacy guarantee. Through these techniques, a systematic noise is added to the revealed data such that some statistical properties of the original data are preserved. In particular, LDP gains increasing attention in private data analysis as it guarantees the user's privacy on her own device before being sent to any third party [3].

Under the LDP setting, several classification algorithms have been trained in the literature, e.g., Naïve Bayes and Neural Network classifiers [5, 24, 26]. However, a comparison of the performance of classifiers in this setting is currently missing. Such knowledge enables the data owner and the analyst to select the most appropriate classification algorithm and training parameters to guarantee high privacy under LDP while minimizing the loss of accuracy. Accordingly, this study aims to answer the following research questions:

- How does the choice of the LDP mechanism affect the performance of LDP-based classifiers?
- Which properties of the dataset affect the performance of LDP-based classifiers?
- How does the level of privacy affect the performance of LDP-based classifiers?

To answer these questions, we investigate the application of LDP in four well-known classification algorithms, namely the Naïve Bayes, Decision Tree, Random Forest, and Logistic Regression classifiers in a locally differential private setting. For each classification algorithm, we analyze the effect of LDP mechanisms, dataset properties, and privacy levels on the LDP-based classifier accuracy.

The remainder of this paper is organized as follows. The next section presents Local Differential Privacy and the classification algorithms studied in this work. Section 3 shows the proposed architecture along with the main entities, and Sect. 4 presents the LDP-based classifiers. Section 5 describe our experimental setup and results. Section 6 discusses related work, and Sect. 7 concludes the paper and provides directions for future work.

2   Preliminaries

This section briefly presents the Local Differential Privacy mechanisms and classification algorithms used in this study.

Algorithm 1: Frequency estimation

---

1 **Function** estimate(U, l, ϵ, v_r):

  input: U: The set of users $\{u_1, \ldots, u_n\}$, where each user u_i owns
      data value d_i,
      l: ldp mechanism,
      ϵ: epsilon value,
      v_r: value requesting frequency estimation
  output: $F(v_r)$: frequency estimation of value v_r

2 **begin**

   /* Perturb data of each user and send to aggregator */

3   **foreach** v_i **owned by** $u_i \in U$ **do**

4   Aggregator $\leftarrow$ Perturb(v_i, l, ϵ);

   /* Perform frequency estimation for value v_r */

5   **return** Aggregator.estimate(v_r);

2.1 Local Differential Privacy

In Local Differential Privacy (LDP), an aggregator collects information from users (data owners) who do not fully trust the aggregator but are willing to participate in the aggregator's analysis. To protect the confidentiality of data, each user's value is perturbed using a randomized algorithm locally before being sent out to the aggregator [13]. The perturbation might require a pre-processing algorithm over input data named encoding. The aggregator then collects the perturbed values and estimates the true statistic.

Definition 1 (ϵ-Local Differential Privacy (ϵ-LDP) [11]). *A randomized mechanism $\mathcal{M}$ satisfies ϵ-LDP if and only if for any pair of input values $v, v' \in \mathcal{D}$ and for any possible output $S \subseteq Range(\mathcal{M})$, we have*

$$Pr[\mathcal{M}(v) \in S] \leq e^\epsilon Pr[\mathcal{M}(v') \in S] \tag{1}$$

when the value of ϵ is known from the context, we omit ϵ from ϵ-LDP and simply write LDP.

In this study, we employ two main LDP mechanisms, namely *frequency* and *mean* estimation, as summarized in Algorithms 1 and 2, respectively. A complete definition of the LDP-based mechanisms has been provided in Appendix.

2.2 Classification Algorithms

Next, we briefly introduce these classifiers employed in this study (for more detail refer to [1]).

Naïve Bayes (NB) algorithms are statistical classifiers based on the Bayes Theorem for calculating probabilities and conditional probabilities. It makes use of all

---

Algorithm 2: Mean estimation

---

1 **Function** estimateMean(U, l, ϵ, W):

    input: U: users $\{u_1, \ldots, u_n\}$, where each user u_i owns data (X_i^*, c_i),

              l: ldp mean mechanism,

              ϵ: privacy value,

              W: set of weights $(w_1, \ldots, w_k)$

    output: mean gradient for each feature, $(\nabla_1, \ldots, \nabla_k)$

2   **begin**

        /* Calculate gradient of each user and perturb   */

3   **foreach** (X_i^*, c_i) owned by $u_i \in U$ **do**

4             $c_i' = x_1^* \cdot w_1 + \ldots + x_k^* \cdot w_k$;

5             $cost_i = (c_i - c_i')$;

6   **foreach** $x_j \in X^*$ **do**

7                 $\nabla[j] = cost * x_j$;

8             $\psi[i] = $ Perturb(∇, l, ϵ)

        /* Calculate average over all perturbed gradients   */

9   **return** $\frac{1}{n} \sum_{i=0}^{n} \psi[i]$;

Table 1. Notations.

Notation	Description	Notation	Description
N_T	Number of occurrences in T	N_t	Number of occurrences of t in T
P(x)	Probability of x	$P(x \mid c)$	Conditional probability of x given c
n	Number of records	k	Number of feature vectors
D	Dataset	A_j	Feature vector j
X^*	An individual record	x_i^*	Feature value i
C	Set of labels	c'	Predicted class label
η	Learning rate	∇	Set of gradients
W	Set of weights	w_i	Weight i of W
d	Depth of tree	s	Size of forest

attributes contained in the data, and analyses them individually as though they are equally important and independent (naïve assumption) from each other. Naïve Bayes model is easy to build and particularly useful for very large data sets.

Decision Trees (DT) are classification algorithms with a tree-based structure drawn upside down with its root at the top. Each internal node represents a test/condition based on which the tree splits into branches/edges. The end of the branch that does not split anymore (respecting some stopping criteria) is the decision/leaf. The paths from root to leaf represent classification rules. One advantage of DTs is the comprehensibility of the classification structures. This enables the analyzer to verify which attributes determined the final classification. The drawback is that DTs might be non-robust for datasets with a large number of attributes.

Random Forest (RF) is an ensemble learning method for classification which operates by constructing a multitude of decision trees at training time and outputting the class that is the mode of the classes of the individual trees. RF corrects for decision trees' habit of overfitting to their training set. The RF has also been recognized to be among the most accurate classifiers.

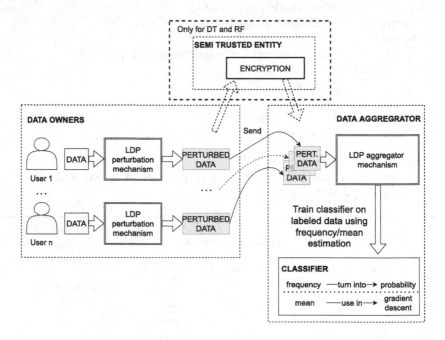

Fig. 1. Architecture of framework.

Logistic Regression (LR) is a statistical model that is largely employed in statistical data analysis to classify binary dependent variables. In regression analysis, logistic regression (or logit regression) is used to estimate the parameters of a logistic model returning the probability of occurrence of a class. To this end, the LR classifier builds a logit variable that contains the natural log of the odds of the class occurring or not. Then, a maximum likelihood estimation algorithm is applied to estimate the probabilities.

Table 1 summarizes the notations that are used in this study.

3   Architecture

The architecture of our framework as depicted in Fig. 1 constitutes of three main entities: 1) the data owner, 2) the data aggregator, and 3) the semi trusted entity.

Data Owner (or User): The data owner is responsible for sending its data to the aggregator (or semi trusted party in DT and RF). It uses a perturbation mechanism that aligns with the mechanism used by the aggregator. In our algorithms, the data of each user is represented by a single record of a dataset. We assume that each user only participates once in the training of our classifier.

Data Aggregator: The data aggregator is responsible for collecting all the perturbed data and training the classifier. It determines the perturbation scheme that the user should employ. The aggregator performs three actions: data aggregation, frequency/mean estimation, and training of the classifier.

Semi Trusted Entity: The LDP-based privacy mechanisms are not standalone enough to guarantee the users' privacy in the construction of DT and RF algorithms. The information leakage occurs when the data are directed to new child nodes. As each user's data will belong to a unique child node, the aggregator can understand the feature-value of the previous level that the user's information satisfied. To avoid it, we propose a new framework that combines LDP and Homomorphic Encryption to securely build the DT and RF algorithms on individual data.

In this setting, the aggregator generates the public and private keys, while the public key is shared with data owners and the private key is kept private. The data owners encrypt the feature-value of the feature they belong to in the previous level of tree and employ LDP for estimating the information gain of upcoming split feature. The data owners then send this tuple, including the encrypted and noisy values to the semi trusted entity. This entity shuffles the data and sends them to the aggregator. The aggregator decrypts the ciphertexts to understand which data should be used for aggregation in each new node.

4 LDP-Based Classification Algorithms

This section presents the algorithms for implementing the LDP-based classifiers.

4.1 LDP-Based Naïve Bayes Classifier

The LDP version of Naïve Bayes classifier has been adopted from the work presented in [26]. In the proposed approach, frequency estimation is used to calculate the different probabilities that are required in Bayes functions. In the first step, the prior probabilities are estimated using frequency estimation. To this end, the user provides the aggregator its class label in a perturbed format. The data aggregator estimates the frequency F_c of each class label c. The prior probability $P(c)$ is then estimated as $P(c_j) = \frac{F_{c_j}}{N_C}$, where N_C (the number of class labels) is known by the aggregator.

The likelihood computation requires some more work at the side of the user. To maintain the relationship between the class and feature values from the training data, it needs to be *connected* before sending it to the server. After the connection step, the result is a representation of the feature and class label connected together into a unique integer as presented in Algorithm 3. Once the connecting is done, the data is perturbed and sent to the aggregator. The aggregator uses the frequency of the connected feature value and class labels to calculate the conditional probabilities as follows:

$$P(x_i \mid c) = \frac{F_{x_i,c}}{\sum_{x_i \in X} F_{x_i,c}} \tag{2}$$

Algorithms 4 and 5 present the estimation of class prior probability and likelihood probabilities, respectively.

4.2 LDP-Based Logistic Regression Classifier

The design of our LDP-based Logistic Regression classifier has been inspired by the work presented in [22]. Logistic Regression works by performing gradient descent. At each iteration, it needs to find a mean gradient that is used to update

---

Algorithm 3: Connect feature value and class label

1 **Function** getConnectedLabel(d, k, c)

    input: d: feature value, encoded numerical representation of the feature value,

               k: number of class labels,

               c: class label, encoded numerical representation of the class label,

    output: $\hat{v}$: connected feature-class label;

2 **begin**

3     $\hat{v} = (d - 1) * k + c$;

4   **return** $\hat{v}$

Algorithm 4: LDP-based Naïve Bayes class prior probability

1 **Function** computeClassPrior(U, l, ϵ, C)

    input: U: set of users $\{u_1, \ldots, u_n\}$ each user u owning class label c_u,

               l: ldp-mechanism,

               ϵ: privacy value,

               C: class domain $C = \{c_1, \ldots, c_m\}$

    output: classPriorProbabilities

2 **begin**

3   classPriorProbabilities = [];

4   **foreach** $c \in C$ **do**

5   F_c = estimate (U, l, ϵ, c);   ▷ (see Algorithm 1)

6         $P(c) = F_c \;/\; n$;

7   classPriorProbabilities $[c] = P(c)$;

8   **return** classPriorProbabilities

the weights of a function. With the LDP frequency estimation technique, we are not able to calculate a gradient directly from the perturbed data. The solution here could be to make the user calculate its own gradient and supply that to the aggregator. Frequency estimation still requires the data to be binned into categories before perturbation. In theory, we could calculate a mean from this data but it is not accurate enough to use in Logistic Regression.

To solve this problem, we use a mean estimation technique instead of frequency estimation. Three different LDP mean estimation mechanisms are described in Sect. 2.1. Every mechanism has its own way of perturbing the data. Once the data is perturbed, the mean is estimated by taking the average of all perturbed records. The gradient descent is done by supplying the user with a set of weights. The user determines a prediction based on their data and calculates their own gradient. This gradient is then perturbed and sent to the aggregator.

On the aggregator side, the mean gradient can be determined from all the data. This mean value is used to update the weights like it is done in the normal

---

Algorithm 5: LDP-based Naïve Bayes likelihood probabilities

1 **Function** computeLikelihood(U, l, ϵ, A, C)

    input: U: set of users $\{u_1, \ldots, u_n\}$ each owning (X_i^*, c_i),

             l: ldp-mechanism,

             ϵ: privacy value,

             A: set of feature domains $A = \{A_1, \ldots, A_k\}$,

             C: class domain $C = \{c_1, \ldots, c_m\}$

    output: likelihood;

2 **begin**

3   likelihood $= []$;

      /* Create a version of U that has connected

          feature-class labels   */

4     $\hat{U} = $ connectFeatureAndClass(U);

5   **foreach** $c \in C$ **do**

6   **foreach** $A_j \in A$ **do**

            /* Obtain estimates of connected feature-class

               labels   */

7   estimates $= []$;

8   **foreach** $d \in A_j$ **do**

9                 $\hat{v} = $ getConnectedLabel(d, c);

10   estimates$[\hat{v}] = $ estimate$(\hat{U}, l, \epsilon, \hat{v})$;

            /* Calculate likelihood for each connected label

               */

11   **foreach** $F_{\hat{v}} \in estimates$ **do**

12   likelihood $[A_j][P(c \mid \hat{v})] = F_{\hat{v}}$ / sum(estimates);

13   **return** likelihood

Logistic Regression algorithm. This process is repeated for a number of iterations. The epsilon value is divided by the total number of iterations to ensure the privacy budget of each user is not overridden. The mechanisms used in this work require the perturbed values be in the range $[-1, 1]$. Any value that is out of this range is transformed to either -1 or 1.

The gradient is calculated by first making a prediction with the current weights. The prediction is then subtracted from the actual class label to obtain the error or cost. The feature values are now multiplied by the error and this is the gradient we use to update the weights as $\nabla = (c - c') \cdot X$ [16].

Note that this step of updating the weights locally is performed on the user side who knows the class label of her own record. Algorithm 6 summarizes the construction of a Logistic Regression algorithm that satisfies ϵ-LDP.

4.3   LDP-Based Decision Tree Classifier

We designed the LDP-based Decision Tree algorithm by the combination of encryption and LDP-based frequency estimations as explained in Sect. 3 (Semi trusted role).

Algorithm 6: LDP-based Logistic Regression Classifier

---

1 **Function train(U, I, η, ϵ):**

   input: U: set of users $\{u_1, \ldots, u_n\}$ each user u_i owning (X_i^*, c_i),

   I: number of iterations to perform,

   η: learning rate,

   ϵ: privacy value

   output: W: trained weights

2 **begin**

3   W = array of 0's with size k;

4   **for** I *iterations* **do**

       /* estimate mean gradients from all users   */

5   mean∇ = estimateMean(U, l, ϵ, W);

       /* Update weights using mean gradients   */

6   **foreach** $w_z \in W$ **do**

7           $w_z = w_z + \eta \cdot mean\nabla_z \cdot w_z$;

8   **return** W

For the part where frequency estimation is used, we essentially compute the Information Gain (IG) for selecting the split attribute. The IG value is computed based on entropy H, where

$$H(A_j) = - \sum_i P(x_{i,j}) log_2 P(x_{i,j}) \tag{3}$$

The feature A^* that maximizes $H(A_j)$ is selected for data division. To compute $P(x_{i,j})$, we connect each feature value and class label using Algorithm 3.

As explained before, after finding the optimum attribute for data division, directing data to child nodes reveals the sensitive information of users. We solve this by introducing a semi-trusted party. First, we get the perturbed data from all users. We use this to calculate the IG and the most important feature. Then, we ask all users which value they have for this feature. They respond by resending their perturbed data together with this value. However, they first encrypt this value using a public key provided by the aggregator. Then, they send this combination to the semi-trusted party. This agent cannot decode the value (not owning the private key), so she can not figure out the value the users have sent it. Next, this intermediate party shuffles the data, so the aggregator does not know which user sent which data.

The aggregator then receives this shuffled data, decrypts the value with the private key, and assigns the perturbed data to the accompanying value. Then for each value, the aggregator can again estimate the frequency and calculate the IG again in new child nodes. This process continues until the tree reaches its pre-determined depth. In the leaves, the aggregator uses frequency estimation to count the labels and assigns the plurality label. We have chosen not to prune out the tree, as it again poses the risk of information leakage.

4.4   LDP-Based Random Forest Classifier

For Random Forests (RF), we use the LDP-based DT classifier as presented in Algorithm 7. The only difference is that in RF the trees are growing through a random selection of features for data division instead of using IG. Algorithm 8 summarizes the process of building the RF classifier in LDP setting.

Algorithm 7: LDP-based Decision Tree Classifier

---

    input: D: dataset $\{(X_1, c_1), \ldots, (X_n, c_n)\}$,
                 A: set of feature domains $A = \{A_1, \ldots, A_k\}$,
                 d: depth of the tree, IF: information gain algorithm,
                 $parent$: start node, l: LDP mechanism, ϵ: privacy budget
    output: DT anchored on root node

1 **begin**

    | /* Get frequency estimates for all values   */
2 | **foreach** A_i *in* A **do**
3 | | **foreach** v_r *in* A_i **do**
4 | | | $count_i r \leftarrow estimate(D, l, \epsilon, v_r)$; $\triangleright$ (see Algorithm 1)
5 | | | $count_i$ add $count_i r$;
6 | | $count$ add $count_i$;

    | /* Select feature with information gain using the
    | estimated frequencies   */
7 | $A_j \leftarrow IF (A, count)$;
    | /* Create leaf if d is reached   */
8 | **if** $d = 0$ **then**
9 | | **foreach** $x_i^* \in A_j$ **do**
10 | | | $lab \leftarrow$ label of $\max(count_j)$;
11 | | | $lf \leftarrow$ leaf with value x_i^* and label lab;
12 | | | attach lf to $parent$;

    | /* Create node for every value of feature and rerun
    | algorithm from that node   */
13 | **else**
14 | | **foreach** $x_i^* \in A_j$ **do**
15 | | | $no \leftarrow$ node with value x_i^*;
16 | | | attach no to $parent$;
    | | | /* The semi-trusted party returns D_t */
17 | | | $D_t \leftarrow$ all data from D where A_j has x_i^*;
18 | | | $A_t \leftarrow A$ without A_j;
19 | | | LDP-based Decision Tree Classifier$(D_t, A_t, d-1 , IF, no, l, \epsilon)$;

---

5   Experimental Analysis

This section presents the experimental set-up and experimental results implementing algorithms presented in Sect. 4.

Algorithm 8: LDP-based Random Forest Classifier

---

input: D: dataset $\{((X_1, c_1), \ldots, (X_n, c_n)\}$,
A: set of feature domains, $A = \{A_1, \ldots, A_k\}$, d: depth of the trees,
s: size of the forest, IF: select random value function,
$parent$: root node, l: LDP mechanism, ϵ: privacy budget

output: RF ← Random Forest

1 **begin**
    /* Create s DT   */
2   **for** $i \le s$ **do**
3   tree ← LDP-based DT algorithm(D, A, d,IF, $parent$, l,ϵ);
4   add tree to RF;
5   **return** RF

Table 2. Dataset information.

Dataset	Data type	# Features	# Records
Adult	Mixed	12	48842
Iris	Continuous	4	150
Mushroom	Categorical	22	8124
Vote	Categorical	16	435
Car	Categorical	6	1728
Nursery	Categorical	8	12960
SPECT	Categorical	22	267
Weight lifting	Continuous	152	3936
Htru2	Continuous	9	17898

5.1 Experimental Set-up

We have implemented the Algorithms 4, 5, 7, 8 in Python using DE, LH, HR, HE, UE, and RAP mechanisms (Sects. 2.1 and A), and Algorithm 6 using Dutchi, Piecewise, and Hybrid mean estimation mechanisms (Sects. 2.1 and A)[2]. The privacy levels ε used in ε-LDP algorithms are taken from the set $\mathcal{E} = \{0.01, 0.1, 0.5, 1, 2, 3, 5\}$. The input variables of the privacy mechanisms have been set to their default parameters as proposed in [6].

Dataset: For our experiments, we have selected nine datasets, namely *adult, iris, mushroom, vote, car, nursery, spect, weightlifting* and *htru2*, from UCI machine learning repository[3]. Table 2 summarizes the dataset information. To make sure all the data we use in our tests is in the same format, we preprocess it. LR

---

[2] The codes of our experiments are available in https://github.com/PaaEl/LDP-classifiers.

[3] https://archive.ics.uci.edu.

and NB can only handle numerical data, thus we convert all categorical data to integers. No information is lost in this step. DT and RF use the same data, for ease of use and to ensure standardization.

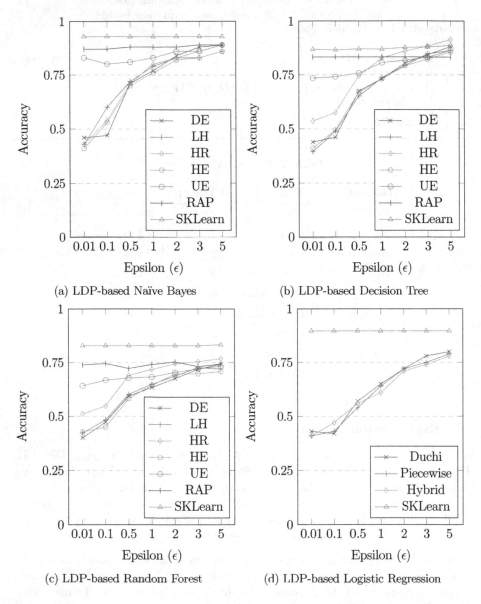

(a) LDP-based Naïve Bayes

(b) LDP-based Decision Tree

(c) LDP-based Random Forest

(d) LDP-based Logistic Regression

Fig. 2. Average accuracy of LDP-based classifiers per LDP mechanism.

5.2   Experimental Results

The experimental results aim to verify the performance of the LDP-based classifiers on the set of selected benchmark datasets.

LDP Mechanism Impact: Figure 2 shows the accuracy of LDP-based classifiers averaged over nine datasets using different LDP mechanisms. It can be observed that for the classifiers employing frequency estimation mechanisms, *i.e.*, NB, DT, and RF classifiers, the RAPPOR and UE provide high accuracy (close to SKLearn accuracy in non-private setting); the other frequency estimation mechanisms show almost the same behaviour, except from HR which slightly performs better than the others. For the LR classifier, all three mean estimation mechanisms show similar performance.

Table 3. Dataset properties.

Dataset property	Datasets
Large	Adult, htru2, nursery
Small	Iris, SPECT, vote, car
Many features	Weightliftingexercises
Few features	Iris, car
Binary classification	Adult, mushroom, SPECT, vote, htru2
Multinomial classification	Nursery, car, iris, weightlifting

Dataset Impact: To evaluate the impact of datasets on the performance of LDP-based classifiers, we consider three different categories of datasets based on their properties, namely large vs small, many vs few features, and binary vs multinomial classification. A large dataset has a number of records more than 10,000 records. A dataset with many features is considered to have more than 100 feature columns, whereas the one with few features has less than 5 features. Table 3 indicates which dataset fits in each category.

Figure 3 depicts the performance of LDP-based classifiers based on dataset properties. It can be observed that as expected large datasets serve as better sources for these classifiers compared to small datasets. This is resulted from the inherent property of LDP in which the noises are cancelled when the number of instances is increased.

The number of features seems to have no direct impact on the performance of LDP-based classifiers. Still, it can be seen that very few features do not provide enough information for our private classifiers to correctly label the new instances.

Finally, the datasets with two labels are considerably better resources for LDP classifiers compared to multi-label datasets. This is because the classifiers tend to better classify the instances when there are only two labels compared to more options.

Privacy Level Impact: From Figs. 2 and 3, it can be seen that as expected in general when the privacy requirement is relaxed (greater ϵ values), the LDP-based classifiers' performance improves. The optimal value of a privacy budget

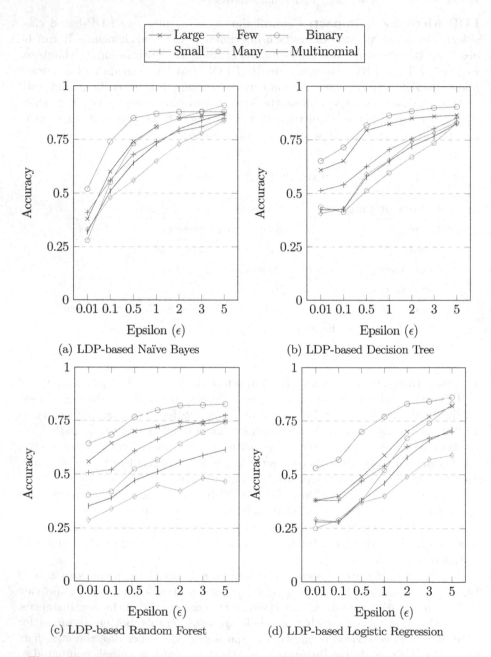

Fig. 3. The impact of datasets properties on LDP-based classifiers' performance.

that trades off between the privacy gain and utility loss can be found on the elbow point of graphs in Figs. 2 and 3. It can be observed that in general, a privacy budget between 1 to 3 (on average $\epsilon = 2$) offers the best value in protecting enough privacy and providing high accuracy. If high privacy (low ϵ value) is required, then it can be seen that non of the LDP mechanism embedded in LDP-based LR provide high accuracy.

5.3 Findings

Our findings can be summarized as follows.

- For the LDP-based classifiers that use frequency estimation, *i.e.*, Naïve Bayes, Decision Tree, and Random Forest, the RAP and UE outperform the other LDP mechanisms. As RAP brings its high accuracy with the expense of implementation runtime, the UE is better to be used when there is a time restriction. For the LDP-based Logistic Regression classifier that relies on mean estimation, the LDP mechanisms show a negligible difference.
- The performance of the LDP-based classifiers is improved when they are trained on large datasets with only two class labels. We could not find any direct link between the number of features and classifiers' performance.
- The optimal value of ϵ for all LDP-based classifiers lies somewhere between 1 and 3. If a higher privacy constraint is required, the combination of RAP/UE and Naïve Bayes/Decision Tree is proposed.
- From our understanding, there is no logical solution to build a Decision Tree or a Random Forest classifiers with the use of only LDP mechanisms (unless with huge accuracy loss in adding noise to the all combination of feature-values). A hybrid algorithm that combines LDP with another privacy enhancing methodology solves the problem of not fully trusting a third party. However, it might cause computation overhead, *e.g.*, here we added Homomorphic Encryption. This should certainly be considered as the limitation of DT and RF algorithms when they are planned to be fitted in LDP setting.

In summary, if the runtime, accuracy, and high privacy are all the matter of importance, we propose the application of UE-based Naïve Bayes classifier as the best solution.

6 Related Work

In the last few years, privacy-preserving machine learning has received increasing attention. Several privacy enhancing techniques, including but not limited to encryption, anonymization, and randomization, have served as effective solutions to protect the users' privacy when direct access to original sensitive data is not possible [2, 14, 15, 21].

In particular, the application of Differential Privacy (DP) and Local Differential Privacy (LDP) in protecting the confidentiality of users' information over distributed data for training the classifiers has gained momentum. In what follows, we present some recent studies in this regard.

In the DP setting, in general, one party owns when one party owns the data and another party is interested in obtaining a classifier model on this sensitive non-public data [9]. This approach has been used to enforce differential privacy on Naïve Bayes classifier [20], which replaces the dataset queries in the standard Naïve Bayes algorithm with differentially private ones. This methodology has been improved in [27] by using smooth sensitivity, a differential privacy technique that lowers the amount of random noise on each query, while retaining the same level of privacy. An overview of differentially private Decision Tree algorithms is given in [9]. In other DP-based approaches, the noise is added to the model's parameters before the model is published. In [10], an evaluation of differential privacy mechanisms for two machine learning algorithms is presented to understand the impact of different choices of ϵ and different relaxations of differential privacy on both utility and privacy.

Local Differential Privacy has also been employed in several studies to guarantee the users' privacy in building classifiers. Naïve Bayes classifier is constructed under LDP in [26] using two approaches to be suitable for both categorical and continuous features. Later in [25] an alternative framework based on the private computation of join distribution is designed for calculating the probabilities. In [22], LDP-based techniques are proposed to compute gradient descent applicable in three classifiers (and specifically Logistic Regression).

Few studies in the literature compare the performance of different classifiers in a private setting. The performance of different classifiers that are trained over private inputs using secure two-party computation [19], anonymization techniques (*e.g.*, k-anonymity) [4], and differential privacy [14], have already been explored. In all of these researches, the impact of the dataset, the inherent properties of classifiers, and privacy requirement on the performance of private classifiers have been investigated.

However, to the best of our knowledge, no previous study has compared the performance of classifiers under local differential privacy. Our research gives an insight into the most optimal use of an LDP machine learning classifiers for specific problems. We bridge the gap between the individual research on specific classifiers and provide a comparison of LDP embedded classifiers.

7 Conclusion and Future Directions

This paper provides a comparison of classifiers' performance when they are trained on Locally Differential Private (LDP) data. The assumption is that each record of data is owned by a single user and all users are interested in obtaining an accurate classifier's model without sharing their original data. Four well-known classification algorithms, namely Naïve Bayes, Decision Tree, Random Forest, and Logistic Regression, have been trained under the LDP setting. Our experimental results show that the selection of LDP mechanism, dataset properties, classifier structure, and privacy level, all affect the performance of the LDP-based classifiers.

In future work, we plan to extend our work in designing LDP-based classifiers for more classification algorithms, e.g., Neural Networks, Support Vector Machines, and k Nearest Neighbors. The other research path is the comparison of LDP-based classifiers' resistance against privacy attacks, e.g., membership inference or attribute attacks. Future studies can provide methodologies on how to improve LDP machine learning to make it safer and more private compared to what it is now.

A   Appendix

This section presents the LDP-based mechanisms used in this study.

A.1   Frequency Estimation

We first present the definition of randomized response in frequency estimation [7]:

Definition 2 (Randomized Response). *Let v be a user's binary value, v' be its encoded version (if any) and $Perturbv'$ be its perturbed response. Then, for any value v,*

$$Pr[Perturbv' = v] = \begin{cases} \frac{e^\varepsilon}{e^\varepsilon + 1} & \text{if } v' = v, \\ \frac{1}{e^\varepsilon + 1} & \text{if } v' \neq v \end{cases} \qquad (4)$$

The randomized response returns the true value with probability $\frac{e^\varepsilon}{e^\varepsilon + 1}$ and the random value with probability $\frac{1}{e^\varepsilon + 1}$.

Based on the concept of randomized response, in what follows we present frequency estimation mechanisms have been used in our research.

Direct Encoding (DE): In this mechanism there is no encoding done, input data is sent in the original format. To determine if the sent data will be perturbed two probabilities are used: p and q.

$$P[Perturb(y) = i] = \begin{cases} p = \frac{e^\varepsilon}{e^\varepsilon + D - 1} & \text{if } v' = i \\ q = \frac{1}{e^\varepsilon + D - 1} & \text{if } v' \neq i \end{cases} \qquad (5)$$

The user sends their true data with probability p or perturbs their data with probability q. The actual perturbation is done by adding noise to the data. For discrete values Generalized Random Response (GRR) can be used. This technique selects a random other value from the domain to be used as the perturbed value.

Advantages of this mechanism are ease of performance and low computational cost. Disadvantage is its poor performance when the dimension of the domain of the data is high.

Local Hashing (LH): OLH is conceptually similar to RAPPOR, but instead of encoding v as a bitvector it uses a vector of integers. The perturbation is done by performing GRR over the integer vector as follows.

$$P[\text{Perturb}(y) = i] = \begin{cases} p = \frac{e^\varepsilon}{e^\varepsilon + g - 1}, & \text{if } v' = i \\ q = \frac{1}{e^\varepsilon + g - 1}, & \text{if } v' \neq i \end{cases} \tag{6}$$

Hadamard Random Response (HR): HR transforms the v into a single bit and then performs RR on this bit. Transformation is done using a random $2^D \times 2^D$ matrix φ, where φ is multiplied with the standard basis vector e with the v'th position equal to 1. Each column vector ϑ of this multiplication then represents a v. Users select a random index and send out the index and the corresponding ϑ. The aggregator adds all the vectors and calculates the inner product of those vectors with φe to estimate frequencies. Main advantage is constant communication cost, but more information is lost during the perturbation.

Threshold with Histogram Encoding (HE): In this technique, v is encoded as a histogram B, of length D, with all components set to 0 except for the one in the v-th position, which is set to 1. The data is then perturbed by adding Laplacian noise to each component. The aggregator considers each component above a threshold ϱ as a 1, each below as a 0. The perturbation is performed as the following:

$$\text{Perturb}(B'[i]) = B[i] + Lap(\frac{2}{\varepsilon}) \tag{7}$$

with Lap being the Laplace distribution.

Unary Encoding (UE): In this mechanism the value to be perturbed v is encoded as a bitvector B of length d with all bits set to 0 except for the one in the v-th position. Perturbation is done by changing the value of every bit based on the probabilities p and q, as mentioned in the *perturbation* definition below. For example an original value of 0 will be changed to 1 with probability q. UE handles higher dimensional data better than DE but takes longer time to be executed. The perturbation function is defined as the following:

$$P[\text{Perturb}(B'[i]) = 1] = \begin{cases} p = \frac{1}{2} & \text{if } B[i] = 1 \\ q = \frac{1}{e^\varepsilon + 1} & \text{if } B[i] = 0 \end{cases} \tag{8}$$

Randomized Aggregatable Privacy-Preserving Ordinal Response (RAPPOR/RAP): The encoding of the data in RAPPOR is done by making a Bloom filter of the data. It does this by using multiple different hash functions to produce multiple hash-values of v. These hashes are used to set the bits in a bit vector B of length k.

Perturbation is done in two steps. The first step is called permanent randomized response. Each bit in B is using a probability based on a parameter f. The following describes this first perturbation step:

$$P[B_1[i] = 1] = \begin{cases} 1 - \frac{1}{2}f, & \text{if } B_0[i] = 1 \\ \frac{1}{2}f, & \text{if } B_0[i] = 0 \end{cases} \tag{9}$$

This is followed by a second perturbation called instantaneous randomized response. This is similar to the first but uses probabilities p and q, which are set to $p = 0.75$ and $q = 0.25$. The following describes this second perturbation step:

$$P[B_2[i] = 1] = \begin{cases} p, & \text{if } B_1[i] = 1 \\ q, & \text{if } B_1[i] = 0 \end{cases} \tag{10}$$

Advantages of using hash functions are the reduction of communication costs and variance, at the cost of increased computational costs and the risk of collisions. To estimate frequencies of values RAPPOR uses LASSO, a regression analysis method, and linear regression [23]. The value for ϵ in RAPPOR is represented by f. The pure-LDP module used in our code provides a conversion function to get the corresponding value for f, given ϵ.

A.2 Mean Estimation

The following mean estimation mechanisms have been used in our research.

Duchi: The first mechanism we use is by Duchi et al. [8] and is taken from the paper by Wang et al. [22]. Given a value $x_i \in [-1, 1]$ and the privacy parameter ϵ, the algorithm returns a perturbed value x_i' that is equal to either $\frac{e^\epsilon + 1}{e^\epsilon - 1}$ or $-\frac{e^\epsilon + 1}{e^\epsilon - 1}$, with the probability:

$$P(x_i' = v \mid x_i) = \begin{cases} \frac{e^\epsilon - 1}{2e^\epsilon + 2} \cdot x_i + \frac{1}{2} & \text{if } v = \frac{e^\epsilon + 1}{e^\epsilon - 1} \\ -\frac{e^\epsilon - 1}{2e^\epsilon + 2} \cdot x_i + \frac{1}{2} & \text{if } v = -\frac{e^\epsilon + 1}{e^\epsilon - 1} \end{cases} \tag{11}$$

Piecewise: The Piecewise mechanism is described by Wang et al. [22]. Given a value $x_i \in [-1, 1]$ and the privacy parameter ϵ, the algorithm returns a perturbed value x_i' that is in $[-C, C]$, where

$$C = \frac{e^{\epsilon/2} + 1}{e^{\epsilon/2} - 1} \tag{12}$$

The perturbed value is returned with the probability:

$$P(x_i' = v \mid x_i) = \begin{cases} p & \text{if } v \in [l(x_i), r(x_i)] \\ \frac{p}{e^\epsilon} & \text{if } v \in [-C, l(x_i)) \cup (r(x_i), C] \end{cases} \tag{13}$$

where

$$p = \frac{e^\epsilon - e^{\epsilon/2}}{2e^\epsilon + 2}, \quad l(x_i) = \frac{C+1}{2} \cdot x_i - \frac{C-1}{2}, \quad r(x_i) = l(x_i) + C - 1. \tag{14}$$

Hybrid: The Hybrid mechanism by Wang et al. [22], uses a combination of both Duchi and Piecewise. The algorithm itself is quite simple. Given an input value x_i, a coin is flipped to see which of the two mechanisms will be used for perturbation.

References

1. Aggarwal, C.C.: Data Classification: Algorithms and Applications. Chapman and Hall CRC (2014)
2. Alishahi, M., Moghtadaiee, V.: Collaborative private classifiers construction. In: Collaborative Approaches for Cyber Security in Cyber-Physical Systems. Springer, Cham (2022)
3. Alishahi, M., Moghtadaiee, V., Navidan, H.: Add noise to remove noise: local differential privacy for feature selection. Comput. Secur. 102934 (2022)
4. Alishahi, M., Zannone, N.: Not a free lunch, but a cheap one: on classifiers performance on anonymized datasets. In: Barker, K., Ghazinour, K. (eds.) DBSec 2021. LNCS, vol. 12840, pp. 237–258. Springer, Cham (2021). https://doi.org/10.1007/978-3-030-81242-3_14
5. Arachchige, P.C.M., Bertok, P., Khalil, I., Liu, D., Camtepe, S., Atiquzzaman, M.: Local differential privacy for deep learning. IEEE Internet Things J. **7**(7), 5827–5842 (2019)
6. Cormode, G., Maddock, S., Maple, C.: Frequency estimation under local differential privacy. Proc. VLDB Endow. **14**(11), 2046–2058 (2021)
7. Cormode, G., Maddock, S., Maple, C.: Frequency estimation under local differential privacy [experiments, analysis and benchmarks]. CoRR abs/2103.16640 (2021). https://arxiv.org/abs/2103.16640
8. Duchi, J.C., Jordan, M.I., Wainwright, M.J.: Minimax optimal procedures for locally private estimation. J. Am. Stat. Assoc. **113**(521), 182–201 (2018)
9. Fletcher, S., Islam, M.Z.: Decision tree classification with differential privacy: a survey. ACM Comput. Surv. (CSUR) **52**(4), 1–33 (2019)
10. Jayaraman, B., Evans, D.: Evaluating differentially private machine learning in practice. In: USENIX Conference on Security Symposium, SEC 2019, pp. 1895–1912 (2019)
11. Kasiviswanathan, S.P., Lee, H.K., Nissim, K., Raskhodnikova, S., Smith, A.: What can we learn privately?*. SIAM J. Comput. **40**(3), 793–826 (2011)
12. Khodaparast, F., Sheikhalishahi, M., Haghighi, H., Martinelli, F.: Privacy-preserving LDA classification over horizontally distributed data. In: Kotenko, I., Badica, C., Desnitsky, V., El Baz, D., Ivanovic, M. (eds.) IDC 2019. SCI, vol. 868, pp. 65–74. Springer, Cham (2020). https://doi.org/10.1007/978-3-030-32258-8_8
13. Kim, J.W., Edemacu, K., Kim, J.S., Chung, Y.D., Jang, B.: A survey of differential privacy-based techniques and their applicability to location-based services. Comput. Secur. **111**, 102464 (2021)
14. Lopuhaä-Zwakenberg, M., Alishahi, M., Kivits, J., Klarenbeek, J., van der Velde, G.J., Zannone, N.: Comparing classifiers' performance under differential privacy. In: International Conference on Security and Cryptography (SECRYPT) (2021)
15. Martinelli, F., SheikhAlishahi, M.: Distributed data anonymization. In: IEEE International Conference on Dependable, Autonomic and Secure Computing (DASC), pp. 580–586 (2019)
16. Poole, D., Mackworth, A.: Artificial Intelligence: Foundations of Computational Agents, 2nd edn. Cambridge University Press, Cambridge (2017)
17. Resende, A., Railsback, D., Dowsley, R., Nascimento, A., Aranha, D.: Fast privacy-preserving text classification based on secure multiparty computation. IEEE Trans. Inf. Forensics Secur. **17**, 428–442 (2022)
18. Sheikhalishahi, M., Saracino, A., Martinelli, F., Marra, A.L., Mejri, M., Tawbi, N.: Digital waste disposal: an automated framework for analysis of spam emails. Int. J. Inf. Sec. **19**(5), 499–522 (2020)

19. Sheikhalishahi, M., Zannone, N.: On the comparison of classifiers' construction over private inputs. In: IEEE International Conference on Trust, Security and Privacy in Computing and Communications (TrustCom), pp. 691–698. IEEE (2020)
20. Vaidya, J., Shafiq, B., Basu, A., Hong, Y.: Differentially private Naive Bayes classification. In: International Joint Conferences on Web Intelligence (WI) and Intelligent Agent Technologies (IAT), vol. 1, pp. 571–576. IEEE (2013)
21. Vu, D.H.: Privacy-preserving Naive Bayes classification in semi-fully distributed data model. Comput. Secur. **115**, 102630 (2022)
22. Wang, N., et al.: Collecting and analyzing multidimensional data with local differential privacy. In: International Conference on Data Engineering (ICDE), pp. 638–649. IEEE (2019)
23. Wang, T., Blocki, J., Li, N., Jha, S.: Locally differentially private protocols for frequency estimation. In: USENIX Security Symposium, pp. 729–745 (2017)
24. Wu, X., Qi, L., Gao, J., Ji, G., Xu, X.: An ensemble of random decision trees with local differential privacy in edge computing. Neurocomputing (2021)
25. Xue, Q., Zhu, Y., Wang, J.: Joint distribution estimation and Naïve Bayes classification under local differential privacy. IEEE Trans. Emerg. Top. Comput. (2019)
26. Yilmaz, E., Al-Rubaie, M., Chang, J.M.: Locally differentially private Naive Bayes classification. arXiv preprint arXiv:1905.01039 (2019)
27. Zafarani, F., Clifton, C.: Differentially private Naive Bayes classifier using smooth sensitivity. arXiv preprint arXiv:2003.13955 (2020)
28. Zheng, X., Zhao, Y., Li, H., Chen, R., Zheng, D.: Blockchain-based verifiable privacy-preserving data classification protocol for medical data. Comput. Standards Interfaces **82** (2022)

IMSI Probing: Possibilities and Limitations

Daniel Fraunholz[1]([✉]), Dominik Brunke[1], Simon Beidenhauser[1],
Sebastian Berger[1], Hartmut Koenig[1], and Daniel Reti[2]

[1] ZITiS, Communications Department, Munich, Germany
Daniel.Fraunholz@zitis.bund.de
[2] German Research Center for Artificial Intelligence, Kaiserslautern, Germany

Abstract. Mobile networks are vital for modern societies. Recent generations of mobile communication systems have introduced increased security and privacy features to enhance their trust and reliability capabilities. Several well-known vulnerabilities, however, have not been mitigated due to design choices so far. An example is the IMSI probing attack considered in this paper which exploits vulnerabilities of the paging mechanism in mobile networks, whereas the reference to the International Mobile Subscriber Identifier (IMSI) is arbitrary and misleading. The IMSI probing attack can be used to locate and track mobile phones to infer the behavior their users. Although first published already ten years ago, it can be applied to all cellular network generation up to the upcoming 5G Stand Alone. The attack requires a certain effort to be successful. It is therefore considered less practicable. In this paper, we present an in-depth analysis of the IMSI probing attack and discuss the likelihood for its success including the required presumptions. We show that under certain conditions the attack may be successful and that the success rate can significantly be improved. Finally, we present a novel attack variant that doubles the success rate and enables location determination at the cell granularity level.

Keywords: IMSI probing attack · Privacy violation · 4G · 5G SA · Paging · RRC protocol

1 Introduction

Mobile devices have become ubiquitous in recent decades. The number of services offered on mobile devices is increasing with an astonishing speed. Sensitive services, such as online banking and health data capturing, have become standard. The growing impact of mobile technologies on human beings improves their life quality in various ways, but they also provide a lucrative target for misuse by exploiting their vulnerabilities.

With each generation, mobile telecommunications networks have become more and more secure. At the very beginning of the development the lack of mutual authentication between base station and the mobile phone (UE, user

H. P. Reiser and M. Kyas (Eds.): NordSec 2022, LNCS 13700, pp. 80–97, 2022.
https://doi.org/10.1007/978-3-031-22295-5_5

equipment) in 2G was the main reason for the well-known privacy attacks based on false base stations (FBSs) [9]. For this attack type, solutions were discussed through all mobile network generations, e.g., the authentication of System Information Block (SIB) broadcast messages to prevent the use of false base stations. With 5G Stand Alone (5G SA), the use of the permanent subscription identifier has been restricted over the air interface which significantly limits the possibility of privacy attacks. Another example of a vulnerability existing since 3G is the so-called *Linkability of Failure Messages* (LFM) attack [2] which exploits a weakness in the authentication and key agreement (AKA) procedure. With paging, used to wake up disconnected mobile devices, the situation is similar. The IMSI probing attack exploits the fact that paging messages include the M-TMSI (Temporary Mobile Subscriber Identity) of the phone to wake up, which is typically not changed frequently [6]. The attack was first published in 2012 [8], but it was not considered a severe attack at that time, since the same result could readily be achieved with other attacks. The reference to the International Mobile Subscriber Identifier (IMSI) was arbitrarily chosen for this attack because the initial attack scenario published did not use the IMSI as target identifier but the phone number. In principle, the attack can use any identifier to initiate interactions with a target device.

In 4G and 5G, the attack can be applied for degrading privacy guarantees. So in 5G SA, for instance, an attacker should not be capable to verify the presence or absence of a user because no permanent identity is transmitted over the air, but the paging vulnerability allows one to link the reuse of temporary identities, e.g., the GUTI (Globally Unique Temporary Identifier), to verify the presence and absence of a certain user. The 3rd Generation Partnership Project (3GPP) - the relevant body for the specification of cellular networks - has been already aware of this problem and proposed to change the 5G GUTI after certain events (3GPP TS33.501, 6.12.3), e.g., after receiving paging messages (GUTI re-allocation). However, 3GPP has not specified exactly how the GUTI reallocation should be implemented. Recent research has found out that several operators did so even before it was required by the standard [6]. In many cases, however, the new GUTI was based on the previous one with only slight and predictable modifications. The 3GPP standard (3GPP TS33.501, 6.12.3) explicitly states that the change of the GUTI is up to the operator. So, the re-allocation of GUTIs was not implemented as required in the three investigated 5G SA networks in China, rendering IMSI probing attacks still feasible [10].

In this paper, we present an in-depth analysis of IMSI probing attacks and examine the effectiveness as well as the limitations of the attack. This is necessary because no such investigation has been performed since the introduction of the attack. We discuss the conditions when the attack may be successful and present an attack variant that doubles the success rate and allows for a location accuracy at cell granularity. Currently, the use of paging messages is the only available probing method in public. Therefore, we refer to paging-based probing here. Paging messages can only be triggered when the target phone has no radio connectivity, i.e., when it is in the so-called *idle* mode. We explore the idle mode with and without user interactions, called *active* and *passive* phone, respectively. The remainder of the paper is organized as follows. In the following Sect. 2, we introduce the IMSI probing attack and discuss various aspects of its use. Section 3 analyzes the behavior with passive phones in a testbed consisting of 4G and 5G mobile network lab environments and commercial off-the-shelf (COTS) mobile phones. Section 4 then considers the behavior with active phones. For this, a user behavior model has been developed to enable simulation-based analysis of the IMSI probing attack. The impact of applications installed on mobile phones is analyzed in depth also in this section. In Sect. 5, we present measurements from public land mobile networks (PLMNs) to augment the results of the lab network and the simulation. Based on these analyses, we quantify the overall success probability of IMSI probing attacks in Sect. 6 and analyze the impact of the most relevant parameters for the success probability is analyzed. In Sect. 8 we present a novel, more efficient attack vector. Some final remarks conclude the paper.

2 IMSI Probing Attack

The goal of the IMSI probing attack is to verify whether a given device is currently in a certain cell or tracking area. This can be used to track a person in certain area (e.g. city), to observe its movement in a shopping area, or to prepare further activities, e.g., to check whether a person is at home to prepare a burglary. The presence can be determined with cell (200 m–20 km) or tracking area (multiple cells) granularity, respectively.

The software for this attack is freely available. The hardware cost for commercial-of-the-shelf software-defined radios, which are sufficient for launching the attack, is below $2000. Only minimal programming knowledge is required to adapt open-source software like srsRAN [14], OpenAirInterface [11], or other open-source monitoring tools, such as Falcon [5], LTEEye [7], OWL [3], and C3ACE [4] for the attack. Qualcomm baseband chips offer access to layer-2/3 messages via the DIAG protocol. Open-source frameworks, such as QCsuper [12], built upon this DIAG protocol can also be used.

2.1 Attack Presumptions

To launch the attack the attacker has to trigger a paging message. This can be done by sending a message to the target device. For this, the attacker needs to know at least one identity of the target device, e.g., the social media account or others, as discussed below. The attacker must further be connected to the mobile network of the target device, either directly or via a proxy network, e.g., the Internet. Moreover, the attacker must be able to passively monitor and analyze the paging channel of the given cell or of at least one cell within the tracking area in which the target device's presence should be checked. The analysis itself can be either performed in real time or offline afterwards. Finally, it requires that the attacker is close to the target device. In practice, this can be several hundred meters in urban cells and some kilometers in rural environments. It is difficult to determine the proximity in advance as beam propagation is subject to different factors, e.g., weather or position. The distance to the target device can be increased using high-end antennas and other monitoring equipment.

Target Device Identities. Attacks on mobile devices often use different identities for their purpose, such as GUTI, IMSI, IMEI (International Mobile Equipment Identity), or MSISDN (Mobile Subscriber Integrated Services Digital Network Number). IMSI probing, in contrast, can use any identity that trigger paging messages. From the attacker's perspective, this is a substantial advantage because social media or e-mail accounts can be exploited as well. Additionally, the attack can also be performed without knowledge of any mobile network-related identity, if other identities are known as shown by Shaik et al. [13]. Thus, the attack can be used in versatile scenarios.

2.2 Triggering Paging Messages

Assuming that all presumptions of the attacker model are met the attack can be launched triggering a paging message. For this, the attacker has to select an appropriate triggering method based on the available identities. Almost all instant messaging applications trigger a paging message at the base station. Since an attacker usually does not know the instant message apps installed, default applications, such as telephony or SMS, can also be used for triggering. There is also the option to secretly trigger paging messages. Shaik et al. [13] proposed the use of the typing notification of Whatsapp for this because it is not shown on the target device, even if the application is used by the device owner during the reception of the paging message. There is one exception when the attacker's Whatsapp account is already known to the target Whatsapp's one. In this case, the attacker's account is indicated as *"typing"*, i.e., the account is currently writing a message. A similar behavior is also expected in other instant messaging apps. Another less concealed option is the use of Facebook [13]. This proposal relies on the fact that the Facebook application does not prominently show messages of unknown users, but instead stores them in a folder, called *"Other messages"*, not be seen by the user. In addition, an attacker must know in advance whether various additional conditions are fulfilled: does the target use the application, also the mobile version of it, and whether it is active. Therefore, it is most likely that attacks prefer to use phone or vendor default applications which require less assumptions on installed applications. We did not examine any other means in the context of this investigation to trigger paging messages in an open or concealed manner.

2.3 Connection Mode

The connection mode is of crucial importance for the success of the attack. It is idle or connected. A phone is in the *connected* mode when it has established a layer-2 (Access Stratum, AS) and a layer-3 (Non Access Stratum, NAS) connection. It is in the *idle* mode when only a layer-3 (NAS) connection has been established but no layer-2 (AS) connection. Only if the phone is in the idle mode the attack is successful. Therefore, the switching between these two modes has to be detected. This has to be done by simultaneously monitoring the paging channel of the target cell or tracking area, respectively.

2.4   Monitoring the Paging Channel

Regarding the monitoring two kinds are distinguished: regular and smart paging. *Regular paging* sends paging messages in each cell of a tracking area, whereas *smart paging* only in the cell in which the mobile device is located, i.e., with smart paging, the presence of the target device can be verified with cell-granularity. An attacker can easily figure out whether smart paging is used by triggering a paging message and monitoring a neighbor cell of the same tracking area. If the paging message is received only tracking area-granularity can be achieved.

In order to recognize the paging messages triggered by the attack the paging messages must be sent with defined sending frequency. This frequency can arbitrarily be chosen by the attacker, e.g., every 10 s, and can also be non-equidistant. In this case, the paging channel analysis tries to recognize whether there are messages to a certain device that follow this pattern.

2.5   Result Verification

Regarding the sending two types of errors can be distinguished. If the frequency pattern is detected although the target device is currently not located in the cell or tracking area we have a *false positive* (FPs). This type of error occurs if a short pattern has been chosen. Kune et al. [8] triggered a paging message with a probe j ($j \in 1 \leq j \leq n$) and stored any temporary identifier in a set I_j that were addressed in paging messages within a specified time interval $t_{min} \leq t \leq t_{max}$ after triggering the paging message to the target device.

$$I_j = \begin{cases} TMSI_t, & t_{min} \leq t \leq t_{max} \\ \varnothing, & \text{otherwise} \end{cases} \quad (1)$$

This step was repeated n times until only one identifier occurred in each of the stored set I, i.e. the intersection of temporary identifiers send after each probe is the temporary identifier of the target device ($I_1 \cap I_2 \cap ... \cap I_n$). While using a distinct pattern, the likelihood of a false positive is lower than in the approach of Kune et al. Simple repetitions of the pattern further decreases the likelihood. *False negatives* (FNs), in contrast, occur when the device is located in the monitored cell or tracking area, but the frequency pattern is not found on the paging channel. This happens if the target device is not in idle mode when the attack is carried out or the monitoring system misses to capture the message. It is enough to fail the attack, when one paging message to the target device is missing in at least one set because there is no identifier in this case that occurs in each list $(I_1 \cap I_2 \cap ... \cap I_n = \emptyset)$. Pattern matching algorithms that employ thresholds for list comparison achieve more reliable results. After sending 10 probes, for example, it is sufficient to have a single identity in 80% of the lists, i.e., eight lists to conclude that the target is present, while the algorithm of Kune et al. would fail in this example. We apply the results of this examination to develop optimized attack success strategies which we present in Sect. 6.

3   Analyzing Idle Behavior with Passive Phones

The most significant limitation of the IMSI probing attack is that an attacker does not know whether the target device is in idle mode. When it is not in idle mode the attack results in a false negative, i.e., the target presence cannot be verified even if the target device is in the cell or tracking area. We consider two cases for the further analysis: (1) the device is not in use at all during the attack. Even then, there is a probability that the device is not in idle mode. This case is referred to as *passive mode* and is considered in this section. (2) The device is in use during the attack, e.g., for a telephone call or for browsing the Internet. This is referred to as *active mode* and is analyzed in a subsequent section.

3.1   Test Setup

To assess the passive mode we set up a testbed to measure idle times using an Amarisoft Callbox Classic [1]. The Callbox consists of a base station with 5G SA support, the respective core, and an IP Multimedia Subsystem (IMS). Base station and core also support 4G and multiple cell scenarios, such as 5G NSA. In our experiments, we used 5G SA for phones that support it, otherwise 4G. The phones were Android ones from various vendors, e.g., Samsung, Google, Huawei, Oppo, and Sony. The Callbox also possesses other basic monitoring capabilities, e.g., the possibility to verify whether a device has a layer-2 identifier (Cell-Radio Network Temporary Identifier, C-RNTI) associated with. If no such identifier is associated, the device is in idle mode and possesses only the layer-3 identity (GUTI). A script has been written to monitor the association of a layer-2 identifier in 1 s periods. Thus, the idle times of any device connected to the test setup could be determined. All phones had a factory-reset prior to experimentation and no additional software was installed. Any software installed on the phones can potentially alter the idle time behavior because any software with network connection can initiate a communication and thus forcing the phone to switch from idle to connected. It can be assumed that the more software, i.e., apps, are installed on the target phone the more likely is that the device is not in the idle mode, so that the presence verification leads to a false negative. Because only default software was installed on the phones, the results can be interpreted as best case scenarios in which the attack can be launched on each phone model.

3.2   Idle Time Behavior of Passive Phones

We found out that the examined mobile phones (Phone A, Phone B, Phone C, Phone D, Phone E) were between 89% and 96% of the overall monitoring period

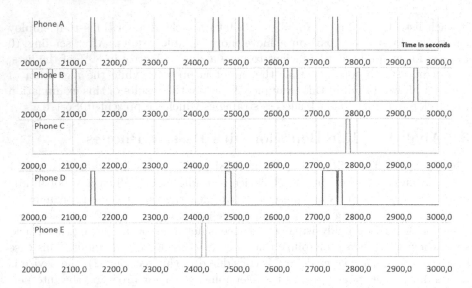

Fig. 1. Idle behavior of the investigated phones with default configuration

in the idle mode. An exception was Phone E* for which we used Phone E with disabled data connectivity and an idle ratio of 99.8%. In all cases other than E*, an increased connectivity period in the first minutes of the experiment was observed followed by a cyclic periodicity of idle time behavior after about 5 min. An exemplary visualization of the idle behavior of the investigated mobile phones is given in Fig. 1. The shortest observed idle time period was 1s for Phone A, the longest 4972 s for Phone E* with disabled mobile data connectivity. With enabled mobile data connectivity, Phone E had a maximal idle duration of 530 s, indicating the significant influence of the data connectivity. An overview of the results is given in Table 1. When the mobile data connection between the mobile phone and the network was disabled, the mobile phone connected only once during the monitoring. From this, it can be derived that the phones' idle phases are significantly correlated with the Internet connectivity, which is controlled in the upper layers of the phones' protocol stack. It can also be concluded that the idle behavior of passive phones in default configuration is characterized by short but frequent connection phases, which are temporally grouped in many cases.

3.3   Analysis of Process Behavior in Passive Mode

In order to assess which processes are relevant in the idle and connected mode, a mobile application has been developed to collect information about the network packets and the corresponding processes. The app uses the *proc* file system to gather this information. It requires a rooted phone for installation. Two 24h experiments were conducted. In the first experiment, the test phone was in the default configuration, i.e., no apps (besides our monitoring app) were installed. A total of 6287 packets was observed resulting in an average of 4.4

Table 1. Overview of the idle time behavior of selected mobile phones with default settings and default software installed, Phone E* is like Phone E but with disabled data connectivity

	Phone A	Phone B	Phone C	Phone D	Phone E	Phone E*	Av. wo E*
Exp. duration	4271 s	3592 s	3870 s	3942 s	4095 s	6790 s	3954 s
Number conn.	34	32	17	12	27	2	24,40
Idle conn. ratio	91%	89%	91%	96%	90%	99,8%	91%
Av. conn. phase	11 s	13 s	21 s	15 s	16 s	6 s	15.20 s
Min. conn. phase	4 s	10 s	10 s	10 s	10 s	1 s	8.80 s
Max. conn. phase	26 s	27 s	76 s	40 s	73 s	10 s	48.40 s
Av. idle phase	118 s	96 s	207 s	290 s	136 s	2260 s	169.40 s
Min. idle phase	1 s	2 s	3 s	5 s	2 s	290 s	2.60 s
Max. idle phase	287 s	328 s	821 s	821 s	530 s	4972 s	557.40 s

packets per minute. However for IMSI probing, the temporal distribution is significant. Therefore, we further analyzed the phases in which no packets were sent. We found out that most packets (6015) had a distance less than 1s to the preceding packet. There were several phases in which no packets were sent, up to 1680 s, which provide multiple options for successful IMSI probing attacks. Google services, such as *GMS persistent* and *quicksearchbox*, accounted for the majority of network traffic and dominated the connectivity phase. Since cellular phones are usually not in default configuration, the opportunities for IMSI probing may differ from the previously discussed scenarios. To take the impact of mobile applications on the IMSI probing success probability into account we installed and registered in the second experiment a number of popular applications on the phones. The complete list is given in Appendix A. Where necessary, user accounts were registered. However, no further interactions with apps were induced, e.g., no subscriptions, friend requests, likes etc. Interestingly, the behavior changed drastically. With these popular applications, the number of packets transferred in 24 h increased almost 35 times, resulting in a total of 217748 packets transferred and on average of 151 packets per minute. As expected, the number of idle phases reduced significantly to only 15 phases between 20 s and 30 s. The maximal idle duration observed was 25.4 s. The effective time is even smaller in reality, since we measured the time between two consecutive packets in the experiment. The actual idle phases are initiated by the network after a certain threshold (phone's inactivity timer) which further reduces the time slot available for the attack. On process-level, the most significant change is that Google services have no significant share in the number of packets sent over the network. Instead the process *com.zhiliaoapp.musically* (60.76%) and *com.zhiliaoapp.musically:push* (5.21%) account caused more than 65% of the observed packets. As the two processes can be attributed to the *TikTok* application, this observation indicates that an installed *TikTok* application significantly reduces the probability of successful IMSI probing attacks. With 1.32% of the observed packets, the aforementioned *Google GMS* service is ranked third. This process also almost doubled the number of packets sent from 1589 to 2885, suggesting that at least one of the installed applications affects Google services as well.

4   Analyzing Idle Behavior with Active Phones

IMSI probing attacks can only be successful when the target phone besides being in idle mode is close to the target person. However most likely, the phones are actively used over time thus reducing the idle mode times. To enable an in-depth analysis of IMSI probing attacks under these conditions the idle behavior model of the mobile phones must include the user behavior. For this purpose, we have developed an additional user behavior model based on the following assumptions: The average screen time of a person varies by many factors, such as weekday, habits, and age. To evaluate the effectiveness of the IMSI probing attack several assumptions about the target must be made. We assume here that an average person spends about 3:15 h with its phone per day and that this time spreads over 58 sessions [15], 70% of them are shorter than 2 min, 25% are between 2–10 min, and 5% longer than 10 min. Moreover, the sessions are equally distributed between 8 a.m. and 7 p.m. The time spent on smartphones is significantly lower between 9 p.m. and 7 a.m., what increases the probability of a successful attack. It was also found that on average the time spent on mobile phones is less on weekdays than on weekends [15]. During the pandemic the screen time increased about 20% to 30% rendering probes less likely to be successful. A visualization of an exemplary idle behavior of the developed model of such a behavior for an 8h period is contained in Fig. 2 (lower graph, cyan and magenta solid lines).

5   Empirical Evaluation in Real World Mobile Networks

To further quantify the success probability of IMSI probing attacks other parameters were examined. An important parameter is the number of consecutive probes required for a successful attack. The capture rate of the available monitoring systems is another parameter that needs to be considered because there is a likelihood of probes being missed.

5.1   Experimental Environment

Figure 3 depicts the number of paging messages in 10 s time interval over a 24 h period in the network used for the experimental evaluation. The tracking area is located in the north-east metropolitan region of Munich, but it is no longer part of the Munich city. As it can be seen, up to almost 1400 paging messages per 10 s interval need to be captured and processed by the monitoring system.

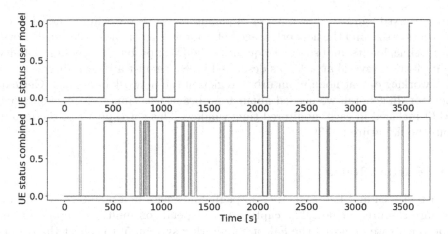

Fig. 2. Upper graph: Exemplary visualization of the idle and connected times of the assumed user behavior model. Lower graph: Exemplary visualization of the idle and connected phases resulting from the combined user and processes model

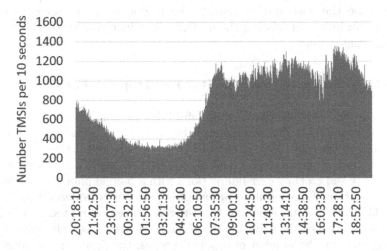

Fig. 3. Visualization of the number of received temporal user identities (TMSI) per 1680 s over the course of about 24 h in a cell in the northern metropolitan area of Munich.

5.2   Required Number of Probing Repetitions

The determination of the required probe number for a successful identification of a phone is crucial for further investigations. This is because the number of required probes in combination with the duration of a single probe determines the total idle period necessary for a successful attack. The required number of probes is not known in advance and can only be estimated. As previously described, an attacker needs to define a time window in which paging messages are collected. This must be repeated until only one or none GUTI is included in each observed window. The number of paging messages per window depends on the window size and the network usage behavior which depends, as argued above, on daytime, habits, and so on. To quantify the IMSI probing success probability we performed several attacks (as described in [8]) against a known target phone on a working day at noon in an urban region in the network of a major German operator. In general, we needed about 6 probes at this time to receive only one GUTI included in each monitored time window. This corresponds to the results from the literature [8,13].

5.3   Capture Rates

An attacker cannot know whether all paging messages in a monitored time window are captured or not. The capture rate depends on multiple factors. In our experiments we deployed the Falcon monitoring system [5] to collect the paging messages and to determine the capture rate. We found that the value significantly depends on the signal quality and the network usage. The achieved capture rates were between 70% and 99%. Mobile phones do also not have a capture rate of 100% because the base station repeats the paging messages several times to reduce the likelihood of missing them. This effect increases the capture rate of the monitoring system.

6   Attack Success Probability and Impact Factors

To determine the probability of a successful IMSI probing attack two cases have to be distinguished. (1) The success probability is estimated using the developed model based on the experimental results of the idle behavior of the mobile phones that are not in use (passive) and have no applications installed (default configuration). (2) Based on this, user interactions with a mobile phone are included in the quantification. False positive probabilities are not considered here because this would require assumptions on third-party devices connected to the cell or tracking area in which the attack is launched. In the two cases, the success probability depends on the number of required probes, the time window to monitor the probes, the capture rates, and the idle times of the mobile phones. Given that an attacker cannot know the exact idle behavior of the mobile phones, any attack time is equally sufficient.

6.1   Passive Mobile Phone with Default Configuration

In our experiments, we used the Amarisoft Callbox as test network and the aforementioned script to monitor the phone's idle times. Additionally, a Python script was written to use the JSON API to periodically send SMSs every 20 s via the test network to the target phone. 20 s were chosen because the network typically releases the phone after 5–15 s of inactivity and 20 s ensure that the previous SMS does not influence the subsequent ones. The script used the JSON API of the Callbox. The paging channel of the test network was again monitored

Table 2. Overview of the idle time behavior of selected mobile phones with default settings and default software installed

	Ph. A	Ph. B	Ph. D	Ph. E	Ph. E*
True-pos	98	128	96	100	108
False-pos	7	19	27	14	1
True-neg	2823	2767	2295	2151	2053
False-neg	45	18	9	12	10
Precision	0.933	0.871	0.780	0.877	0.991
Recall	0.685	0.877	0.914	0.893	0.915
F1-score	0.790	0.874	0.842	0.885	0.952

with the Falcon tool. A statistical evaluation of the complete experiment is given in Table 2.

The success rate for IMSI probing attacks against passive phones in default configuration varies significantly depending on the number of probes required and the phone model. This is because the false negative classifications, i.e., the missed probes, were significantly higher than for other phones. The reason for this is the shorter idle time or the more frequent connection phases, respectively, since the same monitoring system was used in all experiments. The success probability for one probe is about 70% and reduces to about 1% for 12 consecutive probes for Phone A. All other phones had a success probability of about 90% for one and between 20% and 35% for the 12 consecutive probes. The success probability for 7 consecutive probes, as identified as typical number in the experiment, is about 7% for Phone A and between 40% and 53% for the other phones.

From this experiment, the time between a received SMS and the return to idle mode was estimated to be about 12 s. This is important to quantify the waiting period between two consecutive probes in the subsequent evaluation.

6.2   Active Mobile Phone with Default Configuration

To determine the success probability for active phones the idle behavior model as described in Subsect. 4 was investigated. An exemplary visualization of the distribution of the connections and idle phases is shown in Fig. 4b, whereby the threshold of 7 consecutive probes with a 12 s window between probes is marked with a vertical solid red line.

It shows that there are several idle phases that are long enough to perform a successful IMSI probing attack. An attacker, however, cannot know the begin or end of these phases, i.e., the likelihood of a successful attack is the same at any point in time from the attackers perspective. Therefore, the attacker's probability to launch the attack is equally distributed over the considered time. Consequently, the number of required probes and the capture rate of the monitoring system are the two parameters that cannot be known in advance because they depend on the cell or tracking area load during the attack. An exemplary

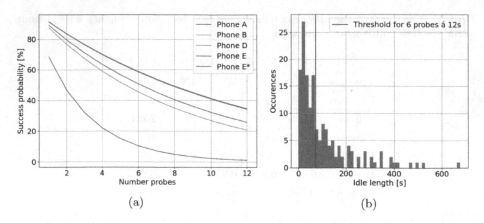

(a)   (b)

Fig. 4. (a) Visualization of the relation of the attack success probability and the number of probes required for presence verification. Phone D (green) and Phone E* (purple) are almost similar. (b) Histogram of the resulting length of idle times in the user behavior simulation and the threshold for the minimal idle time required for a successful attack (6 consecutive probes á 12 s) (Color figure online)

visualization of the success rates for several required numbers of probes and capture rates is given in Fig. 5.

Several of the considered scenarios have a success probability close to zero. This is because the availability of idle phases is limited if the user behavior is taken into account. The required number of consecutive probes linearly increases the needed duration of the idle phase. The gradient depends on the minimal time between two probes which is the sum of the time between sending the probe, receiving by the phone, connecting to the network, receiving the data (i.e., the SMS in our experiment), and switching back to idle mode after a short inactivity period. In best-case scenario, the IMSI probing attack only achieves a success probability of 36.88%. This is the case with a 100% capture rate and only 4 probes being necessary to differentiate the target phone from all other phones in the cell or tracking area. In our experiments with different provider networks, four probes was the minimum number of probes that were required for a successful attack.

7   Optimizing the Attack Success Probability

The results obtained suggest that IMSI probing is not a reliable attack technique at all. If we consider the typical user behavior with eight required probes and a capture rate of 99%, the success probability is below 20%. Moreover, this only holds if no applications are installed. The in-depth process analysis revealed that the required idle phases are even less if applications are installed on the phone, which is the normal case in real world scenarios.

The success probability is determined based on the assumption that the pattern detection algorithm cannot handle errors, leading to an unsuccessful

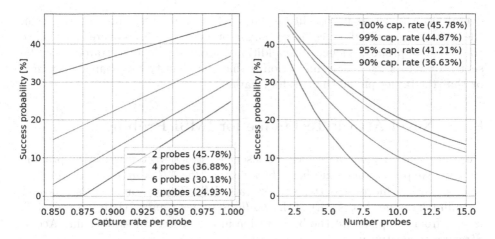

Fig. 5. Left: Impact of the capture rate on the success probability for different number of required probes. Right: Impact of the required number of probes on the success probability for different capture rates.

probe if one probe is missed (e.g., because of the capture rate or because the phone was not in idle mode). More advanced pattern detection algorithms can take these factors into account and increase the success probabilities as follows. There are two strategies. (1) An attacker can simply repeat the IMSI probing attack after completion. In this case, the overall success probability of the attack is generally determined by the discrete binominal distribution $P(X \geq 1) = P(X = 0) + \ldots + P(X = n)$, whereby $P(X) = \binom{n}{k}p^k(1-p)^{n-k}$ and P is the overall success probability, n the number of attacks, k the number of successful attacks and p the success rate of a single probe. For example, if the attack success rate is 40%, the probability of at least one successful attack after 4 attacks is about 87%. This strategy is limited by the overall number of idle phases that are long enough to perform a successful attack, i.e., if there are no idle phases long enough for a successful attack the attack fails regardless of the number of repetitions. In all other cases, this strategy will succeed given infinite time. (2) A more advanced strategy is to adapt the pattern detection during the attack. As presented in Table 2, the recall for a single probe is about 90% (excluding Phone A), i.e., there is only a 10% probability to miss a paging message. If one paging message is missed the intersection does not converge to one remaining identity but to none. In such a situation, additional probes can be sent to verify the result. The formula from above applies here as well. For example, if the likelihood of a single successful probe is 90%, the likelihood of seven consecutive successful probes is about 48%, i.e., when seven probes were sent the probability that at least one was missed is about 52%. However, by simply sending another probe, i.e., eight probes are sent and only seven are required to be successful, the overall success probability reaches 81%. Adding a ninth probe, i.e., nine probes are sent and only seven of them are required for success, would increase the overall attack success probability to 95%. This strategy is more effective than the first one presented, since only a single probe has to be repeated instead of the complete probe sequence. The additional probes in the two strategies can be sent at any time. The only limitation is that the identity can change over time or that the target phone changes its location.

8   A Novel Attack Technique for IMSI Probing

Currently only paging messages are used as attack vector for IMSI probing attacks. We present here another attack vector - *the RRCConnectionSetup message* - which achieves a better success rate. RRCConnectionSetup is a layer-2 downlink message that is part of the *Radio Resource Control* (RRC) protocol. It is sent from the phone to the base station in the process of establishing Access Stratum connectivity.

Performing the IMSI probing attack using the RRCConnectionSetup message has two major advantages. (1) The location accuracy can be improved from tracking area granularity to cell one. RRCConnectionSetup messages are not sent in the tracking area but only on layer-2 of the cell the phone is in. For paging messages, this granularity has been only possible up to now when smart paging (i.e., paging messages are only sent in the last known cell instead of the last known tracking area) was applied in the target cell. (2) The number of probes reduces drastically because the number of RRCConnectionSetups is generally lower than the number of paging messages. This is because RRCConnectionSetup messages are only sent when the paging procedure is successful and the phone establishes a connection, or when the phone establishes a connection without prior paging.

For the evaluation of this attack technique, we performed an experiment comparing paging- and RRCConnectionSetup-based attacks. We performed twenty consecutive attacks and compared the efficiency of the two attack vectors regarding the required number of probes to verify the target presence which ultimately impacts the attack success probability, as argued above. It was found that paging-based IMSI probing attacks required between 4 and 10 probes with on average 5.6 probes and a standard deviation of 1.2 probes. For the RRCConnectionSetup-based attack, 2 or 3 probes were needed with on average of 2.2 probes and a standard deviation of 0.4 probes. These results show the greater efficiency of the new attack vector. The number of messages collected during the specified time window (4.5 s) after the probe was ten RRCConnectionSetup messages compared to on average ninety paging messages before. This is the reason why the new attack method converges faster leading to a better correlation between the number of required probes and the number of messages collected after each probe.

Based on these experimental results, we further assessed the attack success probability of the two vectors. We run hundred simulations with a given capture rate of 95% and a minimal waiting period of 12 s between the probes, and a minimal required number of two probes for RRCConnectionSetup and six for paging. Our model showed an average attack success probability for the RRCConnectionSetup-based method of 39.72% with a standard deviation of 4.42% and for the paging-based one 20.71% with a standard deviation of 3.00%, i.e., the number of RRCConnectionSetup messages is about one tenth of the number of paging messages in the same time window (90 vs. 10 messages). This results in a reduction of about one third in the number of probes required (six vs. two probes) which itself doubles the success probability of the IMSI probing attack (20% vs 40%).

The RRCConnectionSetup attack vector, however, increases the uncertainty of the calibration of the time window after the probe. This is because measuring paging messages is subject to uncertainties of the phone, the API that initiates the probe, and the network that receives the probe and subsequently sends the paging message to the target phone. For monitoring RRCConnectionSetup messages, the uncertainty is extended by the target phone receiving the paging message and subsequently sending the RRCConnectionRequest message back to the base station which then in turn responds with the RRCConnectionSetup to the phone. We found that the delay of this process is on average 0.4 s, while the standard deviation increases from 0.77 s to 1.06 s. This effect must be compensated by adjusted time windows when performing the attack. For paging-based IMSI probing, the calibration of the time window is also necessary.

We identified a limitation in our experimental setup because the Falcon tool [5] captured paging messages with an accuracy of about 98.8% and RRCConnectionSetup messages with an accuracy of about 76%. This may be caused by the increased complexity in decoding for the RRCConnectionSetup messages. We made the measurements from the phone's baseband chip which we accessed via the Qualcomm DIAG protocol with QCsuper [12] as baseline. The ratio of messages received at the baseband chip and SMS triggered was 92.8% for both paging and RRCConnectionSetup messages. The remaining messages (7.2%) were not being sent, since the phone was not in idle mode. We mitigated this limitation by considering positive results only. This is valid because the target phone was present in the monitored network and only the number of required probes for verification was evaluated.

9 Conclusions

In this paper, we have studied on the effectiveness of the IMSI probing attack that allows for invading user privacy. With the advance of cellular network generations, this relative old attack is becoming more attractive for attackers in the context of modern telecommunication networks like 5G. The effectiveness of the attack significantly depends on the manner how the target phone is used. Modern devices with many installed apps and a frequent device usage through phone calls, video streaming, messaging etc. render IMSI probing attacks more complex with a relative low success rate. Nevertheless, 3GPP has proposed mitigation mechanisms (3GPP TS33.501, 6.12.3) which are ineffective though [6]. The attack leaves traces on the device, i.e., in the baseband processor, and hence can be detected. The results of our empirical study have shown that the IMSI probing attack based on the algorithm of Kune et al. using paging messages is rather ineffective and only successful under optimal conditions. We have investigated the success rate for phones in passive and active mode. Especially the passive mode contradicts the current trends of phone and data service usage. These use cases are pretty unlikely. We have shown, however, that the use of additional probes and more robust detection algorithms can improve the success rate significantly. Nevertheless the execution of the attack remains complex. We have proposed a novel attack vector based on the monitoring of the RRCConnectionSetup messages of the RRC protocol. It significantly reduces the number of probes thus increasing the attack success likelihood. This makes the deployment of the attack less complicated. Using the RRCConnectionSetup message instead of paging messages doubles the attack success rate and also improves the localization accuracy to cell granularity level. The impact of network and phone delays, e.g., from network utilization, on the IMSI probing time window needs to be investigated further. In particular, the trade-off between the number of messages (i.e., paging or RRCConnectionSetup) per time interval and the necessary window size for capturing in the context of messages captured after a single probe are of special interest here. Moreover, only smartphones were considered. Other device types, such as IoT devices or vehicles, may have a different susceptibility to IMSI probing attacks. In this domain, the influence of the Discontinuous Reception (DRX) or Extended Discontinuous Reception (eDRX) cycles may play a significant role for the attack success rate, as paging occasions might be reduced drastically.

A   Installed Applications in Section 4

Facebook, Whatapp, Facebook Messenger, Instagram, TikTok, Subway Surfers, Facebook Lite, Microsoft Word, Microsoft PowerPoint, Snapchat, SHAREit, Netflix, Twitter, Flipboard, Candy Crush Saga, Skype, Spotify, Dropbox, Viber, LINE.

References

1. Amarisoft: Amari callbox (2022). https://www.amarisoft.com
2. Arapinis, M., et al.: New Privacy Issues in Mobile Telephony: Fix and Verification. CCS, North Carolina, USA (2012)
3. Bui, N., Widmer, J.: Owl: a reliable online watcher for LTE control channel measurements. In: Proceedings of the 5th Workshop on All Things Cellular: Operations, Applications and Challenges, pp. 25–30. ATC 2016, Association for Computing Machinery, New York, NY, USA (2016). https://doi.org/10.1145/2980055.2980057
4. Falkenberg, R., Ide, C., Wietfeld, C.: Client-based control channel analysis for connectivity estimation in LTE networks. In: 2016 IEEE 84th Vehicular Technology Conference (VTC-Fall), pp. 1–6 (2016). https://doi.org/10.1109/VTCFall.2016.7880932

5. Falkenberg, R., Wietfeld, C.: FALCON: an accurate real-time monitor for client-based mobile network data analytics. In: 2019 IEEE Global Communications Conference (GLOBECOM). IEEE, Waikoloa, Hawaii, USA (2019). https://doi.org/10.1109/GLOBECOM38437.2019.9014096, https://arxiv.org/abs/1907.10110

6. Hong, B., Bae, S., Kim, Y.: GUTI reallocation demystified: cellular location tracking with changing temporary identifier. In: NDSS (2018)

7. Kumar, S., Hamed, E., Katabi, D., Erran Li, L.: LTE radio analytics made easy and accessible. SIGCOMM Comput. Commun. Rev. **44**(4), 211–222 (2014). https://doi.org/10.1145/2740070.2626320

8. Kune, D.F., Koelndorfer, J., Hopper, N., Kim, Y.: Location leaks on the GSM air interface. ISOC NDSS (2012)

9. Mjølsnes, S.F., Olimid, R.F.: Easy 4G/LTE IMSI catchers for non-programmers. In: Rak, J., Bay, J., Kotenko, I., Popyack, L., Skormin, V., Szczypiorski, K. (eds.) MMM-ACNS 2017. LNCS, vol. 10446, pp. 235–246. Springer, Cham (2017). https://doi.org/10.1007/978-3-319-65127-9_19

10. Nie, S., Zhang, Y., Wan, T., Duan, H., Li, S.: Measuring the deployment of 5g security enhancement. In: Proceedings of the 15th ACM Conference on Security and Privacy in Wireless and Mobile Networks, pp. 169–174. WiSec 2022, Association for Computing Machinery, New York, NY, USA (2022). https://doi.org/10.1145/3507657.3528559

11. OpenAirInterface software alliance: openairinterface (2022). https://openairinterface.org

12. P1sec: QCSuper (2022). https://github.com/P1sec/QCSuper

13. Shaik, A., Borgaonkar, R., Asokan, N., Niemi, V., Seifert, J.P.: Practical attacks against privacy and availability in 4g/LTE mobile communication systems. NDSS16 (2016)

14. Software Radio Systems: srsRAN (2022). https://github.com/srsran/srsRAN

15. Zalani, R.: Screen time statistics 2021: your smartphone is hurting you (2021). https://elitecontentmarketer.com/screen-time-statistics/

Attacks and Attack Detection

Honeysweeper: Towards Stealthy Honeytoken Fingerprinting Techniques

Mohamed Msaad[1], Shreyas Srinivasa[1(✉)], Mikkel M. Andersen[1],
David H. Audran[1], Charity U. Orji[1], and Emmanouil Vasilomanolakis[2]

[1] Aalborg University, Copenhagen, Denmark
{mmsaad18,mman21,daudra21,corji21}@student.aau.dk, shsr@es.aau.dk
[2] Technical University of Denmark, Kgs. Lyngby, Denmark
emmva@dtu.dk

Abstract. The increased number of data breaches and sophisticated attacks have created a need for early detection mechanisms. Reports indicate that it may take up to 200 days to identify a data breach and entail average costs of up to $4.85 million. To cope with cyber-deception approaches like honeypots have been used for proactive attack detection and as a source of data for threat analysis. Honeytokens are a subset of honeypots that aim at creating deceptive layers for digital entities in the form of files and folders. Honeytokens are an important tool in the proactive identification of data breaches and intrusion detection as they raise an alert the moment a deceptive entity is accessed. In such deception-based defensive tools, it is key that the adversary does not detect the presence of deception. However, recent research shows that honeypots and honeytokens may be fingerprinted by adversaries. Honeytoken fingerprinting is the process of detecting the presence of honeytokens in a system without triggering an alert. In this work, we explore potential fingerprinting attacks against the most common open-source honeytokens. Our findings suggest that an advanced attacker can identify the majority of honeytokens without triggering an alert. Furthermore, we propose methods that help in improving the deception layer, the information received from the alerts, and the design of honeytokens.

Keywords: Honeytokens · Fingerprinting · Counter-deception

1 Introduction

Cyber attacks have reached a record level in 2021, making it the highest in 17 years with a 10% increase from the previous year [14]. A $1.07 million cost increase is related to the spike in remote work due to the COVID-19 pandemic [15] in addition to the continuous growth of IoT devices [8,23]. Further, the time needed to identify and contain a security breach may take up to 287 days [13]. To combat this, the cyber-defense community is moving toward more active lines of defense that leverage deception-based techniques. Deception techniques confuse and divert attackers from real assets by placing fake data and

H. P. Reiser and M. Kyas (Eds.): NordSec 2022, LNCS 13700, pp. 101–119, 2022.
https://doi.org/10.1007/978-3-031-22295-5_6

vulnerable systems across an organization's network. Any interaction with a deceptive entity may be considered an attack. In practice, there are two leading deception technologies: *honeypots* and *honeytokens*.

Honeypots are deceptive systems that emulate a vulnerable program [16,17, 20,24], for instance, a vulnerable version of the Linux operating system (OS), an HTTP server, or an IoT device. They lure attackers and deflect them from real assets while gathering information about the techniques and tools used during the interaction. Honeypots differ by their low, medium or high-interaction level [9,25,26]. As the name implies, interaction refers to how much capabilities are offered to the adversary. The process of discovering the existence of a honeypot in a system is known as honeypot fingerprinting [22,26]. The drawback of many honeypots is that their emulation of systems/protocols exposes some artifacts that attackers can detect.

Honeytokens are digital entities that contain synthetic/fabricated data. They are usually stored in a system under attractive names as a trap for intruders, and any interaction with them is considered an attack. Honeytokens can be files such as PDFs, SQL database entries, URLs, or DNS records that embed a token. Once accessed they trigger and alert the system about the breach [3]. Additionally, honeytokens are less complex and easier to maintain when compared to honeypots.

The honeytokens' efficiency resides in their indistinguishability; hence, identifying that an entity is a honeytoken (known as fingerprinting), diminishes its value. In this paper, we explore and extend the research on honeytoken fingerprinting techniques and demonstrate a fingerprinting tool that can successfully fingerprint 14 out of 20 honeytokens offered by the most popular open-source honeytoken service. Our contributions in this work are as follows:

- We analyze the design of open-source honeytokens to identify potential gaps for fingerprinting purposes.
- We introduce additional techniques to detect open-source honeytokens without triggering alerts.
- We propose techniques to improve the deceptive capabilities of honeytokens and introduce features that can enhance the use of information received from alerts triggered by intrusions.

The rest of this paper is structured as follows. In Sect. 2, we discuss the background of the working mechanism and the fingerprinting mechanism of honeytokens. Section 3 summarizes the related work of honeytoken fingerprinting. Section 4 presents our proposed stealthy techniques for honeytoken fingerprinting. Moreover, in Sect. 5 we present a proof of concept for honeytoken fingerprinting. In Sect. 6, we discuss countermeasures against honeytoken fingerprinting. We conclude our work in Sect. 7.

2   Background

Cyber-deception is an emerging proactive cyber defense methodology. When well crafted, deception-based tools can be leveraged as source of threat intelligence data. Deception techniques have two correlated defense strategies: first, to diverge the attacker from tangible assets by simulating vulnerable systems to lure attackers and attract attention, protecting tangible assets from being attacked. Second, to notify about ongoing suspicious activities, which can minimize the impact of an attack.

Honeytokens are deceptive entities that work by essentially triggering a notification when the user initiates an action on them. The actions can vary depending on the honeytoken type, such as read, write, query and others. The concept is to embed a token in the deceptive entity and rely on the deceptive layer to consume the token and trigger the alert. Figure 1 shows the conceptual flow of a honeytoken. The honeytoken is deployed on a user's system at either OS, application, or network levels. On any attempt of access, the honeytoken triggers an alert to the user through the notification mechanism. The recipient's information is obtained by placing a request to the honeytoken service. The honeytoken service acts as an endpoint and provides a back-end for managing the honeytokens and the metadata of the deployed honeytokens. Upon obtaining recipient information, a notification is sent either as an email or a text message.

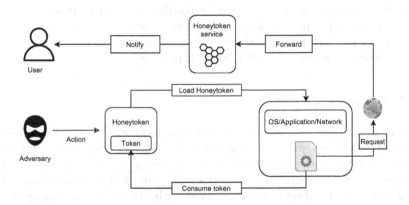

Fig. 1. Honeytoken concept and alert mechanism

To explain the honeytoken mechanism in detail, we use the Canarytokens (honeytokens service) as a case study to provide concrete examples. Canarytokens is an open-source honeytoken provider that offers 20 different honeytoken types. All the honeytokens provided share the same deployment life-cycle as illustrated in Fig. 2.

To explain the deceptive layer and trigger mechanism, we use the PDF honeytoken from the Canarytoken service. The Adobe Acrobat Reader (AAR) offers a range of functionality for the PDF format to increase the document's interaction. One of these functionalities is the URI function, which allows linking a local URI to the world wide web via the AAR plugin Weblink [1]. The weblink plugin exposes its functionalities to other applications through the Host-Function-Table API. Once the honeytoken is accessed with AAR, the URL is loaded by the

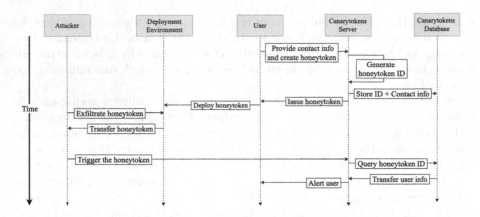

Fig. 2. Canarytokens life-cycle

weblink plugin, which on its turn will start a DNS request to resolve the domain name. This DNS request will alert the owner of the PDF honeytoken.

Unlike honeypots, honcytokens are accessible only if the attacker is within the system where the honeytokens reside. The attacker can gain access through an attack or be an insider. In both cases, honeytokens are very useful as an early alarm against successful data exfiltration if triggered.

3   Related Work

Since the invention of deception techniques, much research has been proposed for fingerprinting the deceptive entities [2, 4, 7, 26]. These fingerprinting techniques fall into two categories: passive and active fingerprinting. Passive techniques do not require interaction with the deceptive entity and focus on monitoring. However, active fingerprinting can be either stealthy or noisy. We define stealthy fingerprinting as the process of revealing a deceptive mechanism without triggering any alarm.

3.1   Honeypot Fingerprinting

Holz et al. list some artifacts produced by the honeypot simulation to detect a honeypot [12]. For instance, by verifying the User-Mode-Linux (UML). UML is a way of having a Linux kernel running on another Linux. The initial Linux kernel is the host OS, and the other is the guest OS. By default, the UML executes in Tracing Thread mode (TT) and is not designed to be hidden and can be used to check for all the processes started by the host OS main thread. By executing the command: *"ps a"*, one can retrieve a list of processes and identify UML usage's existence. Another sign of UML is the usage of the TUN/TAP back-end for the network, which is not common on a real system and can identify UML usage. Another place to look for artifacts is at the file *proc/self/maps* that contains the current mapped memory regions on a Linux system. On a real OS, the end of the stack is usually *0xc0000000*, which is not the case on a guest OS. These artifacts can be used against honeypots, rendering them visible to the attacker.

Other fingerprinting techniques, such as the network latency comparison, focus on the network layer. For instance, by calculating the differences between an HTTP server and a honeypot HTTP server. Mukkamala et al. utilized timing analysis to reveal if a program is a honeypot. Comparing the timing analysis of ICMP echo requests, they showcased that an HTTP-server honeypot will respond slower than a real HTTP-server [18]. In another work by Srinivasa et al., a framework for fingerprinting different honeypots is proposed. The utilized techniques include so-called probe-based fingerprinting (such as port-scans or banner-checks), and metascan-based fingerprinting (e.g., using data from the Shodan API) [22].

3.2   Honeytoken Fingerprinting

Honeytokens can take the form of different data types, such as files, database entries, and URL/DNS records. The first step of fingerprinting is to classify honeytokens to build a standard fingerprint method for each type. Fraunholz et al. have classified honeytokens based on the entity type it emulates [6]. For instance, so-called honeypatches are classified as server-based honeytokens as they emulate a vulnerable decoy. The decoy may host monitoring software that collects important attack information and deceptive files that misinform the attackers. The attacker is redirected to a decoy once the system detects an exploit. Similarly, the database, authentication, and file honeytokens emulate data records and authentication credentials, such as passwords and documents. Similarly, Han et al. proposed a multi-dimensional classification of deception techniques based on the goal, unit, layer, and deployment of the deception [11]. The majority of the surveyed honeytokens are classified based on the detection goal. However, they differ in the four deception layers—the network, system, application, and data layer. In another work, Zhang et al. proposed a two-dimensional taxonomy, which eases the systematic review of representative approaches in a threat-oriented mode, namely from the domains of honeypots, honeytokens, and MTD techniques. They classify deception techniques depending on which phase of the Cyber Kill-Chain they can deceive an attacker. Honeytokens can be used in eight out of twelve phases to deceive attackers [27].

To the best of our knowledge, the only work that examines honeytoken-specific fingerprinting to date is by Srinivasa et al. [21]. The work showcases a proof of concept regarding fingerprinting a public honeytoken provider as a case study. Additionally, they suggest a honeytoken classification based on the four levels of operation and their fingerprinting technique, respectively:

- **Network level**: The honeytokens operating on this level emulate a network entity or use the network as the channel for delivering the alerts. The respective fingerprinting technique for this deceptive layer relies on sniffing the network traffic to detect such calls. In their example with the PDF honeytoken,

Srinivasa et al. observed the usage of DNS queries. However, this fingerprinting method remains passive and not stealthy as it leads to triggering the alert.

- **Application/File-Level**: These honeytokens take the format of a specific file, e.g., PDF or DOCX, and obfuscate an alert mechanism within the file. The alert is triggered if specific applications like Adobe Reader or Microsoft Word opens the honeytoken. The fingerprinting techniques relies on file decompression and obtaining the file honeytoken metadata.
- **System-Level**: These honeytokens utilize operating systems' features such as event logs and *inotify* calls as alert mechanisms. For fingerprinting these, Srinivasa et al. suggest monitoring background-running processes to check for the *inotify* call and to look out for changes in the file or the directory path.
- **Data-Level**: These honeytokens emulate data and can be hard to distinguish from actual data. The technique for fingerprinting honeytokens operating on the data level could vary depending on the data emulated and its alert mechanism. However, as mentioned by Srinivasa et al., viewing the file's metadata can help an attacker determine whether the file is a possible honeytoken. For instance, Honeyaccount [5] creates fake user-accounts for a system to deceive attackers in using them and hence trigger the alert. On a compromised Windows machine, adversaries can list the user accounts to verify the last known activity. Additionally, adversaries can use Windows PowerShell scripts to recover meta-data about the accounts in Active Directory. This can assist in identifying fake user accounts.

Srinivasa et al. also present different fingerprinting techniques for each honeytoken type. For instance, to fingerprint a PDF honeytoken and determine its trigger channel, they monitored the network traffic when interacting with the file. This fingerprinting technique is noisy as the honeytoken triggers after the interaction. However, a stealthier fingerprinting approach for the same honeytoken was also applied. They used a PDF parser[1] to extract information from the PDF stream. The information consisted of a URL where the domain name belonged to the honeytoken provider. All their proposed fingerprinting techniques relied only on black box testing (i.e., triggering the honeytoken to find the deceptive layer and the alerting mechanism). Lastly, the authors did not consider multiple honeytokens but focused only on a few as a base for their proof of concept.

4   Methodology

To build the fingerprinting techniques, we used different methods to extract information from the honeytoken implementation. The methods include white box and black box testing.

---

[1] https://github.com/DidierStevens/DidierStevensSuite/blob/master/pdf-parser.py.

4.1   Honeytoken Analysis

To analyze the honeytokens, we started by building a classification to help us create fingerprinting techniques for each honeytoken class. Srinivasa et al. have established a Canarytoken honeytoken classification, and we use it as a building block for our extended version [21].

In particular, we extend the previous classification and propose a new one that maps all the publicly offered honeytokens from Canarytokens, as shown in Table 1. We added the dependency layer as a category of classification. The dependency can be at the application or the OS layer. The PDF, *.docx* honeytokens can only trigger when used with a specific application. For instance, *.docx* will only trigger with the application Microsoft Word and would not if opened with the online version Microsoft 365, concluding that it is an application-dependent honeytoken. In contrast, other honeytokens, such as the SQL-DUMP, will trigger with any query from an SQL-capable application. This classification also relates to the privileges needed to stop the triggering mechanism (e.g., the OS-dependent honeytokens will require higher privileges to interrupt the trigger process than the application-dependent ones).

The first analysis step is to classify the honeytokens based on their underlying operation. We leverage the syntax form of the token as the base for the classification. From all the 20 available honeytokens, we find four base usages: DNS, URL, SMTP, IP, and access keys base.

The second step is to classify the honeytokens based on the location of the honeytoken identifier in the token. After analyzing all the URL/DNS-based honeytokens, we observed that the token is a subdomain or a path identifier in the URL. This brought us to conclude the trigger channel based on the location. Subdomain honeytokens will use DNS as a trigger channel, while the URL honeytokens will use the HTTP protocol.

With the classification as a base, we focus on developing fingerprinting techniques that target the dependency layer and the trigger channel. We use white and black box testing in our methodology to identify the gap in the implementation of the honeytokens that can be leveraged for developing fingerprinting techniques.

White Box Testing. The Canarytokens (honeytoken provider) service is open source, and we used white box testing to investigate the implementation to find artifacts. In particular, we utilized manual static analysis to check the honeytokens' generation code for any predicted output or patterns that can be used as a fingerprinting base. From our testing, we discover the following:

- ID length: We identify the usage of a fixed length in the honeytoken ID.
- Hardcoded data: We analyzed the source code to search for hardcoded data in the honeytoken's generation process. For instance, upon analyzing the code for the *.exe* file honeytoken, we discover the usage of hardcoded data used to generate a certificate.

Table 1. Extended Canarytokens classification

Honeytoken base	Honeytoken name	Trigger channel	Alerting entity	Dependency layer
DNS Subdomain Based	Acrobat Reader PDF		Adobe Acrobat Reader & Others	Application
	Custom .exe/ Binary		Windows User Access Control	OS
	MySQL Dump		SQL Server	None
	SQL Server		SQL Server	None
	DNS	DNS	DNS Server	None
	Windows Folder		Windows File Explorer	OS
	SVN Server		SVN Server	None
URL Based	Windows Word Document		Microsoft Word Desktop Application	Application
	Windows Excel Document		Microsoft Excel Desktop Application	Application
	QR Code Fast Redirect Slow Redirect URL Custom Image Web Bug Cloned Website	HTTP	Web Browsers, Curl & others	None
SMTP Based	Email Address	SMTP	SMTP Server	None
IP Based	Kubernetes Config File	TLS	Kubernetes Application	
	Wireguard Config File	Wireguard Protocol	Wireguard Application	
Access Key Based	AWS Key	CloudWatch	CloudWatch	Application

- Template file usage: Canarytokens use a template file to generate the PDF, *.docx* and *.xlsx* honeytokens. This template is not changed and leads to static metadata that can be fingerprinted.
- File size: This is a result of the template file usage and constant file size. We consider this an additional artifact to the template to enhance the probability of accurate fingerprinting.

Black Box Testing. The black box testing did not focus on testing the system's internals. Instead, we used it to extract additional information that is only available after the honeytoken generation and validate our findings. The black box included creating and interacting with the honeytoken to reveal the trigger channel and the entity responsible for triggering the alert. The implemented techniques are as follows:

- Extracting metadata from the honeytokens to inspect if there are any static metadata present.
- Monitoring the network traffic when triggering a honeytoken to discover the trigger channel and confirm the white box testing findings.
- Monitoring what sub-processes were started by the application or the OS that triggers the honeytoken. This gives us an idea of how to circumvent the trigger mechanism and stop the honeytoken alert if possible.

With the knowledge gained from the black box, we classify the honeytokens into three categories depending on the token base: URL/DNS, IP, and access key based. The URL/DNS-based honeytokens have a URL or a DNS subdomain directly in the data or the file's metadata. Regardless of the honeytoken type, they all have the same domain name, canarytokens.com, or the equivalent IP address. The access key is a simple AWS access key with an identifier to link the user information with the honeytoken.

4.2 Honeytoken Fingerprinting

The first step is to be able to fingerprint honeytokens generated from the official website of Canarytokens[2]. We create and download all possible honeytokens to familiarize ourselves and gain information about all the different honeytokens offered by the Canarytokens service. In particular, we are interested on the underlying trigger mechanism, the trigger channels, and the honeytoken dependency.

To begin, the fingerprinting technique was a simple keyword search in the honeytoken data. The keyword is usually related to the honeytoken provider or publicly known information. We searched for the "canarytokens" keyword in the data or the metadata of all the URL/DNS base honeytokens. Regarding the IP-based honeytokens, our initial fingerprinting method was to perform a reverse DNS lookup of the "canarytokens.com" domain name and compare it to the one in the honeytoken. Finally, we did not discover any fingerprinting strategy for the access key-based honeytokens since all the information related to the access key, since the all the information is saved at the server of the access key provider, except for a repeated pattern in the AWS key ID as displayed in Listing 1.1. The identifier has 12 constant characters *AKIAYVP4CIPP*, which can be used to fingerprint all the AWS keys originating from Canarytokens.

```
1  # 1st key
2  [default]
3  aws_access_key_id = [AKIAYVP4CIPP]G6FXFYHS
4  aws_secret_access_key = UDxJeQftE3ekx+
       KS7skayD8MuN6CVVxOuemuxBSB
```

---

[2] https://canarytokens.org/generate.

```
 5  output = json
 6  region = us-east-2
 7
 8  # 2nd-key
 9  [default]
10  aws_access_key_id = [AKIAYVP4CIPP]CF45DQPM
11  aws_secret_access_key = 8iTskHJBDDnYpUt1a2KY/
        hTlbScFoAS51cJl4n05
12  output = json
13  region = us-east-2
14
15  # 3rd-key
16  [default]
17  aws_access_key_id = [AKIAYVP4CIPP]A3TB575H
18  aws_secret_access_key = mb8HpotCq27p4rCsQGwYpXoOxx+
        oQcIMpjdT+qOJ
19  output = json
20  region = us-east-2
```

Listing 1.1. Canarytokens AWS access key repeated characters

The second major milestone is fingerprinting the honeytokens regardless of the domain name. We use the Canarytokens source code to set up the honeytoken service on our private honeytoken server. The keyword search or the IP address comparison approach is ineffective with this setup. However, the keyword search is still valid for the *.exe/.dll* honeytoken files due to the hardcoded data found in the certificate generation source code.

As mentioned before, the white box testing revealed that the URL/DNS-based honeytokens follow a specific pattern. The DNS/URL contains a 25-character alphanumeric identifier (ID) as displayed in Table 2, which is used to link the honeytoken with the user's contact information. The ID is the subdomain for the DNS-based honeytokens and is the path for the URL-based ones. The placement of the URL/DNS value in the honeytoken is known to us. However, there are other URLs/DNS in some honeytokens. For instance, the URL in the *.docx* honeytoken resides in the metadata, which already includes other URLs to microsoft.com. In order to determine the existence of a honeytoken URL, we loop through each URL and see if they have a 25-character alphanumeric string in the DNS/URL. If they do, we label it as a possible honeytoken URL.

Table 2. URL/DNS Honeytokens followed pattern

Identifier	uq3501pu9mo56obz6kn5auhpq
URL	http://domain.name/url/path/ uq3501pu9mo56obz6kn5auhpq/contact.php
DNS	uq3501pu9mo56obz6kn5auhpq.domain.name

Our analysis suggests that the file type honeytokens use a static template to generate the PDF, *.docx*, and *.xlsx* files. For instance, the *template.pdf* file in the source code leads to constant metadata in the PDF honeytoken. Normally, some metadata attributes, such as the Document UUID, should be unique for each file. A constant UUID will make it easy to identify any PDF file from Canarytokens, even if the domain name is private. Additionally, other data can make the attacker more confident that this is a honeytoken file (e.g., created and modified dates). However, the file creation and modification dates are old (7 years), and any data in it might not be valid anymore from the attacker's point of view. See Appendix Listing 1.2 for more details.

The Canarytokens implementation uses template files to generate all the file type honeytokens, which results in fixed file sizes. We observe that all the PDF, *.docx*, and *.xlsx* have the same size of 5KB, 15KB, and 7.7KB respectively. This additional artifact can be used with the template static metadata to raise the confidence of our fingerprinting method. Additionally, this constant small file size indicates that the file is empty and may not lure the attacker into interacting with it.

5   Proof of Concept: *Honeysweeper*

This section demonstrates the applicability of our honeytokens' fingerprinting techniques based on the Canarytoken implementation [19]. The fingerprinting tool's, namely *honeysweeper*, source code is available at our GitHub repository[3].

5.1   Overview

From all the information gained from the black/white box testing, we built an OS-independent tool that can successfully fingerprint 14 out of the 20 honeytokens offered by Canarytokens. The tool relies on a primary fingerprinting technique matching the 25-character string identifier. However, this fingerprint method introduces the problem of false positives. As we discussed earlier, some honeytokens (i.e., file-type ones) contain more than one URL/DNS. If by any chance, another link contains a 25 characters string, the tool will label it as a possible honeytoken. Nevertheless, from an attacker's perspective, we argue that false negatives are more critical since they would raise an alarm.

Honeysweeper begins by revealing the honeytoken extension for the file-type ones and then extracting the DNS/URL. URL/DNS/Email honeytokens can be added in a text file and passed to the tool. As in the case of PDF, *.docx* and *.xlsx* files, the tool needs to decompress the file as shown in Appendix Listings 1.3 – 1.4, and loops through each file to extracts all the tokens. Once obtained, *honeysweeper* runs the *_find_canarytoken(string)* to match any pattern that matches the 25-character string in the honeytoken content. The PDF, *.docx*, and *.exe/.dll* honeytokens have higher confidence due to the earlier additional

---

[3] https://github.com/aau-network-security/canarytokens_finger_printer.

artifacts, i.e., the static template as shown in Appendix Listing 1.2 and the small file size as shown in Fig. 3. The tool includes checks for the PDF template as a proof of concept and can easily be enhanced to detect other files such as *.docx* and *.xlsx*.

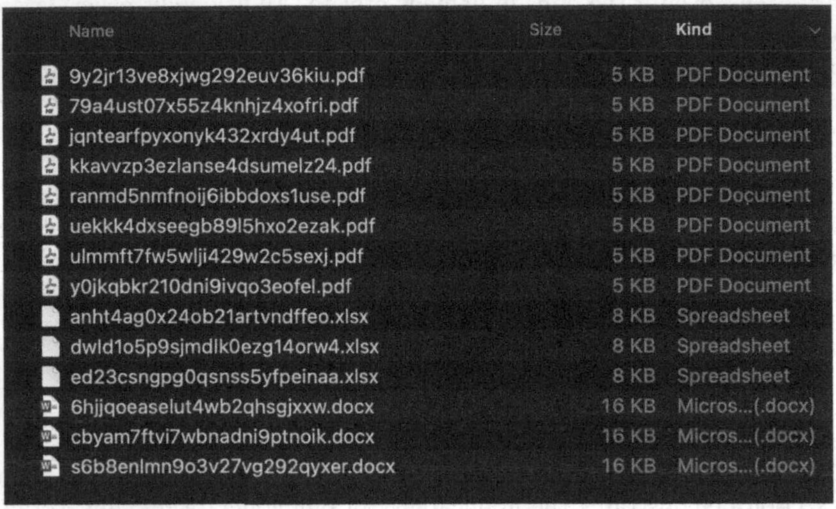

Fig. 3. Honeytokens file-type constant size artifact

5.2 Limitations

The Wireguard and Kubernetes honeytokens are not included in *honeysweeper* as we found no possible way of fingerprinting them when deployed with a private IP. All the data in the honeytokens are randomly generated, e.g., the public and private keys. However, this technique remains effective if the honeytokens are deployed with a known honeytoken provider IP address. The fingerprinting techniques for SVN and SQL-server are not included in the fingerprinting tool since both honeytokens are not directly accessible to the attacker. A possible fingerprinting method for the SQL server can be to check the size of the table where the honeytoken resides. If the table is empty, it may not deceive the attacker for any further interaction. The other honeytokens e.g., PDF, *.docx*, and SQL-dump are available directly on the system and the fingerprinting methods are covered in *honeysweeper*.

6 Countermeasures Against Fingerprinting

The fixed ID length is the primary artifact shared among the studied honeytokens. We propose that the honeytoken identifier should be randomized in length or set in a range. For instance, the ID length could be between 25 and 32 characters, making the fingerprinting process harder and removing the 25-character ID artifact. This mitigation is valid for all the honeytokens containing a URL/DNS with 25 character identifiers. However, this only solves one problem.

The following recommendations are valid for all the template-dependent honeytokens. The PDF honeytokens should have random metadata. In the case of PDF, the attacker can generate a PDF Canarytokens and compare it to any PDF exfiltrated. Even if the honeytoken administrator changes the domain name and removes the 25-character ID artifact, the metadata alone is enough to raise suspicion. To address this, we propose to randomize the PDF XMP metadata. There are a few rules to keep the metadata consistent and not leave a metadata-modification footprint [10]. We present our solution in Appendix Listing 1.5.

Moreover, the honeytoken administrator should modify the content of the *.docx*, *.xlsx*, and PDF files before deployment to change the document size which are *.docx* files are always 15 KB, the *.xlsx* files with 7.7 KB, and the PDF files with 5 KB. Once modified, the honeytokens will resemble an actual file with data and lure the attacker into opening it. Otherwise, the attacker can combine the honeytoken file size with other artifacts to ensure the existence of a trap.

The signing process for the *.exe/binary* honeytokens should be with certificates unrelated to any honeytoken provider. As seen in the Canarytokens source code, a new certificate is generated to sign the *.exe/.dll* files. We generate an executable honeytoken using the source code locally to investigate the generation process. We see that a private key and a certificate is generated to sign the honeytoken and are removed after the process is complete. Nevertheless, the information included in the signature is hard-coded. Figure [4] shows the hard-coded information in the certificate. This hard-coded information will be the same for all the *.exe/*binary honeytokens and can be an artifact.

```
[ ca_dn ]
countryName                 = "ZA"
organizationName            = "Thinkst Applied Research"
organizationalUnitName      = "Thinkst Applied Research CA"
commonName                  = "Thinkst Root CA"
```

Fig. 4. Certificate hardcoded data

When deploying the stored procedure for a table on the SQL server, the administrator can set explicit permissions on the stored procedure by denying the public users from viewing the stored procedure's definition. The same approach applies for the SQL functions as a honeytoken. The function permission can be fragmented. For example, allow the public to select the functions and views but disallow viewing the definitions (syntax). Additionally, the trap table should be populated with random fake data to lure the attacker into interacting with it.

The Wireguard and Kubernetes honeytokens should use an IP address not linked with a honeytoken domain name. If no domain name is available and there is no alternative but to use the Canarytokens servers due to development and maintenance costs, an administrator can use a local server IP and redirect the traffic to Canarytokens servers.

7   Conclusion

Deception techniques like honeytokens are an essential extra layer of defense, and deploying them is becoming more and more common. However, for the deception technique to achieve its goal, it should be well crafted to deceive and should not include easy to exploit fingerprinting artifacts. This paper proposes fingerprinting techniques against most existing Canarytokens' honeytokens proposals and implementations. We analyze all the publicly offered honeytokens and propose countermeasures against the suggested techniques. As ethical disclosure, we informed Canarytokens of our findings. For future work, we plan on exploring other fingerprinting methods. For instance, the signature verification of the *.exe/.dll* files and other techniques. Additionally, we consider improving the honeytoken ID generation process by including a non-repudiation concept.

Appendix

Static Data on PDF Canarytoken

Listing 1.2 shows the static data identified on parsing the composite XML file of the PDF Canarytoken. We can observe static data on the modify date, create date and metadata date.

```
1   <x:xmpmeta xmlns:x="adobe:ns:meta/" x:xmptk="Adobe XMP
        Core 5.6-c015 81.157285, 2014/12/12-00:43:15       ">
2     <rdf:RDF xmlns:rdf="http://www.w3.org/1999/02/22-rdf-
        syntax-ns#">
3       <rdf:Description rdf:about=""
4           xmlns:xmp="http://ns.adobe.com/xap/1.0/"
5           xmlns:dc="http://purl.org/dc/elements/1.1/"
6           xmlns:xmpMM="http://ns.adobe.com/xap/1.0/mm/"
7           xmlns:pdf="http://ns.adobe.com/pdf/1.3/">
8         <xmp:ModifyDate>2015-07-22T16:41:31+02:00</
            xmp:ModifyDate>
9         <xmp:CreateDate>2015-07-22T16:38:51+02:00</
            xmp:CreateDate>
10        <xmp:MetadataDate>2015-07-22T16:41:31+02:00</
            xmp:MetadataDate>
11        <xmp:CreatorTool>Acrobat Pro 15.8.20082</
            xmp:CreatorTool>
12        <dc:format>application/pdf</dc:format>
```

```
13              <xmpMM:DocumentID>uuid:a2364080-b5a8-1b46-b156-
                  ea05c4972d03</xmpMM:DocumentID>=
14              <xmpMM:InstanceID>uuid:7656c56e-b1e6-f444-801f
                  -06e28a50831f</xmpMM:InstanceID>
15              <pdf:Producer>Acrobat Pro 15.8.20082</
                  pdf:Producer>
16           </rdf:Description>
17        </rdf:RDF>
18    </x:xmpmeta>
```

Listing 1.2. PDF honeytoken static metadata

Fingerprinting of PDF Canarytoken

Listing 1.3 shows the pseudo code for fingerprinting of PDF Canarytoken. The
method checks for URLs embedded in the PDF and against a list of known
honeytoken service URLs.

```
1  def find_token_in_pdf(file_location):
2      check_template(file_location) # check for template
          artifact
3      # List for URLs found
4      list_of_urls = []
5      pdf = open(file_location, "rb").read()
6      stream = re.compile(b'.*?FlateDecode.*?stream(.*?)
          endstream', re.S)
7      for s in re.findall(stream, pdf):
8          s = s.strip(b'\r\n')
9          line = ""
10         try:
11             line = zlib.decompress(s).decode('latin-1')
                   # changed this from UTF-8 to latin-1 as
                   it throws errors. We
12             # want the app to be silent :)
13         except Exception as e:
14             print(e)
15         token = Tokenfinder.find_tokens_in_string(line)
16         if token:
17             list_of_urls.extend(token)
18     if len(list_of_urls) == 0:
19         print("No canaries detected")
20         return None
21     else:
22         print(str(len(list_of_urls)) + " canary URLs
              detected in the file")
23         for url in list_of_urls:
24             print("Canary detected!: ", url)
25             print()
```

Listing 1.3. PDF fingerprinting

Fingerprinting of .docx and .xlsx Canarytokens

Listing 1.4 shows the pseudo code for fingerprinting of .docx and .xlsx Canary-tokens. The techniques unzips the composite file formats to check for URLs embedded in the files.

```
1  def check_office_files(file_location):
2      list_of_urls = [] # List to hold all urls in the
            file
3      try:
4          # Unzip the office file without saving to
                folder
5          unzipped_file = zipfile.ZipFile(file_location,"
                r")
6          # List of all the content of the zip
7          namelist = unzipped_file.namelist()
8          # Reads every file in the zip file and looks if
                 it contains the string you wish to search
                for
9          for item in namelist:
10             content = str(unzipped_file.read(item))
11             token = Tokenfinder.find_tokens_in_string(
                   content)
12             if token:
13                 list_of_urls.extend(token)
14     except OSError as e:
15         print(f"Exception: {e}")
16     # If no results of the search
17     if len(list_of_urls) == 0:
18         return None
19     else:
20         print(str(len(list_of_urls)) +" canary URLs
                detected in the file")
21         for url in list_of_urls:
22             print("Canary detected: ", url)
23             print()
```

Listing 1.4. .docx and .xlsx fingerprinting

Mitigation of Metadata in Canarytoken

Listing 1.5 shows the mitigation by randomization of the file creation date and time. The randomness avoids static creation dates that is implemented by Canarytokens.

```
1  from pikepdf import Pdf
2  import  uuid, random, datetime, os
3
4  # make creation date with random Time-Zone [+1 to +3]
```

```
 5  def creation_date():
 6      time = datetime.datetime.now()
 7      rand_region =str(random.randint(1, 3))
 8      stamp = time.strftime('2022-%m-%d')+'T'+ time.
            strftime('%H:%M:%S')+ '+0'+ rand_region+ ':00'
 9      return stamp
10
11
12  def modification_date():
13      time = datetime.datetime.now()
14      return time.strftime('%Y-%m-%d')+'T'+ time.strftime
            ('%H:%M:%S')
15
16  def add_metadata(source_pdf, out_dir):
17      mod_date = modification_date()
18      with Pdf.open(source_pdf) as pdf:
19          with pdf.open_metadata(set_pikepdf_as_editor=
                False) as meta:
20              meta['xmp:CreatorTool'] = 'Acrobat Pro
                    22.001.20112'
21              meta['xmpMM:DocumentID'] = str(uuid.uuid4()
                    )
22              meta['xmpMM:InstanceID'] = str(uuid.uuid4()
                    )
23              meta['xmp:CreateDate'] = creation_date()
24              meta['xmp:ModifyDate'] = mod_date
25              meta['xmp:MetadataDate'] = mod_date
26              meta['pdf:Producer'] = 'Acrobat Pro
                    22.001.20112'
27      pdf.save(os.path.join(out_dir, os.path.basename(
            source_pdf)))
28      print('Done!')
29
30  source_pdf = "/Users/mm/Downloads/pdftoken.pdf"
31  out_dir = '/Users/mm/Desktop/'
32  add_metadata(source_pdf, out_dir)
```

Listing 1.5. Metadata mitigation

References

1. Acrobat: Acrobat API reference (2021). https://opensource.adobe.com/dc-acrobat-sdk-docs/acrobatsdk/html2015/Acro12_MasterBook/API_References_SectionPage/API_References/Acrobat_API_Reference/AV_Layer/Weblink.html
2. Aguirre-Anaya, E., Gallegos-Garcia, G., Luna, N.S., Vargas, L.A.V.: A new procedure to detect low interaction honeypots. Int. J. Electr. Comput. Eng. (IJECE) **4**(6), 848–857 (2014)
3. Čenys, A., Rainys, D., Radvilavicius, L., Goranin, N.: Database level honeytoken modules for active DBMS protection. In: Nilsson, A.G., Gustas, R., Wojtkowski,

W., Wojtkowski, W.G., Wrycza, S., Zupančič, J. (eds.) Adv. Inf. Syst. Dev., pp. 449–457. Springer, US, Boston, MA (2006)

4. Dahbul, R.N., Lim, C., Purnama, J.: Enhancing honeypot deception capability through network service fingerprinting. J. Phys: Conf. Ser. **801**, 012057 (2017). https://doi.org/10.1088/1742-6596/801/1/012057

5. Faveri, C.D., Moreira, A.: Visual modeling of cyber deception. In: 2018 IEEE Symposium on Visual Languages and Human-Centric Computing (VL/HCC), pp. 205–209 (2018). https://doi.org/10.1109/VLHCC.2018.8506515

6. Fraunholz, D., et al.: Demystifying deception technology: a survey. CoRR abs/1804.06196 (2018). https://arxiv.org/abs/1804.06196

7. Fu, X., Yu, W., Cheng, D., Tan, X., Streff, K., Graham, S.: On recognizing virtual honeypots and countermeasures. In: 2006 2nd IEEE International Symposium on Dependable, Autonomic and Secure Computing, pp. 211–218 (2006). https://doi.org/10.1109/DASC.2006.36

8. Ghirardello, K., Maple, C., Ng, D., Kearney, P.: Cyber security of smart homes: development of a reference architecture for attack surface analysis. In: Living in the Internet of Things: Cybersecurity of the IoT - 2018, pp. 1–10 (2018). https://doi.org/10.1049/cp.2018.0045

9. Guarnizo, J.D., et al.: Siphon: towards scalable high-interaction physical honeypots. In: Proceedings of the 3rd ACM Workshop on Cyber-Physical System Security, pp. 57–68. CPSS 2017, Association for Computing Machinery, New York, NY, USA (2017). https://doi.org/10.1145/3055186.3055192

10. Gungor, A.: Pdf forensic analysis and XMP metadata streams (2017). https://www.meridiandiscovery.com/articles/pdf-forensic-analysis-xmp-metadata/

11. Han, X., Kheir, N., Balzarotti, D.: Deception techniques in computer security: a research perspective. ACM Comput. Surv. **51**(4), 1–36 (2018). https://doi.org/10.1145/3214305

12. Holz, T., Raynal, F.: Detecting honeypots and other suspicious environments. In: Proceedings from the Sixth Annual IEEE SMC Information Assurance Workshop, pp. 29–36 (2005). https://doi.org/10.1109/IAW.2005.1495930

13. IBM: how much does a data breach cost? (2021). https://www.ibm.com/security/data-breach

14. IBM: Insights into what drives data breach costs (2021). https://www.ibm.com/account/reg/uk-en/signup?formid=urx-51643

15. IBM: key findings (2021). https://www.ibm.com/downloads/cas/OJDVQGRY

16. La, Q.D., Quek, T.Q.S., Lee, J., Jin, S., Zhu, H.: Deceptive attack and defense game in honeypot-enabled networks for the internet of things. IEEE Internet Things J. **3**(6), 1025–1035 (2016). https://doi.org/10.1109/JIOT.2016.2547994

17. Mokube, I., Adams, M.: Honeypots: Concepts, approaches, and challenges. In: Proceedings of the 45th Annual Southeast Regional Conference. p. 321–326. ACM-SE 45, Association for Computing Machinery, New York, NY, USA (2007). https://doi.org/10.1145/1233341.1233399

18. Mukkamala, S., Yendrapalli, K., Basnet, R., Shankarapani, M.K., Sung, A.H.: Detection of virtual environments and low interaction honeypots. In: 2007 IEEE SMC Information Assurance and Security Workshop, pp. 92–98 (2007). https://doi.org/10.1109/IAW.2007.381919

19. Research, T.A.: Canarytokens. https://github.com/thinkst/canarytokens

20. Sethia, V., Jeyasekar, A.: Malware capturing and analysis using dionaea honeypot. In: 2019 International Carnahan Conference on Security Technology (ICCST), pp. 1–4 (2019). https://doi.org/10.1109/CCST.2019.8888409

21. Srinivasa, S., Pedersen, J.M., Vasilomanolakis, E.: Towards systematic honeytoken fingerprinting. In: 13th International Conference on Security of Information and Networks. SIN 2020, Association for Computing Machinery, New York, NY, USA (2020). https://doi.org/10.1145/3433174.3433599
22. Srinivasa, S., Pedersen, J.M., Vasilomanolakis, E.: Gotta catch'em all: a multistage framework for honeypot fingerprinting. arXiv preprint arXiv:2109.10652 (2021)
23. Srinivasa, S., Pedersen, J.M., Vasilomanolakis, E.: Open for hire: attack trends and misconfiguration pitfalls of iot devices. In: Proceedings of the 21st ACM Internet Measurement Conference, pp. 195–215. IMC 2021, Association for Computing Machinery, New York, NY, USA (2021). https://doi.org/10.1145/3487552.3487833,https://doi.org/10.1145/3487552.3487833
24. Vasilomanolakis, E., et al.: This network is infected: hostage - a low-interaction honeypot for mobile devices. In: Proceedings of the Third ACM Workshop on Security and Privacy in Smartphones & Mobile Devices, pp. 43–48. SPSM 2013, Association for Computing Machinery, New York, NY, USA (2013). https://doi.org/10.1145/2516760.2516763
25. Vasilomanolakis, E., Karuppayah, S., Mühlhäuser, M., Fischer, M.: Hostage: a mobile honeypot for collaborative defense. In: Proceedings of the 7th International Conference on security of information and networks. SIN 2014, vol. 2014, pp. 330–333. ACM (2014)
26. Vetterl, A., Clayton, R.: Bitter harvest: systematically fingerprinting low- and medium-interaction honeypots at internet scale. In: 12th USENIX Workshop on Offensive Technologies (WOOT 18). USENIX Association, Baltimore, MD (2018). https://www.usenix.org/conference/woot18/presentation/vetterl
27. Zhang, L., Thing, V.L.: Three decades of deception techniques in active cyber defense-retrospect and outlook. Comput. Secur. **106**, 102288 (2021). https://arxiv.org/abs/2104.03594

Towards Self-monitoring Enclaves: Side-Channel Detection Using Performance Counters

David Lantz, Felipe Boeira, and Mikael Asplund[✉]

Department of Computer and Information Science, Linköping University,
Linköping, Sweden
{felipe.boeira,mikael.asplund}@liu.se

Abstract. Trusted execution environments like Intel SGX allow developers to protect sensitive code in so-called enclaves. These enclaves protect their code and data even in the cases of a compromised OS. However, such enclaves have also been shown to be vulnerable to numerous side-channel attacks. In this paper we propose an idea of self-monitoring enclaves and investigate the viability of using performance counters to detect a side-channel attacks against Intel SGX, specifically the Load Value Injection (LVI) class of attacks. We characterize the footprint of three LVI attack variants and design a prototype detection mechanism. The results show that certain attack variants could be reliably detected using this approach without false positives for a range of benign applications. The results also demonstrate reasonable levels of speed and overhead for the detection mechanism. Finally, we list four requirements for making self-monitoring based on such a detection mechanism feasible and point out that three of them are not satisfied in Intel SGX.

Keywords: TEE · Intel SGX · LVI · Side-channel attacks · Intrusion detection · Performance counters

1 Introduction

With the growth of cloud computing, increasingly more sensitive data is being handled and processed in mixed or untrusted environments. Achieving trust in these services is thus both difficult and important, and one way to address this problem is through the concept of a *Trusted Execution Environment* (TEE). A TEE provides a shielded execution environment separated from the (potentially untrusted) Operating System (OS). This means that even if the cloud service itself is compromised and controlled by an attacker, a TEE instance (called an enclave) can still guarantee confidentiality and integrity for the code and data contained in the TEE.

Companies like Intel and ARM have offered their own implementations (or specifications) of TEEs, and there are also research-driven efforts like Keystone [12]. However, many of the current solutions have been shown to be vulnerable to numerous Side-Channel Attacks (SCAs) [17,32], where architectural

H. P. Reiser and M. Kyas (Eds.): NordSec 2022, LNCS 13700, pp. 120–138, 2022.
https://doi.org/10.1007/978-3-031-22295-5_7

side effects of a program like cache behaviour, power consumption, etc., are used to infer secret data used by a program. A large amount of research has been conducted regarding SCAs targeting Intel SGX, and several SCAs have thus been discovered in recent years. One class of such attacks is called Load Value Injection (LVI) [26], which allows an attacker to temporarily hijack the execution of a victim process.

Many of the existing attacks targeting Intel SGX can be mitigated, but often at a high cost in terms of performance. New generations of TEE solutions are also likely to mitigate known attacks, but we argue that a trusted component should not only be designed to be secure against all known attacks, but also capable of detecting when it is under attack. If an attack can be detected in time, the enclave can take protective action like suspending its operation until the threat has been removed.

In this paper, we investigate one potential approach with which an enclave could detect a side-channel attack through Hardware Performance Counters (HPCs). There have been many examples in the literature of using HPCs to detect side-channel attacks in other contexts, particularly attacks targeting cache behaviour [1]. For example, Mushtaq et al. [16] developed a tool called WHISPER that uses machine learning and HPCs to detect cache-based SCAs. However, we are not aware of any work that explores using performance counters for detecting attacks targeting TEEs.

Our threat model assumes an attacker that is able to run (almost) arbitrary code in the untrustusted domain, with the aim of trying to extract information from within the trusted domain (the enclave). Some of the attacks we consider, might not be easily implementable without having at least some way of affecting also the code within the enclave, but such analysis is out of scope for this paper. If the attacker is able to actively influence the performance counters from the untrusted domain, the detection mechanisms discussed in this paper would not work which we also discuss further in Sect. 5.

We have chosen to investigate Intel SGX since it is still one of the dominating TEE implementations available, and there are several interesting attacks against SGX. Of these, we found LVI to be most interesting due to it being relatively recent, still not fully mitigated, and exists in several variants. This work is primarily intended to characterize and describe the relationship between side-channel attack against enclaves in terms of performance counters as a first step towards a long-term goal of allowing enclaves to become self-monitoring. As we show in this paper, such monitoring is not supported by current hardware, and we provide recommendations for how future hardware solutions could better support such mechanisms. To summarize, the contributions of this paper are:

- A characterization of the resource footprint of three LVI attack variants.
- Design and evaluation of a prototype detection mechanism for LVI-style side-channel attacks based on an idea of self-monitoring enclaves.
- Requirements for future hardware designs related to performance counters and TEEs to allow self-monitoring enclaves to be properly implemented.

The remainder of the paper is structured as follows. Section 2 presents the background and related work, in Sect. 3 we analyze the LVI attacks based on how they affect a number of hardware performance counters, Sect. 4 describes details of side-channel attack detection mechanisms and their performance, in Sect. 5 we discuss how such mechanisms could potentially support self-monitoring enclaves and what practical limitations hinder it today, and finally, Sect. 6 concludes the paper.

2 Background and Related Work

In this section we briefly go through some fundamental concepts relating to trusted execution environments and how they can be targeted by side-channel attacks (with a focus on Intel SGX), followed by an overview of existing detection methods for side-channel attacks.

2.1 Attacks on Trusted Execution Environments

In the SGX threat model, only the enclave can be trusted while all other parts of the system are deemed untrustworthy. However, SGX has been shown to be vulnerable against a number of side-channel attacks [17]. Interestingly, side-channel attacks are excluded from the SGX threat model [7], and Intel instead leaves it up to enclave developers to write their programs in a manner which makes it resistant to those types of attacks.

Xu et al. [31] introduced the concept of *controlled-channel-attacks* where secret information is gained by repeatedly causing page faults during enclave execution. In another work related to controlled channel attacks, Bulck et al. developed the attack framework *SGX-Step* [27]. SGX-Step provides a kernel framework that allows attackers to track page table entries directly from user space. SGX-Step is an open-source framework[1] and has been used to construct a number of other attacks.

Cache-based SCAs (CSCAs) have been shown to be possible on SGX [3,8], due to SGX enclaves still making use of shared caches. Several more advanced attacks making use of CSCAs have since been constructed, like CacheZoom [14] and Memjam [13]. A unique attack by Schwarz et al. [22] used cache attacks from within an enclave itself to attack other enclaves.

SGX has also been shown to be vulnerable to transient execution attacks, for example the similarly named attacks SgxPectre [5] and SgxSpectre [18] demonstrated that SGX was vulnerable to Spectre-type attacks. The first version of Foreshadow [25] also targeted SGX, and several Microarchitectural Data Sampling attacks [4,21,28] were shown to be able to leak data across several protection boundaries, including SGX enclaves. Other attacks include CacheOut [29] and CrossTalk [20].

Load Value Injection (LVI) [26] is an example of a transient execution attack specialized for SGX which was found by Bulck et al. [26]. The authors describe

---

[1] https://github.com/jovanbulck/sgx-step

LVI as a "reverse Meltdown"-type attack since it essentially turns the process of a Meltdown attack around by injecting data instead of leaking data. The attack operates under the assumption that the attacker can provoke page faults or microcode assists during enclave execution, optionally using features offered by a framework such as SGX-Step.

2.2 Detection Methods

Most of the research regarding detection of SCAs has been done for non-SGX contexts, but there are also some detection tools developed specifically for SGX. One such SGX-specific detection tool is T-SGX [24], that makes use of TSX to prevent controlled-channel attacks. The authors claim that T-SGX works faster than previous state-of-the-art mitigation schemes, but T-SGX still induces performance overheads of 50% on average and storage overheads of about 30%. Similarly, Chen et al. present Déjà Vu [6], which exists as an extension to the LLVM compiler, and also uses TSX to protect against controlled channel attacks. The authors of SGX-Step [27] state that tools like T-SGX and Déjà Vu would be able to detect an ongoing attack by the frequent interrupts caused by single-stepping an enclave. However, they also bring up some of the drawbacks such as the fact that TSX is not available on all SGX-enabled processors, and that TSX defenses significantly increase run-time performance overheads.

In contexts outside of SGX, a number of methods and tools for detecting side-channel attacks have been proposed. Most of the research regarding SCA detection concerns cache-based SCAs. In a survey by Akram et al. [1], the authors present much of the known work concerning CSCA detection, and note among other things that almost all of the methods use hardware performance counters for detecting the attacks. There are also examples of both signature-based and anomaly-based detection.

Mushtaq et al. [16], develop a tool called WHISPER for detecting CSCAs during runtime with the help of machine learning and hardware performance counters. The tool is designed to collect values from HPCs during runtime, which are then used as features for the ensemble learning model. The authors demonstrate the capability of the tool by using it to detect three CSCA variants targeting the AES cryptosystem: Flush+Reload, Flush+Flush, and Prime+Probe.

While many CSCA detection methods use machine learning methods together with HPCs for detection [2,15], some also present tools based on value thresholds for certain HPC events. HexPADS [19] is one such tool which uses HPC events like LLC accesses, LLC misses and total number of retired instructions to detect certain attacks, like Rowhammer attacks [23] as well as some cache-based SCAs according to known attack signatures. It does this by monitoring performance counters of all currently running processes in the system using the *perf_event_open* interface. By comparing to existing attack signatures for CSCAs and Rowhammer attacks among others, a process is either deemed to be benign or is detected as a potential attack.

3   Characterization of LVI Invariant Footprint

We now proceed to present a characterization of the footprint of LVI attacks. First, we describe which attacks we have analyzed. Then, experiments are made to compare LVI attack processes to other benign processes by running a range of different attack and non-attack scenarios. The objective is to show in which ways LVI differs from benign applications with regards to footprint in performance counters.

3.1   LVI Attacks

For running the LVI attacks, the existing PoC implementation was used, which is included as a part of the SGX-Step [27] repository. The three variants of LVI along with their equivalent variant according to the classification to Bulck et al. [26], are shown in Table 1. From this point, the names from the LVI classification tree will be used to refer to the PoC attacks, with the exception of LVI-SB-ROP which will be referred to as LVI-US-SB-ROP (to highlight that it also relies on the User/Supervisor attribute).

Table 1. The three LVI PoC variants and their corresponding LVI variant according to the classification done by Bulck et al. [26].

PoC variant	LVI classification
LVI-SB (store buffer injection)	LVI-US-SB
LVI-SB-ROP (trans. control flow hijacking)	LVI-US-SB
LVI-L1D (L1D cache injection)	LVI-PPN-L1D

It is important to note that these attack PoCs are simplified and don't demonstrate real attacks, but since they still contain all the major steps behind LVI attacks they can still be used for investigating the impact of LVI on performance counters. One should also note that while the PoC is part of the SGX-Step repository, it only makes use of its page table manipulation features and not its single-stepping capabilities (however, more practical LVI attacks can).

These LVI-US-SB and LVI-US-SB-ROP variants both preempt enclave execution by using page faults that occur when a Page Table Entry (PTE) is marked as belonging to the kernel with the User/Supervisor (U/S) attribute of a page table entry.

There are (for most systems) two types of valid page faults, minor and major page faults, which both can happen during normal program execution. Major page faults for example occur when the requested page is not yet present in memory. Minor faults occur when pages exist in memory but have not yet been marked by the Memory Management Unit (MMU). The types of page faults caused by LVI (and Meltdown-type attacks) however, occur due to one of several invalid conditions (e.g. accessing a page without high enough privileges), and can therefore be seen more as errors that shouldn't occur in a normal program.

Both the LVI-US variants also exploit the store buffer to inject malicious data. The LVI-US-SB variant then uses victim enclave instructions following the faulting instruction to directly encode enclave data via a cache covert channel. The LVI-US-SB-ROP attack on the other hand, uses the same method of data injection, but instead faults a return instruction in order to get it to load the attacker value. This allows the attacker to redirect control flow to an arbitrary second-stage code gadget located within the existing enclave code base, where secrets are again encoded through a cache-based covert channel. This variant thus demonstrates the possibility of using LVI to hijack control flow, using techniques similar to Return Oriented Programming (ROP).

The LVI-PPN-L1D variant instead exploits a type of page fault unique for SGX, by the attacker remapping the PTE for a page B to point to the Physical Page Number (PPN) of another page A. This is done before entering the enclave function. Then, inside the enclave, page A is dereferenced, bringing the physical memory containing A into the L1 data cache. However, when page B is accessed, the Enclave Page Cache Map checks of SGX detect the virtual-to-physical remapping and a page fault is raised. However, the poisoned physical address is still sent to the L1D cache before the fault is architecturally raised, and due to A already being in the L1D cache, this leads to a cache hit. A can thus be injected into transient execution, allowing the attacker again can use a cache-based covert channel to leak enclave data.

3.2   Measuring LVI Impact

The purpose of these tests is to compare the values of these performance counters when an LVI attack is ongoing, to their values for other benign processes. In order to achieve this, a number of different scenarios were constructed in order to showcase both attack applications and a variety of benign processes with varying loads on the system, like web browsers, games, benchmark programs, etc. The selected scenarios are seen in Table 2. We performed the same tests with an additional 20 scenarios (based on different uses of the Atom text editor, web browsing and different games on the Steam platform) [11]. These are excluded from this paper for conciseness since they show similar results.

The first three scenarios simply demonstrate the unchanged LVI attacks variants. To compare with situations where an attack doesn't take place, scenarios where the victim enclave is simply run without an attack were included (scenarios 4–6). Since all three attack variants have designated victim code loops that it attacks, there are also three different baseline scenarios without an attack, one for each variant. Scenarios 7–10 can be seen as normal, benign computer usage processes, while scenarios 11–13 demonstrate benchmark applications that put a high load on the system.

Experiment Setup: Measuring the selected events can only for a maximum of 4 hardware counters in addition to the INSTRUCTIONS event at a time. Using

Table 2. Explanation of different scenarios for measuring performance counters.

Nr	Scenario	Description
1	LVI-US-SB	Normal LVI-US-SB PoC attack scenario
2	LVI-PPN-L1D	Normal LVI-PPN-L1D PoC attack scenario
3	LVI-US-SB-ROP	Normal LVI-US-SB-ROP PoC attack scenario
4	NA (SB)	No Attack (NA) scenario (LVI-US-SB)
5	NA (L1D)	No Attack (NA) scenario (LVI-PPN-L1D)
6	NA (SB-ROP)	No Attack (NA) scenario (LVI-US-SB-ROP)
7	Text editor	User creating and writing to a file in the Atom text editor
8	Firefox - Youtube	User watching a youtube video in the Firefox browser
9	Firefox - Twitter	User scrolling down a twitter feed in the Firefox browser
10	Game	User playing a game (Civilization 5) via the Steam platform
11	Stress -c 1	Loop performing CPU computation sqrt()
12	Stress -m 1	Loop performing malloc() and free() for 256MB arrays
13	Stress -i 1	Loop calling I/O function sync()

more counters than this limit results in either very low values or no values at all for any running processes. Therefore, we selected groups of related counters and measured in batches. Each run consists of running the corresponding scenarios while at the same time running the measurement tool for 150 iterations, with one second between each iteration. In each iteration, the tool scanned for running processes and sampled counter values (in counting mode) before resetting the counters again. For each complete run, the first 120 samples for the relevant processes in each scenario were gathered. From this data, averages for every event could be analyzed and compared across the different scenarios. The INSTRUCTIONS event was also used in order to provide normalized averages of each event.

LVI Footprint Results: Figure 1 shows the results of the experiments split over three plots. In each plot the number of events per 1000 instructions are shown. Note the logarithmic Y-axis in the plots which is used since otherwise the small values are hard to see at all. The top plot shows the normal use-case scenarios, the middle one the stress tests, and the bottom the LVI proof of concept scenarios, with and without an external attacker.

One can see that the number of page faults for the two LVI-US-SB attack variants is quite large compared to other processes. While the number of page faults for stress_m is very high, further examination with the perf command line tool showed that all of these consisted of minor page faults. The LVI attacks on the other hand generate a lot of visible page faults in the cases of LVI-US-SB and LVI-US-SB-ROP, but almost none of these are minor faults. In fact, it could be seen that the amount of minor page faults for an LVI-US-SB attack scenario is the same as when the LVI application is run without an attack taking place. A high total of page faults paired with low amounts of minor and major faults

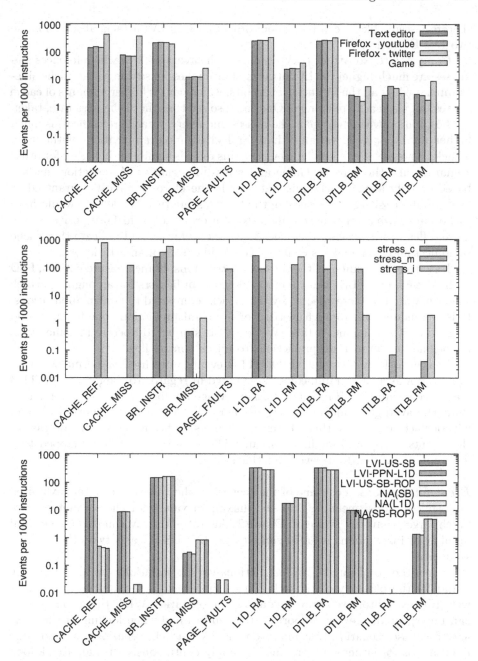

Fig. 1. Number of events per 1000 instructions for each performance counter and scenario.

therefore seems like it can be a good indicator of an LVI attack, at least for the two LVI-US variants.

Compared to No Attack (NA) scenarios, the averages for cache references and misses are much higher for LVI attacks. This makes sense due to the cache side-channel used by all the LVI attack variants, which causes higher amounts of cache misses but also cache references. One can also see that the cache miss rate, taken as the ratio between average cache misses and average cache references, is much higher for LVI attack variants than for LVI example applications without an attack. However, it can also be seen that this ratio is significantly higher for other scenarios, like the Firefox, Game and stress_m scenarios. A detection method based on only a high cache miss rate would therefore be almost guaranteed to lead to false positives for several of the benign scenarios. While they would have to be paired with other attack indicators in order to avoid false positives, the large difference between attack and no attack scenarios still indicate that cache references and cache misses could be good indicators of an attack.

Based on our results, neither branch instructions, branch mispredictions, L1D cache events, or dTLB events seem to be good indicators for an ongoing attack since they are not more affected by the attacks compared to benign applications. It is reasonable that branch instructions and mispredictions don't make good indicators of an ongoing attack. While LVI is similar to Spectre in some ways, it does not use branch mispredictions to hijack control flow.

In the work by Gruss et al. [9], iTLB events were used to normalize other events. However, it can immediately be noted in regards to the number of iTLB read accesses and iTLB read misses, the average number of misses is often larger than the average number of accesses. For the LVI scenarios, both with and without actual attacks, this difference is quite significant. This is in contrast to the results in [9], and might be because iTLB misses events are mapped to a different, actual hardware event for this system.

Event Fluctuations: For some of the scenarios, the values of counters exhibited large fluctuations, meaning that the maximum values for those counters were much larger than the averages. Figure 2 illustrates this by comparing the total number of instructions over 50 samples for LVI-US-SB and two other benign scenarios.

When the total number of instructions varies, variations are also naturally found for the other events as well. The scenarios with the largest fluctuations were the text editor, web browsing, and game scenarios. While these fluctuations can be expected, they are important to keep in mind when looking at the averages for those scenarios. In comparison, the LVI attack scenarios shows no large fluctuations for either counter, since it simply continuously runs an attack loop for several iterations, and doesn't change behaviour significantly across sample iterations. The same is true for the stress benchmark scenarios.

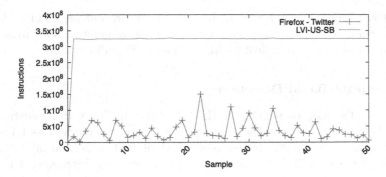

(a) Total number of instructions for the LVI-US-SB and Firefox - Twitter scenarios.

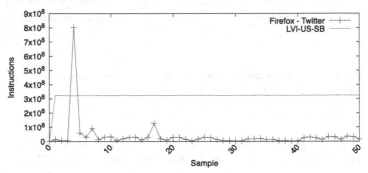

(b) Total number of instructions for the LVI-US-SB and Text editor scenarios.

Fig. 2. Fluctuations in total number of instructions.

4   Detecting LVI Attacks

This section describes the design and evaluation of a prototype mechanism to detect LVI attacks.

4.1   Chosen Attack Indicators

Given the results in Sect. 3, the performance events that were deemed to show the most promise for detection, were total number of instructions, page faults (total as well as minor and major), LLC cache misses, and LLC cache references. These events (except instructions) showed a large difference between attack and no-attack LVI scenarios, and were quite significant in attack scenarios compared to other, benign scenarios. Page faults, LLC cache misses and references can also be directly tied to the behaviour of an LVI attack, which is not true for many of the other events. For the page faults, a distinction was made between valid and invalid page faults since the invalid page faults seemed to be the best indicator of an attack. Since a counter event for specifically invalid page faults doesn't exist, a high amount of total page faults but a low amount of both minor and major faults was used to indicate a high amount of invalid faults.

4.2   Footprint-Based Detection

US Variant: Pseudocode for DET_LVI_US is shown in Fig. 3, with constants for all thresholds. The intuition for this detector can be summarised as follows. If there are many page faults that cannot be attributed as normal faults (major or minor), then it is likely an attack (partial detection). Moreover, if there is a high cpu usage (many instructions per second), and at the same time a high cache usage and miss rate, then this is a strange process that is neither a normal process that uses moderate amounts of cpu or a cpu-intensive process that should have a confined memory locality. Combined with the first indication we decide that this is a full detection.

```
1  cache_miss_rate = cache_misses / cache_references;
2  if (total_page_faults > TPF &&
3    minor_faults < MINF_1 &&
4    major_faults < MAJF_1) {
5    // Attack potentially detected! (Partial detection)
6    if (instructions > INSTR_1 && cache_references > CR_1 &&
7        cache_misses > CM_1 && cache_miss_rate > CM_RATE_1) {
8      // Attack detected! (Full detection)
9    }
10 }
```

Fig. 3. Pseudocode for DET_LVI_US, detector for the LVI-US-SB attack variants.

The average number of page faults for the LVI-US-SB attack is more than 10,000 per sample while the benign process with the highest number of total page faults (apart from the outlier scenario stress_m) is a web scenario with 2322 page faults per sample [11]. For the purpose of the experiments with our prototype detector we chose values that were spaced reasonably between the attack and non-attack variants. For a proper detection mechanism, we believe that more platforms (i.e., other CPUs) and scenarios (more use-cases) would need to be analyzed and potentially be based on a learning-based approach. Such analysis is out of scope for this work as our goal is to showcase that the detection is at all viable in this context. All the chosen values for the thresholds used with the DET_LVI_US detector are shown in Table 3.

PPN Variant: The second detector, DET_LVI_PPN, is similar to the first one except that it cannot detect based on a high total of page faults, since the results showed that the invalid page faults caused by LVI-PPN-L1D weren't reported to the performance counters (leading to a low number of total page faults). Instead,

Table 3. Chosen values for the thresholds used with the DET_LVI_US detector.

Threshold	Value	Threshold	Value
TPF (>)	6000	CR_1	3000000
MINF_1	10	CM_1	1000000
MAJF_1	1	CM_RATE_1	0.3
INSTR_1	100000000		

another attack indicator was added in an attempt to minimize the possibility of false positives. From the results we observe that the values of counters for many benign applications varies a lot between samples, while the LVI processes showed very little variation between samples, since they all run a continuous attack loop without major variations between iterations. A measurement on this variation could be obtained by dividing the total number of instructions for the current iteration with the same value for the last iteration. In order to fully detect an attack with DET_LVI_PPN, this value was assumed to be within a certain interval. While this indicator can increase the time to detect an attack, it can also lessen the risk of false positives. Aagin we differentiate between processes that some of the chosen indicators (partial detection) from processes that match all indications (full detection) (Fig. 4).

```
1  cache_miss_rate = cache_misses / cache_references;
2  instr_diff = instructions / instructions_prev_iteration;
3  if (total_page_faults < TPF && minor_faults < MINF_2 &&
4      major_faults < MAJF_2) {
5    if (instructions > INSTR_2 && cache_references > CR_2 &&
6        cache_misses > CM_2 && cache_miss_rate > CM_RATE_2) {
7      // Attack potentially detected! (Partial detection)
8      if (instr_diff > IDIFF_LOW && instr_diff < IDIFF_HIGH ) {
9        // Attack detected! (Full detection)
10     }
11   }
12 }
```

Fig. 4. Pseudocode for DET_LVI_PPN, detector for the LVI-PPN-L1D attack.

The detection thresholds were chosen in a similar way as for the US-variant, but with some adjustments. Since DET_LVI_PPN couldn't rely on invalid page faults as an attack indicator, the risk of false positives was deemed to be larger for this detector. The thresholds for number of instructions, cache references and cache misses were therefore increased. Furthermore, the number of minor page faults was assumed to be zero instead of close to or equal to zero. Finally, the value for the difference in instructions between iterations was assumed to be within 0.9–1.1. When observing the LVI attacks, this value was found to often be less than a hundredth away from 1. The specific values used as thresholds for the DET_LVI_PPN detector are shown in Table 4.

Table 4. Chosen values for the thresholds used with the DET_LVI_PPN detector.

Threshold	Value	Threshold	Value
TPF (<)	6000	CM_2	2000000
MINF_2	1	CM_RATE_2	0.3
MAJF_2	1	IDIFF_LOW	0.9
INSTR_2	150000000	IDIFF_HIGH	1.1
CR_2	6000000		

4.3 Detection Performance

To evaluate the effectiveness of the prototype detectors for LVI, the same scenarios as described above were used to offer both attack and non-attack scenarios. In addition to these, an idle scenario (only detection tool running) and a benchmarking scenario using Geekbench5[2] were added. The scenarios were run for 120 s while the detection tool measured performance counters for all running processes (with the standard sampling interval of 1 s) and noted whenever a potential attack was detected. It was also noted whether a potential attack process matched all the attack indicators (Full detection) or some of them (Partial detection).

Table 5 shows the results of detection for the different scenarios, detectors (partial and full) and how a combined detector that uses both variants (full detection) combined would perform. Each attack scenario was fully detected by the suitable detector, and no other scenarios lead to a benign process being fully detected as an attack. The LVI-US-SB attacks were both detected after either 2 or 3 sample iterations of the detector. This could vary depending on the number of minor page faults caused during the setup phase of the attack (creation of enclave, etc.), which could remain above the threshold for multiple sample iterations. Afterwards, the attacks were however consistently and reliably detected.

The LVI-PPN-L1D attack was also detected fully and consistently with the DET_LVI_PPN detector, but it should be noted that Partial detection took 2 sample iterations while Full detection took 3 iterations, since the transition from setup phase to main attack loop in the attack application also means a bigger difference in number of instructions. This shows that the attack has to run for a longer time in order to match the final indicator. But as can be seen for the Geekbench scenario, which was reported as a potential attack (Partial) twice, not having the final indicator would have lead to benign processes being fully reported as attacks.

---

[2] https://www.geekbench.com/.

Table 5. Detection results during different scenarios, each running for at least 120 s and a sampling interval of 1 s.

	DET_US		DET_PPN		Combined
	Part.	Full	Part.	Full	
Attack scenarios					
LVI-US-SB	Y	Y	N	N	Y
LVI-PPN-L1D	N	N	Y	Y	Y
LVI-US-SB-ROP	Y	Y	N	N	Y
Benign scenarios					
NA (SB)	N	N	N	N	N
NA (L1D)	N	N	N	N	N
NA (SB-ROP)	N	N	N	N	N
Text editor	N	N	N	N	N
Firefox - Youtube	N	N	N	N	N
Firefox - Twitter	N	N	N	N	N
Game	N	N	N	N	N
Stress_c	N	N	N	N	N
Stress_m	N	N	N	N	N
Stress_i	N	N	N	N	N
Idle	N	N	N	N	N
Geekbench5	N	N	Y	N	N

5   Towards Self-monitoring Enclaves

Having analyzed the LVI attacks in terms of their affect on a number of HPCs and demonstrated how they can be detected using relatively simple thresholds we now proceed to discuss what would be required to make this useful in for a self-monitoring enclave. Next, we discuss why this cannot be done in current Intel SGX systems.

Self-monitoring Enclaves: A self-monitoring enclave which could reliably detect that it is being subject to a side-channel attack launched from the untrusted environment would provide some real added security compared to the current situation. Side-channel attacks tend to require a relatively long time period to succeed since the bandwidth of such channels is often quite limited. Thus, being able to detect the attack and then potentially stop operations would likely also prevent the attack from succeeding. Moreover, based on the results in this paper, we can with relative certainty state that the currently available HPCs can be effective in detecting SCAs that target enclaves (at least in some cases). So, does that mean that we could implement this functionality within the enclave so that it becomes self-monitoring? Unfortunately, the answer to this question is no.

For any measuring mechanism to be useful and not counterproductive as a security monitoring primitive the following requirements must be met:

1. The interface to invoke measurement operations must be accessible from within the enclave.
2. The confidentiality, integrity and availability of the measurements must be upheld even if the untrusted environment is compromised.
3. Measurements performed from within the enclave must be able to record events taking place either inside or outside the enclave.
4. Measurements performed from the untrusted environment must not be affected by any events within the enclave.

Requirement 1 is obvious for a self-monitoring enclave since it follows from the very idea of an enclave performing the monitoring activity. Requirement 2 is composed of three properties. Confidentiality of measurements (and the fact that a measurement is being performed) is important to uphold since otherwise this could risk becoming a new side-channel that can be used to exfiltrate information from the enclave. Integrity and availability of measurements are also self-evident as otherwise the attacker can hinder the protection. Requirement 3 is the minimum level of measurement that is needed to detect anything useful. In this work, we relied on events taking place outside the enclave but could also see that the ability to monitor events within the enclave would be very useful (e.g., the EPCM page faults). Finally, requirement 4 is similar to the confidentiality requirement of the measurements since it is needed to prevent the creation of new side-channel attacks. Unfortunately, only requirement 4 is upheld by Intel SGX.

HPCs Cannot be Accessed by Enclaves: Accessing HPCs from within an SGX enclave using an interface such as PAPI, seems to be impractical if not impossible, even for enclaves running in debug-mode (thus violating requirements 1 and 3). Firstly, using third party libraries within Intel SGX (and other TEEs) is non-trivial because of the additional security requirements that comes with enclave execution. In a paper by Wang et al. [30], this matter is discussed and explored in more detail. Secondly, reading HPCs requires making use of an underlying instruction, RDPMC (hardware instruction for reading HPCs), that is classified by Intel as illegal within enclaves, along with many other hardware instructions. According to Intel the RDPMC instruction can result in a VMEXIT (transferring control to the VMM) when executed within an enclave, and since the VMM cannot be allowed to update the enclave, Intel classifies the instruction as illegal. RDPMC is also by default restricted to privilege level 0. In order to use the instruction from within the enclave, a certain flag in register CR4 would have to be manually set in order to allow performance monitoring counters for all privilege levels [10]. However, due to RDPMC being illegal within enclaves according to Intel, this was not investigated further.

HPCs are not Protected: Another fundamental limitation of the method used in this work that prevents it from being practical today as a basis for self-monitoring enclaves is that the detection tool exists in untrusted code. It is therefore not protected against an adversary that has compromised the entire OS, which is the exact type of threat that SGX is supposed to protect against (and that an LVI attack assumes). A privileged attacker could also mess with the values or configurations of hardware performance counters, making their results unreliable. Software performance counters are particularly unreliable in this case since they originate from the OS and not from hardware. This breaks requirement 2.

Enclaves Don't Impact HPCs: Moreover, hardware performance counters are disabled for SGX enclaves (except in debug mode), so the method used here relied on using the performance pattern of the attacker (host application) instead. Having access to performance counter information for an enclave itself would perhaps allow detection methods to easier identify attacks towards it, since they could compare to normal execution performance and see if there is anomalous behaviour indicating an attack. However, as it stands now, it is not realistic to have hardware performance counter support for enclave processes, since it is currently disabled for good reasons. If it was enabled in the same way as for normal processes, it would give insight to the enclave process not only for a potential detection process, but for attackers as well. Attackers could then use the information from the HPC registers to easier mount attacks against the enclaves. In some sense one can say that the current approach upholds requirement 4 at the cost of making HPCs impractical to use for detecting SGX attacks.

6 Conclusions

A trusted enclave in an untrusted cloud environment can be likened to a small fishing boat surrounded by sharks. Hopefully the boat is robust enough, but if someone is starting to chew on the boat it would be good to know about it. Currently, such self-monitoring is not supported for Intel SGX enclaves making the metaphorical fisherman both blind and deaf. In this work we try to showcase the benefits of being able to make enclaves self-monitoring by characterizing three LVI attacks against Intel SGX in terms of how they affect a set of performance counters and based on this design and evaluate a prototype capable of detecting LVI attacks. We also discuss the practical limitations of translating such a prototype into a functioning self-monitoring enclave.

The attack footprint of the LVI attacks have both differences and similarities. They all interrupt a victim by way of page faults or microcode assists, which can be recorded with software or hardware performance counters. They are all also dependent on some sort of side-channel (often cache) at the end to transmit secret data, which also has a measurable impact on performance counters related to that channel. With regards to using the performance counters as a detection mechanism we found that it is possible using a relatively simple threshold-based detection, with acceptable speed and levels of overhead. Moreover, this shows a concrete example of a side-channel attack targeting SGX enclaves being detectable with the help of performance counters. We also describe the four requirements needed for such a mechanism to be useful to make a self-monitoring enclave a reality and find that three of them are violated by Intel SGX.

In summary, there are numerous practical limitations of using performance counters to detect SGX-specific attacks as a self-monitoring mechanism. There are also some challenges with performance counters in general, most notably non-determinism and overcounting. Yet, we hope that future designs for trusted environments consider the need for monitoring not just as a debugging mechanism but also for security reasons that it fulfills the necessary security requirements.

Acknowledgements. This work was supported by the national project RICS (Resilient Information and Control Systems) financed by the Swedish Civil Contingencies Agency (MSB).

References

1. Akram, A., Mushtaq, M., Bhatti, M. K., Lapotre, V., Gogniat, G.: Meet the Sherlock Holmes' of side channel leakage: a survey of cache SCA detection techniques. IEEE Access **8**, 70836-70860 (2020)
2. Allaf, Z., Adda, M., Gegov, A.: A comparison study on flush+ reload and prime+ probe attacks on AES using machine learning approaches. Adv. Intell. Syst. Comput. **650**, 09 (2017)
3. Brasser, F., Müller, U., Dmitrienko, A., Kostiainen, K., Capkun, S., Sadeghi, A.R.: Software grand exposure: SGX cache attacks are practical. In: 11th USENIX Workshop on Offensive Technologies (WOOT 17), Vancouver, BC. USENIX Association (2017)
4. Canella, C., et al.: Fallout: leaking data on meltdown-resistant CPUs. In: Proceedings of the ACM SIGSAC Conference on Computer and Communications Security (CCS). ACM (2019)
5. Chen, G., Chen, S., Xiao, Y., Zhang, Y., Lin, Z., Lai, T.H.: SgxPectre: stealing intel secrets from SGX enclaves via speculative execution. In: 2019 IEEE European Symposium on Security and Privacy (EuroS & P), pp. 142–157 (2019)
6. Chen, S., Zhang, X., Reiter, M.K., Zhang, Y.: Detecting privileged side-channel attacks in shielded execution with déjà vu. In: Proceedings of the 2017 ACM on Asia Conference on Computer and Communications Security, ASIA CCS 2017, New York, NY, USA, pp. 7–18. Association for Computing Machinery (2017)
7. Costan, V., Devadas, S.: Intel SGX explained. IACR Cryptol. ePrint Arch. **2016**, 86 (2016)
8. Götzfried, J., Eckert, M., Schinzel, S., Müller, T.: Cache attacks on Intel SGX. In: Proceedings of the 10th European Workshop on Systems Security, EuroSec 2017, New York, NY, USA. Association for Computing Machinery (2017)
9. Gruss, D., Maurice, C., Wagner, K., Mangard, S.: Flush+Flush: a fast and stealthy cache attack. In: Caballero, J., Zurutuza, U., Rodríguez, R.J. (eds.) DIMVA 2016. LNCS, vol. 9721, pp. 279–299. Springer, Cham (2016). https://doi.org/10.1007/978-3-319-40667-1_14
10. Herath, N., Fogh, A.: These are not your grand Daddys CPU performance counters-CPU hardware performance counters for security (2015)
11. Lantz, D.: Detection of side-channel attacks targeting Intel SGX. Master's thesis, Linköping University, Department of Computer and Information Science (2021)

12. Lee, D., Kohlbrenner, D., Shinde, S., Asanović, K., Song, D.: Keystone: an open framework for architecting trusted execution environments. In: Proceedings of the Fifteenth European Conference on Computer Systems, EuroSys 2020, New York, NY, USA. Association for Computing Machinery (2020)

13. Moghimi, A., Wichelmann, J., Eisenbarth, T., Sunar, B.: *MemJam*: a false dependency attack against constant-time crypto implementations. Int. J. Parallel Program. **47**(4), 538–570 (2018). https://doi.org/10.1007/s10766-018-0611-9

14. Moghimi, A., Irazoqui, G., Eisenbarth, T.: CacheZoom: how SGX amplifies the power of cache attacks. In: Fischer, W., Homma, N. (eds.) CHES 2017. LNCS, vol. 10529, pp. 69–90. Springer, Cham (2017). https://doi.org/10.1007/978-3-319-66787-4_4

15. Mushtaq, M., Akram, A., Bhatti, M.K., Chaudhry, M., Lapotre, V., Gogniat, G.: Nights-watch: a cache-based side-channel intrusion detector using hardware performance counters. In: Proceedings of the 7th International Workshop on Hardware and Architectural Support for Security and Privacy, HASP 2018. ACM (2018)

16. Mushtaq, M., et al.: Whisper: a tool for run-time detection of side-channel attacks. IEEE Access **8**, 83871–83900 (2020)

17. Nilsson, A., Bideh, P.N., Brorsson, J.: A survey of published attacks on Intel SGX (2020). https://arxiv.org/abs/2006.13598

18. O'Keeffe, D., et al.: Spectre attack against SGX enclave (2018). https://github.com/lsds/spectre-attack-sgx

19. Payer, M.: HexPADS: a platform to detect "Stealth" attacks. In: Caballero, J., Bodden, E., Athanasopoulos, E. (eds.) ESSoS 2016. LNCS, vol. 9639, pp. 138–154. Springer, Cham (2016). https://doi.org/10.1007/978-3-319-30806-7_9

20. Ragab, H., Milburn, A., Razavi, K., Bos, H., Giuffrida, C.: CrossTalk: speculative data leaks across cores are real. In 2021 IEEE Symposium on Security and Privacy (SP). Intel Bounty Reward (2021)

21. Schwarz, M., et al.: ZombieLoad: cross-privilege-boundary data sampling. In: CCS (2019)

22. Schwarz, M., Weiser, S., Gruss, D., Maurice, C., Mangard, S.: Malware guard extension: using SGX to conceal cache attacks. In: Polychronakis, M., Meier, M. (eds.) DIMVA 2017. LNCS, vol. 10327, pp. 3–24. Springer, Cham (2017). https://doi.org/10.1007/978-3-319-60876-1_1

23. Seaborn, M., Dullien, T.: Exploiting the DRAM rowhammer bug to gain kernel privileges. Black Hat **15**, 71 (2015)

24. Shih, M. W., Lee, S., Kim, T., Peinado, M.: T-SGX: eradicating controlled-channel attacks against enclave programs. In: The Network and Distributed System Security (NDSS) Symposium, vol. 01 (2017)

25. Van Bulck, J., et al.: Foreshadow: extracting the keys to the Intel SGX kingdom with transient out-of-order execution. In: Proceedings of the 27th USENIX Security Symposium, USENIX Association, vol. 8 (2018)

26. Van Bulck, J., et al.: LVI: hijacking transient execution through microarchitectural load value injection. In: 41th IEEE Symposium on Security and Privacy (S&P 2020). IEEE (2020)

27. Van Bulck, J., Piessens, F., Strackx, R.: SGX-Step: a practical attack framework for precise enclave execution control. In: Proceedings of the 2nd Workshop on System Software for Trusted Execution, SysTEX 2017. ACM (2017)

28. Van Schaik, S., et al.: RIDL: Rogue in-flight data load. In: S&P (2019)

29. van Schaik, S., Minkin, M., Kwong, A., Genkin, D., Yarom, Y.: CacheOut: leaking data on Intel CPUs via cache evictions. In: 2021 IEEE Symposium on Security and Privacy (SP), pp. 339–354 (2021)

30. Wang, P., et al.: Building and maintaining a third-party library supply chain for productive and secure SGX enclave development. In: Proceedings of the ACM/IEEE 42nd International Conference on Software Engineering: Software Engineering in Practice, ICSE-SEIP 2020, New York, NY, USA, pp. 100–109. Association for Computing Machinery (2020)
31. Xu, Y., Cui, W., Peinado, M.: Controlled-channel attacks: deterministic side channels for untrusted operating systems. In: 2015 IEEE Symposium on Security and Privacy, pp. 640–656 (2015)
32. Zhang, Y., Zhao, M., Li, T., Han, H.: Survey of attacks and defenses against SGX. In: 2020 IEEE 5th Information Technology and Mechatronics Engineering Conference (ITOEC), pp. 1492–1496 (2020)

DeCrypto: Finding Cryptocurrency Miners on ISP Networks

Richard Plný[1]📵, Karel Hynek[1,2](✉)📵, and Tomáš Čejka[2]📵

[1] Faculty of Information Technology, Czech Technical University in Prague,
Prague, Czech Republic
{plnyrich,hynekkar}@fit.cvut.cz
[2] CESNET z.s.p.o., Prague, Czech Republic
{hynekkar,cejkat}@cesnet.cz

Abstract. With the rising popularity of cryptocurrencies and the
increasing value of the whole industry, people are incentivized to join and
earn revenues by cryptomining—using computational resources for cryptocurrency transaction verification. Nevertheless, there is an increasing
number of abusive cryptomining cases, and it is reported that "coin miner
malware" grew by more than 4000% in 2018. In this work, we analyzed
the cryptominer network communication and proposed the DeCrypto
system that can detect and report mining on high-speed 100 Gbps
backbone Internet lines with millions of users. The detector uses the
concept of heterogeneous weak-indication detectors (Machine-Learning-
based, domain-based, and payload-based) that work together and create
a robust and accurate detector with an extremely low false-positive rate.
The detector was implemented and evaluated on a real nationwide high-
speed network and proved efficient in a real-world deployment.

Keywords: Cryptocurrency · Miner · Detection · Flow · Security ·
Network · Monitoring

1 Introduction

The first widely recognized cryptocurrency—Bitcoin—was proposed by Satoshi
Nakamoto [26] in 2008. At that time, the world was in a global financial crisis, when central banks rapidly increased the monetary bases (printing money),
which decreased the trust in money. Bitcoin targeted the decreased trust with
decentralized and anonymous peer-to-peer networks based on cryptographic and
consensus mechanisms, which allowed trustworthy financial transactions without the need for a central authority [44]. Since the Bitcoin introduction, we have
seen immense development in the cryptocurrency market. Nowadays, there are
more than 3600 publicly exchangeable cryptocurrencies. It is estimated that the
crypto market is worth more the 1.13 trillion USD (August 2022 [9]).

The cryptocurrency transactions are validated without any central authority
using a consensus mechanism. Bitcoin and similar cryptocurrencies use a "proof-
of-work" consensus protocol [26,44]. In this scheme, the community (i.e., miners)

H. P. Reiser and M. Kyas (Eds.): NordSec 2022, LNCS 13700, pp. 139–158, 2022.
https://doi.org/10.1007/978-3-031-22295-5_8

spends its computational resources to solve a difficult mathematical problem to verify the transactions (mining). The first miner who successfully verifies the transactions is rewarded with newly created coins, transaction fees, or both. The chance of receiving the reward depends on the miner's computational performance since only the first one is rewarded. Therefore, miners are incentivized to maximize their computational power using specialized mining hardware or create large mining GPU arrays [2].

Mining can consume a large portion of electricity, which is the main cost of mining and reduces the net earnings of an individual cryptominer. Therefore, there are examples from the past where miners tried to avoid electricity bills by placing the mining hardware in offices or public buildings without appropriate permission. The property owners (such as universities) are then unaware of the mining activity. However, they have to cover the increased costs of the electricity [1]. Similarly, rogue researchers already misused the computational power of research supercomputers to mine cryptocurrency [13,23].

Miners also use illegal practices to abuse compromised computational resources leaving their owners unaware [8,15,43]. Cryptomalware or abusive cryptomining refers to mining carried out by criminals using resources stolen from their victims [28]. It is a way to use more devices and increase the overall hash rate and the chances to gain reward. Especially Monero became very popular when it comes to cryptomalware since it is known to be hard to trace [12]. Nearly 5% of all Monero coins in circulation in 2018 (valued at almost $40 million at that time) were mined by malware [20]. Specialists from McAffee [22] reported that "coin miner malware" grew by more than 4000% in the year 2018, and nearly 58% of all attacks on IoT devices intended to mine cryptocurrency [33]. Abusive mining attacks were listed as the top three threats by [18]. According to the FBI's Internet Crime Report [11], a total of $1.6 billion was lost due to incidents involving the use of cryptocurrency. The cryptomining communication can thus be a severe indicator of compromise. In multiple use-cases, it is beneficial to detect and notify the device owner, property owner, or administrators about such suspicious activity.

Nowadays, most miners use pooled mining [36] since it provides a much higher chance for a reward compared to solo mining. Therefore, this work targets the network-traffic-based detection of cryptocurrency miners joined in mining pools while avoiding IP-address-based detection due to its unreliability [16,29]. We analyzed the traffic shape of mining communication using a large dataset obtained from a nationwide Internet Service Provider (ISP) network and proposed a novel DeCrypto (Detection of Cryptominers) system that can be deployed to high-speed (100 Gbps) backbone lines and potentially protect millions of devices and users. The proposed DeCrypto system uses described weak-indication architecture, aggregating multiple heterogeneous classifiers into a single, robust, and accurate detector (accuracy reaching up to 96.5% and precision up to 99.9971%) with negligible false-positive detections. We implemented DeCrypto and evaluated it on the nationwide ISP network used by half a million users.

The contributions of our work can be summarized as follows:

- We developed a Rules Generator script, used to daily update a block list of cryptomining pools, that can be used for reliable block-list-based mining detection. The software is publicly available in [31] and was used for the creation of large cryptomining communication datasets.
- We created two annotated datasets containing real-world traffic. Together they contain more than 1 million extended bidirectional flow records of cryptominers communication and around 1.8 million records of other types of traffic used as a counter class. We are unaware of any mining dataset of similar size, and thus we made it publicly available in [32].
- We proposed a novel mining detection system called DeCrypto that uses weak mining indicators. The detector can accurately recognize mining network traffic using extended flows in real-time. The high accuracy combined with extended flows makes the detector deployable on high-speed ISP backbone lines, where it can protect millions of devices.
- We implemented the proposed detector and evaluated it on nationwide ISP infrastructure used by half a million users. The implementation was made publicly available as an open-source project on GitHub [30].

This paper is divided as follows: Sect. 2 summarizes the related work of cryptominers detection. Section 3 provides information about novel datasets. Section 4 describes DeCrypto system in detail. Section 5 contains results of our experiments. Section 6 describes the deployment of DeCrypto system and experiences with ML-based detection on high-speed ISP lines. Section 7 concludes this paper.

2 Related Work

Since mining is considered suspicious activity, it is essential to let network operators know when such activity takes place on their network. One of the possible approaches is to recognize mining using IP-based block-lists of well-known mining pools such as [45]. However, the block-list-based detection can be considered unreliable [16,29], since the block-lists can never be complete. Moreover, they can also suffer for false-positive detection since each domain or IP address can host multiple services. Therefore, multiple studies have proposed mining detection using various approaches. Jingqiang et al. [21] focused on detecting browser-based "silent miners". Their method uses a sandbox to load a website and then analyzes its resources to detect JavaScript (JS) miners. Kharraz et al. [19] also focused on JS miners. In their study, they utilized JS compilation time, JS engine execution time, garbage collection, and other statistics to train the Machine Learning (ML) detector, which achieved more than 95% of the true-positive rate. Nevertheless, these approaches do not use computer-network telemetry to detect miners; instead, they require access to in-browser statistics. Additionally, they consider only browser-based mining software, leaving other types of abusive mining undetected.

Swedan et al. [40] proposed a system called MDPS—Mining Detection and Prevention System, that detects miners in network traffic. The proposed MDPS uses a man-in-the-middle proxy for deep packet inspection. The decrypted payload is then inspected by URL block lists, detectors of mining code, and by Virus-Total[1] to find malicious external JS libraries. Nevertheless, the system's applicability is limited to networks, where man-in-the-middle inspection is acceptable. Compared to the MDPS, the proposed DeCrypto system does not require traffic decryption, which maintains users' privacy while allowing the deployment to service provider networks.

Žádník et al. [42] examined the possibility of cryptominers communication detection using flow-based telemetry. Their work combined passive detection and a secondary verification of false positives by active probing. The passive detection utilized an ML-based model with a manually created feature vector. During the data analysis, they discovered that cryptominers traffic has the following characteristics:

1. Mutual communication between a cryptominer and a mining pool server often lasts for several hours
2. Packets are generally small, often in the range from 40 to 120 bytes
3. Most flows are observed with TCP ACK and PUSH flags set
4. The destination port is either a well-known port of a different service or not well-known but definitely lower than the source port
5. TCP connections are generally long-lasting, often exceeding the maximal flow duration
6. Communication is not disrupted, i.e., most flows do not contain the RST flag

Moreover, Žádník et al. [42] provide a brief overview of all cryptomining protocols, including Stratum protocol [27]. According to Recabarren et al. [35], the Stratum is a de-facto standard in pooled mining. Stratum protocol uses TCP as the underlining transport protocol and transfers messages in JSON format. Since Stratum is a request-response type protocol with long gaps between the messages, it forms a distinctive pattern that the network detectors could recognize. However, Žádník et al. [42] used traditional flow data that contains only basic information such as the number of transferred bytes and packets, and the passive detection suffered from a large false-positive rate. To mitigate the false positives, they used active probing to confirm that the detected destination IP address is a mining pool server. Even though the Žádník et al. [42] proposal achieves good accuracy, the active probing brings performance limitations, and thus it is unsuitable for high-speed networks.

Another flow-based detector was proposed by Muñoz et al. [25], who designed an ML-based detector. They generated a cryptominers traffic dataset and analyzed its characteristics. It was determined that cryptominers flows are long duration and have a small number of transferred packets. Moreover, a server typically sends 20 times more data than a client. Based on their analysis, they proposed the following feature vector:

---

[1] https://virustotal.com.

Table 1. Properties of traditional basic flow and its extensions provided by ipfixprobe flow exporter that are part of the created dataset

Basic flow part	Extended flow part
IP addresses	TLS SNI
Ports	Per Packet Information
Number of transferred bytes and packets from each direction	The first 100 bytes of payload from each direction
Transport Protocol	

1. Inbound and outbound packets/second
2. Inbound and outbound bits/second
3. Inbound and outbound bits/packet
4. Bits_inbound/bits_outbound ratio
5. Packets_inbound/packets_outbound ratio

The best model was Decision Tree which achieved an average accuracy of 99.9%. However, they did not consider real-world deployment and worked with a small portion of lab-created cryptominers traffic that represented only 0.03% (less than 700 flows) of their whole dataset. Therefore, the accuracy can significantly differ when deployed to real-world network monitoring infrastructure.

Compared to the related works, the DeCrypto system uses extended flow data as input network telemetry from high-speed networks. Moreover, the DeCrypto system does not rely on a single ML-based detector. Instead, it combines multiple information carried in the flow to achieve higher accuracy while lowering the false-positive rate to a minimum. Compared to all mentioned related work, the DeCrypto system was deployed to the actual nationwide ISP infrastructure and thus was thoroughly evaluated during multiple months of operation. For instance, Žádník et al. [42] used only 15 min of real-network traffic for evaluation.

3   Datasets

Since none of the previous works provided a sufficient dataset that could be used for proper design and verification, we decided to create our own. The main difference compared to previous works is the size of our dataset and also that we used extended bidirectional flow data created by ipfixprobe[2]—a high-performance flow exporter that can monitor 100 Gbps traffic. Contrary to traditional IP flow record, which contains only basic information about the communication, such as the number of transferred bytes, and packets, ipfixprobe flow exporter also adds information about the first 30 individual packets (packet size, timestamp, TCP flags, and direction) that carried payload. Ipfixprobe also extends each flow for

---

[2] https://github.com/CESNET/ipfixprobe.

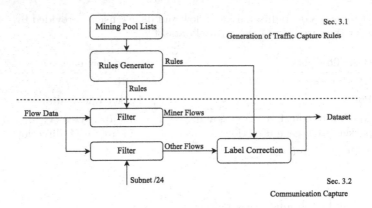

Fig. 1. Dataset creation scheme

the first 100B of payload from each direction and Server Name Indication (SNI) from TLS Client Hello packets. The flow properties exported by ipfixprobe are shown in the Table 1, and the individual field names and their description are provided with the dataset that we made publicly available in [32].

The dataset creation methodology is depicted in the Fig. 1 and was divided into two steps: 1. Generation of Traffic Capture Rules and 2. Communication Capture.

3.1 Generation of Traffic Capture Rules

We have used an initial mining pool list from [45] together with our own created list, available in [31]—we chose top 10 mining pools by size [4,24] for Bitcoin (BTC), Ethereum (ETH) and Monero (XMR). The initial lists of mining pools remained unchanged for whole dataset generation process. Nevertheless, we checked once per day the validity of domain names using our own active probing software called Rules Generator [31]. The Rules Generator takes a list of mining-pool domain names and ports as input and performs DNS resolution to obtain IPv4 and IPv6 addresses. When multiple addresses are received in the DNS response, all of them included in the list are further processed. These addresses are then tested using active probing using mining protocol via TLS or plain TCP connection. Since Stratum protocol is the de-facto standard of pooled mining [35], we only used Stratum to verify that a pair (IP address and port) is an actual mining pool. Verified pairs are then passed to the output to be used as a filtration rule in the Communication Capture phase.

3.2 Communication Capture

To ensure the real-world nature of the dataset, we reached CESNET, a large internet provider with more than half a million individual users. Their customers are mainly big institutions such as universities. The CESNET network monitoring infrastructure follows the traditional IPFIX monitoring approach described

Table 2. Overview of the created datasets

Dataset	Captured during	# Miners	# Others	# Total
Design	Dec 14-Feb 10 2022	693,237	1,331,666	2,024,903
Validation	Feb 28-Mar 31 2022	392,577	682,999	1,075,576

by Hofstede et al. [14] with five minutes of active timeout[3]; thus, the capturing was performed on the flow collector by filtering communication of the pair of IP addresses and ports obtained from the Rules Generator script (described in Sect. 3.1). Since we aimed for long-term data capture, the Rules Generator verified the pools each day and provided an updated list of IP addresses to minimize possible mislabeling due to the natural continuous obsolescence of block-list-based annotations.

We also captured general network traffic transferred via CESNET as a counter class for miner communication. We captured all traffic from the selected/24 IPv4 address sub-space to limit the amount of data and enable long-term capture. Since we are dealing with the ISP traffic, each IP address may correspond to multiple physical/virtual devices due to Network Address Translation and can thus represent multiple devices and users. Additionally, we performed filtration of the general network traffic and removed communication to confirmed mining pools to ensure correct labels. The filtration was done using the daily-updated list of mining pools' IP addresses and ports.

Traffic capture (of both miner and the regular class) was performed between December 2021 and February 2022. Together we collected 2,024,903 extended bidirectional flows from which we created the Design dataset. Moreover, we performed one more traffic capture in March 2022 to create a dataset for evaluation. The Evaluation dataset contains 1,075,576 flows in total. See the Table 2.

The Ethical Aspects of Real Traffic Capture and Active Probing

Users' privacy is an essential priority, so our research was done with extreme carefulness. The indisputable advantages of real traffic generated by hundreds of thousands of people come with the cost of potential privacy abuse of real users. Therefore, we used only automatic data processing with immediate data anonymization. With this, we declare that we did not analyze or manually process deanonymized data and did not perform any procedures that could lead us to the user's identity.

Active probing which we performed is considered an ethical research practice [17]. Nevertheless, the probing procedure was extremely slow, with five-second intervals between individual connections to avoid overloading the target's resources and minimizing the impact. Moreover, the number of checked host was very small and the scan procedure checked hundreds of hosts per day.

---

[3] Longer TCP connections are split into multiple flows.

4   Introduction to DeCrypto System

The main motivation for using the concept of heterogeneous weak indicators for detection is the minimization of false-positive detection. The weak-indicator approach combines multiple heterogeneous classifiers. Each of them works on different operational principles with its own limitations and inaccuracies, thus providing *weak indication* of mining. By joining these weak-indication detectors together, we form a robust and more accurate detector with a small number of false positives, which are our main concern.

Since we aim for deployment to large ISP infrastructure, the detector needs to process a large volume of data. The CESNET network monitoring infrastructure generates by average 120,000 flow records per second from eight backbone peering lines. With a large number of predictions per second, even 99% accuracy is not enough. For instance, the approach proposed by Muñoz et al. [25] reached an accuracy of 99.998% on the lab-created dataset, which would represent (when we assume the same accuracy in real-world deployment) 2.4 false classifications per second in CESNET. Unfortunately, Muñoz et al. do not provide a false-positive rate; however, since cryptominers represent only a negligible amount of transferred traffic (as can be seen in their imbalanced dataset, where cryptominers flows represent less than 0.03%), we could expect that most false classifications would be false positives. Similarly, Žádník et al. [42] proposal would suffer 3120 (2.6%) false-positive detections per second without the active probing. Nevertheless, active probing is not a solution for reducing false positives on large infrastructures due to performance and ethical questions of mass probing (thousands requests per second)—scanning network nodes could be marked as malicious actors, which could negatively affect network operation.

The minimization of false-positive rate in network detectors is one of the biggest challenges for network security research that aims to use Machine Learning technology. A large number of false-positive detections cause alarm desensitization and alert fatigue—even professional security analysts lose their trust in the validity of the alarm resulting in ignored and unresolved alerts [5].

In the following sections, we describe the DeCrypto system architecture, which does not require the active probing mechanism and enables high-speed deployment with negligible false-positive detections.

4.1   Weak Indicators of Cryptomining

Previous works [25,42] summarized that the cryptomining packets are usually smaller than packets in other traffic and inter-packet intervals are generally very long (more than 10 s). We confirmed these observations by analysis of the Design dataset (see the Table 2). Moreover, we found that the mining traffic in the Design dataset is mostly unencrypted, carrying Stratum protocol in plain text. Almost **80%** of cryptominers traffic was unencrypted, even though the traffic encryption can be considered a de-facto standard nowadays. The distinctive cryptominer traffic properties that we found in our Design dataset can be summarized as:

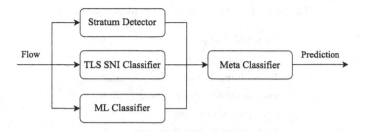

Fig. 2. High-level scheme of the DeCrypto detection procedure

1. Traffic is long-lasting and typically lasts for several hours.
2. Low amount of data are transferred (packers are usually small, ~270 bytes).
3. Longer intervals (more than 10 s) between packets.
4. Almost all packets have a TCP PUSH flag set.
5. Significant amount of traffic is still unencrypted.
6. The encrypted traffic is almost always transferred on different than well-known ports.
7. Domain names in TLS SNI extension contain distinctive words such as `pool`, `mine` and `mining`.

Based on the analysis of the Design dataset, we propose three weak indicators to exploit these traffic characteristics: 1. Stratum Detector, which detects Stratum protocol in unencrypted communication, 2. a Machine-Learning model that leverages statistical properties of mining communication, and 3. TLS SNI Classifier that inspects domain names in SNI. The results of all three detectors are then processed by the Meta Classifier that produces the final result, as indicated in the Fig. 2. The detailed description of each component and experiments performed on the dataset's design part are described in the following sections.

4.2 Stratum Detector

Since ipfixprobe flow exporter supports extraction of the first bytes of payload even from the high-speed networks, we decided to use these bytes as one of the weak indicators. Specifically, Stratum Detector is designed to look for the Stratum mining protocol. The ipfixprobe provides us with the first 100 bytes from each direction of communication. Therefore, a total of 200 bytes is used for the detection, which are inspected by two regular expression patterns that were created based on the Stratum protocol specification [27]:

1. `("(("(?P<I>id)|(?P<R>result)|(?P<E>error)"):\s?).*){3,}`
2. `("(jsonrpc|method|worker)":\s?")|(params":|mining\.(set|not))`

The first pattern can recognize Stratum protocol messages called request and notification, and the second pattern recognizes Stratum responses from the mining pools. Moreover, Stratum Detector checks that all three groups (`id`, `result`

Table 3. TLS SNI values of cryptominer flows

TLS SNI value	Count
asia2.ethermine.org	1228
fee.nanominer.org	1020
rvn-us-west1.nanopool.org	565
rvn-jp1.nanopool.org	561
xmr-us-west1.nanopool.org	402
xmr-jp1.nanopool.org	316
eu1.ethermine.org	39
other	230
total	4361

Table 4. Overview of selected features for ML models. The feature importance was calculated using Gini index.

Feature name	Description	Importance
BYTES	Number of bytes from src	0.0473
BYTES_REV	Number of bytes from dst	0.0510
PACKETS	Number of packets from src	0.0163
PACKETS_REV	Number of packets from dst	0.0238
SENT_PERCENTAGE	Ratio of packets from src	0.1532
RECV_PERCENTAGE	Ratio of packets from dst	0.1829
AVG_PKT_INTERVAL	Average seconds between packets	0.1550
OVERALL_DURATION	Overall flow duration	0.0716
AVG_PKT_LEN	Average length of a packet	0.0695
PSH_RATIO	Ratio of packets with PUSH flag set	0.0709
MIN_PKT_LEN	Minimal length of a packet	0.1009
DATA_SYMMETRY	Ratio of received and sent bytes	0.0576

and **error**) have been matched by the first pattern. Such kind of detector can be considered very reliable since it performs a payload-based analysis. The proposed expressions could find all the flows in our Design dataset with an unencrypted payload containing Stratum. Nevertheless, the Stratum Detector only works with unencrypted communication. The encrypted miner traffic detection is then performed in other weak-indication classifiers.

4.3   TLS SNI Classifier

TLS SNI Classifier is designed to detect suspicious keywords in domain names in the Server Name Indication (SNI) extension of the TLS protocol. However, SNI is only sent when the TLS is used, meaning it can be present only in flows representing encrypted communication.

Mining pools can operate more mining servers and provide services for multiple cryptocurrencies. There is a total of 4361 cryptominer flows with non-empty SNI in the Design dataset; see the Table 3 with mining pool SNI values. It can be seen that these mining-pool domain names contain the cryptocurrency's name and the particular server's identification. Domain names of mining pools also contain keywords suggesting the mining process. As we can see in the Table 3, many domain names contain *pool* or *mine*. Therefore, the TLS SNI classifier performs pattern matching on domain names looking for distinctive keywords.

The first group of keywords contains a list of cryptocurrency abbreviations. We planned to include a wide range of cryptocurrency names in this list, but to achieve the best possible performance, we only included `rvn`, `xmr` and `eth`, because only these were mined in the Design dataset. The `rvn` is contained in 1239 SNI values, `xmr` in 835, and `eth` in 1267 of them. However, not all pools use this scheme; therefore, only around ~75% of the cryptominer flows are covered by this group of keywords. In addition, the TLS SNI Classifier creates four enhanced patterns based on the observed domain names for matching from each list entry: `-$NAME`, `$NAME-`, `.$NAME` and `$NAME.` ($NAME is the short cryptocurrency name).

The second group contains the keywords indicating the mining process. Based on the SNI values in the Design dataset, we chose `mine` and `pool`. The `mine` is contained in 2287 and the `pool` in 2074 of them. In addition, none of the flows contained both keywords in its SNI. Therefore, our two selected keywords match all the cryptominer flows, which have the SNI value non-empty.

The TLS SNI Classifier's output indicates if both, one, or none groups were matched. The group is matched if at least one of its keywords is present in the TLS SNI. The Meta Classifier then processes the TLS SNI Classifier's output to perform the final classification.

4.4   ML Classifier

The third weak-indication detector uses ML to distinguish cryptomining traffic based on its distinctive traffic shape properties. To maintain explainability and enable in-depth inspection and debugging of models in the future, we decided to use a basic shallow-learning approach (such as Decision Trees). Contrary to sophisticated Deep-Learning techniques, shallow learning algorithms provide much better explainability and interpretability even for non-experts in ML domain [5].

During the experiments performed on the Design dataset, we identified 12 distinctive traffic features to recognize cryptominers that are written in the Table 4 together with their importance computed using the mean decrease of Gini impurity index [38]. These features were used in all of our experiments with ML. We experimented with four shallow-learning models, such as AdaBoost (with underlying Decision Tree) [37], Decision Tree [34], Random Forest [3], and Logistic Regression [41]. For each model, we performed hyperparameter tuning and feature selection using 5-fold cross-validation. The Random Forest classifier with all identified features (showed in the Table 4) achieved the best results; thus, we used it in the DeCrypto system. The best hyperparameters are listed in the Table 5.

Table 5. Hyperparameters of the best Random forest model

Hyperparameter	Value
Split criterion	*gini*
Max depth	10
Max features	*sqrt*
Min samples leaf	2
Min samples split	5
Estimators	100

Nevertheless, the Random Forest model does not perform final classification. Instead, it outputs the probability of flow affiliation with cryptomining traffic, which is then used in the Meta Classifier to derive the final detection.

```
 1 def doDetection(flow):
 2     if stratumDetector.isStratum(flow) == True:
 3         return True
 4 # when Stratum was not detected, use ML or
 5 # Dempster—Shafer Theory (DST)
 6     features = getFeatures(flow)
 7     ml_proba = mlClassifier.predictProba(features)
 8
 9 # when we do not have SNI, use only ML score
10     if not flow.hasTlsSni():
11         return ml_proba > ML_THRESHOLD
12
13 # when we have SNI, combine SNI and ML score using DST
14     tls_sni_score = tlsSniClassifier.scoreSni(flow)
15     dst_pignistic = DST.combine(ml_proba, tls_sni_score)
16
17     return dst_pignistic > DST_THRESHOLD
```

Listing 1.1. The Meta Classification Decision

4.5   Meta Classifier

The ML Classifier, the Stratum Detector, and the TLS SNI Classifier form a group of weak-indication classifiers. As mentioned above, the Meta Classifier processes and combines outputs of these support classifiers and performs final detection (see the Fig. 2).

The pseudocode of classifier combination is written in the Listing 1.1. Since detecting a Stratum protocol in the payload is a trustworthy mining indicator, Stratum detection is performed first. If Stratum protocol was detected, a flow is marked as a miner immediately, and other support classifiers are not invoked to save computational resources. If Stratum is not detected, features for the ML

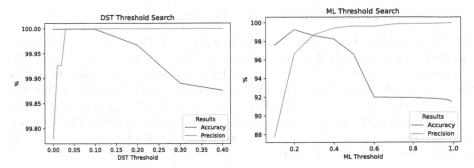

(a) Accuracy and Precision of DST classifier based on selected decision threshold

(b) Accuracy and Precision of ML classifier based on selected decision threshold

Fig. 3. Accuracy and Precision plots when finding the optimal decision thresholds

model are calculated, and the ML Classifier is used to get the probability of affiliation to mining communication. If the TLS SNI is not present, the probability is compared to the ML threshold to get the final prediction. See the Sect. 4.6 for more details on the ML threshold.

If a TLS SNI value is present, it is processed by TLS SNI Classifier. The TLS SNI classifier output is then combined with the output of the ML Classifier via the Dempster-Shafer Theory (DST) [10,39]. The DST is a mathematical framework allowing a combination of multiple data sources, each with different certainty. The beliefs of each data source are expressed as probabilities, which are combined via Dempster's Rule of Combination, resulting in the final belief value (pignistic probability of affiliation to mining class). The pseudocode of combination TLS and ML detection using DST is shown in the Listing 1.2. The final belief is then compared with the DST threshold to make the final prediction.

```
def DSTCombinator(tlsSniScore, mlProba):
    mlBpa = MassFunction({
        'Miner': mlProba,
        'Other': 1 − mlProba
    })
    tlsSniBpa = MassFunction({
        'Miner': tlsSniScore,
        'Other': 1 − tlsSniScore
    })
    combinedBpa = mlBpa.combine(tlsSniBpa)
    combinedPignistic = combinedBpa.pignistic()

    return combinedPignistic['Miner']
```

Listing 1.2. Combination via the DST

4.6   Selection of the Optimal Detection Parameters

In the Meta Classifier, there are three possible paths by which a flow can be marked as a miner—1. Stratum is detected (Stratum path), 2. DST pignistic function exceeds the DST threshold (DST path), or 3. the ML probability exceeds the ML threshold (ML path). To find the optimal value of both DST and ML thresholds, we evaluated threshold values from 0 to 1 with a step of 0.01 in a loop and chose the value producing the minimum false positives. The accuracy and precision measures based on the used threshold can be seen in the Fig. 3, and the best threshold values are:

$$DST\_THRESHOLD = 0.03$$

$$ML\_THRESHOLD = 0.99$$

The DST threshold value of 0.03 is the lowest value that does not generate any false-positive detection. The DST path achieved accuracy of 99.9995% and precision of 100.00%, see the Fig. 3a. The ML threshold value of 0.99 was selected, since it generated only 18 false positives with accuracy of 93.0107% and precision of 99.9663%. The overall accuracy of the ML path is lower than in related works [25,42] due to the minimization of the false-positive rate and could be much higher with a less strict value of the threshold. Nevertheless, we argue that in our deployment scenario is the lowest possible false-positive rate crucial for real-world deployment [5].

The whole DeCrypto system achieved an accuracy of 96.4972% and precision of 99.9971% during the design phase on the Design dataset with the chosen thresholds. The Table 6 depicts the resulting confusion matrix.

Table 6. Confusion matrix of the DeCrypto system on the Design dataset

		Actual	
		Miner	Other traffic
Predicted	Miner	624,585	18
		30.8451%	0.0008%
	Other traffic	70,911	1,329,389
		3.5019%	65.6519%

5   Evaluation

We evaluated the whole DeCrypto system using the Validation dataset described in the Sect. 3, which we did not use in the design phase. The Validation dataset enables independent testing, which is necessary to avoid detector overfitting.

When tested on the Evaluation dataset with previously defined thresholds (see Sect. 4.6), the detector achieved the overall accuracy of 93.7261% and the precision of 99.9945%. The detailed performance results of the DeCrypto system

Table 7. Confusion matrix of the DeCrypto system on the Evaluation dataset

		Actual	
		Miner	Other traffic
Predicted	Miner	325,114	18
		30.2269%	0.0016%
	Other traffic	67,463	682,981
		6.2722%	63.4990%

are shown in the confusion matrix in the Table 7. It can be seen that the results are similar to the design phase, and the detector still maintains a low false-positive rate. The DeCrypto system created only 18 false positives while making 1,075,576 predictions. The 18 false positives were produced only by the ML path of the system (see the Table 8 in the Appendix) and come from 10 different IP addresses; however, due to the anonymization process in the dataset creation, we could not use IP addresses to identify the type of traffic that causes false-positive detection.

The false-negative rate has increased twofold compared to the design phase, and the detector did not identify around 17% mining flows. The increase in the false-negative rate is expected due to the strict settings of thresholds and mini-mization of false positives. However, since the cryptomining process is typically long-lasting, one active cryptominer usually generates more than one flow— long TCP connections are split into five-minute flows in the IPFIX monitoring infrastructures of CESNET. Therefore, even if some flows representing one active cryptominer will be evaluated as false negatives, we can assume that the detector will correctly recognize the miner when processing subsequent flows representing the same mining TCP connection.

We tested our hypothesis and aggregated all flows based on flow key (IP addresses, ports, and protocol) in the Evaluation dataset and found 113,324 unique mining TCP connections (unique cryptominers). The DeCrypto system successfully marked as a miner at least one flow for each mining TCP connection. Therefore, all unique miners in the Evaluation dataset were detected even though the false-negative rate (calculated on individual flows) is not negligible.

6 Deployment

The DeCrypto detection system was implemented in Python using NEMEA [7], a high-performance network traffic analysis framework. The efficiency of our Python implementation was evaluated on the computer with AMD Ryzen 7 3700X 8-Core Processor, 3.59 GHz, and 16 GB RAM. The DeCrypto system was able to process up to 41,500 flows per second in a single thread. Such performance is sufficient for high-speed network monitoring since, in deployment, we put a filter removing flows carrying less than eight packets that would represent at least four Stratum messages. On the CESNET network, the filtration reduces amount of data from 120,000 to around 13,000 flows per second. The large drop in the number of flows is expected since the Internet traffic follows heavy-tail distribution [6] and thus, most flows are very short.

We successfully deployed the DeCrypto implementation to the CESNET network monitoring infrastructure in April 2022, which performs stream-wise flow processing in real-time. In the early phases of deployment, we recorded a ~2500 false positives per day due to the ML detector path. The ML falsely identified chatting services (such as Facebook Messenger, Telegram, or Signal) as cryptominers. Therefore, additional alert processing was implemented to suppress the false positives. The security personnel received alerts from ML-only detection when at least three consecutive flows belonging to the same TCP connections (the flows describing long TCP connections are split after 5 min) were marked as a miner. Since the implementation of the restriction of ML-only detection, we record less than ten false-positive alerts per day, while the DeCrypto creates around 10,000 cryptomining alerts per day.

The deployment of ML technology to high-speed network monitoring infrastructure was successful due to deployment of other non-ML weak indicators. A large number of predictions that has to be made by ISP-level detector still precludes the deployment of algorithms that are solely based on ML technology because even 99% precision is not enough when making thousands of predictions per second. Even though the DeCrypto system provides possible solutions for ML deployment to large monitoring infrastructure, it concerns only a single use-case of cryptomining detection. Other use-cases or a general framework for creating detectors using weak indicators poses a challenge for our future work.

7   Conclusion

With the rising value of the cryptocurrency sector, people are more incentives to join the community and earn revenues by cryptomining. Nevertheless, security companies and governmental agencies have reported an increasing number of abusive mining [11,22,33]. Cryptomining can thus be considered an indicator of compromise, and detecting miners is viable in multiple use-cases.

In this paper, we proposed a novel and efficient detection method, DeCrypto, which can reliably detect mining entities on ISP networks. The proposed DeCrypto system uses the concept of heterogeneous weak-indication detectors to minimize false positives, which is crucial for actual deployment on large monitoring infrastructures. By analysis of real-world cryptominer traffic, we proposed and implemented three heterogeneous weak-indication detectors: 1. the Stratum Detector, 2. the TLS SNI Classifier, and 3. the ML Classifier. All three indicators of cryptomining traffic are merged together and provide reliable detection.

The proposed DeCrypto system was designed and evaluated using novel datasets obtained from real-world ISP backbone lines operated by the CESNET, which we made publicly available [32]. According to our evaluation, the concept of heterogeneous weak indicators proved to be efficient in false positives reduction while recognizing all mining entities in the dataset. The DeCrypto system implementation was published as an open-source project [30] and it is already deployed on real ISP monitoring infrastructure and currently protects half a million users against abusive mining.

Acknowledgments. This research was funded by the Ministry of Interior of the Czech Republic, grant No. VJ02010024: Flow-Based Encrypted Traffic Analysis and also by the Grant Agency of the CTU in Prague, grant No. SGS20/210/OHK3/3T/18 funded by the MEYS of the Czech Republic.

A   Appendix

A.1   Detailed Results of Weak-Indication Classifiers

Table 8 and Table 9 show detailed results of the DeCrypto system together with true positives (TP), false positives (FP), false negatives (FN) and true negatives (TN).

Table 8. Results of all paths of the DeCrypto system on the Design dataset with the DST threshold set to 0.03 and ML threshold set to 0.99

Path	TP	FP	FN	TN	Accuracy	Precision
Stratum Path	567,138	0	0	0	100.0000%	100.0000%
DST Path	4105	0	256	442,246	99.9427%	100.0000%
ML Path	53,342	18	70,655	887,143	93.0107%	99.9663%

Table 9. Results of all paths of the DeCrypto system on the Evaluation dataset with the DST threshold set to 0.03 and ML threshold set to 0.99

Path	TP	FP	FN	TN	Accuracy	Precision
Stratum Path	313,670	0	0	0	100.0000%	100.0000%
DST Path	2882	2	280	262,438	99.8938%	99.9307%
ML Path	8562	16	67,183	420,543	86.4601%	99.8135%

References

1. Baciu, P.: Czech prime minister accuses pirate party of mining bitcoin (2018). https://bitcoinist.com/prime-minister-accuses-czech-pirate-party-of-mining-bitcoin-so-what/
2. Bedford Taylor, M.: The evolution of bitcoin hardware. Computer **50**(9), 58–66 (2017). https://doi.org/10.1109/MC.2017.3571056
3. Breiman, L.: Random forests. Mach. Learn. **45**(1), 5–32 (2001)
4. BTC.com: Professional data service for global blockchain enthusiasts. https://explorer.btc.com/

5. Bushra Alahmadi, L.A., Martinovic, I.: 99% false positives: a qualitative study of SOC analysts' perspectives on security alarms. In: 31st USENIX Security Symposium (USENIX Security 2022). USENIX Association, Boston (2022). https://www.usenix.org/conference/usenixsecurity22/presentation/alahmadi

6. Cappé, O., Moulines, E., Pesquet, J.C., Petropulu, A.P., Yang, X.: Long-range dependence and heavy-tail modeling for teletraffic data. IEEE Signal Process. Mag. **19**(3), 14–27 (2002)

7. Cejka, T., et al.: NEMEA: a framework for network traffic analysis. In: 12th International Conference on Network and Service Management (CNSM) (2016)

8. Cimpanu, C.: Malvertising campaign mines cryptocurrency right in your browser (2017). https://www.malwarebytes.com/malvertising

9. CoinMarketCap: Coinmarketcap. https://coinmarketcap.com. Accessed 8 Aug 2022

10. Dempster, A.P.: Upper and lower probabilities induced by a multivalued mapping. Ann. Math. Stat. **38**(2), 325–339 (1967). https://doi.org/10.1214/aoms/1177698950

11. FBI: FBI: internet crime report 2021. https://www.ic3.gov/Media/PDF/AnnualReport/2021_IC3Report.pdf

12. Hayward, A.: What are privacy coins? Monero, zcash, and dash explained (2021). https://decrypt.co/resources/what-are-privacy-coins-monero-zcash-and-dash-explained

13. Hill, K.: Government researcher misused supercomputers to mine a surprisingly small amount of bitcoin (2014). https://www.forbes.com/sites/kashmirhill/2014/06/06/government-researcher-misused-supercomputers-to-mine-bitcoin/

14. Hofstede, R., et al.: Flow monitoring explained: from packet capture to data analysis with NetFlow and IPFIX. IEEE Commun. Surv. Tutor. **16**(4), 2037–2064 (2014). https://doi.org/10.1109/COMST.2014.2321898

15. Hruska, J.: Browser-based mining malware found on pirate bay, other sites (2017). https://www.extremetech.com/internet/255971-browser-based-cryptocurrency-malware-appears-online-pirate-bay

16. Hynek, K., Cejka, T., Žádník, M., Kubátová, H.: Evaluating bad hosts using adaptive blacklist filter. In: 2020 9th Mediterranean Conference on Embedded Computing (MECO), pp. 1–5 (2020). https://doi.org/10.1109/MECO49872.2020.9134244

17. Jamieson, S.: The ethics and legality of port scanning. Technical report, SANS Institute (2001). https://www.sans.org/white-papers/71/

18. JustFirewalls: 2022 cyber security trends: Top 5 threats to watch out for this year. https://www.justfirewalls.com/2022-cyber-security-trends-top-5-threats-to-watch-out-for-this-year

19. Kharraz, A., et al.: Outguard: detecting in-browser covert cryptocurrency mining in the wild. In: The World Wide Web Conference, WWW 2019, pp. 840–852. Association for Computing Machinery, New York (2019). https://doi.org/10.1145/3308558.3313665

20. Khatri, Y.: Crypto mining malware has netted nearly 5% of all monero, says research (2019). https://www.coindesk.com/markets/2019/01/10/crypto-mining-malware-has-netted-nearly-5-of-all-monero-says-research/

21. Liu, J., Zhao, Z., Cui, X., Wang, Z., Liu, Q.: A novel approach for detecting browser-based silent miner. In: 2018 IEEE Third International Conference on Data Science in Cyberspace (DSC), pp. 490–497 (2018). https://doi.org/10.1109/DSC.2018.00079

22. McAffee: Mcafee labs threats report (2018). https://www.mcafee.com/enterprise/en-us/assets/reports/rp-quarterly-threats-dec-2018.pdf

23. McMillan, R.: Harvard researcher was caught mining the bitcoin derivative, dogecoin (2014). https://www.wired.com/2014/02/harvard-dogecoin/
24. MiningPoolStats: Miningpoolstats. https://miningpoolstats.stream/monero
25. Muñoz, J.Z.I., Suárez-Varela, J., Barlet-Ros, P.: Detecting cryptocurrency miners with NetFlow/IPFIX network measurements. In: 2019 IEEE International Symposium on Measurements Networking (M N), pp. 1–6 (2019). https://doi.org/10.1109/IWMN.2019.8804995
26. Nakamoto, S.: A peer-to-peer electronic cash system. Bitcoin.org **4**, 2 (2008). https://bitcoin.org/bitcoin.pdf
27. Palatinus, M.: Stratum mining protocol. Slushpool.com (2019). https://slushpool.com/help/manual/stratum-protocol
28. Pastrana, S., Suarez-Tangil, G.: A first look at the crypto-mining malware ecosystem: a decade of unrestricted wealth. In: Proceedings of the Internet Measurement Conference, IMC 2019, pp. 73–86. Association for Computing Machinery, New York (2019). https://doi.org/10.1145/3355369.3355576
29. Pektaş, A., Acarman, T.: Deep learning to detect botnet via network flow summaries. Neural Comput. Appl. **31**(11), 8021–8033 (2018). https://doi.org/10.1007/s00521-018-3595-x
30. Plný, R., Hynek, K., Čejka, T.: Decrypto. https://github.com/plnyrich/DeCrypto
31. Plný, R., Hynek, K., Čejka, T.: Rules generator. https://github.com/plnyrich/RulesGenerator
32. Plný, R., Hynek, K., Čejka, T.: Datasets of cryptomining communication (2022). https://doi.org/10.5281/zenodo.7189292
33. PurpleSec LLC: Cyber Security Statistics: The Ultimate List of Stats, Data, & Trends for 2022 (2022). https://purplesec.us/resources/cyber-security-statistics/#Start
34. Quinlan, J.R.: C4.5: Programs for Machine Learning. Morgan Kaufmann Publishers Inc., San Francisco (1993)
35. Recabarren, R., Carbunar, B.: Hardening stratum, the bitcoin pool mining protocol. Proc. Priv. Enhanc. Technol. **3**, 54–71 (2017)
36. Ren, L., Ward, P.A.: Pooled mining is driving blockchains toward centralized systems. In: 2019 38th International Symposium on Reliable Distributed Systems Workshops (SRDSW), pp. 43–48 (2019). https://doi.org/10.1109/SRDSW49218.2019.00015
37. Schapire, R.E.: Explaining AdaBoost. In: Schölkopf, B., Luo, Z., Vovk, V. (eds.) Empirical Inference, pp. 37–52. Springer, Heidelberg (2013). https://doi.org/10.1007/978-3-642-41136-6_5
38. Scornet, E.: Trees, forests, and impurity-based variable importance. arXiv preprint arXiv:2001.04295 (2020)
39. Shafer, G.: A Mathematical Theory of Evidence. Princeton University Press, Princeton (2021). https://doi.org/10.1515/9780691214696
40. Swedan, A., Khuffash, A.N., Othman, O., Awad, A.: Detection and prevention of malicious cryptocurrency mining on internet-connected devices. In: Proceedings of the 2nd International Conference on Future Networks and Distributed Systems, ICFNDS 2018. Association for Computing Machinery, New York (2018). https://doi.org/10.1145/3231053.3231076
41. Tsangaratos, P., Ilia, I.: Comparison of a logistic regression and naïve bayes classifier in landslide susceptibility assessments: the influence of models complexity and training dataset size. CATENA **145**, 164–179 (2016). https://doi.org/10.1016/j.catena.2016.06.004

42. Veselý, V., Žádník, M.: How to detect cryptocurrency miners? By traffic forensics! Digit. Invest. **31**, 100884 (2019). https://doi.org/10.1016/j.diin.2019.08.002
43. Vuijsje, E.: Cryptocurrency malvertising campaign hijacks users' browsers. https://www.geoedge.com/cryptocurrency-malvertising-campaign-hijacks-users-browsers/
44. Watorek, M., Drożdż, S., Kwapinń, J., Minati, L., Oswiecimka, P., Stanuszek, M.: Multiscale characteristics of the emerging global cryptocurrency market. Phys. Rep. **901**, 1–82 (2021). https://doi.org/10.1016/j.physrep.2020.10.005. Multiscale characteristics of the emerging global cryptocurrency market
45. Zvik, E.W.: The crypto mining threat: the security risk posed by bitcoin and what you can do about it (2018). https://www.catonetworks.com/blog/the-crypto-mining-threat/

Detection of Voice Conversion Spoofing Attacks Using Voiced Speech

Arun Sankar Muttathu Sivasankara Pillai[1](✉), Phillip L. De Leon[2], and Utz Roedig[1]

[1] School of Computer Science and Information Technology, Cork, Ireland
{asankar,u.roedig}@ucc.ie
[2] Klipsch School of Electrical and Computer Engineering, New Mexico State University, Las Cruces, NM, USA
pdeleon@nmsu.edu

Abstract. Speech consists of voiced and unvoiced segments that differ in their production process and exhibit different characteristics. In this paper, we investigate the spectral differences between bonafide and spoofed speech for voiced and unvoiced speech segments. We observe that the largest spectral differences lie in the 0–4 kHz band of voiced speech. Based on this observation, we propose a low-complexity, pre-processing stage which subsamples voiced frames prior to spoofing detection. The proposed pre-processing stage is applied to two systems, LFCC+GMM and IA/IF+KNN that differ entirely on the features and classifier used for spoofing detection. Our results show improvement with both systems in detection of the ASVspoof 2019 A17 voice conversion attack, which is recognized to have one of the highest spoofing capabilities. We also show improvements in the A18 and A19 voice conversion attacks for the IA/IF+KNN system. The resulting A17 EERs are lower than all reported systems where the A17 spoofing attack is the worst attack except the Capsule Network. Finally, we note that the proposed pre-processing stage reduces the speech date by more than 4× due to subsampling and using only voiced frames but at the same time maintaining similar pooled EER as that for the baseline systems, which may be advantageous for resource constrained spoofing detectors.

Keywords: Spoofing detection · Speech processing · Computer security · Voice bio-metric

1 Introduction

Traditionally, usernames and passwords are used for authentication. However, handling usernames and passwords securely has been proven to be difficult and compromised passwords have lead to many security breaches. The burden of using passwords can be eliminated by using biometric authentication. For example, finger prints, retina scans or voice prints can be used as input for authentication.

Automatic Speaker Verification (ASV) systems are popular as a low-cost and flexible technology for biometric authentication. However, even these systems

© The Author(s), under exclusive license to Springer Nature Switzerland AG 2022
H. P. Reiser and M. Kyas (Eds.): NordSec 2022, LNCS 13700, pp. 159–175, 2022.
https://doi.org/10.1007/978-3-031-22295-5_9

are known to be vulnerable to spoofing which can be classified into attacks via impersonation, replay, speech synthesis, twins, and voice conversion [1]. Among these, replay, speech synthesis, and voice conversion remain threats due to the availability of successful open-source tools for generating high-quality spoofed speech which can be used in a targeted attack [2].

Countermeasures to detect spoofed speech and thus prevent an attack, are in active development and the ASVspoof challenge, initiated in 2015, has assisted with advancing the research through organized trials and evaluations [3]. Most developed methods perform feature extraction in the frequency domain using filter banks to obtain sub-band spectral features. The features are analysed using sophisticated classifiers such as Gaussian Mixture Model (GMM) or Deep Neural Networks (DNN), and the best performing systems use a number of classifiers in combination, i.e. ensemble classifier. There have been significant advances in spoofing detection to the point where top-performing systems evaluated using the ASVspoof 2019 dataset report pooled min-tandem-Decision Cost Function (t-DCF) below 0.1 and Equal Error Rate (EER) below 3.5% (see [4]). Recently 12 state-of-the-art detection systems have been reported in [5] and evaluated using the ASVspoof 2019 dataset. It was found that the most successful spoofing attacks are A08 (most successful for 2 systems), A17 (most successful for 9 systems), and A18 (most successful for 1 system). Attack A08 is speech synthesis and attacks A17 and A18 are voice conversion. However, state-of-the-art systems' performance against the worst ASVspoof 2019 attacks have an average EER of 12.94% [5]. Of the 9 systems reporting A17 as the worst attack, the average EER is 14.2% with Capsule Network reporting 3.76% EER [5]. Thus for some specific attacks, detection accuracy is still lacking.

The speech signal is composed of voiced and unvoiced segments that differ by the production mechanism and characteristic features [6]. These segments are separately used for many speech processing applications due to the difference in the type and depth of information contained in these segments. For example, the speaker-specific unique information can be found much in voiced segments due to vocal cord vibration and so on [7]. In general, spoofing attacks are applied to the entire speech signal without considering separately voiced and unvoiced segments and hence the location and level of artefacts vary with these segments.

In this paper, we investigate the spectral differences between human (bonafide) and spoofed speech for voiced and unvoiced speech segments. When comparing spectra of bonafide and spoofed speech, we find the largest differences lie in voiced segments in the 0–4 kHz band. With this observation, we propose a low-complexity pre-processing stage which *subsamples voiced frames* prior to spoofing detection. We evaluate this novel pre-processing stage using different detection systems. The core contribution of this work is the insight that voiced and unvoiced speech segments contribute very differently to the task of spoofing detection.

Our specific contributions are as follows:

– We show that voiced speech segments are more useful for spoofing detection than unvoiced speech segments. We also describe the distribution of information for spoofing detection over frequency bands in voiced and unvoiced speech segments.

- We propose a low-complexity pre-processing stage which subsamples only voiced frames prior to spoofing detection. This pre-processing stage reduces the amount of necessary data by a factor of 4 while maintaining overall detection accuracy (similar pooled EER).
- We show that this pre-processing stage can be combined with different existing spoofing detection systems.
- We show an improvement in the detection accuracy for the challenging ASVspoof 2019 A17 voice conversion attack using two different detection systems together with the novel pre-processing stage. We also show improvements for the A18 and A19 voice conversion attacks in some settings.

This paper is organized as follows. The details of the ASVspoof database used for conducting experiments are given in Sect. 2. In Sect. 3, we provide a brief review of speech production focusing on voiced speech and place of articulation as motivation for the investigation of using voiced speech for spoofing detection. In Sect. 4, we present our observations on the spectral differences between bonafide and spoofed speech for voiced and unvoiced segments. In Sect. 5, we propose a pre-processing stage which takes as input the speech signal and passes to the countermeasure a signal containing only voiced segments and in Sect. 6 we provide detection results for two different countermeasures with and without the pre-processing stage. Section 7 summarizes the works done in spoofing detection and how our work differs from others. In Sect. 8, we discuss the results paying close attention to the A17 attack which is considered the most difficult attack to detect. Finally, in Sect. 9, we conclude the paper.

2   ASVspoof Challenge Dataset and Evaluation Metric

The ASVspoof challenge series was initiated in 2015 with the motivation of advancing spoofing detection and countermeasures. The first challenge was focused on voice conversion and synthetic speech attacks while the second spoof challenge organized in 2017 concentrated on replay attacks as they are much easier to generate without any technical expertise. The third spoof challenge took place in 2019 and considered speech synthesis, voice conversion, and replay attacks. The fourth challenge organized recently in 2021 focused on discriminating between genuine and spoofed or deepfake speech using ASVspoof 2019 database.

The ASVspoof 2019 challenge database consists of a logical access (LA) partition containing voice conversion and speech synthesis examples in addition to the physical access (PA) partition which contains replay examples. Each partition contains training, development and evaluation subsets. The training and development subsets are used for conducting experiments related to the development of the detection model while the evaluation set is utilized for measuring detection performance of the developed model. The training and development subsets of LA contain 6 spoofing attacks which are considered as known attacks and used for the construction of the detection model. The evaluation subset of LA has 11 unknown attacks to determine the efficiency of the developed model on attacks that are unknown to the system or in other words on attacks that are not used for training the model. In addition, each subset also contains examples of human-produced speech. All speech examples, including the source utterances for creating the spoofed speech, are taken from the VCTK corpus [8]. The utterances consist of 107 speakers (46 male and 61 female) that are partitioned into three disjoint subsets. Details of the database are summarized in Table 1.

Table 1. Description of the logical access partition of the ASVspoof 2019 challenge database.

Database attributes	Training set	Development set	Evaluation set
Spoofing attackalgorithms	A01-A06	A01-A06	A07-A19
Spoofing methods	TTS (4) VC (2)	TTS (4) VC (2)	TTS (6) VC (2) Hybrid (3)
Known attacks	6	6	2 (A16 = A04, A19 = A06)
Unknown attacks	0	0	11
No. of genuine samples	2580	2548	7355
No. of spoofed samples	22800 (3800 × 6)	22296 (3716 × 6)	63882 (10647 × 6)
No. of male speakers	8	4	21
No. of female speakers	12	6	27

The training and development data sets are built using the same set of spoofing attacks (A01–A06). Spoofing attacks A01 to A04 are based on Text-to-Speech (TTS) methods while attacks A05 and A06 use voice conversion (VC) methods. The attacks A01-A03 are neural network based TTS systems and attack A04 does TTS using waveform concatenation method. The evaluation data set consists of 13 spoofing attacks (A07-A19) out of which 2 attacks (A16 and A19) are considered as known attacks and the remaining 11 spoofing attacks are unknown attacks. Attacks A16 and A19 use the same spoofing techniques as attacks A04 and A06 respectively. The unknown attacks consist of six TTS based methods (A07-A12), two VC methods (A17 and A18) and three hybrid models (A13-A15). The hybrid models use a combination of VC and TTS for the generation of spoofed speech.

The following metrics are used for quantifying the detection performance of spoofing detector.

- *Equal Error Rate (EER)* - An ideal spoofing detector should flag spoofed speech and pass genuine speech but in reality there is always some error which is quantified using False Acceptance Rate (FAR) and False Rejection Rate (FRR).

  False Acceptance Rate: It is the ratio of spoofed speech samples wrongly classified as genuine speech and can be written as

$$\text{FAR} = \frac{\text{FP}}{\text{FP+TN}} \tag{1}$$

where False Positive (FP) is the number of spoofed speech samples misclassified as genuine speech and True Negative (TN) denotes the number of correctly identified spoofed speech samples.

False Rejection Rate It is defined as the ratio of genuine samples misclassified as spoofed speech. FRR can be expressed as

$$\text{FRR} = \frac{\text{FN}}{\text{FN+TP}} \tag{2}$$

where True Positive (TP) is the correctly identified bonafide speech samples and False Negative (FN) is the number of genuine speech samples misclassified as spoofed speech.

It is desirable to minimize both FAR and FRR for improving the efficiency of detection systems. But adjusting the detection threshold to reduce either of the errors harm the other. The detection threshold plot has a point where both the error rates are equal and that common value is called the EER which is considered a metric in ASV spoof 2019 challenge.

- *tandem-Decision Cost Function* The EER metric is sufficient to quantify the performance of a stand alone spoofing detector. But when this detector is integrated into an ASV system, the impact of countermeasure on verification performance cannot be evaluated by EER metric. In such scenario, the t-DCF metric [9] measures the impact of spoofing and countermeasure on the reliability of ASV system by combining the verification and spoofing errors. The minimum normalized tandem-Decision Cost Function is expressed in the form

$$\text{t-DCF}_{\min} = \min_{Thr} \left\{ \beta P_{cm\,MISS}(Thr) + P_{cm\,FAR}(Thr) \right\}. \tag{3}$$

The parameter β depends on the spoofing prior and cost parameters and on miss and false alarm rates of speaker verification. $P_{cm\,MISS}(Thr)$ and $P_{cm\,FAR}(Thr)$ are the false alarm and miss rates of the counter measure at threshold Thr.

For additional information, please see [10].

3   Brief Review of Speech Production

Speech is an acoustic wave produced by the air expelled from lungs which serves as the excitation for the acoustic filter consisting of vocal and nasal tracts [6].

The frequency spectrum of the excitation is shaped by the frequency selectivity of these tracts. The vocal tract contains different sections called articulators that play a crucial role in the generation of different sounds by shaping the airflow. During speech production, the airflow is modulated according to the sound to be generated by the movement of active articulators toward the passive articulators which remain stationary throughout the process [11]. This relative placement of articulators will create different types of constrictions for generating various voiced (vowels) and unvoiced (plosives, consonants) sounds. The features of vocal and nasal tracts change continuously with time and make speech radiated from lips non-stationary.

The basic difference between voiced and unvoiced sound is due to the behavior of vocal cords during sound production [6]. During vocal cord vibration, air flowing from the lungs will be interrupted periodically by the vocal cords providing a series of pulses for excitation of the vocal tract which produces voiced speech signals. Voiced speech is dominated by periodic pulses and a set of formants which are peaks in the frequency spectrum due to the acoustic resonance of vocal tract. These spectral peaks are in the low-frequency region and hence the energy of voiced speech mostly lies below 4 kHz. When vocal cords remain stationary, the vocal tract will have a random excitation and constriction by different articulators will generate unvoiced sound. These unvoiced sounds are non-periodic, sounds random and their energy is mainly contained in region from 2–8 kHz [12]. The speech production mechanism is thus modelled as a source excitation passing through a time-varying filter that corresponds to the dynamic characteristics of vocal tract. The excitation is random noise for unvoiced sounds and a series of pulses for voiced sounds which represents the fundamental frequency in speech.

Spoofed speech is generated using TTS and VC techniques in order to change the voice identity of speech to that of a target speaker to be perceived true by humans and/or speaker verification systems. In ASVspoof 2019 challenge database, the spoofed speech is generated using four TTS (A01-A04) and two VC (A05-A06) spoofing attack algorithms for training and development sets and by using ten TTS (A07-A16) and three VC (A17-A19) spoofing attack algorithms for the evaluation set [13].

The spoofed speech generation using the TTS system converts the input text to speech that feels like to be spoken by the target speaker. This process involves conversion of text to linguistic features and then to acoustic features which are used to generate the waveform of desired speech. The VC techniques change the voice identity of speech without changing the linguistic content. When parallel training data (utterances with the same linguistic content for both source and target speakers) is available, the VC can be easily done using methods such as dynamic time wrapping and spectral mapping [14,15]. Due to the difficulty in obtaining parallel training data, many VC methods are developed using non-parallel training data. In all these methods, the input speech undergoes an intermediate transformation to remove the source speaker characteristics followed by the addition of target speaker characteristics and reconstruction of speech.

The various VC models include variational auto-encoder (A05 and A17), GMM-UBM with speech source filter model (A06), i-vector Probabilistic Linear Discriminant Analysis (PLDA) based transfer learning, and so on [13,16]. The spoofing attack A06 does VC for the generation of spoofed speech by mapping the source-filter characteristics of input speech on a frame-by-frame basis to that of the target speaker. The input audio signal is analyzed and the derived acoustic features (Mel frequency Cepstrum Coefficients (MFCC) and Linear Prediction Cepstrum Coefficients (LPCC)) are modified to match the filter characteristics with that of the target speaker and in order to produce the spoofed speech. The spoofing attack A18 uses a transfer learning method to predict the i-vectors of target speaker from the i-vectors of source speaker. The knowledge about predicted i-vectors are used to generate the MFCCs of target speaker and thereby for the production of spoofed speech. The attacks A05 and A17 use variational auto-encoder for mapping the spectral features of input audio from source to target speaker. The auto-encoder is trained to encode the incoming spectral feature vectors to speaker independent vectors and then to decode them with the characteristics for the target speaker. This is followed by a speech reconstruction process in which attacks A05 and A17 differ.

The spoofing attack A17 uses direct waveform modification method for the generation of target speech but the spoofing attack A06 uses WORLD vocoder. In direct waveform modification, spectral details are preserved that help in producing high-quality speech. The target speech waveform is generated in spoofing attack A17 by passing the $F0$ transferred residual signal through a synthesis filter designed for the target speaker using the converted spectral features. The $F0$ transferred residual signal is sensitive to the spectral estimation error due to the difficulty in modelling speaker characteristics which is a problem associated with conversion models based on non-parallel training data. The interaction of $F0$ transformed residual signal with inaccurately estimated spectrum will produce noise in the reconstructed speech. It is evident from the spectral plots of source speech and target speech obtained using waveform modification method given in [17] that spectral errors are prominent in the low-frequency region.

Motivated by the spectral estimation errors and the fact that speech (excluding silence) is dominated by voiced sounds that contain mainly low-frequency components, use of these voiced segments may provide better features for discriminating between genuine and spoofed speech generated using VC methods based on direct waveform modification.

4   Spectral Differences in Voiced/Unvoiced Segments from Human and Spoofed Speech

Initial work in detection of spoofed speech, extracted discriminating features from the entire speech signal and using pre-trained models, classified speech signals as genuine or spoofed [18,19]. Later work extracted features from specific components of the decomposed speech signal which contained more discriminating information than the signal as a whole, in order to improve detection accuracy. For example, spoofing detectors based on specific words [20], based on specific spectral bands [21,22], or based on specific modes in Empirical Mode Decomposition (EMD) have been investigated [23]. Speech signals are generally composed of voiced, unvoiced, and silence segments [11]. Typically, little if any discriminating features exist in silence segments and thus we focus on analyzing unique discriminating features within voiced and unvoiced segments. To the best of our knowledge spoofing detectors based on voiced or unvoiced segments have not been investigated.

In order to analyze spectral differences in voiced and unvoiced segments from genuine and spoofed speech, we choose from ASVspoof 2019 LA training sets A01-A04 (TTS), two male speakers (LA92 and LA95) and two female speakers (LA79 and LA80). Next, we identified identical sentences from genuine and spoofed speech for each speaker. Next, for each identical sentence pair, we segmented phonemes according to voiced or unvoiced. Finally for each voiced/unvoiced segment we computed the difference in magnitude spectra between the genuine and spoofed segment. For training sets A05-A06 (VC), identical sentences did not exist so we identified identical words from genuine and spoofed speech for each speaker and proceeded as above with phoneme segmentation and computation of the difference spectra. The difference spectra were then averaged and are shown in Figs. 1 and 2.

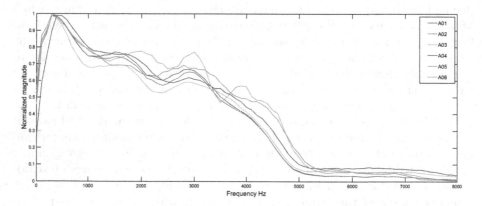

Fig. 1. Average difference (between bonafide and spoofed speech) magnitude spectra for voiced segments from ASVspoof 2019 attacks A01 to A06. We observe a large, well-defined spectral difference in the 0–4 kHz frequency band.

When comparing spectra of human (bonafide) and spoofed speech, we find the largest differences lie in voiced segments over the 0–4 kHz band; smaller differences exist in unvoiced segments over the 4–8 kHz band. From this observation, we find that we are able to accurately classify bonafide versus spoofed speech using only voiced speech segments from the 0–4 kHz band. When viewed as a general pre-processing stage, we can show this technique, i.e. using only voiced segments from 0–4 kHz, can be applied to various detectors including

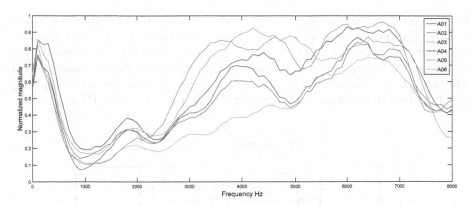

Fig. 2. Average difference (between bonafide and spoofed speech) magnitude spectra for unvoiced segments from ASVspoof 2019 attacks A01 to A06. Unlike voiced speech (Fig. 1), we observe an uneven spectral difference in the unvoiced speech, however, most of the spectral difference lies in 4–8 kHz frequency band.

Linear frequency Cepstrum Coefficients (LFCC)+GMM while maintaining similar accuracy. By using only voiced segments and downsampling the signal to 4 kHz bandwidth, the data rate and hence computation can be reduced.

From Fig. 1 we observe differences in spectra for voiced segments in the 0–4 kHz band where the largest differences are in the 0–1 kHz band. A simple linear interpolation over 300–4000 Hz shows an approximate difference rate of −17 dB/kHz. On the other hand, in the band from 4–8 kHz the spectral difference is minor. This suggests that for voiced segments, most of the spectral discriminating features lie in 0–4 kHz band. From Fig. 2 we also observe differences in spectra for unvoiced segments but in the 4–8 kHz band. Furthermore, these differences are not as great as in the voiced segments. Given these observations, in the next section we propose a pre-processing stage for which features are extracted from voiced segments only.

5   Subsampling and Voiced Segmentation as a Pre-processing Stage

From our observations of the spectral differences in voiced segments from bonafide and spoofed speech, we propose a pre-processing stage which takes as input the speech signal and passes to the countermeasure a signal containing only voiced segments. Furthermore, because most of the spectral difference in the voiced segment lies in the 0–4 kHz band, we may subsample the signal by 2×. In the implementation, shown in Fig. 3, we first use 20 ms speech frames and a Zero Crossing Rate (ZCR) detector to label the frames as voiced or unvoiced.

We subsample the speech signal by 2× and retain only the corresponding voiced frames. The proposed pre-processing stage lowers the date rate approximately by a factor of 4, i.e. removal of silence and unvoiced segments shortens the signal by approximately half and downsampling reduces the data by another half. This reduction in data may be important in applications where low-complexity spoofing detection is important, e.g. Personal Voice Assistants (PVAs).

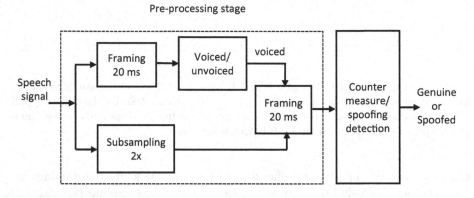

Fig. 3. Block diagram of the proposed pre-processing stage.

6   Spoofing Detection Results Using Proposed Pre-processing Stage

In order to test the proposed pre-processing stage, we consider two detectors which use different features and have results which are among the top performing systems, excluding ensemble systems, using the ASVspoof 2019 evaluation set. We exclude neural networks and deep learning systems in order to focus on the generalization of this approach as a pre-processing stage to conventional systems. The first system uses LFCC features with a ML detector based on a GMM [22] and the second system uses statistics of the Instantaneous Amplitude (IA)/Instantaneous Frequency (IF) from Intrinsic Mode Functions (IMFs) decomposed using EMD [24].

6.1   Brief Overview of Anti-spoofing Systems Used in This Work

The first system under consideration is the LFCC-based system proposed in [22]. The LFCC features are extracted from the entire speech signal spectrum using a filter order of 70. The training and development sets of ASVspoof 2019 challenge are used to generate the LFCC features and to train the GMM using 1024 components. Classification uses ML estimation. For additional details on this system, we refer the reader to [22]. As software for this system was unavailable, we implemented our own version. Results of this system for ASVspoof 2019 evaluation set A07-A19 and pooled baseline results are given in the second row of Table 2. Our implementation has a slightly higher EER (3.85%) than the published result (3.51%) which may be due to the difference in the environment.

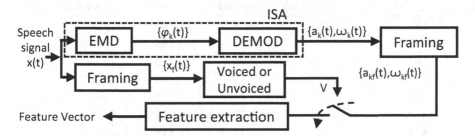

Fig. 4. Block diagram of the EMD based feature vector creation for spoofing detection.

The second system under consideration is based on statistics of the IAs and IFs from IMFs resulting from EMD as proposed in [24]. In this system shown in Fig. 4, EMD is used to decompose the entire speech signal into IMFs. IMFs are each demodulated in order to obtain the IAs and IFs. For each of the first 10 IMFs, we compute the statistics $\{\mu, \sigma^2, \gamma, \kappa\}$ of the IA and IF resulting in an 80×1 feature vector. We use a k-Nearest Neighbours (KNN) classifier to determine whether the speech signal is bonafide or spoofed. For additional details on this system, we refer the reader to [24]. Results of this system for ASVspoof 2019 evalaution set A07-A19 and pooled baseline results are given in the third column of Table 2.

6.2 Results Using Proposed Pre-processing Stage

The proposed pre-processing stage can be viewed as a front-end to the anti-spoofing countermeasure. This front-end subsamples the speech signal by $2\times$ and retains only those frames which have been classified as voiced. Since voiced frames are approximately half of the speech signal (unvoiced and silence frames are the other half), this front-end reduces the data presented to the counter-measure by approximately $4\times$ and hence lowers computation. The LFCC-GMM detector with the proposed pre-processing stage gives a pooled EER and min-t-DCF of respectively 3.99% and 0.10% which is slightly worse compared to the baseline system's EER and roughly the same for the min-t-DCF. While comparing the performance for each individual attack (A7-A19), the proposed methods improves the EER for 3 attacks (A12, A15, and A17); gives worse EER for 5 attacks (A10, A13, A14, A18, and A19); and nearly the same (within 0.05%) EER for 5 attacks (A7, A8, A9, A11 and A16) in comparison with the baseline

Table 2. The spoofing detection error metrics (%) for LFCC+GMM and IA/IF-KNN systems using only voiced segments or the entire speech signal (baseline). Error rates in red denote worse performance when using voiced segments, while those in blue denote better performance when using voiced segments.

Spoofing attack algorithms	Spoofing detectors			
	LFCC-GMM (Baseline)	LFCC-GMM (voiced)	IAIF-KNN (baseline)	IAIF-KNN (voiced)
A07	0.02	0.02	2.09	3.50
A08	0.00	0.02	2.09	3.50
A09	0.00	0.02	2.09	3.50
A10	12.74	14.89	2.09	3.50
A11	0.00	0.02	2.09	3.50
A12	1.87	1.77	2.09	3.50
A13	2.87	3.44	2.09	3.50
A14	0.00	0.76	2.09	3.50
A15	2.01	1.63	2.09	3.50
A16	0.02	0.02	2.09	3.50
A17	7.47	3.97	11.90	4.56
A18	0.04	2.73	10.15	4.46
A19	0.08	0.14	6.63	3.50
Pooled tDCF	0.10	0.10	0.09	0.09
Pooled EER	3.85	3.99	3.51	3.50

detection system. This is highlighted in Table 2 using red color for worse EER, blue color for better EER, and black color for nearly the same EER.

The IA/IF-KNN detector with the proposed pre-processing stage gives a pooled EER and min-t-DCF of respectively 3.50% and 0.09% which is roughly the same compared to the baseline system's EER and min-t-DCF. While comparing the performance for each individual attacks (A7-A19), the proposed method improves the EER for 3 attacks (A17, A18, and A19) and gives worse EER for 10 attacks (A7-A16) in comparison with the baseline detection system.

For the IA/IF-KNN system, all VC attacks (A17-A19) have lower EER with the pre-processing stage than without it. For A17, A18, and A19 attacks, EER is reduced to 4.56%, 4.46%, 3.50% from 11.90%, 10.15%, 6.63% respectively.

Of particular interest is attack A17 where we note that "...this method was judged to have the highest spoofing capability in Voice Conversion Challenge 2018" [25]. More recently in [5] (see Table 3) A17 is generally considered the worst attack with the best performing system (Capsule Network) reporting an EER of 3.76% on this attack. For two systems in this work, EER is substantially improved to 3.97%, 4.56% from 7.47%, 11.90% respectively for the LFCC-GMM, IA/IF-KNN systems. With the exception of the Capsule Network (LFCC+Deep Learning) which reports EER of 3.76% for A17, the systems in this work with the pre-processing stage perform better than all the other systems, i.e. Res-TSSDnet (6.01%), ResNet18-LCML-FM (6.19%), LCNN-LSTM-sum (9.24%), ResNet18-OC-Softmax (9.22%), ResNet18-AM-Softmax (13.45%), ResNet18-GAT-T (28.02%), ResNet18-GAT-s (21.74%) and PC-DARTS (30.20%) where the A17 attack is the worst attack [5]. Performance of these systems for the A17 attack, may be improved with the proposed pre-processing stage.

7   Related Work

The various LA spoofing detection methods developed differ by the front-end features used to acquire discriminative information and by the back-end classifiers used for generating the decision score based on which genuine/spoof speech classification is performed. The promising features used for spoofing detection are especially but not limited to Constant-Q Cepstrum Coefficients (CQCC), LFCC, MFCC, Inverse Mel frequency Cepstrum Coefficients (IMFCC), and neural network embedding [19, 26–29]. In some mechanisms, the above-mentioned features are used in combination with source features such as epochs, peak to side lobe ratio to obtain the complementary information that aids detection [18, 30, 31]. The conventional feature extraction is carried out in the frequency domain using filter banks to obtain the short-term sub band spectral features. Some DNN based spoofing detection methods use these features to extract the network embeddings that serve as the feature for categorization [32].

Despite the information richness, the time domain is not considered generally for countermeasure except in a few cases. These include the processing of incoming speech signals in the time domain to separate out the temporal dependency feature which is used in conjunction with the source features for detection [33], temporal convolution for spoofing detection [30] and the usage of variation in temporal distribution of amplitudes for genuine and spoofed speech classification. The statistical features of IA and IF derived using EMD are calculated along time domain in [24] for spoofing detection. The raw speech waveform is used as input in some DNN based spoofing detectors and this has been made possible by using sinc filters [5, 34, 35].

Rather than extracting features from either time or frequency domain, some spoofing detection methods have used a combined approach [32, 35, 36]. Here the spectral and temporal domains are combined either at feature level by combining the features extracted form both domains or at score level by fusing the individual scores of classifiers by using the features extracted from each domain or by combining the intermediate feature representations of domains within the detector model itself.

In all these spoofing detection approaches, the speech signal is considered as whole without considering the level of impact on various types of segments within a speech signal. That is how our work differs from others where the voiced and unvoiced segments of a speech signal is separately analyzed to quantify the impact of spoofing on them and used that for spoofing detection.

8   Discussion

Further elaborating for the pooled EER and worst attack performance, we refer the reader to [5]. The IA/IF-KNN system with the pre-processing stage, has better pooled EER performance and better performance against the worst attack than systems ResNet18-GAT-T, ResNet18-GAT-s, PC-DARTS, and RawNet2. With the exception of Capsule Network, the other systems have better pooled EER but worse performance on the worst attack than the worst attack (A17) on IA/IF-KNN system with the pre-processing stage.

For the systems considered in this paper (LFCC+GMM and IA/IF+KNN), in general the pooled results (t-DCF and EER) are roughly the same when using the entire speech signal or with the pre-processing stage (voiced segments and downsampled) where we note that with the pre-processing stage we use approximately 1/4 of the signal samples. We measured execution time for our implmentations of the LFCC+GMM and IA/IF+KNN baseline systems and compared to the systems with the proposed pre-processing stage. We find that, including the overhead for the voiced/unvoiced detector, execution times are reduced by 1.86%, 1.95% for the LFCC+GMM, IA/IF+KNN respectively when using the pre-processing stage.

9   Conclusions

In this paper, we present our observations that the largest spectral differences between bonafide and spoofed speech, lie in the 0–4 kHz band of voiced speech segments. Based on this observation, we propose a pre-processing stage which subsamples voiced frames prior to spoofing detection. The application of the proposed method to the LFCC+GMM and IA/IF+KNN systems reduces the input speech data while maintaining similar pooled EER as that for the baseline systems. Furthermore, our results show substantial improvements in the detection accuracy by both the systems for A17 voice conversion attack and in the A18 and A19 voice conversion attacks for the IA/IF+KNN system. The ASVspoof 2019 A17 voice conversion attack is recognized to have one of the highest spoofing capabilities and has the worst EER for most of the top performing spoofing detectors. We note that the proposed pre-processing stage reduces the speech data by approximately a factor of 4, due to subsampling and using only voiced frames, which may be important for resource-constrained spoofing detectors. Although only two systems were considered, this pre-processing stage may be beneficial to other systems as well.

Acknowledgement. This publication has emanated from research supported in part by a Grant from Science Foundation Ireland under Grant number 19/FFP/6775 and 13/RC/2077_P2.

References

1. Wu, Z., Li, H.: On the study of replay and voice conversion attacks to text-dependent speaker verification. Multimed. Tools Appl. **75**(3), 5311–5327 (2015). https://doi.org/10.1007/s11042-015-3080-9
2. Lindberg, J., Blomberg, M.: Vulnerability in speaker verification-a study of technical impostor techniques. In: Sixth European Conference on Speech Communication and Technology, pp. 5–9 (1999)
3. Wu, Z., et al.: ASVspoof 2015: the first automatic speaker verification spoofing and countermeasures challenge. In: Sixteenth Annual Conference of the International Speech Communication Association (2015)
4. Todisco, M., et al.: ASVspoof 2019: future horizons in spoofed and fake audio detection. In: Proceedings of the Annual Conference of the International Speech Communication Association (INTERSPEECH), pp. 1008–1012 (2019)
5. Ge, W., Patino, J., Todisco, M., Evans, N.: Raw differentiable architecture search for speech deepfake and spoofing detection. In: Proceedings of the 2021 Edition of the Automatic Speaker Verification and Spoofing Countermeasures Challenge, pp. 22–28 (2021)
6. Quatieri, T.F.: Discrete-Time Speech Signal Processing: Principles and Practice. Pearson Education India, New Delhi (2006)
7. Lovekin, J.M., Yantorno, R.E., Krishnamachari, K.R., Benincasa, D.S., Wenndt, S.J.: Developing usable speech criteria for speaker identification technology. In: Proceedings of the 2001 IEEE International Conference on Acoustics, Speech, and Signal Processing (ICASSP), vol. 1, pp. 421–424 (2001)
8. Veaux, C., Yamagishi, J., MacDonald, K., Corpus, V.C.T.K.: English multi-speaker corpus for CSTR voice cloning toolkit. The Centre for Speech Technology Research (CSTR), University of Edinburgh (2017)
9. Kinnunen, T., et al.: t-DCF: a detection cost function for the tandem assessment of spoofing countermeasures and automatic speaker verification. arXiv preprint arXiv:1804.09618 (2018)
10. Consortium: ASVspoof 2019: automatic speaker verification spoofing and countermeasures challenge evaluation plan (2019). https://www.asvspoof.org/asvspoof2019/asvspoof2019_evaluation_plan.pdf
11. Rabiner, L., Schafer, R.: Digital Processing of Speech Signals. Prentice Hall, Englewood Cliffs (1978)
12. Monson, B.B., Hunter, E.J., Lotto, A.J., Story, B.H.: The perceptual significance of high-frequency energy in the human voice. Front. Psychol. **5**, 587 (2014). https://www.frontiersin.org/article/10.3389/fpsyg.2014.00587
13. Wang, X., et al.: ASVspoof 2019: a large-scale public database of synthesized, converted and replayed speech. Comput. Speech Lang. **64**, 101114 (2020). https://www.sciencedirect.com/science/article/pii/S0885230820300474
14. Sisman, B., Yamagishi, J., King, S., Li, H.: An overview of voice conversion and its challenges: from statistical modeling to deep learning. IEEE/ACM Trans. Audio Speech Lang. Process. **29**, 132–157 (2020). https://doi.org/10.1109/TASLP.2020.3038524
15. Kobayashi, K., Toda, T., Nakamura, S.: Intra-gender statistical singing voice conversion with direct waveform modification using log-spectral differential. Speech Commun. **99**, 211–220 (2018). https://www.sciencedirect.com/science/article/pii/S0167639317303710

16. Hsu, C.C., Hwang, H.T., Wu, Y.C., Tsao, Y., Wang, H.M.: Voice conversion from non-parallel corpora using variational auto-encoder. In: 2016 Asia-Pacific Signal and Information Processing Association Annual Summit and Conference (APSIPA), pp. 1–6. IEEE (2016)

17. Huang, W.C., et al.: Generalization of spectrum differential based direct waveform modification for voice conversion. arXiv preprint arXiv:1907.11898 (2019)

18. Xiao, X., Tian, X., Du, S., Xu, H., Chng, E., Li, H.: Spoofing speech detection using high dimensional magnitude and phase features: the NTU approach for ASVspoof 2015 challenge. In: Proceedings of the Annual Conference of the International Speech Communication Association (INTERSPEECH), pp. 2052–2056 (2015)

19. Todisco, M., et al.: Integrated presentation attack detection and automatic speaker verification: common features and Gaussian back-end fusion. In: Proceedings of the Annual Conference of the International Speech Communication Association (INTERSPEECH), pp. 77–81 (2018)

20. De Leon, P.L., Stewart, B.: Synthetic speech detection based on selectedword discriminators. In: 2013 IEEE International Conference on Acoustics, Speech and Signal Processing, pp. 3004–3008. IEEE (2013)

21. Mankad, S.H., Garg, S.: On the performance of empirical mode decomposition-based replay spoofing detection in speaker verification systems. Prog. Artif. Intell. **9**(4), 325–339 (2020). https://doi.org/10.1007/s13748-020-00216-0

22. Tak, H., Patino, J., Nautsch, A., Evans, N., Todisco, M.: Spoofing attack detection using the non-linear fusion of sub-band classifiers. In: Proceedings of the Annual Conference of the International Speech Communication Association (INTER-SPEECH), p. 1844 (2020)

23. Tapkir, P., Patil, H.A.: Novel empirical mode decomposition cepstral features for replay spoof detection. In: Proceedings of the Annual Conference of the International Speech Communication Association (INTERSPEECH), pp. 721–725 (2018)

24. Sankar, M.A., De Leon, P.L., Sandoval, S., Roedig, U.: Low-complexity speech spoofing detection using instantaneous spectral features. In: 2022 29th International Conference on Systems, Signals and Image Processing (IWSSIP), pp. 1–4. IEEE (2022). https://hdl.handle.net/10468/13215

25. Kinnunen, T., et al.: A spoofing benchmark for the 2018 voice conversion challenge: leveraging from spoofing countermeasures for speech artifact assessment. Proc. Odyssey **2018**(06), 187–194 (2018)

26. Yu, H., Tan, Z.-H., Ma, Z., Martin, R., Guo, J.: Spoofing detection in automatic speaker verification systems using DNN classifiers and dynamic acoustic features. IEEE Trans. Neural. Netw. Learn. Syst. **29**(10), 4633–4644 (2018)

27. Sahidullah, M., et al.: Integrated spoofing countermeasures and automatic speaker verification: an evaluation on ASVspoof 2015. In: Proceedings of the Annual Conference of the International Speech Communication Association (INTERSPEECH) (2016)

28. Lavrentyeva, G., et al.: STC antispoofing systems for the ASVspoof2019 challenge. In: Proceedings of the Annual Conference of the International Speech Communication Association (INTERSPEECH), pp. 1033–1037 (2019)

29. Chetttri, B., et al.: Ensemble models for spoofing detection in automatic speaker verification. In: Proceedings of the Annual Conference of the International Speech Communication Association (INTERSPEECH), pp. 1018–1022 (2019)

30. Tian, X., Xiao, X., Chng, E.S., Li, H.: Spoofing speech detection using temporal convolutional neural network. In: Asia-Pacific Signal and Information Processing Association Annual Summit and Conference (APSIPA), pp. 1–6 (2016)

31. Jelil, S., Das, R.K., Prasanna, S.M., Sinha, R.: Spoof detection using source, instantaneous frequency and cepstral features. In: Proceedings of the Annual Conference of the International Speech Communication Association (INTERSPEECH), pp. 22–26 (2017)

32. Tak, H., Jung, J.W., Patino, J., Todisco, M., Evans, N.: Graph attention networks for anti-spoofing. In: Proceedings of the Annual Conference of the International Speech Communication Association (INTERSPEECH) (2021)

33. Witkowski, M., Kacprzak, S., Żelasko, P., Kowalczyk, K., Gałka, J.: Audio replay attack detection using high-frequency features. In: Proceedings of the Annual Conference of the International Speech Communication Association (INTERSPEECH), pp. 27–31 (2017)

34. Tak, H., Patino, J., Todisco, M., Nautsch, A., Evans, N., Larcher, A.: End-to-end anti-spoofing with RawNet2. In: Proceedings of the IEEE International Conference on Acoustics, Speech and Signal Processing (ICASSP), pp. 6369–6373 (2021)

35. Tak, H., Jung, J.W., Patino, J., Kamble, M., Todisco, M., Evans, N.: End-to-end spectro-temporal graph attention networks for speaker verification anti-spoofing and speech deepfake detection. In: Automatic Speaker Verification and Spoofing Countermeasures Challenge, pp. 1–8 (2021)

36. Jung, J.W., et al.: AASIST: audio anti-spoofing using integrated spectro-temporal graph attention networks. In: Proceedings of the IEEE International Conference on Acoustics, Speech and Signal Processing (ICASSP), pp. 6367–6371 (2022)

A Wide Network Scanning for Discovery of UDP-Based Reflectors in the Nordic Countries

Alexander Bjerre, Andreas Philip Westh, Emil Villefrance,
A S M Farhan Al Haque, Jonas Bukrinski Andersen, Lucas K. Helgogaard,
and Marios Anagnostopoulos$^{(\boxtimes)}$

Department of Electronic Systems, Aalborg University, Copenhagen, Denmark
mariosa@es.aau.dk

Abstract. Distributed Reflective Denial of Service (DRDoS) attacks exploit Internet facing devices with the purpose to involve them in DoS incidents. In turn, these devices unwittingly amplify and redirect the attack traffic towards the victim. As a result, this traffic causes the extortion of the target's network bandwidth and computation resources. The current work evaluates the amplification and reflective potentials of four UDP-based protocols, which are constantly reported as facilitators to DoS attacks. These are Simple Service Discovery Protocol (SSDP), Simple Network Management Protocol (SNMP), Constrained Application Protocol (CoAP) and Web Services Dynamic Discovery (WSD). Specifically, we conduct a countrywide network scanning across the four main Nordic countries, i.e., Denmark, Finland, Norway and Sweden, and enumerate the devices that respond to any of our probes and hence they can be exploited in DoS attacks. For each of the discovered devices, we assess its amplification capabilities in terms of Bandwidth Amplification Factor (BAF) and Packet Amplification Factor (PAF) that can contribute to a DoS incident. The outcomes show that from the four examined protocols, SSDP and SNMP are the most beneficial protocols from an attacker's perspective, as a multitudinous group of reflectors is identified in each of the considered countries. Even worst, a significant portion of these devices produced a BAF over 30, a BAF that can multiply significantly the attack traffic stemming from the attacker's side and hence causes a devastating impact on the victim's infrastructure.

Keywords: DDoS · Amplification attacks · Reflection attacks · SSDP · SNMP · CoAP · WSD · Internet measurement

1 Introduction

Without a doubt, denial of service (DoS) attacks are considered as a crucial threat against the stability and resilience of the Internet's critical infrastructure. This fact is reported in many recent security reports, which they estimate that the number and impact of the Distributed DoS (DDoS) incidents will steadily

H. P. Reiser and M. Kyas (Eds.): NordSec 2022, LNCS 13700, pp. 176–193, 2022.
https://doi.org/10.1007/978-3-031-22295-5_10

rise every year [1]. The objective of such attacks is to saturate the bandwidth of the target with numerous and large packets and exhaust its computational resources.

Distributed Reflective DoS (DRDoS) attacks, which are the focus of our work, typically exploit the application protocols that rely on the User Datagram Protocol (UDP) of the transport layer. Due to its connectionless nature, UDP facilitates the spoofing of the requests' source IP address, which are reflected by the third parties that service these applications, and eventually they redirect the attack traffic to the target. Moreover, such attacks take advantage of the amplification capabilities of the application layer protocols, where specific protocols or type of requests provide a much larger response than the size of the request, thus, multiplying the attack traffic [2]. In short, DRDoS attacks combine the amplification and reflection characteristics with the aim to saturate the victim's network and computational resources. This is achieved by flooding the target with network traffic triggered by small but legitimate requests originated by the attacker to a service. In turn, this service redirects the traffic as responses towards the victim [3].

Usually, the evildoers take advantage of protocols and services that support specific types of requests that generated much greater responses. Examples of such protocols are the Domain Name System (DNS) [4], the Network Time Protocol (NTP) [5], and others. A requirement for the success of a DRDoS is that these services should operate openly, which means that they should accept and respond to requests from anyone on the Internet. Typically, such services should be restricted to the intended internal users, however, the researchers and the real-life security incidents have shown that this is not the case.

Contributing to this topic, our work provides a fresh, multi-country and multi-protocol Internet measurement study on the amplification and reflection capabilities of the Simple Service Discovery Protocol (SSDP), Simple Network Management Protocol (SNMP), Constrained Application Protocol (CoAP) and Web Services Dynamic Discovery (WSD). These four UDP-based protocols are constantly reported in the related literature as enablers of devastating DRDoS attacks. For this reason, we exhaustively investigate the IP ranges of the four major Nordic countries, namely Denmark (DK), Finland (FI), Norway (NO) and Sweden (SE) –in alphabetical order–, with the purpose to discover the devices that openly respond to any of the four aforementioned protocols and analyse their amplification capabilities. In particular, the main contributions of the current work are summarized as follows:

- We conduct a wide network scanning and probing of the IP address ranges in the four main Nordic countries, i.e., Denmark, Finland, Norway and Sweden, with the purpose to discover devices accessible from the open Internet that run any of the SSDP, SNMP, CoAP, and WSD service, and possibly provide a high amplification factor. Such type of devices can be implicated in DRDoS incidents as the unwittingly reflectors.
- We evaluate their potential contribution to DRDoS attacks by assessing the amplification they yield, both in terms of Bandwidth Amplification Factor

(BAF) and Packet Amplification Factor (PAF). We examine variant payload values that trigger different set of responses and hence different magnitudes of amplification factors.
- To obtain a clearer view of the trends and differences between the four countries, we analyse the Autonomous Systems (AS) that the reflectors reside and categorize them to the type of the network that they are connected.

The rest of the paper is organized as follows. The next section provides the background that will facilitate to grasp the inner workings of the DRDoS attacks, while it also presents the SSDP, SNMP, CoAP and WSD protocols with the various type of requests and payloads. The followed methodology is described in Sect. 3, while Sect. 4 presents the results and highlights our main outcomes. The related work is discussed in Sect. 5, whereas the paper concludes in Sect. 6.

2   Background

2.1   Source IP Address Spoofing

The capability of source IP address spoofing is essential to how UDP-based DoS attacks unfold. The UDP is a connectionless protocol which, unlike the TCP, has no handshake phase. Even more, in the case the ingress filtering mechanism [6], aka BCP 38, is not implemented adequately, then the spoofing can pass undetected. A study from the Spoofer Project [7] in 2005 showed that roughly 25% of the ASs allowed spoofed IP packets to be sent out of their network, thus, facilitating the aggressors to launch reflection attacks. This was still a problem in 2016, when it was estimated that 20% of the ASs can still be used to send out spoofed IP packets [8]. More recent statistics by the CAIDA Spoofer Project [9] indicate that the 20% of the AS are still spoofable, regardless if Network Address Translation (NAT) is enabled or not.

2.2   Calculation of Amplification Factor

In simple terms, the amplification characteristic is accomplished, when the size of the response is much greater than that of the request. The attacker first needs to choose a protocol and utilize a specific type of request, that produces a response that has the maximum possible size. This capability is measured as the amplification factor (AF), and it is an indication of the effectiveness of the attack. In short, the higher the AF, the more voluminous the attack traffic and the quicker the bandwidth and resource consumption at the target's side. In the literature, they are used two formulas for assessing the amplified effect [5]. The PAF (Eq. 1) considers the number of response packets that the amplifier sends towards the target, when it responds to a single request.

$$PAF = \frac{\text{response's number of packets}}{\text{request's number of packets}} \tag{1}$$

On the other, the BAF (Eq. 2) [5,10] denotes the bandwidth increment as the amount of bytes that the amplifier sends, as a response to the request, divided by the amount of bytes of the request. According to common practices in the literature, in our work we calculate the BAF based on the length of the IP payload of the request packet and the total number of bytes in the response [8].

$$\text{BAF} = \frac{\text{length(response)}}{\text{length(request)}} \tag{2}$$

2.3 Evaluated Protocols

In our research, we focus on the assessment of the SSDP, SNMP, CoAP, and WSD, as facilitators in DRDoS attacks. Following, we detail on their functionality, how they are abused for launching a DRDoS attack, and what type of requests are used to trigger an amplified response. The main issue with these protocols is that although they are meant to be used within a Local Area Network (LAN), a Service Provider Network or an enterprise's Wide Area Network (WAN), they are instead deployed on public Internet-facing devices in an unauthenticated and open way. Consequently, these devices accept and are forced to fulfil the requests.

Simple Service Discovery Protocol (SSDP)
Within environments that do not operate a centralized configuration mechanisms, such as DHCP, and contain a vast number and diverse type of appliances, there is a need for a simple and easy way for discovering the network services. This can be accomplished with the help of the SSDP protocol [11]. A device in an SSDP setup is either a control point (client) or root (server) which offers one or more SSDP services. Whenever the client sends an *M-SEARCH* command, then the root devices should answer with the details of the services they offer. For each different service, a root should send a separate response. SSDP is based on UDP to send a request either to the multicast (239.255.255.250) or unicast address of the root device on port 1900. It supports two generic query types:

- `upnp:rootdevice`, which searches for all root devices.
- `ssdp:all`, which searches for all UPnP-supporting devices and services.

Simple Network Management Protocol (SNMP)
SNMP is used for network monitoring and specifically to configure and collect information from network devices such as routers, switches, servers and workstations. Typically, the administrative computer, called manager, undertake to monitor the networking devices, called agents. The agents provide the management data in the form of variables, which describe their status and configuration. The manager is capable to request or set the value of these variables. SNMPv2 is considered the most suitable version for amplification attacks, as it supports the `GetBulk` request and allows requests without the requirement for authentication.

GetBulk returns a list of SNMP variables and typically is used for iterating all monitoring variables of an agent. The response size, and thus the amplification factor, is determined by the total amount and length of the variables contained in the returned list. In addition, the following parameters for the GetBulk probe are found to be efficient for amplifying the response [12]:

- Community must be set to "public", this allows access to the SNMP variables without authentication and is commonly the default configuration.
- Max-repetitions must be set to a high value. This field represents how many GetNext operations should be performed by the receiver. In other words, it forces the agent to include multiple variables in its response.
- Non-repeaters must be '0' to indicate the number of objects that are expected to return a single instead of multiple instances.

Constrained Application Protocol (CoAP)
CoAP, defined in RFC 7252 [13], is a specialized web transfer protocol for use by constrained nodes and allows them to communicate with the Internet. It is designed for constrained environments, e.g., low-power and lossy networks, or between constrained nodes and general nodes on the Internet. CoAP is an application protocol, similar to HTTP, but for usage over UDP. It is mainly utilized in IoT devices and aims to operate as HTTP over UDP, effectively enabling these devices to interact over the Internet. Since CoAP is based on UDP transport protocol, even a simple GET request can be used for triggering a much larger response. However, in our probe, the /.well-known/core URI is utilized to perform a CoRE Resource Discovery on UDP port 5683 and thereby request the list of resources hosted by a server [14].

Web Services Dynamic Discovery (WSD)
WSD, also known as WS-Discovery, is a multicast discovery protocol to locate services on a LAN over UDP. Its intended use is to facilitate the network discovery of consumer devices, such as printers, CCTV and DVR systems. Notably, various components of Windows OS employ WSD for network discovery. It uses only the IP multicast address 239.255.255.250, which typically should not be routed through the Internet. However, the implementation of WSD daemon responds to the requests even when they come from an unicast IP address and there is only a single recipient [15]. In our probe, we utilized the malformed XML-payload provided in the pkt file for ZMap [16].

3   Methodology

Our objective is to scan the whole IPv4 range of the main Nordic countries, e.g., Denmark, Finland, Norway and Sweden, with the purpose to detect and identify exploitable, possibly unattended, devices running any of the four evaluated protocols and assess their potential amplification capabilities for different types

of requests. Similarly to our methodology, an attacker can follow the same approach to locate these devices and engage them as reflectors and amplifiers in their
DDoS campaigns. To acquire the IP address ranges for the Nordic countries, we
use the ip2location.com[1] database.

For the scanning, we utilize the ZMap tool [16]. ZMap is a fast Internet-wide
scanning tool capable of scanning millions of IP addresses within few minutes. It
can also take as parameter the payload, either in text or hex format, and issue
a properly formatted request to every IPv4 address in the specified IP range.
Simultaneously with the scanning process, we monitor the incoming responses.
Whenever a response is captured from a specific IP address, it means that in
this address a device operates the service openly, and thus a candidate reflector
is identified. Afterwards, we evaluate for each of the discovered device its amplification capabilities. This means, we calculate the PAF and BAF produced by
the response using the Eq. 1 and 2, respectively.

4   Results

For the analysis of the results, we utilize the `tshark` tool to extract the IP
payload length and other useful fields from the responses contained in the captured traffic. Overall, for each protocol, we provide a table including interesting
statistics for the specific probe. The column **Reflectors** indicates the unique
number of the detected devices, while the column **PCM** shows the per cent
mille or the one-thousandth percent of the reflectors based on the total number of IP addresses scanned for the specific country. The columns **MeanBAF**
and **MaxBAF** show the mean and the maximum BAF calculated from all the
responses of a country, correspondingly. Similarly, the columns **MeanPAF** and
MaxPAF give the mean and the maximum PAF. Finally, the column **Mean-
BAF>=30** presents the mean BAF of the responses that generated a BAF over
or equal to 30. While, the column **MeanTop10%** provides the mean BAF of
the Top 10% highest BAF results. The rest of the columns are protocol specific.
Note that in boldface are denoted the highest values for each country.

For further visualizing the population of the identified reflectors, we provide
the distribution of the BAF results in histograms grouped into different ranges,
e.g., less than 1, from 1 to less than 10, from 10 to less 20, from 20 to less than
30, and 30 or above.

4.1   IP Demographics

As mentioned previously, this work examines the main Nordic countries, those
are Denmark, Finland, Norway and Sweden. As evident from Table 1, these countries have a similar allocation of IP addresses, which is around 13–15M, except
for Sweden that reaches 30M.

---

[1] IP2Location: https://lite.ip2location.com/database/ip-country.

Table 1. Demographics per examined country

Country	Total IP addresses
Denmark	13,001,728
Finland	15,256,576
Norway	15,779,840
Sweden	30,212,096

4.2 SSDP

For the SSDP scanning, we conducted two probes, one that contains the unicast address as the host field of the SSDP request, that is, the IP address of the host that our probe is heading. The other contains the SSDP multicast address, e.g., 239.255.255.250. These two probes are indicated as **U** and **M** in the column **Target**, respectively. Both of these two probes utilize the ssdp:all query type.

Table 2 shows the results from the SSDP scans. It is evident that the highest distribution of SSDP reflectors resides within the Swedish IP range with around 2.8K reflectors, while the lowest within the Finish with less than 300 reflectors. This is evident in the difference of the PCM values, where Sweden has the highest and Finland the lowest density of reflectors.

Additionally, we can observe that the highest BAF and PAF are similar for all countries, except Denmark unicast probe, which exhibits notably lower values. Also, the mean BAF lies between a factor of 20 and 31 for both probes. Furthermore, when focusing on the reflectors with a BAF over 30, the mean is lowest in Denmark with a BAF of 39 and up to 151 in Finland. Note that in Finland, they were identified only 32 reflectors with a BAF over 30, where 28 of these are part of its top 10% group. Another interesting finding is the PAF statistics. All countries have a max PAF of 84 except for unicast probe in Denmark which has 46.

Table 2. Detailed results for SSDP scanning

Country	Target	Reflectors	PCM	MeanBAF	MaxBAF	MeanPAF	MaxPAF	MeanBAF > 30	MeanTop10%
Denmark	U	764	5.88	**23.26**	128.47	7.85	46	38.32	42.26
	M	**766**	**5.89**	22.11	**290.21**	**7.92**	**84**	**39.34**	**43.01**
Finland	U	284	1.86	**21.51**	309.59	6.26	84	**151.70**	**168.94**
	M	**286**	**1.87**	20.31	290.58	**6.36**	84	143.38	155.09
Norway	U	1,186	7.52	**30.78**	309.20	10.41	84	**41.15**	**48.49**
	M	1,186	7.52	29.60	290.21	**10.66**	84	39.58	45.81
Sweden	U	**2,821**	**9.34**	**23.05**	309.20	7.82	84	40.78	**48.62**
	M	2,807	9.29	21.72	290.21	**7.83**	84	**41.16**	46.46

Figure 1 visualizes the proportions of the SSDP reflectors in the examined countries. The highest mean BAF is achieved for the probe that had unicast IP address as target. It is evident, that the Norwegian IP range contains the highest number of SSDP reflectors with a BAF over 30. Specifically, this is the 61% of the discovered devices for the unicast and 56% for the multicast probe. Denmark comes second with 44% and 32%, while Sweden comes third with 34% and 26%, and finally Finland with 11% and 10%, for unicast and multicast respectively. On the contrary, the majority of the reflectors contained in the Finish IP range exhibits a BAF in the group 1 to 10. Overall, the multicast probe reveals a trend for lower BAF across all countries.

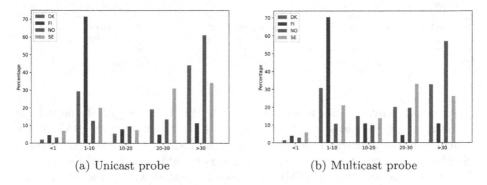

(a) Unicast probe   (b) Multicast probe

Fig. 1. Histograms of BAF results for SSDP

Furthermore, we categorize the SSDP reflectors according to their administrative organization. Table 3 provides the population of devices located on the same AS. For privacy reasons, we exclude the name and the identifier of the AS, but rather we mention the type of the network. In Table 3, Telco means that the IP range belongs to a telecommunication company that offers data, voice and mobile services, while ISP represents a network that provides solely broadband services. Regional ISPs are ISP companies that offer services to a specific geographical region. From Table 3, we can observe that the majority of the reflectors reside within the networks of ISPs, which gives an indication that these reflectors are end-users appliances. Further examination of the SSDP payload, namely the advertised services contained in the SSDP responses, indicates that the devices are both of Linux and Windows OS, as well as OS found on networking devices and smart IoT devices, like Cisco, pfSence OS, Synology/DSM, Net OS and others. Overall, there are a few number of ASs that cumulative are responsible for the majority of the devices, while many more ASs contain a handful of devices. A special case is that of Finland, where we can see that more than the half of the reflectors (67.96%) are located in a cloud provider, which can interpreted that most probably the reflectors correspond to cloud services.

4.3 SNMP

For the SNMP protocol, we experiment with different values for the `max-repetition` field in the `GetBulk` request, specifically, with 500, 1000 and

Table 3. SSDP reflectors by organization. Percentage values, rounded to 2 decimal places, are given in parentheses.

Denmark		Finland		Norway		Sweden	
AS	Devices	AS	Devices	AS	Devices	AS	Devices
Regional ISP	161 (21.07)	Cloud provider	193 (67.96)	Telco	638 (53.79)	ISP	499 (17.69)
Telco	157 (20.55)	Telco	19 (6.69)	Telco	160 (13.49)	Regional ISP	407 (14.43)
Regional ISP	78 (10.21)	Telco	11 (3.87)	ISP	133 (11.21)	ISP	365 (12.94)
ISP	54 (7.07)	Telco	10 (3.52)	ISP & Cloud provider	106 (8.94)	Research network	226 (8.01)
ISP	48 (6.28)	ISP	8 (2.82)	Regional ISP	27 (2.28)	Cloud provider	191 (6.77)
ISP	46 (6.02)	Telco	4 (1.41)	Corporate network	16 (1.35)	Telco	130 (4.61)
ISP	42 (5.50)	Corporate network	4 (1.41)	Regional ISP	15 (1.26)	ISP	123 (4.36)
Regional ISP	27 (3.53)	Regional ISP	3 (1.06)	Regional ISP	12 (1.01)	Corporate network	103 (3.65)
Regional ISP	25 (3.27)	ISP	3 (1.06)	Regional ISP	9 (0.76)	ISP & Cloud provider	78 (2.76)
ISP & Cloud provider	23 (3.01)	ISP	2 (0.71)	Regional ISP	7 (0.59)	Regional ISP	54 (1.91)
Corporate network	14 (1.83)	Telco	2 (0.71)	Corporate network	6 (0.51)	Regional ISP	53 (1.88)
Regional ISP	10 (1.31)	Corporate network	2 (0.71)	Cloud provider	4 (0.34)	ISP	42 (1.49)
Other	79 (10.35)	Other	23 (8.08)	Other	53 (4.47)	Other	550 (19.50)

2250. In this way, we aim to investigate how this field can affect the volume of the returned variables in a response, and thus it increases the BAF of the attack. Table 4 summarizes the outcomes for the SNMP scans, where the column **MaxRep** corresponds to the value of the `max-repetition` field of the request. The highest population of SNMP reflectors is located within the Swedish IP range with around 13K devices, while the lowest within the Finish with almost 1.5K. As a result, the highest PCM is 44.44 from the scan of Sweden with 500 as the `max-repetition` value and the lowest is 9.48 PCM from the scan of Finland with 2250. The highest observed BAF is 683.15 from a host in the Swedish IP range, when it was probed using 2250 as the `max-repetition` value.

Table 4. Detailed outcome for SNMP scanning

Country	MaxRep	Reflectors	PCM	MeanBAF	MaxBAF	MeanPAF	MaxPAF	MeanBAF > 30	MeanTop10%
Denmark	500	**3,069**	**23.60**	**11.65**	268.42	**1.49**	16	**65.08**	**75.08**
	1000	3,016	23.20	8.72	574.98	1.33	34	46.57	49.37
	2250	3,007	23.13	7.43	**580.93**	1.25	34	36.66	37.60
Finland	500	**1,553**	**10.18**	38.46	322.31	2.74	22	74.20	177.86
	1000	1,495	9.80	**42.62**	**627.95**	**2.99**	37	**90.99**	**229.94**
	2250	1,447	9.48	24.39	123.51	1.93	10	40.29	53.94
Norway	500	**3,718**	**23.56**	**20.73**	360.69	**1.63**	21	**89.82**	**87.89**
	1000	3,637	23.05	15.16	145.92	1.3	11	39.32	36.44
	2250	3,682	23.33	18.24	242.65	1.48	15	70.37	64.32
Sweden	500	**13,427**	**44.44**	**20.80**	395.71	**1.98**	23	**91.12**	**120.30**
	1000	12,867	42.59	12.92	673.79	1.54	40	49.75	51.42
	2250	12,964	42.91	12.93	**683.15**	1.54	40	46.35	49.22

Figure 2 illustrates the proportions of the SNMP reflectors. From Fig. 2, it is evident that Finland has the highest distribution of reflectors with more than 35% that provide a BAF over 30 for the three different payloads, while the rest of the countries with a percentage of around 7%–15% have similar distribution for this category. On the contrary, the majority of reflectors within the Danish IP range with a percentage around 75% fall in the category of 1 to 10, which stands true for all probes irrelevant of the value of `max-repetition` field.

Another interesting outcome is that the `max-repetition` value of 500 triggers the best results, although that these responses are not expected to have the largest size. This makes the `max-repetition` value of 500 as the best candidate for exploitation in DDoS attacks. From these figures, we can only assume that the investigated devices tend to respond to SNMP requests that do not require high computational power to process or trigger lengthy responses, which a higher `max-repetition` value will force the device to perform.

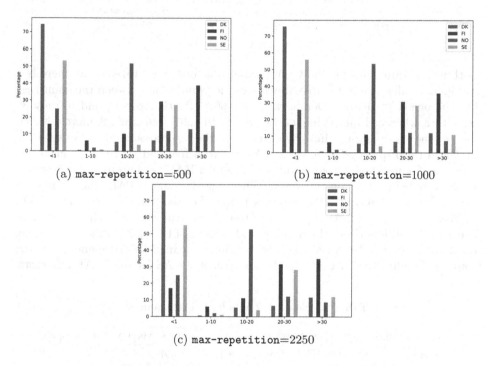

(a) `max-repetition`=500   (b) `max-repetition`=1000

(c) `max-repetition`=2250

Fig. 2. Histograms of BAF results for SNMP

Similarly, Table 5 summarizes the AS of the SNMP reflectors. The figures are similar to that of SSDP, where the IP ranges of Telco and ISP companies contain the majority of the SNMP reflectors. In fact, we can safely argue that, with few exceptions, the same set of AS contain high numbers of SSDP and SNMP reflectors.

4.4 CoAP

For the case of CoAP, we omit to produce the histograms, as most of the BAF values fall in the range of 1 to 10 with only a handful of outliers over 10. Table 6

Table 5. SNMP reflectors by organization. Percentage values, rounded to 2 decimal places, are given in parentheses.

Denmark		Finland		Norway		Sweden	
AS	Devices	AS	Devices	AS	Devices	AS	Devices
ISP and Cloud provider	1,157 (37.70)	Telco	312 (20.09)	Regional ISP	1,637 (44.03)	Regional ISP	5,673 (42.25)
Cloud provider	426 (13.88)	Telco	297 (19.12)	ISP and Cloud provider	371 (9.98)	Telco	1,747 (13.01)
Telco	411 (13.39)	Telco	276 (17.77)	Telco	357 (9.60)	ISP	1,537 (11.45)
Corporate network	102 (3.32)	Cloud provider	141 (9.08)	Telco	282 (7.58)	Telco	615 (4.58)
Telco	94 (3.06)	Telco	83 (5.34)	Telco	249 (6.70)	ISP and Cloud provider	554 (4.13)
ISP	85 (2.77)	Telco	58 (3.73)	ISP	171 (4.60)	ISP	433 (3.22)
Telco	79 (2.57)	ISP	42 (2.70)	Corporate network	65 (1.75)	Cloud provider	365 (2.72)
Regional ISP	73 (2.38)	Cloud provider	38 (2.45)	Telco	50 (1.34)	ISP	249 (1.85)
ISP	71 (2.31)	ISP	27 (1.74)	Regional ISP	49 (1.32)	Cloud provider	160 (1.19)
Regional ISP	58 (1.89)	Telco	25 (1.61)	Corporate network	45 (1.21)	ISP	130 (0.97)
Telco	55 (1.79)	Cloud provider	24 (1.55)	ISP and Cloud provider	41 (1.10)	Corporate network	128 (0.95)
Regional ISP	54 (1.76)	ISP	18 (1.16)	Regional ISP	33 (0.89)	Regional ISP	118 (0.88)
Other	404 (13.16)	Other	212 (13.65)	Other	368 (9.90)	Other	1,718 (12.80)

outlines the outcomes for the CoAP scans. The outcomes reveal that there is a significant difference in the distribution of the population between the countries. On the one side, there is Denmark with 0.66 PCM that correspond to only 86 reflectors, whereas Finland has 12.89 PCM with 1,967 reflectors. A more detailed look at the results shows that the majority of the responses, namely between the first and third quartile, produce a BAF between five and six, which makes the mean BAF consistent across countries. The max BAF goes up to 40 for Norway, while only being 9.41 for Denmark. With regard to mean PAF, the results are similar for all countries, whereas this is not the case for the maximum PAF. In Norway, we see a PAF up to 30. Overall, we can conclude that there is a considerable difference in the number and density of the CoAP reflectors among the four countries. However, they offer similar mean BAF independent of the country. Finally, Table 7 provides the analysis of the AS for the CoAP reflectors.

Table 6. Detailed results for CoAP scanning

Country	Reflectors	PCM	MeanBAF	MaxBAF	MeanPAF	MaxPAF	MeanTop10%
Denmark	86	0.66	4.96	9.41	4.97	7	7.12
Finland	1,967	12.89	5.39	20.69	5.51	7	6.91
Norway	549	3.48	4.86	40.34	4.91	30	7.73
Sweden	3,104	10.27	4.87	25.10	5.00	13	6.88

4.5   WSD

Table 8 provides the outcomes of the WSD scanning, while Fig. 3 depicts the distribution of the WSD reflectors. As presented in Table 8 the highest population of WSD reflectors resides within the Swedish IP range where 811 unique devices were identified with 2.68 PCM, and the lowest within the Danish with 58 devices

Table 7. CoAP reflectors by organization. Percentage values, rounded to 2 decimal places, are given in parentheses.

Denmark		Finland		Norway		Sweden	
AS	Devices	AS	Devices	AS	Devices	AS	Devices
Regional ISP	28 (32.56)	Telco	632 (32.13)	Telco	125 (22.77)	Regional ISP	761 (24.52)
ISP	10 (11.63)	Telco	561 (28.52)	Research network	97 (17.67)	Telco	551 (17.75)
Telco	10 (11.63)	Telco	396 (20.13)	ISP and Cloud provider	76 (13.84)	Telco	481 (15.50)
Telco	8 (9.30)	ISP	58 (2.95)	Telco	51 (9.29)	ISP	308 (9.92)
ISP	8 (9.30)	Cloud provider	53 (2.69)	Telco	33 (6.01)	ISP	262 (8.44)
ISP	4 (4.65)	Cloud provider	31 (1.58)	Telco	28 (5.10)	Cloud provider	178 (5.73)
ISP	3 (3.49)	Telco	29 (1.47)	Corporate network	28 (5.10)	Corporate network	147 (4.74)
Regional ISP	2 (2.33)	Telco	27 (1.37)	Telco	25 (4.55)	ISP and Cloud provider	51 (1.64)
		Telco	23 (1.17)	Telco	17 (3.10)	Telco	32 (1.03)
		Corporate network	19 (0.97)	Regional ISP	16 (2.91)	Regional ISP	30 (0.97)
		Telco	14 (0.71)	ISP	8 (1.46)	Regional ISP	28 (0.90)
		ISP	14 (0.71)	Regional ISP	7 (1.26)	University network	24 (0.77)
Other	13 (15.11)	Other	110 (5.59)	Other	38 (6.92)	Other	251 (8.09)

with 0.45 PCM. Furthermore, we can observe that the mean BAF is similar for all countries, with a value around 30. Sweden exhibits the highest max BAF with 193.55, while Denmark and Finland produced notably reduced max BAF with a value of 97.94. The mean PAF is quite low for the WSD protocol, where all countries exhibit a mean PAF of 1.5. Lastly, Table 9 shows the population of the WSD reflectors according to the AS that they belong.

Table 8. Detailed results for WSD scanning

Country	Reflectors	PCM	MeanBAF	MaxBAF	MeanPAF	MaxPAF	MeanBAF > 30	MeanTop10%
Denmark	58	0.45	31.74	97.94	1.55	3	46.11	70.47
Finland	298	1.96	35.30	97.94	1.56	6	57.35	97.42
Norway	179	1.13	33.50	145.16	1.66	3	43.57	65.31
Sweden	811	2.68	29.32	193.55	1.50	6	50.68	82.83

From Fig. 3, we observe that for all the countries, the proportion of BAF greater than 30 is more than the half of the overall population, with the highest for that of Norway with a 72%. The second-largest proportion is in the range of 1 to 10, consisting of around a quarter of devices. An interesting outcome is that none of the responses, across all countries, produced a BAF less than 1. This is due to the fact that the payload of the request is minimal, containing just three characters. The small payload could be interpreted as that WSD based DRDoS attacks could be suitable for exploiting IoT devices, which often have low bandwidth capabilities. On the other, the low population of WSD reflectors indicates that it would be challenging for a DoS attacker to assemble a crucial army of reflectors, and they may favour for other UDP-based protocols with more dense population.

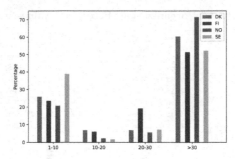

Fig. 3. Histograms of BAF results for WSD probe

Table 9. WSD reflectors by organization. Percentage values, rounded to 2 decimal places, are given in parentheses.

Denmark		Finland		Norway		Sweden	
AS	Devices	AS	Devices	AS	Devices	AS	Devices
Telco	28 (48.28)	Telco	87 (29.19)	ISP and Cloud provider	26 (14.53)	Cloud provider	181 (22.32)
Telco	8 (13.79)	Telco	83 (27.85)	Telco	25 (13.97)	Telco	116 (14.30)
ISP	5 (8.62)	Telco	56 (18.79)	Research network	25 (13.97)	Telco	98 (12.08)
Regional ISP	5 (8.62)	ISP	14 (4.70)	ISP	20 (11.17)	ISP	84 (10.36)
ISP	3 (5.17)	Telco	7 (2.35)	Telco	14 (7.82)	Telco	83 (10.23)
Regional ISP	3 (5.17)	Corporate network	7 (2.35)	Regional ISP	14 (7.82)	ISP	48 (5.92)
Regional ISP	2 (3.45)	Cloud provider	6 (2.01)	ISP	12 (6.70)	Corporate network	28 (3.45)
Cloud provider	1 (1.72)	ISP	5 (1.68)	ISP	7 (3.91)	ISP	21 (2.59)
Telco	1 (1.72)	Telco	4 (1.34)	ISP	5 (2.79)	ISP	15 (1.85)
ISP	1 (1.72)	ISP	4 (1.34)	ISP	4 (2.23)	Corporate network	12 (1.48)
ISP	1 (1.72)	ISP	3 (1.01)	ISP	4 (2.23)	University network	11 (1.37)
		Regional ISP	2 (0.67)	Students organization	3 (1.68)	ISP and Cloud provider	8 (0.99)
Other	0 (0.00)	Other	20 (6.71)	Other	20 (11.17)	Other	106 (13.07)

4.6   Discussion

As expected, SSDP exhibits the highest max and mean PAF. This is due to the fact, that SSDP returns a response for every supported service. All countries achieved a mean PAF between 6 and 10, with a max PAF of 84, except for the unicast probe for Denmark. The max BAF is over 100 for each type of probe, with values that vary between 128.47 for Denmark and 309.59 for Finland. For SSDP, the unicast probe produces a marginal higher BAF than the multicast probe. A possible explanation could be that the payload for an unicast request is usually smaller than that of the multicast request, which is the largest possible and has fixed length. Thus, it results in a larger BAF.

Regarding SNMP scanning, the outcomes reveal that the number of reflectors increases with lower `max-repetition` values, however, the BAF increases with higher `max-repetition` values. The `max-repetition` value of 500 seems to be a good balance in the trade-off between the number of reflectors and BAF, as this value produce the optimal mean BAF for all the reflectors as well as for the reflectors that produce a BAF over 30 or the top 10%. This stands valid for all the countries except Finland, which shows the best mean BAF values for `max-repetition` equal to 1,000. The highest BAF observed throughout our experiments is for SNMP with a value of 229.94, and is produced by a Finish IP address when the `max-repetition` was 1,000.

However, although, the SNMP reflectors resulted in the highest max BAF among the four protocols, the mean BAF is surprisingly low, the second lowest after CoAP. This is because a significant number of the reflectors returned a response with a size smaller than the request, resulting in a BAF smaller than 1. This fact is also evident from the high max PAF and low mean PAF values in Table 4. Nevertheless, if we filter out the optimal amplifiers, either those that provided a BAF over 30 or the top 10%, they produce the highest mean BAF for all countries. Finally, SNMP reflectors exhibit the most dense population among the four investigated protocols, with a population that varies from around 10 PCM for Finland to almost 45 PCM for Sweden.

CoAP results in the lowest outcomes in terms of BAF, significantly lower compared to the other three protocols. The mean BAF does not exceed 6 across all countries, with a max BAF of 40.34 for Norway. The low mean BAF for the top 10% confirms that there are a handful of outliers that produced a beneficial for an attacker BAF. Similarly, the mean PAF values are very close across countries. Noteworthy is the max PAF of Norway with a value of 30 with the remaining countries demonstrating far lower mean PAF.

WSD produces the highest mean BAF. However, it has the lowest distribution of reflectors, which is the lowest observed throughout our experiments. This constitutes challenging to discover and exploit these reflectors in effective DDoS attacks. The PAF outcomes are not considerable as well. These figures can be explained by the fact that the payload of the request is minimal, which can create a high BAF with a relatively small response length or PAF.

Overall, SNMP seems to be the most beneficial to be exploited in DDoS attacks. This is due to the highest proportion of discovered reflectors, the highest max BAF, as long as high results in the statistics for mean BAF over 30 and the top 10%. SSDP is also a reasonable choice for a DDoS attack, with its high mean PAF and considerable mean BAF results. On the other hand, if the attackers aim to launch a lightweight attack and exploit restricted devices, then the appropriate choice could be CoAP protocol, as this requires the creation of a small request which triggers a considerable high mean BAF.

From the point of view of the examined countries, Sweden contains the largest population of reflectors both in terms of absolute values and proportion for all protocols but CoAP. For this country, the distribution of reflectors reaches the highest for the case of SNMP protocol with a value of 44.5 PCM or 13,427 identified devices. On the other hand, Finland has the smallest population for the SSDP and SNMP protocols, the two most beneficial protocols, with 1.9 and 10, respectively. Finally, Denmark has the smallest population for CoAP and WSD with around 0.5 PCM.

5   Related Work

In the literature, there exist a significant corpus of research works that scrutinize various factors in DRDoS attacks. Mainly, these works investigate the contribution of UDP-based protocols as amplifiers and assess their capabilities in terms of BAF and PAF.

To this direction, Rossow [5] conducted an Internet scanning measurement and investigated 14 UDP-based protocols as potential amplifiers in DDoS attacks. Regarding SNMP, the authors assessed that the discovered reflectors produced a mean BAF of 6.3 with the top 10% achieving a BAF of 11.3. For the case of SSDP protocol, they deduced that SSDP devices could provide a mean BAF of 30.8 with the top 10% accomplishing a BAF of 75.9. In comparison to our work, we can note that the reflectors we have discovered provide a much higher BAF, namely 75 to 230 and 42 to 169 for SNMP and SSDP, respectively. However, the population of the reflectors, we identified, is much smaller, as we only consider 4 countries.

Furthermore, Kührer et al. [17] conducted a global Internet scanning for the discovery of potential reflectors. They focused on several UDP-based protocols, including SNMP and SSDP. They showed that throughout their experiment there existed a number of around 9M SNMP and 5M SSDP reflectors. Another interesting observation is that these reflectors migrate to different IP addresses with a high rate. In fact, only 50% of the initial identified reflectors were still accessible after one week on the same IP address. In comparison with [17], besides the enumeration of the potential reflectors, we also assess their amplification capabilities in terms of BAF and PAF.

More recent, Anagnostopoulos et al. [18] conducted a large scale evaluation of DNS and SSDP reflectors in three countries, these are Greece, Portugal and Singapore. Their outcomes for SSDP verify that there exist a significant portion of SSDP reflectors in the three countries, which contribute a BAF of 52 to 85 for the top 25% reflectors of each country, achieving a maximum BAF of 470 and a PAF of 126.

Another category of research works is the examination of IoT and networking devices by exploiting them as reflectors and stressing them under heavy network load. For example, Lyu et al. [19] investigated the reflective DDoS attack capabilities of eight consumer IoT devices in terms of provided BAF and traffic capacity. From their experiments with SSDP, SNMP and TCP SYN reflection, they observed that M-SEARCH request for SSDP is the most beneficial for an attacker, as it was supported by the half of the examined devices yielding a BAF between 15.13 and 43.3. By deploying the eight devices, the authors were able to carry out and sustain a DDoS attack with a BAF of 20 for 24 h, causing a traffic stream of around 1.2 Mbps towards the victim.

Gondim et al. [12] assessed in a custom testbed the amplification capabilities of SSDP and SNMP protocol, among other UDP-based protocols. They observed a BAF of at most 38 and 610, and a PAF of 10 and 33 for SSDP and SNMP, respectively. However, they recognized that protocols such as SSDP and SNMP, which are mainly deployed in restricted environments such as in IoT networks, suffer from saturation when they are exploited for DoS purposes. That is, the amplification effect is decreasing due to the computation capabilities of the IoT device and the congestion on the outbound traffic.

6 Conclusions

DoS type of attacks in the form of DRDoS, which take advantage of the amplification effect of specific application protocols, as well as the IP spoofing capability, constitutes a constant threat to the Internet infrastructure and a rising concern to the security community. In this work, we conduct a multi-country Internet scan in the Nordic region with the purpose to investigate SSDP, SNMP, CoAP and WSD services. The specific protocols have been reported to provide strong amplification potentials. Through our probes, we aim to examine the distribution of the reflectors in the four countries, namely, Denmark, Finland, Norway and Sweden, and assess their amplification capacity.

Our findings show that there exist a substantial number of potentially exploitable reflectors, a great proportion of which generates a high amplification factor in terms of both BAF and PAF. SNMP and SSDP protocols are proven to be the most beneficial protocols from an attacker's perspective. For SNMP, Sweden contains the most multitudinous group of reflectors, as more than 44 PCM of the overall Swedish IP addresses respond to the SNMP probe, yielding a mean BAF of 20. In addition, Finland has the highest proportion of the most optimal amplifiers. Specifically, in this country, around one third of the detected reflectors provide a BAF over 30, with an overall mean BAF of 90. Even worst, for the most beneficial type of probe, the top 10% of the amplifiers produces a BAF of 230. Regarding SSDP, the distribution of reflectors reaches the highest of 10 PCM for Sweden, with a mean BAF of 23. This country also has the highest proportion of devices that produce a BAF over 30 with of 41. On the other hand, Finland which has the lowest population exhibits the best results for the categories BAF over 30 and top 10%, with a BAF of 152 and 169, respectively. On the contrary, CoAP and WSD show the lowest outcomes in terms of distribution and partially in BAF, which makes them not a strong candidate for DRDoS.

Overall, we believe our work could contribute in the battle against the DDoS ecosystem and help the interested parties in the cybersecurity community, such as professionals, researchers, and service providers, to design their defence strategy against the DDoS attacks. Through our experiments, we can deduce the type and the characteristics of the existing reflectors. The analysis of the IP addresses in terms of AS shows that the majority of these devices reside within IP ranges assigned to ISP and telco companies, meaning that we can safely assume that these devices belong to end-users. Moreover, the payload of the SSDP and SNMP responses denote that these reflectors correspond to home appliances, like networking and smart IoT devices. In addition, the outcomes of this study can help to raise the security awareness of the community regarding the potentials of this critical threat and urge the stakeholders to undertake the appropriate mitigation actions.

References

1. NexusGuard. Threat Report FHY 2021 Distributed Denial of Service (DDoS)
2. Anagnostopoulos, M.: Amplification DoS Attacks, pp. 1–3. Springer, Heidelberg (2019). https://doi.org/10.1007/978-3-642-27739-9_1486-1
3. Heinrich, T., Obelheiro, R.R., Maziero, C.A.: New kids on the DRDoS block: characterizing multiprotocol and carpet bombing attacks. In: Hohlfeld, O., Lutu, A., Levin, D. (eds.) PAM 2021. LNCS, vol. 12671, pp. 269–283. Springer, Cham (2021). https://doi.org/10.1007/978-3-030-72582-2_16
4. M. Anagnostopoulos, G. Kambourakis, S. Gritzalis, and D. K. Y. Yau. Never say never: authoritative TLD nameserver-powered DNS amplification. In: NOMS 2018 IEEE/IFIP Network Operations and Management Symposium, pp. 1–9 (2018)
5. Rossow, C.: Amplification hell: revisiting network protocols for DDoS abuse. In: Proceedings of the 2014 Network and Distributed System Security Symposium (NDSS) (2014)
6. Ferguson, P., Senie, D.: Network ingress filtering: defeating denial of service attacks which employ IP source address spoofing. Technical report (1998)
7. Beverly, R., Bauer, S.: The spoofer project: inferring the extent of internet source address filtering on the internet. In: Steps to Reducing Unwanted Traffic on the Internet Workshop (SRUTI 2005). USENIX Association (2005)
8. Ryba, F.J., Orlinski, M., Waehlisch, M.,Rossow, C., Schmidt, T.C.: Amplification and DRDoS attack defense-a survey and new perspectives. arXiv preprint arXiv:1505.07892 (2015)
9. Center for Applied Internet Data Analysis (CAIDA). State of IP Spoofing. http://spoofer.caida.org/summary.php (2022)
10. van Rijswijk-Deij, R., Sperotto, A., Pras, A.: DNSSEC and its potential for DDoS attacks: a comprehensive measurement study. In: Proceedings of the 2014 Conference on Internet Measurement Conference, IMC 2014, New York, NY, USA, pp. 449–460. ACM (2014)
11. Goland, Y., Cai, T., Leach, P., Gu, Y., Albright, S.: Simple service discovery protocol/1.0 operating without an arbiter (1999)
12. Gondim, J.J., de Albuquerque, R.O., Orozco, A.L.S.: Mirror saturation in amplified reflection Distributed Denial of Service: a case of study using SNMP, SSDP, NTP and DNS protocols. Future Gener. Comput. Syst. 108, 68–81 (2020)
13. Shelby, Z., Hartke, K., Bormann, C.: RFC7252: The Constrained Application Protocol (CoAP) (2014)
14. Mattsson, J.P., Selander, G., Amsüss, C.: Amplification Attacks Using the Constrained Application Protocol (CoAP) (2014)
15. Respeto, J.: New DDoS vector observed in the wild: WSD attacks hitting 35/Gbps. http://www.akamai.com/blog/security/new-ddos-vector-observed-in-the-wild-wsd-attacks-hitting-35gbps (2019)
16. Durumeric, Z., Wustrow, E., Halderman, J.A.: ZMap: fast internet-wide scanning and its security applications. In: 22nd USENIX Security Symposium (USENIX Security 13), pp. 605–620. USENIX Association (2013)

17. Kührer, M., Hupperich, T., Rossow, C., Holz, T.: Exit from hell? reducing the impact of amplification DDoS attacks. In: 23rd USENIX Security Symposium (USENIX Security 14), pp. 111–125 (2014)
18. Anagnostopoulos, M., Lagos, S., Kambourakis, G.: Large-scale empirical evaluation of DNS and SSDP amplification attacks. J. Inf. Secur. Appl. **66**, 103168 (2022)
19. Lyu, M., Sherratt, D., Sivanathan, A., Gharakheili, H.H., Radford, A., Sivaraman, V.: Quantifying the reflective DDoS attack capability of household IoT devices. In: Proceedings of the 10th ACM Conference on Security and Privacy in Wireless and Mobile Networks, WiSec 2017, New York, NY, USA, pp. 46–51. Association for Computing Machinery (2017)

GPU-FAN: Leaking Sensitive Data from Air-Gapped Machines via Covert Noise from GPU Fans

Mordechai Guri[✉][ID]

Cyber Security Research Center, Ben-Gurion University of the Negev,
8410501 Beer-Sheva, Israel
gurim@post.bgu.ac.il
http://www.covertchannels.com

Abstract. Modern computer networks are secured with a wide range of products, including firewalls, intrusion detection and prevention systems (IDS/IPS), and access control mechanisms. But despite the multiple layers of security, these measures can be bypassed by motivated attackers. To cope with this threat, an 'air-gap' is a network security measure that may be taken where highly sensitive information needs to be protected. In this approach, the internal network is isolated from the Internet, physically and logically, to create a physical boundary with the outer digital world.

In this paper, we show that attackers can leak data from air-gapped networks via covert acoustic signals. Our method doesn't require speakers on infected computers. Malware running on the computer can use the GPU (graphics processing unit) fans and evasively control its speed. While the slight changes in the RPM (rotation per minute) speed are not noticeable to users, they can be used to modulate and encode binary information. A nearby receiver, such as a compromised smartphone or a laptop, can receive the covert acoustic signals and demodulate and decode the binary information. We discuss the attack model on air-gapped networks and provide relevant technical background and the characteristics of the GPU fans. We also present the covert channel's design, implementation, and evaluation. The results show that a brief amount of sensitive information can be leaked several meters away via covert noises generated from the GPU fans.

Keywords: Air-gap · Acoustic · GPU · Covert channel · Exfiltration

1 Introduction

Information is an organization's most valuable asset in the modern digitalized era. Accordingly, sensitive data such as personal information, financial data, intellectual properties, and source code are kept secured within the organization's networks. To protect IT networks from online threats, a wide range of

H. P. Reiser and M. Kyas (Eds.): NordSec 2022, LNCS 13700, pp. 194–211, 2022.
https://doi.org/10.1007/978-3-031-22295-5_11

security products are commonly used; antivirus (AV), intrusion detection and prevention systems, data leakage prevention systems, Security Information and Event Management (SIEM), and so on. But despite the multiple layers of security and defense, a major part of the industry has recorded successful attacks on their networks. Such attacks are usually conducted by attack groups or cyber criminals with specific goals, whether to steal, spy, or disrupt. For example, in March 2021 hacking group known as Hafnium attacked a wide range of industries by exploiting vulnerabilities in Microsoft Exchange Server. The attack affected over 30,000 organizations across the United States, including local governments, government agencies, and businesses [1]. In April 2022, a cryptocurrency and NFT games company Ronin reported that they were hacked with a total loss of $540 Million. To infiltrate the organization's network, attackers may employ different types of techniques, including social engineering, 0-day vulnerabilities, Malvertising, exploit kits, browser attacks, and so on [2].

1.1 Air-Gap Networks

Where highly sensitive information is involved, an organization may keep the relevant data in air-gapped networks. An air-gap (or air-wall) is a security measure in which a computer, network, or device is disconnected from the Internet on both physical and logical levels. In air-gap networks, there is no connection to the external networks through cable networks, Wi-Fi, Bluetooth, or other types of connection. Such physical isolation keeps sensitive information protected from the aforementioned types of online cyber threats. Air-gapped networks are known to be used by a wide range of organizations, including defense and military, governmental sectors, finance and banking, health care and hospitals, and critical infrastructure.

1.2 Air-Gap Attacks

Although the level of security provided by the air-gap measure is high, air-gap networks are immune to sophisticated cyber attacks. Events reported in the past show that skilled and persistent adversaries can infiltrate the organization's boundaries and breach air-gap networks. To achieve this goal, the attackers may use strategies such as compromising supply chains, employing social engineering, and using deceived insiders. Agent.btz, revealed in 2008, is a worm that primarily spreads itself via removable devices such as USB thumb drives [3]. The worm infected U.S. classified networks in a military base in the Middle East. The FBI and DHS joint analysis report attributed Agent.BTZ to Russian civilian and military intelligence services [3]. The Stuxnet worm, reported in 2011, is a malicious computer worm that is known for its use to attack nuclear facilities. According to the reports, the worm could attack the systems through a USB drive that was plugged into an affected system and then spread to any subsequent systems that the USB drive was plugged into [4]. In November 2019, the Washington Post reported the Kudankulam Nuclear Power Plant (KKNPP) in India, suffered from a cyberattack. Other malware that targets air-gap environments, such as Ramsay [5], and Tick [6], were reported in recent years.

1.3 Air-Gap Exfiltration

After the infiltration phase, the malware usually collects the data of interest; documents, keystrokes logging, credentials, etc. At some point, the malware needs to exfiltrate the information outward to the attacker. In the case of Internet-connected networks, exfiltration is a trivial task; legitimate Internet protocols such as HTTPS, DNS, or SMTP can be used for the exfiltration [7]. However, in the cases of air-gapped networks, the act of leakage is a more challenging task due to the lack of Internet connectivity. The research domain of exfiltrating data over air-gaps is known as air-gap covert channels. The fundamental idea is to use nonstandard communication mediums to leak the information to the remote attacker. Over the past twenty years, researchers demonstrated different types of air-gap covert channels, including electromagnetic, optical, thermal, and acoustic [8].

1.4 Our Contribution

This paper presents a new type of air-gap covert channel based on the GPU fans that enable attackers to leak data from isolated, air-gapped systems. The contributions of our work are listed below.

1. **Attack model.** We present the offensive attack model on an air-gapped system in which the attacker uses the GPU fans to exfiltrate information. The GPU exists today on many modern systems workstations, servers, data centers, and public and private cloud environments, making this attack highly available to the attacker.
2. **GPU fan acoustics.** We focus on using the Graphical Processing Unit (GPU) for the exfiltration. Although leaking via fan noise has been discussed before, no prior work focuses on GPU fans. We focus on the characteristics unique to GPU fans, technically and acoustically, for the implementation, evaluation, and measurements.
3. **Collaborative attack & modulation.** GPU fans are commonly equipped with multiple fans. We present the exfiltration of data with multiple GPU fans and discuss the topic of collision avoidance and multi-fan modulation.
4. **Implementation and countermeasures.** We present the implementation of a transmitter and receiver that can be used with any ordinary smartphone or nearby microphones and also discuss a set of countermeasures to cope with this threat.

1.5 Contribution to Prior Work

Although the concept of a covert channel using the computer chassis and CPU fans has been presented in prior work [9], no previous work focus on the GPU fans

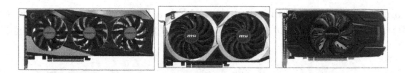

Fig. 1. Graphic cards with one (C), two (B), and three (A) fans

Table 1. Comparison between the characteristics of chassis, CPU, and GPU fans

Fan	Control	Interference	Number
Chassis	Partial	No	Mostly single
CPU	Partial	Interference with CPU workloads	Mostly single
GPU (this paper)	**Full control**	**No interference with CPU**	**Multiple**

for the exfiltration. In this paper, we focus on the GPU fans, which have several unique characteristics for exfiltration, as presented in Table 1. First, compared to the GPU fans, the chassis and CPU fans have limited or no control over the speed. Some CPU controllers have an internal controller that overrides the speed configuration, and some chassis and CPU fans completely lack speed control. Second, using the CPU fans cause interference with the current processes on the CPU, while the GPU fans are separated from the main CPU and hence available most of the time. Third, modern graphic cards are commonly shipped with multiple fans, which can be used for exfiltration. Figure 1 shows typical graphic cards with one, two, and three fans.

This paper is organized as follows. The attack model is introduce in Sect. 2. We overview related work in Sect. 3. The design and implementation of transmitter and receiver are described in Sects. 4 and 5, respectively. Section 6 presents the analysis and evaluation results. Countermeasures are provided in Sect. 7, and we conclude in Sect. 8.

2   Attack Model

The term Advanced Persistent Threat (APT) in cyber-security is used to describe sophisticated, commonly nation-state cyberattacks aimed at gaining strategic advantages. It also includes the type of cybercrime attacks targeted at business sectors. The cyber kill chain framework introduced by Lockheed Martin consists of seven main attack phases [10]. In this cyber kill chain, the remote operations on the network are done over legitimate connections, usually through the Internet. For example, the attacker may compromise the internal network using a phishing email opened by an organization employee, and data can be exfiltrated via HTTPS protocol to a remote server. However, in the case of an air-gapped network, these steps are more challenging since the attacker doesn't have direct connectivity with the target network. In the following subsections, we describe the main phases that are unique to the APT attacks on air-gapped networks. The attack chain consists of the following main stages, illustrated in Fig. 2.

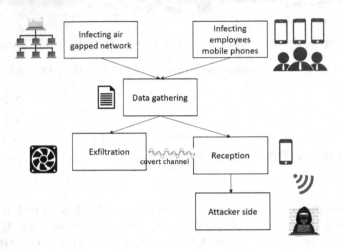

Fig. 2. The different phases of the attack; infection, data gathering, and exfiltration

2.1 Air-Gap Infection

In the case of air-gap networks, malware delivery through the Internet is impossible since the network is isolated. In this case, the adversaries may use sophisticated attack vectors, such as contaminating the organization's supply chains of hardware and software. For example, Blomberg reported in 2018 that state actor spy chips are found in hardware used by Apple, Amazon, and other companies. Attackers can also use malicious or deceived insiders to deliver malware into the air-gap network [11]. The Agent.btz APT from 2008 is a computer worm that compromised U.S. military networks via an infected USB drive used by a deceived employee. Another case is the Stuxnet worm that breached supervisory control and data acquisition (SCADA) systems in 2010 [4]. Other attacks that target air-gap facilities, such as Ramsay [5] and Tick [6], were found by security firms in recent years.

2.2 Mobile Infection

In the second step, the employees' smartphones in the organization are located, and the malicious application is installed on the smartphones. It is important to note that mobile phone carriers are not necessarily malicious insiders. The device can be infected via email attachments, websites, or malicious app downloads without the owner's consent or knowledge.

2.3 Data Gathering

After installing malware in the target network, the attacker may want to collect interest data. The information collected may be documents, keylogging, credentials, biometric information, images, and so on.

2.4 Data Exfiltration

In the exfiltration stage, the malware transmits the data using acoustic signals generated by GPU fans. The binary information is modulated and encoded on the manipulations of one or more GPU fan speeds. Concurrently, the malicious app on the phone scans for the acoustic signals denoting a covert channel. When the signals are received and decoded, the data can be decoded in the smartphone. This data can be forwarded later to the attacker via Wi-Fi or cellular data.

Fig. 3. Attack scenario (illustration). Malware within the infected air-gapped computer (A) transmits sensitive information emanating from the GPU fans. The smartphone or laptop of employees receives the data

The attack scenario is illustrated in Fig. 3. Malware within the infected air-gapped computer (A) transmits sensitive information emanating from the GPU fans. The smartphone or laptop of employees receives the data.

3 Related Work

Air-gap covert channels are particular types of communication channels that allow attackers to leak data from highly isolated, air-gapped systems in non-standard ways. They are commonly categorized into electromagnetic and magnetic, electric, optical, thermal, and acoustic. A wide range of prior works focuses on the electromagnetic spectrum as a medium for covert communication channels in air-gap environments. Emanating radio signals from various components in the system is demonstrated by techniques such as AirHopper [12], GSMem [13], Funthenna [14], and USBee [15]. Other research show how to use magnetic fields to exfiltrate data from isolated computers within Faraday cages [16]. Researchers also introduced techniques that use power lines to leak data from air-gapped systems [17,18]. The optical medium can also be used to leak information. Loughry discussed the option of leaking data over optical emanation using LEDS [19], which was recently extended by other research works [20,21], by using the drive indicator LED [22], router LEDs [23], and screens [24] to exfiltrate over air-gaps. BitWhisper is a unique thermal covert channel that uses heat to modulate data and exfiltrate it from a device [25].

3.1 Acoustic

In acoustic covert channels, data is encoded on top of sound waves. The most common technique used by prior work is to use the computer loudspeakers to generate sonic and ultrasonic waves [26–29]. These work discuss the transmission of information between desktops, laptops, and smartphones via near ultrasonic waves, usually above 18 kHz. The main limitation of the acoustic methods listed above is the required system with sound hardware and loudspeakers. It is known that some policies restrict the installation of loudspeakers in the system to create a hardened, audio- gaped environment. To overcome the audio-gap limitations, Researchers introduced a few methods which do not require loudspeakers. Guri et al. used the noise from the hard disk drive actuator arm and CD/DVD to leak data to short ranges [30,31]. More recently, researchers presented PowerSupplay, a method that uses power supplies to exfiltrate data from air-gapped, audio-gapped systems [32]. The work which is close to our work is Fansmitter, which used computer fans to modulate and leak data [9]. However, the work in [9] discusses chassis and CPU fans, while our work focuses on GPU fans and their unique characteristics for data exfiltration in the discussion, implementation, and evaluation. The contribution of our work is described in detail in Sect. 1.

4   Transmission

In this section, we present the implementation of the transmitter and the data modulation encoding schemes.

4.1   GPU Fan Control

To control the GPU fan speed, a core code must be executed at the kernel level. The GPU manufacturers implement their kernel driver and modules that interface with the GPU thermal information and fan speeds. In many cases, a set of API functions that interact with the kernel driver is provided to the developers to be used in their user-level process. For example, the AMDGPU kernel driver provides fan control for graphics cards via `hwmon` in the `sysfs` interface. In this case, the fan PWN control range from 0 to 255 and can be calculated by multiplying its value by 2.55. For example, setting the fan speed to 25 present can be done by `echo "64" > /sys/class/drm/cardX/device/hwmon/hwmon0/pwm1`. Other manufacturers provide their own control libraries. For example, NVIDIA provides dynamic fan control for NVIDIA graphic cards on Linux and Windows. The NVAPI allows full user-level access to NVIDIA GPUs and drivers in any application. Another option is to use the command line interface to interact with the GPU fans; as in the case of NVIDIA, use the command `nvidia-settings -a GPUTargetFanSpeed=70` to set the fan speed to 70%. The implementation used the standard API to control the GPU fans. The three levels of GPU fan control and their corresponding required privilege levels and prerequisite are listed in Table 2.

Table 2. Levels of GPU fan control

Control level	OS	Privileges	Prerequisite
Kernel module/driver	Windows/Linux/Mac	Root/admin	Signed driver (windows) installing kernel module (Linux, Mac)
User level API	Windows/Linux	User	DLL (Windows) or shared libraries (Linux) provided by the OEM
File system interface (VFS)	Linux/Mac	User	File system write permissions

4.2 Blade Pass Frequency (BPF)

The centrifugal fans installed on the GPUs are emitting acoustic noises in frequencies and amplitudes. The blade passing frequency (BPF) noise is the most dominant acoustic component of centrifugal fans. This noise is an aerodynamic noise that is generated by turbulent flow fields and vibroacoustic noise resulting from structural vibrations. The main tone generated by a fan is calculated by multiplying the number of blades (n) by the rotating speed (R) in revolutions per minute (RPM).

4.3 Modulation

We used the BFSK (binary frequency shift keying) modulation scheme in which the information is modulated over two-speed levels. In this modulation, the two BPF frequencies, BPF_0 and BPF_1, representing 0 and 1, are generated by two distinct RPM speeds. Figure 4 shows the spectrogram of the alternating sequence, with the F_0 (600 Hz) and F_1 (510 Hz) frequencies generated by two RPM in the GPU fan. Note that data can be modulated on the low harmonies as well, but the quality of the signal is low due to the low SNR at the low frequencies.

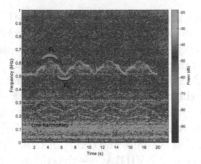

Fig. 4. BFSK modulation with two RPMs

4.4 Encoding and Framing

We encode the data with a frame consists a sequence of 13 bits (Fig. 5). The first four bits are used for synchronization, letting the receiver detect the beginning of a frame and extract the BPF parameters. The following 8 bits are the actual payload representing the byte to transfer. The last bit is a parity bit which is used as a simple error detection mechanism.

Calibrating	Byte 0		Calibrating	Byte 1	
Sync	Payload	Parity	Sync	Payload	Parity
1010	8 bits	1 bit	1010	8 bits	1 bit

Fig. 5. The frames structure

4.5 Multiple Fans

Many modern graphics cards are shipped with multiple fans, most commonly two or three. There are graphic cards that have even four and five fans. Single fan GPU has a small form factor and uses a blower-style method for their cooling. The multiple fans graphic cards have more computation power and are suitable for medium to large-sized computer cases. Multiple fan GPUs are built with PWM support which allows them to automatically adjust the speed according to the heat. In the context of our covert channel, the malware can increase the channel bandwidth by using multiple fans to exfiltrate the data. To modulate the data on multiple fans, we implement a modulator that splits the stream of bytes to transmit into chunks of n, where n is the number of fans that exists on the system. For the transmission, each of the fans is responsible for transmitting the byte in the stream of the location modulo t, where t is the specific fan number. Figure 6 illustrates the exfiltration of six bytes in a stream with three fans.

Multiple Fans Physical Layer. At the physical layer, a transmission with multiple fans requires a collision avoidance mechanism. This is important for the prevention of interference between the concurrent transmissions of the different fans. In our implementation, we split the relevant frequency band to the number of fans (n) where each fan base carrier frequency begins at a distinct band.

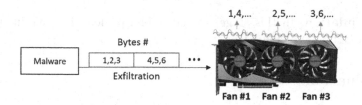

Fig. 6. Exfiltration with three fans ($n = 3$)

5   Reception

A standard audio chip in smartphones and laptops can sample at 48 kHz. Since our covert channel is at the lower frequency bands, we downsampled the audio input to 1000 Hz Hz. Our demodulator app is implemented in Android OS for smartphones. The main functionality of the receiver operates in a dedicated thread, responsible for data sampling and downsampling, signal processing, and data demodulation. Figure 7 on the left shows the Android receiver app state machine. A photo of an app decoding the 'TOP SECRET' keystrokes exfiltrated from a nearby air-gapped workstation is presented on the right.

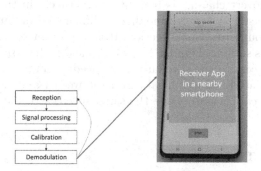

Fig. 7. The Android receiver app state machine (left), and an Android receiver app, decoding the 'TOP SECRET' text exfiltrated from a nearby workstation (right)

- **Reception and Signal Processing.** The first step is to sample the signal, transform it to the frequency domain, and extract the two FSK frequencies by applying a fast Fourier transform (FFT) to the array of the sampled values. The signal is downsampled and stored.
- **Sync Detection and Calibration.** The receiver continuously searches for a syn signal to identify a frame header (1010). The channel parameters are extracted and forwarded to the demodulation methods if the sequence is detected.
- **Demodulation.** In this stage, the eight bits payload is demodulated, and the parity bit is calculated.

6   Evaluation

In this section, we present the evaluation of the covert channels. We show the acoustic range of different GPUs, discuss the transmission speed, present the effective distances given various properties, and the transmission time of different types of information.

6.1   Acoustic Range

The frequency range of GPU fans is a fundamental property of the communication channel at the physical layer for implementing the down-sampling, modulation, and demodulation schemes. In addition, given one or more transmitting fans, it is crucial to split the dynamic range accordingly to avoid collisions and interference between the fans. Table 3 present the acoustic range and number of fans of seven GPUs of major graphic card manufacturers; NVIDIA, ASUS, EVGA, GAINWARD, INNO3D, MSI, and GIGABYTE. As can be seen, the main acoustic components of GPU fans span approximately 0 to 700 Hz. This implies that the covert channel is maintained relatively in the lower frequency ranges of the acoustic spectrum, making it difficult to monitor and block, as discussed in the countermeasures section. It is important to note that although some graphic cards support high RPMs, which yield higher BPF values, we limit the evaluation process to the standard max speeds, commonly 3000 RPM. The number of fans on a typical graphical card is between 1 and 3, whereas multiple fans on a graphic card usually have the same speed, acoustic range, and other characteristics.

6.2   Transition Time

The transmission speed mainly depends on the d parameter, which is the transition time between two RPMs encoding the '0' and '1'. Since the switching between two rotational speeds is a mechanical process, we tested the minimal value of d in which a nearby receiver can identify the acoustic component of the corresponding BPF. In this evaluation we tested the transmission with $d = 250$ ms, $d = 500$ ms, $d = 1$ s, and $d = 2$ s. Figure 8 show the spectrogram of a

Table 3. The acoustic range and number of fans of different graphic cards

#	Model	Upper BPF	Blades	# Fans
1	GeForce GTX 1080Ti Founders	450 Hz	9	1
2	ASUS ROG Poseidon GeForce GTX 1080Ti Platinum Edition	650 Hz	13	2
3	EVGA GeForce GTX 1080Ti FTW3 Elite	550 Hz	11	3
4	GAINWARD GeForce GTX 1080Ti Phoenix Golden Sample	750 Hz	15	2
5	INNO3D iChill GeForce GTX 1080Ti Black	450 Hz	9	1
6	MSI GeForce GTX 1080Ti Lightning	750 Hz	15	3
7	GIGABYTE GeForce GTX 1060 Mini	650 Hz	13	1

signal transmitted with three values of d, as received by a nearby smartphone receiver. The results show that we maintained successful signal demodulation for the values of 2 s, 1 s, and 500 ms. However, the transmission time of 250 ms yields low SNR values that work only for short distances with some of the fans. Hence, we consider the $d = 500$ ms as the stable minimal value for use in the covert channel.

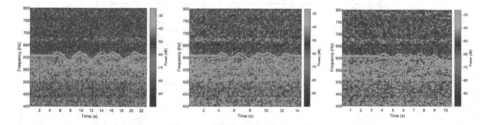

Fig. 8. Spectrogram of transmissions with $d = 2$ s (left), $d = 1$ s (middle), and $d = 500$ ms (right)

6.3 Bit Rates

The bit rate of the covert channel is derived from the transition time and the number of fans on the graphical card. We found that a minimal guarding interval 10 Hz is sufficient to prevent collisions between transmissions in cases of multiple fans. Table 4 shows the different bit rates for the graphical cards provided in Table 3 at the beginning this section. The bit rates are 0.5–2 bit/s for transmissions with a single fan and 1.5–6 bit/s for transmissions with three participating fans. Note that higher bit rates can be maintained where a parameter of $d = 250$ ms is applicable, e.g., short ranges and appropriate GPUs.

6.4 Effective Distance

We measure the effective distance of the covert channel. In this setup, a receiver smartphone with a demodulator app described in Sect. 5 was located at increasing distances from the transmitting computer. Figure 9 shows the power spectral

Table 4. The bit rates for graphic cards with various numbers of fans and different d values

Models #	$d = 250\,ms$	$d = 500\,ms$	$d = 1\,s$	$d = 2\,s$
1,5,7 (1 fan)	4 bit/s	2 bit/s	1 bit/s	0.5 bit/s
2,4 (2 fans)	8 bit/s	4 bit/s	2 bit/s	1 bit/s
3,6 (3 fans)	12 bit/s	6 bit/s	3 bit/s	1.5 bit/s

Table 5. The evaluation results in a range of 0 to 500 cm, with SNR, BER, and different fan speeds

Distance	Fan Speed (%)	SNR (dB)	d	BER
0 cm	40-60	5	500 ms	
	50-70	7	500 ms	
	60-80	17	500 ms	BER = 0%
	70-90	18	500 ms	
	80-100	20	500 ms	
100 cm	40-60	-	500 ms	
	50-70	10	500 ms	
	60-80	11	500 ms	BER = 0%
	70-90	14	500 ms	
	80-100	14	500 ms	
200 cm	40-60	-	500 ms	
	50-70	-	500 ms	
	60-80	7	500 ms	BER = 0%
	70-90	10	500 ms	
	80-100	10	500 ms	
300 cm	40-60	-	500 ms	
	50-70	-	500 ms	
	60-80	5	500 ms	BER = 0%
	70-90	8	500 ms	
	80-100	10	500 ms	
400 cm	40-60	-	500 ms	
	50-70	-	500 ms	
	60-80	5	500 ms	BER = 0%
	70-90	6	500 ms	
	80-100	7	500 ms	
500 cm	40-60	-	1 sec	
	50-70	-	1 sec	
	60-80	5	1 sec	BER = 0%
	70-90	6	1 sec	
	80-100	6	1 sec	

density (PSD) of transmissions up to 500 cm away, which depicts the existence of the signal over time in terms of power. The signals are observed in the spectrum in the whole range. Table 5 present the signal-to-noise ratio (SNR), with different percentage of fan speeds for distances of 0 to 500 cm. For the evaluation we tested five different fan speeds transitions, 40%–60%, 50%–70%, 60%–80%, 70%–90%, and 80%–100%. For each transmission, we present the bit error rate (BER) maintained for the transmission, whereas BER of 0% means data transmitted with no errors. As can be seen, with a transition time of 500 ms ($d = 500\,ms$), we maintained a BER of 0% up to 400 cm between the transmitting computer and the receiving smartphone. For 500 cm away, we had to increase the transition time to 1 s ($d = 1\,s$) to achieve a BER of 0%. This is mainly due to environmental acoustic interferences that emanate from other components in the room and outside, which affect the SNR levels.

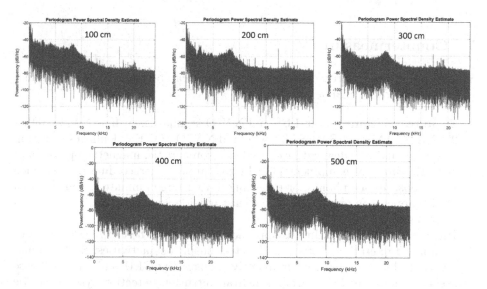

Fig. 9. The power spectral density (PSD) of transmissions up to 500 cm away

6.5 Data Transmission

Table 6 present the time it takes to exfiltrate various types of information for each computer with minimum ($d = 0.250\,ms$) and maximum ($d = 2\,s$) parameters. A brief amount of information such as bitcoin private keys, RSA encryption keys, short texts, keylogging, and credentials can be exfiltrated from each computer in a time ranging from seconds to dozens of minutes, depending on the transmitting parameters and number of fans participating in the covert channel. Note that the attackers may use multiple computers to increase the channel bandwidth.

Table 6. Transmission times min $(d = 0.250\,\text{ms})$/max $(d = 2\,\text{s})$

Information	1 fan	2 fans	3 fans
256-bit bitcoin key	64 s/512 s	32 s/256 s	21 s/170 s
Password (64 bit)	16 s/128 s	8 s/256 s	5 s/43 s
2048 bit RSA key	512 s/4096 s	256 s/2048 s	170 s/1375 s
AES 128 key	32 s/256 s	16 s/128 s	10 s/85 s
Keylogging	8 s/1.2 s	4 s/1 s	3 s/0.5 s
PIN codes (80 bits)	20 s/160 s	10 s/80 s	7 s/53 s
Brief texts (100 bytes)	200 s/1600 s	100 s/800 s	67 s/533 s

7   Countermeasures

Several defensive and protective countermeasures can be taken to defend against the proposed covert channel.

- **Zone restrictions.** Several US and NATO standards, such as NATO SDIP-27, NATO AMSG, USA NSTISSAM, and NATO ZONES, define a separation of zones usually to deal with radiated electromagnetic, magnetic, optical, and acoustic waves of equipment [33]. In this approach, recording devices such as laptops, mobile phones, or recording devices are eliminated from the area of air-gapped computers or kept at least outside a specified radius of several meters away.
- **Intrusion Detection.** In this approach, we monitor the GPU fan's activities within the operating systems and detect suspicious activities. Such anomalies could be a process that frequently changes the GPU fan's speed. These are three different layers from which an intrusion detection system can be operated. **(1) API monitoring:** In this user-level approach, the thermal API provided by the OEM is monitored, and the actual function calls are inspected in runtime. In the case of Windows OS, this can be implemented as proxy dynamic link libraries (DLLs) to the OEM libraries or by using code injection and hooking techniques. **(2) Monitoring kernel driver:** In this kernel level approach, a driver/module is installed at the kernel level and continuously monitors the commands sent to the graphic cards on the specified buses. The main advantage of this approach is the ability to cope with kernel-level rootkits that bypass user-level mechanisms. **(3) File system filter:** This approach is most relevant to Linux/Mac systems, in which the fan can be controlled using the file system interface. This method installs a file system filter and monitors the I/O control commands sent to the GPU fans. Our experiment shows that all the monitoring approach leaks to certain levels of false positive. One of the main reasons is that legitimate software regulates the GPU fans according to the current temperature and workload on the GPU.

- **External acoustic monitoring.** It is possible to use noise detector hardware devices that record and analyze the audio waves in a room at a specified range of frequencies. Although such products exist [34], they are mainly used in the ultrasonic band, which is relatively quiet. As shown in Sect. 6 the relevant range for our covert channel is 0–700 Hz which is a highly noisy range; it would suffer from high rates of false alarms due to environmental noises.
- **Internal jamming.** Another option is to interrupt the covert channel by applying random fluctuations to the GPU fans. Such jamming can be implemented as a process that randomly interferes and performs slight changes to the GPU fan RPMs. The main drawback of this approach is the undesired continuous interference with the GPU fans that can affect its performance.
- **External acoustic jamming.** Acoustic jammers are hardware devices which used to mask potential transmissions on certain frequency ranges, usually ultrasonic. The jamming is done by continuously producing high-power white noise signals in the whole range, masking other signals. While this approach is effective for the inaudible ultrasonic band, it is less relevant to the low-frequency band of our covert channel. Jamming the 0–700 Hz range yields a continuous high noise in the room, which is usually not accepted due to user inconvenience and health reasons.
- **GPU with water cooling.** GPU water coolers, such as Corsair Hydro series, provide effective and quiet cooling for GPUs and graphic cards. However, the users need to purchase the complete cooling kit to facilitate a GPU water block and are also required to work only with compatible graphic cards, which is not always possible.
- **Noise blocking chassis.** There are specialized enclosures for workstations and servers, which can significantly reduce the noise levels on the system's top, bottom, or sides. They also reduce the negative impact of air and structure-borne vibrations. Some of the products we checked can reduce the noise by 70–75%, equivalent to approximately 15 dBA.

8   Conclusion

This paper presents a covert acoustic channel that allows attackers to exfiltrate information from air-gapped, audio-gapped systems. We show that malicious code in the computer can control the momentary speed of the GPU cooling fans and encode binary information over the changes. A nearby receiver, such as a compromised smartphone, can receive the emanated blade frequency acoustic signals and decode the binary data. We present the design, implementation, and evaluation of the covert channel. We also discuss the GPU fan control and the multiple fans modulation. The results show that some sensitive information, such as encryption keys, credentials, and texts, can be successfully leaked from air-gapped computers up to five meters away.

References

1. New nation-state cyberattacks - microsoft on the issues. https://blogs.microsoft. com/on-the-issues/2021/03/02/new-nation-state-cyberattacks/. Accessed 09 Apr 2022
2. Ronin hack: North korea's lazarus behind $540 million axe infinity breach | wired. https://www.wired.com/story/ronin-hack-lazarus-tmobile-breach-data-malware-telegram/. Accessed 09 Apr 2022
3. Agent.btz - Wikipedia. https://en.wikipedia.org/wiki/Agent.BTZ. Accessed 09 May 2022
4. Kushner, D.: The real story of stuxnet. IEEE Spectr. **50**(3), 48–53 (2013)
5. ESET research discovers cyber espionage framework Ramsay | ESET. https:// www.eset.com/int/about/newsroom/press-releases/research/eset-research-discovers-cyber-espionage-framework-ramsay/. Accessed 09 May 2022
6. Tick group weaponized secure USB drives to target air-gapped critical systems. https://unit42.paloaltonetworks.com/unit42-tick-group-weaponized-secure-usb-drives-target-air-gapped-critical-systems/. Accessed 09 May 2022
7. Mazurczyk, W., Wendzel, S., Zander, S., Houmansadr, A., Szczypiorski, K.: Information Hiding in Communication Networks: Fundamentals, Mechanisms, Applications, and Countermeasures. John Wiley, Hoboken (2016)
8. Guri, M., Elovici, Y.: Bridgeware: the air-gap malware. Commun. ACM **61**(4), 74–82 (2018)
9. Guri, M., Solewicz, Y., Elovici, Y.: Fansmitter: acoustic data exfiltration from air-gapped computers via fans noise. Comput. Secur. **91**, 101721 (2020)
10. Assante, M. J., Lee, R. M.: The industrial control system cyber kill chain. SANS Inst. InfoSec Read. Room **1** (2015)
11. The big hack: How china used a tiny chip to infiltrate U.S. companies - Bloomberg. https://www.bloomberg.com/news/features/2018-10-04/the-big-hack-how-china-used-a-tiny-chip-to-infiltrate-america-s-top-companies. Accessed 09 Apr 2022
12. Guri, M., Kedma, G., Kachlon, A., Elovici, Y.: AirHopper: bridging the Air-Gap between isolated networks and mobile phones using radio frequencies. In: Malicious and Unwanted Software: The Americas (MALWARE), 2014 9th International Conference on, pp. 58–67. IEEE (2014)
13. Guri, M., Kachlon, A., Hasson, O., Kedma, G., Mirsky, Y., Elovici, Y.: GSMem: data exfiltration from air-gapped computers over GSM frequencies. In: USENIX Security Symposium, pp. 849–864 (2015)
14. funtenna - GitHub (2016). https://github.com/funtenna. Accessed 09 May 2022
15. Guri, M., Monitz, M., Elovici, Y.: USBee: Air-Gap covert-channel via electromagnetic emission from USB. In: 2016 14th Annual Conference on Privacy, Security and Trust (PST), pp. 264–268. IEEE (2016)
16. Guri, M., Zadov, B., Elovici, Y.: ODINI: escaping sensitive data from faraday-caged, air-gapped computers via magnetic fields. IEEE Trans. Inf. Forensics Secur. **15**, 1190–1203 (2019)
17. Guri, M., Zadov, B., Bykhovsky, D., Elovici, Y.: PowerHammer: exfiltrating data from Air-Gapped computers through power lines. IEEE Trans. Inf. Forensics Secur. **15**, 1879–1890 (2019)
18. Shao, Z., Islam, M.A., Ren, S.: Your noise, my signal: exploiting switching noise for stealthy data exfiltration from desktop computers. Proc. ACM Meas. Anal. Comput. Syst. **4**(1), 1–39 (2020)

19. Loughry, J., Umphress, D.A.: Information leakage from optical emanations. ACM Trans. Inf. Syst. Secur. (TISSEC) **5**(3), 262–289 (2002)

20. Guri, M., Zadov, B., Bykhovsky, D., Elovici, Y.: CTRL-ALT-LED: leaking data from Air-Gapped computers via keyboard LEDs. In: 2019 IEEE 43rd Annual Computer Software and Applications Conference (COMPSAC), vol. 1, pp. 801–810. IEEE (2019)

21. Nassi, B., Shamir, A., Elovici, Y.: Xerox day vulnerability. IEEE Trans. Inf. Forensics Secur. **14**(2), 415–430 (2018)

22. Guri, M., Zadov, B., Elovici, Y.: LED-it-GO: leaking (A Lot of) data from Air-Gapped computers via the (Small) hard drive LED. In: Polychronakis, M., Meier, M. (eds.) DIMVA 2017. LNCS, vol. 10327, pp. 161–184. Springer, Cham (2017). https://doi.org/10.1007/978-3-319-60876-1_8

23. Guri, M., Zadov, B., Daidakulov, A., Elovici, Y.: xlED: covert data exfiltration from Air-Gapped networks via switch and router LEDs. In: 2018 16th Annual Conference on Privacy, Security and Trust (PST), pp. 1–12. IEEE (2018)

24. Guri, M., Bykhovsky, D., Elovici, Y.: Brightness: leaking sensitive data from Air-Gapped workstations via screen brightness. In: 2019 12th CMI Conference on Cybersecurity and Privacy (CMI), pp. 1–6. IEEE (2019)

25. Guri, M., Monitz, M., Mirski, Y., Elovici, Y.: BitWhisper: covert signaling channel between Air-Gapped computers using thermal manipulations. In: 2015 IEEE 28th Computer Security Foundations Symposium (CSF), pp. 276–289. IEEE (2015)

26. Madhavapeddy, A., Sharp, R., Scott, D., Tse, A.: Audio networking: the forgotten wireless technology. IEEE Pervasive Comput. **4**(3), 55–60 (2005)

27. Carrara, B., Adams, C.: On acoustic covert channels between Air-Gapped systems. In: Cuppens, F., Garcia-Alfaro, J., Zincir Heywood, N., Fong, P.W.L. (eds.) FPS 2014. LNCS, vol. 8930, pp. 3–16. Springer, Cham (2015). https://doi.org/10.1007/978-3-319-17040-4_1

28. Guri, M., Solewicz, Y., Elovici, Y.: Mosquito: covert ultrasonic transmissions between two Air-Gapped computers using speaker-to-speaker communication. In 2018 IEEE Conference on Dependable and Secure Computing (DSC), pp. 1–8. IEEE (2018)

29. Deshotels, L.: Inaudible sound as a covert channel in mobile devices. In: WOOT (2014)

30. Guri, M., Solewicz, Y., Daidakulov, A., Elovici, Y.: Acoustic data exfiltration from speakerless Air-Gapped computers via covert hard-drive noise ('DiskFiltration'). In: Foley, S.N., Gollmann, D., Snekkenes, E. (eds.) ESORICS 2017. LNCS, vol. 10493, pp. 98–115. Springer, Cham (2017). https://doi.org/10.1007/978-3-319-66399-9_6

31. Guri, M.: Cd-leak: leaking secrets from audioless Air-Gapped computers using covert acoustic signals from CD/DVD drives. In: 2020 IEEE 44th Annual Computers, Software, and Applications Conference (COMPSAC), pp. 808–816. IEEE (2020)

32. Guri, M.: Power-supplay: Leaking sensitive data from air-gapped, audio-gapped systems by turning the power supplies into speakers. IEEE Trans. Dependable Secure Comput., 1 (2021)

33. Nstissamtempest/2-95 (2000). https://cryptome.org, https://cryptome.org/tempest-2-95.htm. Accessed 09 May 2022

34. Products - pulsar instruments plc (2018). https://pulsarinstruments.com/en/categories. Accessed 09 May 2022

Secure Protocols and Systems

SIMPLEX: Repurposing Intel Memory Protection Extensions for Secure Storage

Matthew Cole[(✉)] and Aravind Prakash

Binghamton University, Binghamton, USA
{mcole8,aprakash}@binghamton.edu

Abstract. The last few decades have seen several hardware-level features to enhance security, but due to security, performance, and/or usability issues these features have attracted steady criticism. One such feature is the Intel Memory Protection Extensions (MPX), an instruction set architecture extension promising spatial memory safety at a lower performance cost due to hardware-accelerated bounds checking. However, recent investigations into MPX have found that is neither as performant, accurate, nor precise as software-based spatial memory safety. Given its ubiquity, we argue that it provides an under-utilized hardware resource that can be salvaged for security purposes. We propose SIMPLEX, an open-sourced library that re-purposes MPX registers as general purpose registers. Using SIMPLEX, we demonstrate securely storing sensitive information directly on the hardware (e.g. encryption keys). We evaluate for performance, and find that deployment is feasible in all but the most performance-intensive code, with amortized performance overhead as low as about 1%.

Keywords: Information hiding · Hardware security · Intel MPX

1 Introduction

Intel Memory Protection Extensions (MPX) is an instruction set architecture (ISA) extension for modern Intel processors providing spatial memory safety using compile-time intentions. MPX is comprised of three key components working in harmony: architectural support through a set of two configuration, one status, and four bounds registers; compile-time instrumentation; and run-time support integrated with the operating system. This run-time manages enabling and disabling CPU interpretation of MPX instructions through the configuration registers, sets up a pointer bounds lookup table for spilling more objects' bounds than four registers can hold, interprets error codes indicated in the status register, and coordinates with the operating system to handle memory management and error handling.

In practice, MPX is unusable in its intended form. It was intended to be performant, inter-operable with un-instrumented legacy code, and configurable for both debug and release environments without rewriting the source. However, Oleksenko et al. and Serebryany independently showed that MPX does not perform as well as software- and language-based memory safety, demonstrating a

H. P. Reiser and M. Kyas (Eds.): NordSec 2022, LNCS 13700, pp. 215–233, 2022.
https://doi.org/10.1007/978-3-031-22295-5_12

50% amortized performance overhead with good compiler optimizations, and a 400% worst-case performance overhead [24,32]. The GNU C Compiler (GCC) recently removed its libmpx library and eliminated the instrumentation code, while Linux recently removed its support for kernel compilation due to a lack of community interest in maintaining the code. In short, MPX never achieved widespread adoption as a memory safety tool as envisioned by its designers, even as its architectural resources remain on widely-deployed processors. Yet even a conservative estimate puts the number of MPX-supported deployments at 100s of millions worldwide, thus MPX is a ubiquitous – yet unused – resource.

In this paper, we leverage MPX as a general storage primitive–specifically for storage of security-sensitive data such as cryptographic keys. Our contribution is named SIMPLEX, which is comprised of a library enabling introspection and manipulation of the MPX context, a minimalist runtime that avoids the overhead associated with the compiler-provided MPX runtime, a test suite verifying correctness, and evaluations demonstrating the practicality of SIMPLEX. Furthermore, our contribution allows manipulation of the MPX context *even in the complete absence of support* for compiler instrumentation or an operating system's runtime.

The SIMPLEX library provides all necessary runtime components and functions for instrumentation, and the MPX context is part of the broader XSAVE context, thus it is still saved and restored on context switches even though Linux formally removed all MPX support as of kernel version 5.6. Only a microcode update from Intel would break SIMPLEX by removing the CPU's ability to interpret the MPX opcodes, however we do not believe that this is likely to occur because there are no extant attacks against a victim which do not also link to an operating system's runtime (i.e. the attack proposed by Dekel and Kasif [7]).

Because the ability to prevent disclosure is a valuable resource in security, we emphasize applications of SIMPLEX for moving information out of main memory. For example, Hargreaves and Chivers, and Kazim et. al showed two different techniques for extracting encryption keys from main memory [13,16]. On the one hand, hiding data in the kernel is often impractical as it incurs performance overhead due to the expensive transitions between user and kernel modes. On the other hand, reserving registers (e.g. [18,20,21,34])) is undesirable for two reasons: (1) it removes a register from the allocation pool, which could impact performance due to sub-optimal register allocation [2], and (2) it affects interoperability when handwritten assembly or binaries not compiled using the modified compiler may accidentally access or modify the reserved register. Because SIMPLEX uses the MPX bounds registers, and because the bounds registers are not used unless the application was also explicitly compiled with MPX support, we can ensure that no other code will access or modify the hidden data or pointer stored inside the bounds register.

Our evaluation shows that SIMPLEX is practical, and confirms initial observations by Otterstad [27] and Oleksenko et al. [24] that the majority of MPX's performance cost comes from handling exceptions and interacting with the bounds lookup table within the runtime. We avoid this overhead because SIMPLEX avoids using the bounds lookup table by writing to the bounds registers directly using the `bndmk` instruction and reading from the bounds registers using the `bndmov` instruction to spill the contents into memory. We evaluated for performance in two different ways. First, we created three custom benchmark fixtures: (1) a microbenchmark testing the rate at which load and store operations can be completed to both the `%r15` general purpose register and the `%bnd0` MPX bounds register, (2) a macro-benchmark simulating information unhiding by traversing and combining two hidden half-buffers, and (3) implementations of a subset of the `string.h` header. Second, we compiled sandboxed versions of two SPEC CPU2017 benchmarks: 519.lbm, a particle-fluid simulation written in C, and 531.deepsjeng, a chess engine written in C++ to demonstrate practicality of moving key data into the MPX bounds registers from global memory. Finally, we evaluated for usability and correctness by modifying the OpenSSL Blowfish cipher, then running the included integration and unit test suites.

The remainder of the paper is structured as follows: We discuss the history of MPX and the reasons prohibiting its widespread adoption as a memory safety tool in Sect. 2.1. Next, we examine the problems in information hiding continuing to plague security researchers in Sect. 2.2. An overview of our threat model and necessary modifications to a compiler to support SIMPLEX appears in Sect. 3. We describe the implementation of the SIMPLEX library, and answer questions about MPX context behavior during common program behavior including multithreading and system process lifecycles in Sect. 4. We present our evaluation in Sect. 5, showing SIMPLEX is both sound and practical. Finally, we survey related work in Sect. 6 and conclude in Sect. 7.

2   Background

2.1   Intel MPX

In 2012, Intel introduced POINTERCHECKER, which provides bounds checking in the software layer through the Intel Composer XE development environment for C and C++ [9]. Recognizing the potential for greatly improved performance through hardware support, Intel moved much of the POINTER CHECKER functionality into MPX, announced in 2013 [14] and subsequently debuted in the Skylake architecture in 2015.

MPX is a combination of an instruction set extension, compiler and operating system support, and runtime library. It provides four new 128-bit bounds registers (`%BND0` through `%BND3`), each of which are split into an upper half and lower half which have the purpose of holding an upper bound and lower bound address. MPX also employs the `%BNDCFGx` register pair to hold user-space and kernel-space configuration, and a `%BNDSTATUS` register to hold status information in case of a bounds check failure. These additional registers are encompassed in the larger Intel64 context, shown in Fig. 1. Intel designed MPX with the overarching goal of compatibility with un-instrumented code and unextended architectures. Where an MPX-supported CPU encounters un-instrumented code, such as a vendor-provided library, program execution continues with the cost that the

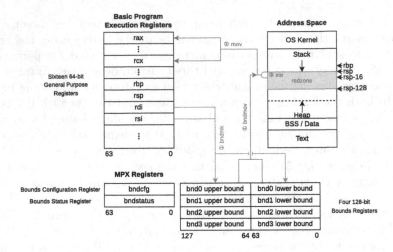

Fig. 1. The MPX context as part of the larger Intel64 context. The blue pathway shows how information is written to the bounds registers. The red pathway shows how information is read from the bounds registers (including sanitizing the stack afterwards). (Color figure online)

CPU can no longer provide memory safety because the bounds checks are not performed unless a `bndcl`, `bndcu`, or `bndcn` instruction is executed. Where an MPX-unsupported CPU encounters instrumented code, or when MPX has not been initialized by setting `%bndcfg[0]`, the instructions are interpreted as `nop` instructions instead of triggering unrecognized instruction exceptions.

Although MPX achieves a four- to five-fold speedup compared to POINTER CHECKER, it suffers prohibitive penalties of worst-case 200% performance overhead, 480% memory overhead, $5.4x$ more page faults [24], significant cache pressure, and a 50% slowdown even when bounds checking instructions are idempotent [32]. Furthermore, MPX cannot catch temporal memory safety issues [24], suffers false positives from otherwise legal C idioms due to restrictions on structure memory layouts [24,32] and false negatives in response to undefined behaviors which cause inappropriate bounds loads [27], conflicts with other Intel ISA extensions such as SGX and TSX [24], and it has no explicit support for multithreading [24]. As a result, support for MPX bounds checking has virtually ceased. Currently MPX's only remaining compiler support is Intel's own ICC since version 15.0 and Microsoft's Visual Studio 2015 Update 1.

2.2 Information Hiding

Information hiding techniques relying on probabilistic mechanisms can be defeated. Göktaş et al. demonstrated *thread spraying* [10] as a means of disclosing the safe regions with a known structure (e.g. the safe stack region used in [18]). By repeatedly creating objects that have both safe and regular allocations, then probing the space to find one of these hidden safe allocations, they can effectively de-randomize the entire address space. They also discovered that information in the thread local storage (TLS) and the thread control block (TCB) provide clues to locating these stacks. Furthermore, Oikonomopoulos et al. introduced *allocation oracles* which eliminate the need for probing [23]. The idea is that an allocation oracle takes the size of an area to allocate as input, and if successful returns the location allocated. From this information and applying a binary search technique, an attacker can locate "holes" in the allocatable memory. If the attacker has knowledge of how a defense's sensitive data is laid out, then these holes reveal where the sensitive data *is not* hidden. With enough queries to the oracle, eventually the sensitive data can be located, and the process avoids crashes or distinguishable behavior usable by a runtime detector. Likewise, Evans et al. used timing side channels to read the contents of hidden metadata with or without crashes (the former is faster, the latter is difficult to detect) [8]. Using this technique, they can de-randomize the location of libraries such as libc, then use this to calculate the start of the safe region. Once complete, modifying the contents of the safe region permits an attacker to violate at least one implementation of Code Pointer Integrity (CPI).

State of the art defenses use registers to simulate segmentation as available in the IA-32 architecture in order to provide deterministic rather than probabilistic information hiding. One common point of these implementations is that they would benefit from dedicated registers. For example, two of the implementations of CPI require a dedicated register for information hiding [18]. In the reference implementation, %fs was reserved, however this may affect other legitimate usages of the register. For example, operating systems sometimes use this register to access TLS. Providing register storage via SIMPLEX helps return reserved general purpose registers to the compiler's allocation list and restores special purpose registers to their expected usage.

The dangers of storing secrets such as cryptographic keys in memory are also well known. For example, CERT Secure Coding Standard MEM06-C warns against writing sensitive data to disk, and Cold Boot Attacks [12,26] are a well explored vector when the key is located in DRAM. As a result, these secrets are often moved to un-swappable memory, such as registers or enclaves in order to maintain secrecy.

3   SIMPLEX

3.1   Threat Model

We assume a threat model similar to that offered by other work on information hiding, namely Koning [17] and Yun [33]. Our system under threat has an effective defense against code reuse, which in turn prevents an attacker from arbitrarily calling the SIMPLEX library functions, even though he or she may have an arbitrary read or write primitive. Although SIMPLEX might be used to store a pointer to a *hidden* memory region, it does not itself provide *isolation*. We presume that the programmer has a *Trusted Code Base* comprised of at least a privileged, trusted operating system and a trusted build toolchain used to build the SIMPLEX library. We concede that an attacker may be able to load a Loadable Kernel Module (LKM) that enables or disables MPX at a privileged operating system level (and in fact, we provide one such implementation within the SIMPLEX code base). However, this would imply a compromised kernel, which is outside our scope. That said, we show in Sect. 3.4 that it is not sufficient for an attacker to emplace values into the bounds registers or leak values from the bounds registers in a way that is beneficial to the attacker. Finally, we assume that SIMPLEX is correctly implemented and is trusted by the programmer. We release our code as open source, and offer a full test suite within that code base as an assurance to that assumption.

3.2   Design Decisions

Previous works seeking to hide information from attackers have chosen one of three options. 1) Storing information in the kernel or in pages that can only be accessed in a privileged hardware mode (e.g. [11,15]) is secure as long as the operating system is not compromised. However these schemes come with the obligation of additional context switches for each query or update, hampering performance. 2) A more performant choice is storing information in a hidden region within the program's address space (e.g. [6,18,21]). Yet it relies on either probabilistic hiding measures which can be defeated if the attacker has knowledge of the type of information being hidden, or if the attacker is able to tolerate crashes and restarts while searching. 3) Alternatively, it is possible to reserve registers from the compiler's allocation pool and use these registers exclusively for storing sensitive data. Once the registers are selected, the defender can formally verify that no other code accesses these registers, guaranteeing security. Nonetheless, there is still the concern that available registers are limited and may conflict with other defenses or dynamically linked code that use the reserved register.

3.3   Simplex-Enabled Compilation

In our evaluations, we manually replaced global pointer objects and their reference/dereference statements with the necessary code to enable bounds register usage. However, we do not feel this is scalable. Consider the modifications made to the SPEC CPU2017 benchmarks: 519.lbm has just 1 KLOC and required 22 modifications, 531.deepsjeng has only 10 KLOC and required 173 modifications – these are very small code bases compared to 502.gcc (1.3 MLOC) and 526.blender (1.6 MLOC), the largest C/C++ benchmarks in CPU2017. Making these modifications are expensive in terms of developer effort and time, requiring both discovering and understanding the global variables' utilization. For example, modifying the two SPEC CPU2017 benchmarks took about two days of development time each. If the number and complexity of changes necessary were to scale, implementing the larger benchmarks by hand becomes infeasible. Therefore, we have designed but not yet implemented a system using Clang's annotation system to mark variables as candidates for placement in a bounds register. This reduces the developer's workload to simply recognizing which variables should go into a bounds register, applying annotations to the declarations, then compiling the source code with the options necessary to enable SIMPLEX.

First, the developer applies the necessary annotation at the variable's declaration. The compiler recognizes the annotation, and maps that variable to one of the bounds registers, depending on its size or throws a compilation error if no more register space is available. Next, the compiler pass replaces references to these variables with appropriate SIMPLEX function calls. If the variable is an *lvalue*, it is replaced with a call to one of the mutator functions; if it is a *rvalue*, it is replaced with a call to one of the accessor functions.

Developer Annotation vs Automated Discovery: On the one hand, developer annotation has the benefit of precisely capturing what is of security relevance and importance as per software design, but on the other hand, developers are prone to make mistakes. Therefore, we recommend three modes of operation that make a trade off between security and performance.

Whitelisting: In this mode, we allow a developer to whitelist security-sensitive data that is stored in the MPX bounds registers by the compiler. This is the most conservative and performance-friendly, yet error-prone option.

Automatic Inference: In this mode, the compiler employs a heuristic approach to automatically profile and identify security sensitive information and accordingly provisions MPX bounds registers to manage such sensitive data. One option is to identify security-sensitive documented API functions and perform backward slicing to identify data of interest. This is the most aggressive option that favors security over performance.

Blacklisting: Finally, as an intermediate option, blacklisting allows a developer to define data items that *should not* be stored in the MPX registers. While blacklisting is just as prone to human error as is whitelisting, it is likely to have less adverse effects on security as compared to mistakes in whitelisting.

3.4   Context Behavior

Motivated by the desire to provide confidentiality between processes and/or threads – even when there is a relationship between the processes or threads – we explored the behavior of the MPX context. At process creation, the child inherits an identical MPX context to that of the parent because the MPX context is itself part of the larger CPU context (see Fig. 1).

Because SIMPLEX provides methods to initialize and finalize its minimal MPX context, the reader may question what would happen if a programmer or attacker called these methods repeatedly (whether by accident or malice). We found that each time the MPX context is initialized, the bounds registers' lower bounds are set to the system maximum unsigned value, and the upper bounds are set to 0. In MPX's design use case, this results in a guaranteed passed bounds check until the bounds register is set to some allocated object's bounds. In the SIMPLEX use case, repeated initialization destroys the values inside the bounds registers by resetting them to the conservative bounds values. Although this may allow an attack against availability, it does not allow an attack seeking disclosure. Furthermore, it is no more dangerous for code-reuse attacks than the numerous xor %reg %reg instructions which are used by the compiler to place a zero value in a register.

4   Implementation

4.1   Components of SIMPLEX

Unfortunately, there is no means of directly accessing the MPX bounds registers via a mov instruction. ICC does offer intrinsics, although these are only available if a MPX runtime is available and providing bounds checking [29]. This means it is not possible to use these intrinsics for accessing the bounds registers without also suffering the continual risk of a bounds check clobbering the bounds registers. Therefore, within SIMPLEX we provide a system readiness check, a minimal runtime to enable and disable MPX execution, accessor and mutator functions, and a test suite to verify proper operation of the library.

System Readiness Check. Although it is possible for a user to test whether their system can support MPX from the command line using commands such as lscpu and sysctl, a program must be able to verify readiness itself and abort further execution if it cannot prove its readiness. This is because CPUs that do not support MPX will silently interpret these MPX instructions as NOP. We verify that %CPUID[14] is set (indicating that the CPU supports the MPX extension), and that %XCR0[3:4] are set (indicating that the CPU should include the MPX registers as part of a context save and restore) during initialization.

Enabling and Disabling Functions. We also provide a way of enabling and disabling MPX operations within both kernel mode and user mode applications. This can be done by setting flags on the %BNDCFGS and %BNDCFGU registers respectively. %BNDCFGx[0] enables interpretation of the MPX instruction extension, and %BNDCFGx[1] enables bounds register preservation when legacy instructions are encountered. Unlike the GCC run-time, we do *not* set %BNDCFGx[63:12] with the base address of the bounds table. This minimizes startup overhead, and also provides a small measure of security since accidentally attempting to access the bounds table will result in a segmentation fault rather than disclosing the contents of a bounds register.

Accessor and Mutator Functions. For each of the four bounds registers, a common accessor and mutator wrapper function provides a handle to the bounds register. There are four varieties of each wrapper function: lower-half 64 bits only, upper-half 64 bits only, all 128 bits, and a "quick" lower-half only which does not attempt to save the upper-half nor clean the stack of any spilled values. The applicable bounds register is selected through an enumerator with four values. When writing to the bounds registers, the value to be written is marshaled from the function arguments into a bndmk instruction using sib-addressing. When accessing, the bounds register is atomically spilled onto the stack above the stack pointer (i.e. at a lower address than the top of the stack) then moved into a register because there is no bounds register-to-general purpose register instruction. This is accomplished using a bndmov instruction. As previously mentioned, all accessor functions except the quick variants will sanitize this value on the stack in case the value stored within the bounds registers is sensitive. We have verified that our extended assembly statements to perform the sanitation are not optimized by either GCC or Clang through manual inspection of disassembled code. See Fig. 1 for more information on data flows to and from the MPX context.

4.2   Security Impact of the SIMPLEX Implementation

Canella et al. recently reported a variety of Meltdown transient execution attacks, one of which is the Meltdown-BR (Bounds Check Bypass) attack [4,19]. Dekel also describes a post-exploitation technique called BoundHook, which allows an attacker to cause a bounds check exception in a user-mode context, and then catch the exception to gain control over the thread execution [7]. With both of these vulnerabilities, SIMPLEX does not increase a program's attack surface because both require a #BR exception to be raised in order to initiate exploitation. Since SIMPLEX does not use the bndcl, bndcu, or bndcn instructions, no such exception will be raised by our code. Additionally, because BoundHook requires that the attacker has also already compromised machine administrator rights, any attacker who can successfully execute a BoundHook intrusion can simply observe and modify the MPX context without the need to further compromise SIMPLEX.

Considerations for Multi-threaded Programs. Because SIMPLEX can be used in multi-threaded applications, we must address the dangers that an attacker-controlled thread could victimize a thread using SIMPLEX to interact with the MPX bounds registers during a brief period after spilling to the stack. We provide one mitigation in that SIMPLEX will zero out the memory used by the bndmov spill instruction immediately after copying to the destination register in all accessor functions except for qgetbndl which is performance- rather than security-optimized. We speculated an attacker-controlled victim thread or process with a pointer to the bottom of the stack could read this memory in a race condition assisted by a scheduler interrupt sometime between the spill from the bounds register to the time the stack memory is sanitized. Therefore we instrumented our library using a PAPI API [1] software defined event to measure the frequency of context switches within the SIMPLEX accessor functions and did not detect that such a sequence of events occurred. We hypothesize that this is because the accessor functions do not require any system calls and are very short-lived, and thus unlikely to trigger the scheduler's watchdog timer. Furthermore, we note that threads cannot directly access other threads' stacks, therefore the risk is limited to an attacker causing a process or thread to disclose its own bounds register values into shared memory during the window. We also note that SIMPLEX spills outside the red zone, and therefore the compiler should not generate instructions that otherwise access this region without attacker input, and therefore such gadgets in the intended instruction stream are extremely rare.

5   Evaluation

We conducted our evaluation on an 8-core Intel Core i7-7700K CPU at 4.20 GHz with 62.8 GiB RAM running Ubuntu 20.04 LTS and the Linux 5.4 kernel. The system under evaluation conforms to POSIX.1-2017, and uses GNU libc and POSIX thread implementation version 2.27.

5.1   Benchmarks

We authored two benchmark fixtures to evaluate whether SIMPLEX attains performance that is comparable to using general purpose registers.

Load-Store Benchmark. First, we authored a micro-benchmark that tests load and store performance when SIMPLEX employs the %bnd0 MPX bounds register compared to handwritten assembly using general purpose registers using %r15, segmentation registers using %gs:0, and the MMX and SSE instruction set extension registers using %mm0 and %xmm1 respectively, see Fig. 2. We find that the mean of writing to the MPX bounds registers is comparable to writing to the general purpose registers ($1.00x$), segmentation registers ($1.01x$), and MMX registers ($0.98x$). This is because all four of these operations have a fast, dedicated assembly instruction for writing to the register - either mov or bndmk. The fastest assembly instruction option for writing to the SSE registers is movaps, which moves four aligned, packed, single-precision floating point values to the register. However, it incurs significant overhead compared to the mov instruction because of microarchitectural limitations and thus the rate of MPX bounds register writes is $13.90x$ faster than these writes.

Loading from the MPX bounds registers is a different story. Additional overhead results because the MPX extension does not contain an instruction to move from a bounds register directly to another register, whether a bounds register or otherwise; bndmov only provides a bounds register to memory spill operation. Therefore load operations from a bounds register require that the data is first spilled to the quadword above the stack pointer through a bndmov instruction, then recovered through two additional mov instructions. General purpose register, segmentation register and MMX register loads can all be accomplished by a single mov instruction and thus MPX bounds register loads are only $0.74x$, $0.32x$, and $0.73x$ as fast, respectively. Segmentation register loads are particularly fast when repeatedly executed because of cache effects. Conversely, MPX bounds register loads are $1.69x$ faster than SSE register loads because these loads also must spill to stack, and because of the aforementioned micro-architectural limitations of the apsmov instruction.

Our findings also confirm the micro-architectural analysis of Oleksenko et al. [24] which found that it was not necessarily the MPX bounds operations that were particularly expensive, but rather the management of the bounds table through a two-level table lookup – particularly the `bndstx` and `bndldx` instructions. Simplex uses neither of these instructions and thus avoids their associated performance overhead.

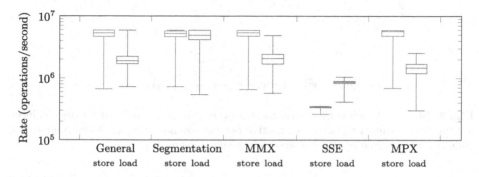

Fig. 2. Rate of load and store operations. Box and whisker plot shows median, minimum/maximum, and first/third quartile operation rates. We use `%r15` for *General*, `%gs:0` for *Segmentation*, `%mm0` for *MMX*, `%xmm1` for *SSE* and `%bnd0` for *MPX*. The test consisted of 10^4 runs, with 10^6 iterations per run. We report the steady-state rate of operations accomplished per second.

String Operations. We also evaluated the block memory operations from the `string.h` header using reference implementations of libgcc. We excluded the string-specific functions so that we could randomly fill buffers from test run-to-run without the concern of whether the buffer formed a single valid C string, and because our choice of functions does not include trivial functions that do not operate on buffers (e.g. `strerror`). We then refactored these functions for Simplex to replace any passed argument that contains the address of a buffer with calls to instead load it from the corresponding bounds register. These benchmarks show that the performance cost of Simplex is easily amortized, as we found that the maximum overhead was only 5.86%, and a 0.69% overall geometric mean. In the specific case of these function implementations, benchmarks that do not short-circuit (i.e. memcpy, memmove and memset) are able to amortize the cost fully compared to functions that do short-circuit (i.e. memcmp, memchr). We do not claim that there is a performance benefit to Simplex, simply that if there is a performance cost, it is small enough to be unnoticeable to the user and that it is offset by the utility of the additional registers provided by Simplex. We report specific data for each benchmark in Fig. 3.

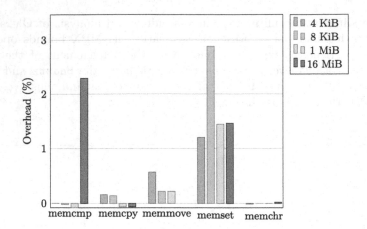

Fig. 3. String.h benchmarks' performance overhead when modified to pass pointer arguments in bounds registers. A negative percentage indicates the SIMPLEX-modified code ran in less time than the reference implementation.

5.2   Modifications to Existing Codebases

SPEC CPU2017. We hand-modified two SPEC CPU2017 benchmarks, 519.1bm which simulates fluid flow through lattices, and 531.deepsjeng which plays chess. In both cases, we selected the two global pointers to data structures that had the highest number of uses in order to fully stress the SIMPLEX library, showing an example of these modifications in Fig. 4. Although we selected global objects, it should be emphasized that SIMPLEX is not limited to just globals; heap or local objects could also be placed in the bounds registers. Using the SPEC benchmarks proves both correctness – the output is verified against a known correct output – and demonstrates performance cost of using SIMPLEX. We measured the performance rate ratio between runs with an unmodified benchmark and one where frequently used pointers to global variables were placed into a bounds register. This performance ratio was between 1.000 and 1.006 for 519.1bm, and 0.975 and 0.985 for 531.deepsjeng (see Table 1). Higher performance rate ratios indicate faster execution, but differ from performance overhead measurements since performance rate takes into account the number of threaded copies running simultaneously.

OpenSSL. We then modified the OpenSSL Blowfish symmetric key cipher to demonstrate how SIMPLEX might be used in a security application. In our modified Blowfish cipher, the address of the cipher's global key schedule structure is stored in a bounds register. Therefore wherever an encryption or decryption function would ordinarily receive a pointer to the key schedule as a function parameter, we instead pass a null value as the parameter and thus de-reference the bounds register at each usage of the parameter. Although the OpenSSL test suite provides test run time in its output, the Blowfish correctness test is very

```
      #include <sys/stat.h>
     +#include "simplex.h"

     -static LBM_GridPtr srcGrid, dstGrid;

     void MAIN_initialize(const MAIN_Param* param) {
     +        process_specific_init();

     -        LBM_allocateGrid((double**) &srcGrid);
     -        LBM_allocateGrid((double**) &dstGrid);
     +        double* ptr;
     +        LBM_allocateGrid(&ptr);
     +        qsetbndl(BND0,(uint64_t) ptr);
     +        ptr = 0;
     +        LBM_allocateGrid(&ptr);
     +        qsetbndl(BND1,(uint64_t) ptr);
     +        ptr = 0;

     -        LBM_initializeGrid(*srcGrid);
     -        LBM_initializeGrid(*dstGrid);
     +        LBM_initializeGrid(*((LBM_GridPtr)qgetbndl(BND0)));
     +        LBM_initializeGrid(*((LBM_GridPtr)qgetbndl(BND1)));
     }
     void MAIN_finalize(const MAIN_Param* param) {
     -        LBM_freeGrid((double**) &srcGrid);
     -        LBM_freeGrid((double**) &dstGrid);
     +        double* p0 = (double*) qgetbndl(BND0);
     +        double* p1 = (double*) qgetbndl(BND1);
     +        LBM_freeGrid(&p0);
     +        p0 = 0;
     +        LBM_freeGrid(&p1);
     +        p1 = 0;

     +        process_specific_finish();
     }
```

Fig. 4. An example of modifications needed to store global pointers in bounds registers from the lbm benchmark. In this example, the global pointers srcGrid and dstGrid are placed in BND0 and BND1 respectively.

short in duration. As a result, our observed runtime overheads are smaller than the reported measurement resolution and not particularly useful as a metric of performance (see Table 2). We conclude that register repurposing presents minimal performance cost for cryptographic applications. We also emphasize that although we placed a pointer to a key schedule structure in the bounds registers for this evaluation, this structure is stored on the heap in the unmodified Blowfish cipher and therefore we have not introduced attack surface in our modified cipher. Additionally, some other OpenSSL ciphers' keys are less than 512 bits in size and would fit entirely within the bounds registers. The MPX bounds registers can hold any value, not just pointer values.

6   Related Work

Existing Evaluations. Explorations of Intel MPX generally find MPX to be flawed as a memory safety tool, and thus inspired our investigation as to whether MPX could be repurposed. Serebryany unfavorably evaluated the performance

Table 1. SIMPLEX SPEC CPU2017 evaluation data. *Run time* refers to how long the benchmark took to complete. *Base Rate* refers to the raw performance of this benchmark relative to the SPEC CPU2017 reference machine and thus provides insight into the underlying system under test. *Ratio* refers to the ratio of the modified benchmark's multi-threaded performance to the unmodified benchmark's multi-threaded performance. *Ratio* < 1 implies the modified benchmark ran slower than the unmodified benchmark.

Variables in bounds register	Copies	Run time	Base rate	Ratio
519.lbm_r				
None	1	202	5.21	
None	4	605	6.96	
srcGrid →bnd0	1	201	5.24	1.006
srcGrid →bnd0	4	605	6.96	1.000
srcGrid →bnd0, dstGrid →bnd1	1	202	5.23	1.004
srcGrid →bnd0, dstGrid →bnd1	4	606	6.96	1.000
531.deepsjeng_r				
None	1	283	4.04	
None	4	290	15.8	
state →bnd0, gamestate →bnd1	1	288	3.98	0.985
state →bnd0, gamestate →bnd1	4	297	15.4	0.975

Table 2. Simplex OpenSSL evaluation data. Measurements were obtained using `time(1)`, and presented columns reflect its output.

Variables in bounds register	usr	sys	cusr	csys	cpu
05-test_bf.t					
None	0.02	0.00	0.03	0.00	0.05
BF_KEY *schedule →bnd0	0.01	0.00	0.03	0.00	0.04
Overhead	−50.0%	0.0%	0.0%	0.0%	−20.0%

of Intel MPX versus the Address Sanitizer memory safety tool [31,32]. Notably, he discovered not only up to a $2.5x$ performance slowdown and $4.0x$ memory overhead on some benchmarks, but that the MPX instructions still exhibit a 50% slowdown even when they should be ignored on a system which does not have MPX support or has disabled it. He also identifies three categories of false positives that Address Sanitizer does not have: atomic pointers, un-instrumented bounds changes, and those caused by compiler optimizations after instrumentation. Otterstad examined the effectiveness of early implementations of MPX, identifying eight new categories of false positives and false negatives beyond those explored by Serebryany [27]. Furthermore, he demonstrates at least one toy program which can be victimized by ROP attacks because of these false positives and false negatives. Oleksenko et al. performed a study of the performance, security guarantees, and usability issues of MPX after it became available in production hardware [24]. Furthermore, their empirical study was backed by an exhaustive investigation of how MPX is actually implemented at the hardware, operating system and software levels, supporting their experimental findings.

Other Uses of Intel MPX. We are not the only members of the community to propose repurposing MPX. Code Pointer Integrity (CPI) maintains a safe region to protect function pointers, return addresses and other pointers to code called a "safe stack" [18]. The authors propose one implementation of CPI using MPX to store the safe region's metadata, gaining performance benefits by moving some of the implementation into MPX's hardware accelerated checks. Burow further investigates using MPX to isolate CPI's shadow stacks and provide a highly-efficient implementation [3]. We note that SIMPLEX performs much of the management functionality they described, and could be used in conjunction with their defenses. Opaque Control-Flow Integrity (O-CFI) combines fine-grained code layout randomization with coarse-grained CFI in order to defeat sophisticated attacks seeking in-memory layout information to launch code-reuse attacks [21]. O-CFI uses MPX instructions to perform branch instrumentation, where legal branch targets are "chunked" together into a minimal address range, similar to a buffer. Oleksenko proposes a system combining MPX for hardware fault detection with Intel Transactional Synchronization Extensions (TSX) for fault rollback [25]. The underlying principle is that if a pointer's value is corrupted by a fault, then it will likely point to a dramatically different address outside the bounds of the referent object. MemSentry is a deterministic memory isolation framework addressing the threats of allocation oracles, thread spraying, crash-resistant memory disclosure primitives, and various side channels [17]. The authors use MPX and Intel Memory Protection Keys (MPK) to describe a more efficient method of intra-process isolation, similar to that provided by the kernel through mprotect and Software Fault Isolation (SFI). CFIXX is a C++ defense for virtual table pointers providing Object Type Integrity (OTI) [3]. CFIXX protects against corruption attacks against OTI by protecting the memory region containing the OTI metadata with selective MPX instrumentation. By reimagining the layout of the address space, they are able to halve the number of bound checks compared to a full memory safety solution provided by MPX. BOGO extends the MPX bounds tables to not only provide spatial memory safety, but also temporal memory safety [35]. Since MPX already initializes bounds table entries at allocation, BOGO additionally invalidates these entries upon deallocation and thus gains temporal memory safety. Since doing this operation at every deallocation can be expensive, the authors also introduce more efficient techniques for managing the deallocation metadata updates and for scanning the bounds table. DataShield provides three methods for coarse-grained bounds checks for non-sensitive pointer dereferences, one of which utilizes MPX to avoid the need to information hide the non-sensitive data regions [5]. Up to four of these regions' addresses are initialized in the MPX bounds register at program startup, with each pointer dereference in order to assure that the pointer does not escape the non-sensitive region. The Linux kernel can be protected against

Just-in-Time code reuse attacks by kRˆX, which hardens benign read operations that an attacker might reuse to disclose code to find useful JIT gadgets [28]. Intel MPX is used in one implementation of kRˆX to accelerate the execute-only range checks to reduce the performance overhead. The Spons & Shields Framework (SSF) for Intel SGX trusted execution environments uses the MPX bounds check instructions to verify memory accesses, however it does so outside of the traditional MPX runtime [30].

Repurposing Hardware Registers. The idea of repurposing hardware registers as with SIMPLEX is not unique. TRESOR is a patch that implements the AES encryption algorithm for the Linux kernel, and also provides additional security by utilizing the Intel AES-NI instruction set extension plus keeping encryption keys in the x86 debug registers instead of in RAM [22]. Ginseng keeps secrets in an encrypted secure stack until they are needed, then moves the secret into dedicated registers [33]. This has the effect of reducing the amount of sensitive data kept in the ARM TrustZone Trusted Execution Environment (TEE) and thus reduces the TEE's attack surface and does not require placing the operating system within the trusted computing base.

7   Conclusion

SIMPLEX is an open-source library repurposing the Intel MPX instruction set extension. We present evidence that suggests that MPX is ubiquitous, and show that MPX bounds registers can be repurposed as general purpose storage. In particular, they can be used to hide security sensitive data. We demonstrate that although the MPX ISA lacks a dedicated instruction to move data directly to and from the bounds registers, it is still possible to do so through the available spill and fill instructions, bndmk and bndmov. Furthermore, we show that such operations are not overly-burdensome, especially once the operations are amortized across the entire execution of a program. We do this through a collection of refactored programs and a partial implementation of the C standard library. Finally, we make SIMPLEX available to the community as open-source software at https://github.com/bingseclab/simplex.

References

1. Browne, S., Dongarra, J., Garner, N., London, K., Mucci, P.: A scalable cross-platform infrastructure for application performance tuning using hardware counters. In: Proceedings of the 2000 ACM/IEEE Conference on Supercomputing, SC 2000 (2000). https://doi.org/10.1109/SC.2000.10029
2. Bruening, D., Garnett, T., Amarasinghe, S.: An infrastructure for adaptive dynamic optimization. In: Proceedings of the International Symposium on Code Generation and Optimization: Feedback-Directed and Runtime Optimization, CGO 2003, pp. 265–275. IEEE Computer Society (2003)

3. Burow, N., Mckee, D., Carr, S.A., Payer, M.: CFIXX: object type integrity for C++. In: Network and Distributed Systems Security Symposium 2018 (2018). https://doi.org/10.14722/ndss.2018.23279

4. Canella, C., et al.: A systematic evaluation of transient execution attacks and defenses. In: 28th USENIX Security Symposium (USENIX Security 2019), pp. 249–266 (2019). https://www.usenix.org/conference/usenixsecurity19/presentation/canella

5. Carr, S.A., Payer, M.: DataShield: configurable data confidentiality and integrity. In: Proceedings of the 2017 ACM on Asia Conference on Computer and Communications Security - ASIA CCS 2017 (2017). https://doi.org/10.1145/3052973.3052983

6. Davi, L., Liebchen, C., Sadeghi, A.R., Snow, K.Z., Monrose, F.: Isomeron: code randomization resilient to (just-in-time) return-oriented programming (2015). https://doi.org/10.14722/ndss.2015.23262

7. Dekel, K.: BoundHook: exception based, kernel-controlled user-mode hooking (2017). https://www.cyberark.com/threat-research-blog/boundhook-exception-based-kernel-controlled-usermode-hooking/

8. Evans, I., et al.: Missing the point(er): on the effectiveness of code pointer integrity. In: 2015 IEEE Symposium on Security and Privacy, pp. 781–796 (2015). https://doi.org/10.1109/SP.2015.53

9. Ganesh, K.: Pointer checker: easily catch out-of-bounds memory accesses (2012). https://software.intel.com/sites/products/parallelmag/singlearticles/issue11/7080_2_IN_ParallelMag_Issue11_Pointer_Checker.pdf

10. Göktas, E., et al.: Undermining information hiding (and what to do about it). In: Proceedings of the 25th USENIX Conference on Security Symposium, pp. 105–119 (2016)

11. Gruss, D., Lipp, M., Schwarz, M., Fellner, R., Maurice, C., Mangard, S.: KASLR is dead: long live KASLR. In: Engineering Secure Software and Systems, pp. 161–176 (2017). https://doi.org/10.1007/978-3-319-62105-0_11

12. Halderman, J.A., et al.: Lest we remember: cold-boot attacks on encryption keys. Commun. ACM **52**(5), 91–98 (2009). https://doi.org/10.1145/1506409.1506429

13. Hargreaves, C., Chivers, H.: Recovery of encryption keys from memory using a linear scan. In: 2008 Third International Conference on Availability, Reliability and Security (2008). https://doi.org/10.1109/ARES.2008.109

14. Intel Corporation: Introduction to Intel Memory Protection Extensions (2013). https://software.intel.com/en-us/articles/introduction-to-intel-memory-protection-extensions

15. Intel Corporation: Control-flow Enforcement Technology Specification, May 2019. https://software.intel.com/sites/default/files/managed/4d/2a/control-flow-enforcement-technology-preview.pdf

16. Kazim, A., Almaeeni, F., Ali, S.A., Iqbal, F., Al-Hussaeni, K.: Memory forensics: recovering chat messages and encryption master key. In: 2019 10th International Conference on Information and Communication Systems (ICICS), pp. 58–64 (2019). https://doi.org/10.1109/IACS.2019.8809179

17. Koning, K., Chen, X., Bos, H., Giuffrida, C., Athanasopoulos, E.: No need to hide: protecting safe regions on commodity hardware. In: Proceedings of the Twelfth European Conference on Computer Systems, pp. 437–452 (2017). https://doi.org/10.1145/3064176.3064217

18. Kuznetsov, V., Szekeres, L., Payer, M., Candea, G., Sekar, R., Song, D.: Code-pointer integrity. In: Proceedings of the 11th USENIX Conference

on Operating Systems Design and Implementation, OSDI 2014, pp. 147–163. USENIX Association (2014). https://www.usenix.org/conference/osdi14/technical-sessions/presentation/kuznetsov

19. Lipp, M., et al.: Meltdown: reading kernel memory from user space. In: 27th USENIX Security Symposium, pp. 973–990 (2018). https://www.usenix.org/conference/usenixsecurity18/presentation/lipp

20. Lu, K., Song, C., Lee, B., Chung, S.P., Kim, T., Lee, W.: ASLR-guard: stopping address space leakage for code reuse attacks. In: Proceedings of the 22nd ACM SIGSAC Conference on Computer and Communications Security, pp. 280–291 (2015). https://doi.org/10.1145/2810103.2813694

21. Mohan, V., Larsen, P., Brunthaler, S., Hamlen, K.W., Franz, M.: Opaque control-flow integrity. In: Network and Distributed Systems Security Symposium 2015 (2015). https://doi.org/10.14722/ndss.2015.23271

22. Müller, T., Freiling, F.C., Dewald, A.: TRESOR runs encryption securely outside RAM. In: Proceedings of the 20th USENIX Conference on Security, SEC 2011 (2011). https://doi.org/10.5555/2028067.2028084

23. Oikonomopoulos, A., Athanasopoulos, E., Bos, H., Giuffrida, C.: Poking holes in information hiding. In: 25th USENIX Security Symposium, Austin, TX, pp. 121–138 (2016)

24. Oleksenko, O., Kuvaiskii, D., Bhatotia, P., Felber, P., Fetzer, C.: Intel MPX explained: an empirical study of Intel MPX and software-based bounds checking approaches (2017). https://doi.org/10.48550/ARXIV.1702.00719

25. Oleksenko, O., Kuvaiskii, D., Bhatotia, P., Fetzer, C., Felber, P.: Efficient fault tolerance using Intel MPX and TSX. In: Fast Abstract in the 46th Annual IEEE/IFIP International Conference on Dependable Systems and Networks, Toulouse, France (2016)

26. Ooi, J.G., Kam, K.H.: A proof of concept on defending cold boot attack. In: 2009 1st Asia Symposium on Quality Electronic Design (2009). https://doi.org/10.1109/ASQED.2009.5206245

27. Otterstad, C.W.: A brief evaluation of Intel MPX. In: 2015 Annual IEEE Systems Conference Proceedings, pp. 1–7. IEEE (2015). https://doi.org/10.1109/SYSCON.2015.7116720

28. Pomonis, M., Petsios, T., Keromytis, A.D., Polychronakis, M., Kemerlis, V.P.: kRⓍX: comprehensive kernel protection against just-in-time code reuse. In: Proceedings of the Twelfth European Conference on Computer Systems, EuroSys 2017 (2017). https://doi.org/10.1145/3064176.3064216

29. Ramakesavan, S., Rodriguez, J.: Intel memory protection extensions enabling guide (2016). https://software.intel.com/en-us/articles/intel-memory-protection-extensions-enabling-guide

30. Sartakov, V.A., O'Keeffe, D., Eyers, D., Vilanova, L., Pietzuch, P.: Spons & shields: practical isolation for trusted execution. In: Proceedings of the 17th ACM SIGPLAN/SIGOPS International Conference on Virtual Execution Environments (2021). https://doi.org/10.1145/3453933.3454024

31. Serebryany, K., Bruening, D., Potapenko, A., Vyukov, D.: Addresssanitizer: A fast address sanity checker. In: 2012 USENIX Annual Technical Conference. pp. 309–318 (2012)

32. Serebryany, K.: Address sanitizer Intel memory protection extensions (2016). https://github.com/google/sanitizers/wiki/AddressSanitizerIntelMemoryProtectionExtensions

33. Yun, M.H., Zhong, L.: Ginseng: keeping secrets in registers when you distrust the operating system. In: Network and Distributed Systems Security Symposium 2019 (2019). https://doi.org/10.14722/ndss.2019.23327
34. Zhang, M., Sekar, R.: Control flow and code integrity for COTS binaries: an effective defense against real-world ROP attacks. In: Proceedings of the 31st Annual Computer Security Applications Conference, pp. 91–100 (2015). https://doi.org/10.1145/2818000.2818016
35. Zhang, T., Lee, D., Jung, C.: BOGO: buy spatial memory safety, get temporal memory safety (almost) free. In: Proceedings of the Twenty-Fourth International Conference on Architectural Support for Programming Languages and Operating Systems, ASPLOS 2019, New York, NY, USA, pp. 631–644. Association for Computing Machinery (2019). https://doi.org/10.1145/3297858.3304017

Automatic Implementations Synthesis of Secure Protocols and Attacks from Abstract Models

Camille Sivelle[1], Lorys Debbah[1], Maxime Puys[1,3]([✉]),
Pascal Lafourcade[2], and Thibault Franco-Rondisson[1]

[1] Univ. Grenoble Alpes, CEA, LETI, DSYS, 38000 Grenoble, France
{Camille.Sivelle,Lorys.Debbah,Maxime.Puys,
Thibault.Franco-Rondisson}@cea.fr
[2] LIMOS, University Clermont Auvergne, CNRS UMR 6158,
Clermont-Ferrand, France
Pascal.Lafourcade@uca.fr
[3] CEA-Leti, 17 rue des Martyrs, 38054 Grenoble Cedex 9, France

Abstract. Attack generation from an abstract model of a protocol is not an easy task. We present BIFROST (Bifrost Implements Formally Reliable prOtocols for Security and Trust), a tool that takes an abstract model of a cryptographic protocol and outputs an implementation in C of the protocol and either a proof in ProVerif that the protocol is safe or an implementation of the attack found. We use FS2PV, KaRaMeL, ProVerif and a dedicated parser to analyze the attack traces produced by ProVerif. If an attack is found then BIFROST automatically produces C code for each honest participant and for the intruder in order to mount the attack.

1 Introduction

The security of a communication protocol involves two different aspects: (i) the security of the protocol itself and (ii) the security of the cryptographic schemes involved. Several tools are now available to formally prove the intrinsic security of both protocols (like ProVerif [19], Scyther [23] or Tamarin [32]) and primitives (like CryptoVerif [20] or Easycrypt [9]) see [8] for a survey. However, another issue comes into play. Security flaws often appear when implementing code for a given protocol, even for a proven secure one. In this case, the attack does not rely on an intrinsic flaw of the protocol, but involves vulnerabilities related to the code design or even from the programming language. It also happens too often that the implementation is a slightly different protocol than the one proven (for instance the order of the content of an encrypted message is changed) and thus have the formal proof becoming meaningless. In 2014, the Heartbleed [27] attack over SSL/TLSv1.0 whose feasibility had been formally proven in [16] is an example of an attack targeting the implementation. We can also mention a famous attack of the SSH protocol in Debian Linux distributions where the generation of a fresh nonce was wrongly implemented [5]. Hence implementing a secure protocol is a sensitive task and every detail is important.

H. P. Reiser and M. Kyas (Eds.): NordSec 2022, LNCS 13700, pp. 234–252, 2022.
https://doi.org/10.1007/978-3-031-22295-5_13

Contributions: We propose an automatic tool-chain named BIFROST (Bifrost Implements Formally Reliable prOtocols for Security and Trust), that takes as input a cryptographic protocol modeled in F*, we call this input a *protocol model* in the rest of the paper, and combines the following existing tools: FS2PV [17], KaRaMeL [38] (formerly known as KreMLin) and ProVerif [19]. BIFROST produces:

1. An implementation in C from a protocol modeled in F*.
2. If the protocol is safe then a proof in ProVerif is produced.
3. If ProVerif finds a flaw then an implementation in C of the attack is given.

BIFROST supports several standard cryptographic primitives that correspond to those supported by ProVerif. We are able to use several symmetric encryption schemes, public key encryption schemes, signatures schemes and hash functions. All these primitives are wrapped around widely-known cryptographic primitive libraries such as MbedTLS. BIFROST unifies their APIs and make them directly compatible with verification tools such ProVerif. BIFROST has been successfully tested on the famous Needham-Schroeder [34] and Otway-Rees [36] protocols, alongside a MAC based password protocol taken from [17].

   Formal verification tools need to over-approximate an attacker's capabilities in order to be sure that a protocol is secure in regards to a given property. Therefore, the attacks generated by such tools can sometimes not be feasible in practice. If the protocol was not found secure, the attack implementation generated by BIFROST can be played along with the protocol implementation previously generated. If the execution of the attack found by formal verification succeeds, it proves its feasibility in a practical context. This can give an automatic confirmation that the protocol is not secure, rather than manually implementing the attack.

Related Work: Several tools can be related to BIFROST. We classify them in three categories: (i) generic code verification tools, (ii) cryptographic protocol verification tools, (iii) tools specifically designed to generate code from verifiable protocol models. Generic code verification and cryptographic protocol verification tools are not directly related works to BIFROST, but they are related to the basic blocks used in the approach. Thus, we will mainly mention the one used within BIFROST and their main competitors.

Generic Code Verification Tools: They have been developed for several tens of years. Among many other reference tools we can list:

- The B method [6] is a formal method software development framework proposed by Abrial et al. in 1996 based on set theory and first order logic in order to write and check code specifications. The goal is to both check consistency of specifications and code.
- Frama-C [24] is a tool developed in 2012 by Cuoq et al. that performs static analysis on C programs. Various analyses are supported such as dead code deletion, value analysis or weakest-precondition calculus.

- F* [40] is a general-purpose functional programming language designed by Swamy et al. in 2013 which allows to specify properties alongside code. Then, various analyses can be performed on the code such as dependent types, monadic effects, refinement types, and a weakest precondition calculus.

We use F* models in BIFROST, due to their compatibility with the other bricks used in our toolchain.

Cryptographic Protocol Verification Tools: They have been developed since 1995, when G. Lowe found an attack on the formerly proven Needham-Schroeder protocol [31]. Such tools often implement the Dolev-Yao [26] intruder model and check all possible actions for an attacker interacting with multiple sessions of a given protocol in parallel to verify security properties such as secrecy or authentication. Multiple tools have been introduced since 1995 [8] and benchmarked [8,30]. Among them we can list:

- Tamarin [32] is a security protocol prover designed by Meier et al. since 2013. Tamarin is able to handle an unbounded number of sessions. Protocols are specified as multi-set rewriting systems with respect to temporal first-order properties. It relies on Maude [28] and supports equational theories such as Diffie-Hellman.
- DY* [14] is a tool developed by Bhargavan et al. in 2021. It is an implementation of the Dolev-Yao intruder model in F* and allows security properties verification on a protocol taking advantage of the internal F* prover. It is however currently unable to produce attack traces.
- ProVerif [19] is developed by Blanchet et al. since 2001 and relies on Horn clause analysis to check an unbounded number of sessions.

We chose ProVerif in our tool chain, since it is stable and that several bricks of our approach are compatible with this well established tool.

Cryptographic Protocol Code Generation Tools: There exist some tools allowing to generate code from verifiable protocol models, such as BIFROST.

- Spi2Java [37] is a framework proposed in 2004 that automatizes the generation of Java implementations from protocols described in spi calculus, an extension of pi-calculus. This method allows for formal verification of security properties through translation of the spi-calculus specifications to a format that can be verified by ProVerif prior to code generation.
- In 1993 and in 2009, Bieber et al. [18] and Benaissa et al. [12] respectively proposed an approach to analyze the security of cryptographic protocols using the Event-B framework. To the best of our knowledge, they partly implement the Dolev-Yao model as a library for the internal verifier of Event-B, allowing them to specify lemmas describing security properties to be proven such as secrecy and authentication. It is however unclear if their approach is able to find an attack trace. As their framework relies on Event-B, specifications can be refined into C-like code.

- In 2009, Bhargavan et al. [15] proposed a compiler allowing to translate protocols modeled in some ad-hoc language into ML-like implementations. They provide various security verifications through a custom type-checker [13] which performs security verifications similar to ProVerif and Tamarin.
- AnBx [33] is an IDE developed in 2015 by Modesti. It extends the Alice & Bob (AnB) protocol model making it compatible with OFMC [10], a protocol verifier such as ProVerif. After verification, the protocol model can be translated into Java.
- Jasmin [7] is a cryptographic primitive verification tool, developed by Almeida et al. in 2017. It takes a primitive model as input, written in a specific language, and checks it against memory flaws or cache timing attacks. The model is then translated in a subset of the C language. Yet, it is worth noting that even if Jasmin shares resemblance with the frameworks described above, it only applies to cryptographic primitives rather than to protocols, which are complementary.

Finally, several previous works mention that they perform *protocol synthesis*. However, if their works share resemblance with ours, this terminology should not be confused with *protocol implementation synthesis* which aims at automatically generating executable protocol implementations. For instance, Bellare et al. [11] and Katz et al. [29] synthesize protocol models resistant to active intruders from protocol models resistant to passive intruders in the context of authenticated group key exchange. Cortier et al. [22] translate a single-session protocol into a multi-session protocol secure against a Dolev-Yao intruder. Sprenger [39] et al. rely on Isabelle/HOL [35] to write secure-by-design protocol models. In 2008, Bhargavan et al. [17] synthesize ProVerif models from F# protocol implementations in a tool called FS2PV. We are using FS2PV in BIFROST because it is compatible with ProVerif and it will help us in our goal to generate attack implementations in C.

Overall, only cryptographic protocol code generation tools are direct competitors to BIFROST. All other presented works are related to internal tools used within BIFROST (e.g., cryptographic protocols verification tools). Moreover, to the best of our knowledge, if all tools mentioned above are able to faithfully translate a protocol from a provable model into a programming language (with their own limitations), none of them are dealing with attacks found by the verification tools.

Outline: In Sect. 2, we introduce the BIFROST framework. In Sect. 3, we delve into the technical challenges regarding automatic code generation from protocol models and explaining the inner-workings of BIFROST. In Sects. 4 and 5, we respectively present the cryptographic primitives supported and how we automatically generate code for attacks found. In Sect. 6 we give a detailed example of the approach on the Needham-Schroeder protocol which will be part of technical report of this paper and in the manual of BIFROST. Finally, we conclude in Sect. 7.

2   Overview of BIFROST

Our aim is, with the same input file, to be able to generate C code with KaRaMeL and a π-calculus file for ProVerif. For this, we use a subset of F* that is compatible both with the subset of F# that is used by FS2PV, and also with low* (the subset of F* that can be compiled into C) in order to be able to use KaRaMeL. In the rest of the paper, we denote this subset $F^{\$}$. When it is clear from the context we also use F*. In Fig. 1, we describe the BIFROST approach. From a cryptographic protocol model (1) the user needs to write an $F^{\$}$ file. In step (2), we generate a π-calculus model using FS2PV, which can then be verified by ProVerif in step (3) with respect to the security properties described in a .query file. If the protocol is safe and ProVerif proves the security of the requested properties in step (4), we apply KaRaMeL in step (5) to the initial model in $F^{\$}$ to generate C code corresponding to the implementation of the roles of each participant in the protocol (6), thus bridging the gap between the formal verification of the protocol and its implementation. If the protocol is not safe it means that ProVerif found an attack in step (7), then we parse the ProVerif attack trace using a tool we have developed (8) to generate the corresponding $F^{\$}$ code. We apply KaRaMeL to the obtained $F^{\$}$ files to automatically generate the C code implementing the role of the attacker in the protocol.

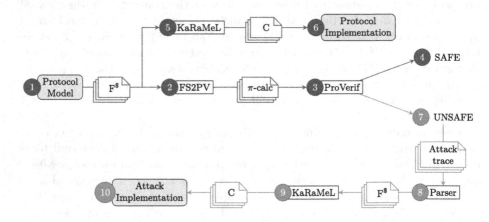

Fig. 1. The BIFROST toolchain.

In the following, we describe in Sect. 3 some of the challenges for transforming abstract models into a practical implementation. We then present, in Sect. 4, the different cryptographic primitives that are available in BIFROST and how we integrate them to allow crypto-agility. Finally, we show, in Sect. 5, how we manage to generate attack implementations from ProVerif traces.

3   From Abstract Model to Implementation

The translation from an abstract model to a concrete implementation brings several challenges. The F$^\$$ model which serves as an input for our toolchain relies on a set of functions for cryptographic primitives, network operations and data manipulation, which are all currently imposed by FS2PV. One important point is that FS2PV only uses an abstract definition of these function to translate the input F$^\$$ protocol description into a ProVerif model. However, when generating the C implementation of the protocol, all these functions must also be defined with their proper implementation. Moreover, their implementation must fit their purpose in the real world. For instance, if the `Net.send` function is internal to FS2PV for its analysis at the abstract model phase, it must actually be sending packets on a network when called by real code. Some abstract functions can have multiple implementations depending on user choices. For instance, a `Crypto.symenc` function can be translated into AES or ChaCha encryption while `Net.send` can translate to a TCP/IP send or a LoraWan send depending on context. On the other hand, some functions defined and called within the abstract model do not serve any purpose in the implementation (such as π-calculus' $fork$).

BIFROST Libraries. To this end, we propose a series of C libraries `Crypto`, `Net`, `Data` and `Pi`, implementing all the necessary functions to link and run the C code produced by KaRaMeL from our model. Figure 2 describes the translation of the different libraries of abstract functions into their implementations.

- `Data` contains several functions necessary for data types manipulation. In FS2PV representation, the principal data type is the Byte, which can represent variables of various size and nature, as it could be a nonce as well as a key, or even a concatenation of different Bytes. This is problematic in C, as those can hardly be represented by the same data structures and might introduce some type flaw attacks, as the one existing on the fixed version of Needham-Schroeder by G. Lowe, where a confusion between identity and nonces allows an intruder to mount an attack [21]. The solution we proposed in our `Data` library is to define the Byte as a C structure, composed of an integer representing the subtype of the object, an integer representing the size of the object and an union of the C structures corresponding to each possible subtype (nonce for example).
- `Crypto` gathers all the functions relative to the cryptographic operations in the protocol. Most of its functions are meant to be crypto-agile and thus are algorithm agnostic wrappers to specific primitives such as RSA or AES.
- The `Net` library of BIFROST includes basic network operations. As of now, they are implemented on either TCP/IP sockets or low level UART connections. However, supporting various protocols is possible with BIFROST but it is important to ensure the compatibility with the network model of ProVerif.

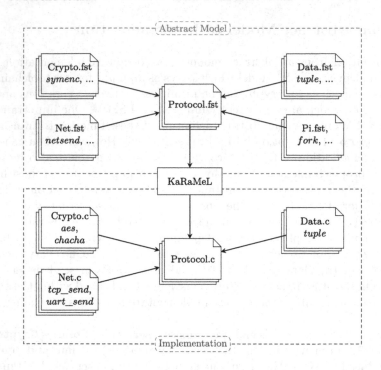

Fig. 2. Abstract functions libraries translated into C code.

- Finally, the Pi library relates to internal π-calculus functions used by ProVerif for its analysis (mainly for process scheduling) and does not have any real purpose in real life. Thus, this module does not need to be translated into C.

Keys Management. Another difference between the protocol model and the role implementation is the way that keys are managed. When verifying a protocol with ProVerif, private keys are often modeled as terms freshly generated at the beginning of the protocol, public keys being derived from these terms and published on a public channel. This is sufficient to consider that each participant knows a given public key in the formal model. However, this traditional setup for verification, consisting in broadcasting keys or supposing that participants already know each other's public keys beforehand is more complicated to pull off on real hosts. Within BIFROST, we use the following key management to reconcile both formal verification and implementation usability (it can also apply to any supposedly pre-shared keys): two distinct main functions are defined for the formal verification and the implementation generation. One is required by FS2PV in which each participant role is called with keys created by abstract methods from FS2PV. This file is then translated as the main *process* clause used by ProVerif to setup roles instances. On the other hand, KaRaMeL produces C code for every participant, plausibly running on different systems, and each of them requires its main function. Thus, the role of each participant is described in a $F^\$$ file containing a role function, which takes in argument the keys, and a main function, in which the keys are loaded from a `.pem` file. This choice presupposes that the keys are generated and stored on each system executing a participant's role beforehand, which is common for embedded devices.

4 Cryptographic Primitives

To allow crypto-agility by letting the user choose a cryptographic algorithm among different options, we decided to handle all the following schemes and to implement several algorithms for each of them.

- **Symmetric encryption** uses a key shared by both participants to encrypt and decrypt data. Symmetric keys are often smaller than asymmetric keys which allows communication to be fast. We support three algorithms for symmetric encryption: AES-128/192/256 in CBC mode, Blowfish in CBC mode and Chacha20.
- **Message Authentication Code** uses symmetric keys to check the integrity and authenticity of data. We support the following four algorithms: AES with CMAC, Poly1305-AES, Chacha20-Poly1305 and HMAC.
- **Hashing** has a lot of applications in cryptography. It can be used to compute fingerprints for example. We support two hashing algorithms: SHA2 and RIPEMD160.
- **Asymmetric encryption** uses a public key, private key pair to encrypt and decrypt. It is often used to transfer symmetric keys. We support two algorithms for asymmetric encryption: RSA-OAEP and RSA-PKCS1-v1.5.
- **Asymmetric signature** uses a public key, private key pair to check for the integrity and the authenticity of data. We support three algorithms for asymmetric signature: RSA-PKCS1-v1.5, RSA-PSS and ECDSA.

Cryptographic primitives management in BIFROST relies on MbedTLS [1], a C library developed by ARMmbed. It implements the TLS [25] protocol and required cryptographic primitives. MbedTLS is designed to fit on small embedded systems. However, one of the key concerns of BIFROST is to allow for crypto-agility, which would in our case translate as the possibility for the toolchain to handle both different algorithms and different cryptographic libraries, such as OpenSSL [3] or OpenQuantumSafe [2], in order to fit as easily to existing code base. In practice, any cryptographic operation requires different MbedTLS function calls (e.g., to set the seed or initialize the context before encrypting). As all these atomic function calls are not defined within FS2PV and ProVerif, granularity differs with MbedTLS. Thus, we created a C library composed of functions that would act as wrappers above MbedTLS's functions. More precisely, we wanted those wrappers to encompass every intermediate function of MbedTLS (or another library) to provide a more generic function to the user, which would also fit the granularity of protocol models. The use of this library also allows the user to choose the primitives to use for a given protocol.

Different options allow us to choose which primitive to use. The choice of which primitive should be used is currently left to the user of BIFROST (which is the protocol modeler and not the final user). This choice is partly motivated by the context of embedded systems where not all primitives are supported by chip vendors and some freedom in the choice can be important. Yet, letting any user choose their cryptographic primitives will often lead to vulnerable systems. While leaving room for freedom of choice, we intend to support cryptographic suites[1] which will automatically include a combination of validated cryptographic primitives with their proper configuration (e.g., ECDHE_PSK_WITH_AES_128_ GCM_SHA256). By defining the right macros, preprocessor will comment out code for unused primitives. In a similar way, the user can choose the size of its keys with preprocessor directives, the idea being to give the user maximum control over the parameters for each primitive. This control is the one that MbedTLS provides so we did not restrict the options provided by the library but we eased the way to select them. This allows a user to custom the protocol by choosing the cryptographic primitives' parameters he wishes to use.

5   Attack Generation

The generation of the attack implementation is based on the output printed by ProVerif in case an attack is found. This output corresponds to an attack trace in applied π-calculus which describes the steps performed by the intruder to violate the specified security property. As already presented in Fig. 1, the approach we chose for this part was to first parse the attack trace from ProVerif's output in order to obtain an abstract syntax tree (8), and to use that tree to generate the $F^\$$ file implementing the actions described in the trace. We then apply KaRaMeL (9) to that $F^\$$ file to generate the C implementation of the attacker's role (10). We motivate the choice of generating $F^\$$ code and using KaRaMeL rather than generating C code directly from the syntax tree for the coherency it guarantees with the C code generated from the protocol model with KaRaMeL. To our knowledge, there is no tool or framework allowing to generate executable code for an attack found by a protocol verification tool. The generated C code can then be compiled and executed alongside a normal protocol session (or more if needed) in order to play the attack.

ProVerif Attack Trace Parsing: To parse the attack traces from the ProVerif outputs, we have chosen to proceed in Python, using the Lark module [4]. Lark is a parsing library able to parse any context-free grammar, using an advanced grammar language based on EBNF, a metalanguage that allows to describe the syntactic rules of programming languages. The first step is therefore to determine the grammar of ProVerif outputs and to describe it in EBNF language. Globally, an attack trace is made up of a succession of lines that can be considered as instructions. We consider four different types of instructions in ProVerif's language: *in*, *out*, *new* and *event*.

---

[1] https://ciphersuite.info/cs/.

```
1 in(c,(Bob,M_1)) with M_1 = pk(skB_1) at {5}
2 out(c,M_6) with M_6 = aenc(n_3,pk(skB_1)) at {12}
```

Listing 1.1. Example of in/out instructions.

The *in* and *out* instructions aim to send and receive messages from a channel and have the same grammar. The elements that we want to retrieve in our syntax tree are:

1. their two arguments (for example c and M_6 for the *out* of Listing 1.1),
2. the equality given after the with keyword (for instance $M\_1 = pk(skB\_1)$ for the *in*),
3. the line number in the process (5 or 12).

In Listing 1.1, c, M_6, and M_1 are variable or channel names, $pk(skB\_1)$ or $aenc(n\_3, pk(skB\_1))$ are functions applied these variables. As terms can be functions applied multiple times to another term, we define values as either ground terms or function results and line numbers correspond to natural numbers. Then, we can define the *in* and *out* instructions as in Listing 1.2.

```
1 out: "out" "(" val "," val ")" "with" val "=" val "at" "{" line "}"
2 in:  "in"  "(" val "," val ")" "with" val "=" val "at" "{" line "}"
```

Listing 1.2. Grammar for in/out instructions.

We also define similar rules for *new* and *event* keywords. The *new* instruction allows a participant or the intruder to generate a fresh term. On the other hand, *event* does not have any effect on the protocol but allows to place markers in the trace which can be used for reachability properties. Their form is shown in Listing 1.3.

```
1 new n_1 creating n_3 at {21}
2 event endB(A,pk(skA_1),Bob,pk(skB_1),n_2) at {25}
```

Listing 1.3. Example of new/event instructions.

Similarly, these instructions are translated in EBNF as shown in Listing 1.4.

```
1 new:   "new" val "creating" val "at" "{" line "}"
2 event: "event" val "at" "{" line "}" "(goal)"
```

Listing 1.4. Grammar for new/event instructions.

Generating F$^\$$ *Code:* From the syntax tree obtained, we write a program that generates a code in F$^\$$. Processing will differ according to the type of instruction. An *out* corresponds for example to a sending by one of the hosts defined in the protocol. As the code generated at this step corresponds to the behavior of the intruder, a call to F$^\$$ *Net_recv* function is performed on the channel indicated by the variable stored in the AST. Similarly, an *in* means that the intruder must send the given message on the channel, leading to a call to *Net_send*. When the declaration in the *with* statement involves functions, for example $M\_6 = aenc(n\_3, pk(skB\_1))$, we translate these into the corresponding functions in our libraries. The events could be ignored since they do not bring anything to the attack in itself. We therefore simply use a logging system when an event is raised. The case of the *new* requires a little more work because ProVerif does not distinguish the generation of nonces from the generation of encryption keys. However, the functions that are assimilated in $F^\$$ are not the same. To remedy this problem, we use a preprocessing function that goes through the tree a first time to determine on one hand if the generation of each variable is done by the intruder, and on the other hand, the type of this variable. The latter is given by the functions that are applied to it after creation. The algorithm used for the generation of the code can therefore be summarized as shown in Listing 1.5.

```
 1  ast_to_fdollar(tree):
 2    initialize the output string to ""
 3
 4    # Preprocessing
 5    for each instruction:
 6      if it is a new:
 7        store the type of the variable declared
 8    output all the declarations with their correct types
 9
10    # Main processing
11    for each instruction:
12      determine the type using the first child node of the tree
13      if it is of type "in":
14        add to output a "let ... = ..." defining the variable
15        add to output a Net_send(...,...)
16      if it is of type "out":
17        add to output a "let ... = ..." defining the variable
18        add to output a Net_recv(...,...)
19      if it is of type "event":
20        add to output a log(...,...)
21      if it is of type "new":
22        do nothing (already processed during the preprocessing)
23    return output
```

Listing 1.5. $F^\$$ code generation.

6   An Example: The Needham-Schroeder Protocol

We show how BIFROST can be applied on the well-known Needham-Schroeder protocol. We first describe this protocol in Sect. 6.1, then we show in Sect. 6.2 how this protocol is modeled in $F^\$$ and it is translated into C code using BIFROST. Finally, we detail in Sect. 6.3 the generation of the implementation of an attack on this protocol from the attack trace found by ProVerif.

6.1   The Needham-Schroeder Protocol

The Needham-Schroeder [34] protocol is a mutual authentication protocol involving two parties A and B. They wish to agree on a shared value that they will use to secure further communications. In this protocol, messages are sent on an insecure channel. N_A, N_B are nonces, pk_A, pk_B are public keys and $(m)_{pk_B}$ symbolizes the public encryption of the message m. The first message $(A, N_A)_{pk_B}$ is used to initiate a new session between A and B. The second message is used by A to authenticate B and the third one is used by B to authenticate A. Nonces are also used to prevent replay attacks.

$$A \longrightarrow B : (A, N_A)_{pk_B}$$
$$B \longrightarrow A : (N_A, N_B)_{pk_A}$$
$$A \longrightarrow B : (N_B)_{pk_B}$$

In 1996 G. Lowe [31] found a famous attack on this protocol. This attack assumes that a dishonest agent I impersonates the honest agent B in the previous protocol, leading to a man-in-the-middle attack.

$$A \longrightarrow I : (A, N_A)_{pk_I}$$
$$I \longrightarrow B : (A, N_A)_{pk_B}$$
$$B \longrightarrow I : (N_A, N_B)_{pk_A}$$
$$I \longrightarrow A : (N_A, N_B)_{pk_A}$$
$$A \longrightarrow I : (N_B)_{pk_I}$$
$$I \longrightarrow B : (N_B)_{pk_B}$$

With this attack, the intruder obtains both N_A and N_B which allows him to derive any secret based on those two nonces. He also impersonates A when speaking to B. This vulnerability was fixed by Gavin Lowe [31] by modifying only one message in the Needham-Schroeder-Lowe (NSL) protocol:

$$A \longrightarrow B : (A, N_A)_{pk_B}$$
$$B \longrightarrow A : (N_A, N_B, B)_{pk_A}$$
$$A \longrightarrow B : (N_B)_{pk_B}$$

One can see that with this variant, the intruder is not able to get the nonce N_B. Indeed, as the intruder tries to perform the attack, A will cipher with pk_I as she is willingly talking with the intruder. However, upon reception of the second message containing the identity of B, A will realize she is not talking to I as she was willing to initially and will not send the last message, thus preventing I from getting the last nonce.

6.2   From Protocol Model to Implementation

The code 1.6 is the role of A in the Needham-Schroeder protocol in $F^\$$, and the code 1.7 is the protocol implementation in C generated by KaRaMeL are given in Fig. 3. The code for B is similar. We can see that in $F^\$$ code 1.6, we start by establishing the communication channel 10.0.0.2, port 80 (which we will use for the IP address of B). Then a pair of keys is generated and public

```
1  let roleA host : Int32.t =
2  let url="10.0.0.2:80" in
3  let c=connect(url) in
4  let skA=(rsa_keygen()) in
5  let pkA=(rsa_pub skA) in
6
7  let x0=Net.send c (concat
       (keytobytes pkA) host
       ) in
8
9  let (pkb,dest)=(iconcat(
       Net.recv c)) in
10
11 // A -> B: (A,nA)_pkB
12 let pk=asympubkey(pkb) in
13  let nA=mkNonce() in
14  log tr (BeginA(host,dest
       ,nA));
15  let x1=Net.send c (
       rsa_encrypt pk (concat
       host nA)) in
16
17  // B -> A : (nA, nB)_pkA
18  let m=(rsa_decrypt skA (
       Net.recv c)) in
19
20   let (nA1, nB)=iconcat m
       in
21  if nA1=nA then
22  (
23   // A -> B : (nB)_pkB
24   let x2=(Net.send c (
       rsa_encrypt pk nB)) in
25   let z=(close c) in 01
26  )
27   else let z=(close c) in
       01
```

Listing 1.6: Role of A in F$^\$$.

```
1  int32_t roleA(Data_bytes host) {
2   Prims_string url ="10.0.0.2:80"
       ;
3   Net_conn c = Net_connect(url);
4   Crypto_key skA =
       Crypto_rsa_keygen();
5   Crypto_key pkA = Crypto_rsa_pub
       (skA);
6   Prims_int x0 = Net_send(c,
       Data_concat(Crypto_keytobytes
       (pkA), host));
7   K____Data_bytes_Data_bytes scrut
       = Data_iconcat(Net_recv(c));
8   Data_bytes pkb = scrut.fst;
9   Crypto_key pk =
       Crypto_asympubkey(pkb);
10  Data_bytes nA = Crypto_mkNonce
       ();
11  Prims_int x1 = Net_send(c,
       Crypto_rsa_encrypt(pk,
       Data_concat(host, nA)));
12  Data_bytes m =
       Crypto_rsa_decrypt(skA,
       Net_recv(c));
13  K____Data_bytes_Data_bytes
       scrut0 = Data_iconcat(m);
14  Data_bytes nA1 = scrut0.fst;
15  Data_bytes nB = scrut0.snd;
16  if (___eq___Data_bytes(nA1, nA))
17  {
18     Prims_int x2 = Net_send(c,
       Crypto_rsa_encrypt(pk, nB));
19     Prims_int z = Net_close(c);
20     return (int32_t)0;
21  }
22  else
23  {
24     Prims_int z = Net_close(c);
25     return (int32_t)0;
26  }
27 }
```

Listing 1.7: Role of A generated by KaRaMeL.

Fig. 3. Input code of A's role in F$^\$$ and generated C code.

keys are published on the network. A listens for the public key of B[2]. After this initialization phase, the protocol can start and A generates a nonce and sends it

---

[2] This is a common modeling practice in protocol verification, allowing the intruder to choose who A is going to talk to.

and her name encrypted with the public key of B according to the first step of the protocol. Then A waits for the answer of B. Once B's response is received, A checks the correspondence between the nonce sent in the first message and the one received from B. If the nonces match them A confirms to B that she has received N_B by sending it back to B encrypted by B's public key.

The C code produced by BIFROST is given in the code 1.7. It follows exactly the same steps and use all libraries proposed by the tool. Moreover, we argue that even for an automatically generated code. It stays fairly understandable and possible to analyze with C static analyzers such as Frama-C or CPPcheck.

6.3   Attacker Implementation Generation

The F$^\$$ code of the role of A displayed in Listing 1.6 is translated into *pi*-calculus by FS2PV and can be analyzed by ProVerif[3]. To do so, we need to provide a *query* (i.e., a security property) for ProVerif to verify. In this example, this query is shown in Listing 1.8 and requires the last message received by B from A to actually be sent by A for B earlier, ensuring authentication of A to B on N_B.

```
1| query ev:Ev(BMessageB(a,b,nb)) ==> ev:Ev(AMessageA(a,b,nb)).
```
Listing 1.8. Query used by ProVerif

Using this query, ProVerif is able to find an attack. The trace is also quite long and we chose to narrow down the output to what is shown in Listing 1.9.

```
1| new T55 creating T55_1 at {90}
2| new T53 creating T53_1 at {92}
3| new T51 creating T51_1 at {94}
4| out(NethttpChan, CryptoAsymPrivKey(DataFresh(M))) with M =
      T51_1 at {96}
5| out(NethttpChan, CryptoAsymPubKey(DataBin(M_1))) with M_1 =
      DataPK(DataFresh(T53_1)) at {97}
6| event Ev(BStart(DataUtf8(SBobS()),DataUtf8(SAliceS())))  at
      {128}
7| event Ev(AStart(DataUtf8(SAliceS()),DataUtf8(SIntruderS())))
      at {100}
8| new T49 creating T49_1 at {102}
9| out(NethttpChan, DataBin(M_2)) with M_2 = DataAsymEncrypt(
      DataBin(DataPK(DataFresh(T51_1))),DataConcat(DataUtf8(
      SAliceS()),DataFresh(T49_1))) at {104}
10| in(NethttpChan,[...]) = DataAsymEncrypt(DataBin(DataPK(
      DataFresh(T53_1))),DataConcat(DataUtf8(SAliceS()),
      DataFresh(T49_1))) at {130}
11| new T29 creating T29_1 at {135}
12| out(NethttpChan, DataBin(M_3)) with M_3 = DataAsymEncrypt(
      DataBin(DataPK(DataFresh(T55_1))),DataConcat(DataFresh(
      T49_1),DataFresh(T29_1))) at {137}
```

---

[3] As this code is really long, we will not show it in this article.

```
13  in(NethttpChan, DataBin(M_3)) with M_3 = DataAsymEncrypt(
        DataBin(DataPK(DataFresh(T55_1))),DataConcat(DataFresh(
        T49_1),DataFresh(T29_1))) at {105}
14  out(NethttpChan, DataBin(M_4)) with M_4 = DataAsymEncrypt(
        DataBin(DataPK(DataFresh(T51_1))),DataFresh(T29_1)) at
        {111}
15  in(NethttpChan,[...]) = DataAsymEncrypt(DataBin(DataPK(
        DataFresh(T53_1))),DataFresh(T29_1)) at {138}
```

Listing 1.9. Attack trace found by ProVerif.

The attack found by using ProVerif is actually the same as the one discovered by Lowe and presented in Sect. 6.1. It can be read as the following (with lines 1–5 prior to the roles of A and B): Line 1: creation of sk_A; Line 2: creation of sk_B; Line 3: creation of sk_I; Line 4: share sk_I for the intruder; Line 5: share pk_B for the intruder; Line 6–7: start event from B and A Line 8: creation of nonce N_A; Line 9: A sends $(A, N_A)_{pk_I}$; Line 10: B receives $(A, N_A)_{pk_B}$. This message is built by the intruder using the message from A. Line 11: creation of nonce N_B; Line 12: B sends $(N_A, N_B)_{pk_A}$; Line 13: A receives $(N_A, N_B)_{pk_A}$; Line 14: A sends $(N_B)_{pk_I}$; Line 15: B receives $(N_B)_{pk_B}$. This message is built by the intruder using the message from A.

The F$^\$$ representation of the role of the intruder generated by the Python parser can be found in Listing 1.10. The reader may take note that it follows the steps of the attack described above. The C implementation is generated by KaRaMeL, similarly to the roles of A and B, and after compilation it can be executed along with the two roles in order to play the attack. Finally, when we add Lowe's correction to the protocol model (described in Sect. 6.1), we can indeed see that ProVerif declares the protocol safe for the given properties.

```
1   let roleI skI pkB adr1 adr2: Int32.t =
2       let c2 = connect adr2 in
3       let c1 = listen adr1 in
4       let m_04 = skI in
5       let m_05 = pkB in
6       let m_09 = Net.recv(c1) in
7       let m_13 = utf8("Alice") in
8       let m_15 = rsa_decrypt m_04 m_09 in
9       let (m_16,m_17) = iconcat m_15 in
10      let m_14 = m_17 in
11      let m_12 = concat m_13 m_14 in
12      let m_10 = rsa_encrypt m_05 m_12 in
13      let m_11 = Net.send c2 m_10 in
14      let m_20 = Net.recv(c2) in
15      let m_21 = Net.send c1 m_20 in
16      let m_22 = Net.recv(c1) in
17      let m_25 = rsa_decrypt m_04 m_22 in
18      let m_23 = rsa_encrypt m_05 m_25 in
19      let m_24 = Net.send c2 m_23 in
20      let z = Net.close c2 in 01
```

Listing 1.10. Role of the intruder in F$^\$$

7   Conclusion

We present BIFROST, a toolchain allowing to automatically generate C code from an abstract model of cryptographic protocols. BIFROST takes as inputs a protocol modeled in $F^\$$ and output C files. To generate these files BIFROST uses KaRaMeL to obtain an implementation of the protocol that corresponds to the model. Moreover, BIFROST transforms the $F^\$$ specifications into a π-calculus file using FS2PV and this file is sent to ProVerif to verify if the protocol is safe or not. If ProVerif finds a flaw, then we produce the additional C files that allow us to mount the attack on the protocol implementation. For this we have designed a parser of ProVerif's output, able to generate $F^\$$ model describing the attack trace. This $F^\$$ file can be translated into C code using KaRaMeL in the same way as other roles. Moreover, BIFROST can deal with several cryptographic primitives and network parameters. The choice of using ARM mBedTLS as a backend relies on its common use within industry products, especially within embedded systems. However, support with HACL*[4] which is a formally verified cryptographic library would be possible and make sense to have a completely verified toolchain. On a similar note, gcc/clang could be switched to CompCert[5], a formally verified compiler.

As a future work, we intend to switch FS2PV for an F* compatible translator that will allow us to support multiple verification tools alongside ProVerif. This will allow us to not rely on F# anymore and have a protocol representation only requiring to be compatible with F*. We also aim to extend BIFROST to be able to consider equational theories and advanced trace-based security properties like forward secrecy and post-compromise security. Security against side-channel and fault attacks could also be studied.

References

1. ARM mBed. https://tls.mbed.org/. Accessed 21 Jan 2022
2. OpenQuantumSafe. https://openquantumsafe.org. Accessed 21 Jan 2022
3. OpenSSL. https://www.openssl.org/. Accessed 21 Jan 2022
4. Python Lark parser. https://lark-parser.readthedocs.io/en/latest/. Accessed 21 Jan 2022
5. Cve-2008-0166: Openssl 0.9.8c-1 (2008). https://security-tracker.debian.org/tracker/CVE-2008-0166
6. Abrial, J.R.: The B-Book: Assigning Programs to Meanings. Cambridge University Press, Cambridge (2005)
7. Almeida, J.B., et al.: Jasmin: high-assurance and high-speed cryptography. In: Proceedings of the 2017 ACM SIGSAC Conference on Computer and Communications Security, pp. 1807–1823 (2017). https://doi.org/10.1145/3133956.3134078
8. Barbosa, M., et al.: SoK: computer-aided cryptography. In: 42nd IEEE Symposium on Security and Privacy, SP 2021, San Francisco, CA, USA, 24–27 May 2021, pp. 777–795. IEEE (2021). https://doi.org/10.1109/SP40001.2021.00008

---

[4] https://github.com/hacl-star/hacl-star.
[5] https://compcert.org/.

9. Barthe, G., Grégoire, B., Heraud, S., Béguelin, S.Z.: Computer-aided security proofs for the working cryptographer. In: Rogaway, P. (ed.) CRYPTO 2011. LNCS, vol. 6841, pp. 71–90. Springer, Heidelberg (2011). https://doi.org/10.1007/978-3-642-22792-9_5

10. Basin, D., Mödersheim, S., Viganò, L.: An on-the-fly model-checker for security protocol analysis. In: Snekkenes, E., Gollmann, D. (eds.) ESORICS 2003. LNCS, vol. 2808, pp. 253–270. Springer, Heidelberg (2003). https://doi.org/10.1007/978-3-540-39650-5_15

11. Bellare, M., Canetti, R., Krawczyk, H.: A modular approach to the design and analysis of authentication and key exchange protocols. In: Proceedings of the Thirtieth Annual ACM Symposium on Theory of Computing, pp. 419–428 (1998). https://doi.org/10.1145/276698.276854

12. Benaissa, N., Méry, D.: Cryptographic protocols analysis in event B. In: Pnueli, A., Virbitskaite, I., Voronkov, A. (eds.) PSI 2009. LNCS, vol. 5947, pp. 282–293. Springer, Heidelberg (2010). https://doi.org/10.1007/978-3-642-11486-1_24

13. Bengtson, J., Bhargavan, K., Fournet, C., Gordon, A.D., Maffeis, S.: Refinement types for secure implementations. ACM Trans. Program. Lang. Syst. (TOPLAS) 33(2), 1–45 (2011). https://doi.org/10.1145/1890028.1890031

14. Bhargavan, K., et al.: DY*: a modular symbolic verification framework for executable cryptographic protocol code. In: EuroS&P 2021–6th IEEE European Symposium on Security and Privacy (2021). https://doi.org/10.1109/EuroSP51992.2021.00042

15. Bhargavan, K., Corin, R., Deniélou, P.M., Fournet, C., Leifer, J.J.: Cryptographic protocol synthesis and verification for multiparty sessions. In: 2009 22nd IEEE Computer Security Foundations Symposium, pp. 124–140. IEEE (2009). https://doi.org/10.1109/CSF.2009.26

16. Bhargavan, K., Fournet, C., Corin, R., Zalinescu, E.: Cryptographically verified implementations for TLS. In: Proceedings of the 15th ACM Conference on Computer and Communications Security, pp. 459–468 (2008). https://doi.org/10.1145/1455770.1455828

17. Bhargavan, K., Fournet, C., Gordon, A.D., Tse, S.: Verified interoperable implementations of security protocols. ACM Trans. Program. Lang. Syst. (TOPLAS) 31(1), 1–61 (2008). https://doi.org/10.1145/1452044.1452049

18. Bieber, P., Boulahia-Cuppens, N., Lehmann, T., van Wickeren, E.: Abstract machines for communication security. In: 1993 Proceedings Computer Security Foundations Workshop VI, pp. 137–146. IEEE (1993). https://doi.org/10.1109/CSFW.1993.246632

19. Blanchet, B.: An efficient cryptographic protocol verifier based on prolog rules. In: 2001 Proceedings of the 14th IEEE Computer Security Foundations Workshop, pp. 82–96. IEEE (2001). https://doi.org/10.1109/CSFW.2001.930138

20. Blanchet, B.: A computationally sound mechanized prover for security protocols (2006). https://doi.org/10.1109/SP.2006.1

21. Ceelen, P., Mauw, S., Radomirović, S.: Chosen-name attacks: an overlooked class of type-flaw attacks. Electron. Notes Theor. Comput. Sci. 197, 31–43 (2008). https://doi.org/10.1016/j.entcs.2007.12.015

22. Cortier, V., Warinschi, B., Zălinescu, E.: Synthesizing secure protocols. In: Biskup, J., López, J. (eds.) ESORICS 2007. LNCS, vol. 4734, pp. 406–421. Springer, Heidelberg (2007). https://doi.org/10.1007/978-3-540-74835-9_27

23. Cremers, C.J.F.: The Scyther tool: verification, falsification, and analysis of security protocols. In: Gupta, A., Malik, S. (eds.) CAV 2008. LNCS, vol. 5123, pp.

414–418. Springer, Heidelberg (2008). https://doi.org/10.1007/978-3-540-70545-1_38

24. Cuoq, P., Kirchner, F., Kosmatov, N., Prevosto, V., Signoles, J., Yakobowski, B.: Frama-C. In: Eleftherakis, G., Hinchey, M., Holcombe, M. (eds.) SEFM 2012. LNCS, vol. 7504, pp. 233–247. Springer, Heidelberg (2012). https://doi.org/10.1007/978-3-642-33826-7_16

25. Dierks, T., Rescorla, E.: The transport layer security (TLS) protocol version 1.2. RFC 5246 (2008)

26. Dolev, D., Yao, A.: On the security of public key protocols. IEEE Trans. Inf. Theory **29**(2), 198–208 (1983). https://doi.org/10.1109/TIT.1983.1056650

27. Durumeric, Z., et al.: The matter of heartbleed. In: Proceedings of the 2014 conference on internet measurement conference, pp. 475–488 (2014). https://doi.org/10.1145/2663716.2663755

28. Escobar, S., Meadows, C., Meseguer, J.: Maude-NPA: cryptographic protocol analysis modulo equational properties. In: Aldini, A., Barthe, G., Gorrieri, R. (eds.) FOSAD 2007-2009. LNCS, vol. 5705, pp. 1–50. Springer, Heidelberg (2009). https://doi.org/10.1007/978-3-642-03829-7_1

29. Katz, J., Yung, M.: Scalable protocols for authenticated group key exchange. In: Boneh, D. (ed.) CRYPTO 2003. LNCS, vol. 2729, pp. 110–125. Springer, Heidelberg (2003). https://doi.org/10.1007/978-3-540-45146-4_7

30. Lafourcade, P., Puys, M.: Performance evaluations of cryptographic protocols verification tools dealing with algebraic properties. In: Foundations and Practice of Security - 8th International Symposium, FPS 2015, Clermont-Ferrand, France, 26–28 October 2015, Revised Selected Papers, pp. 137–155 (2015). https://doi.org/10.1007/978-3-319-30303-1_9

31. Lowe, G.: Breaking and fixing the Needham-Schroeder public-key protocol using FDR. In: Margaria, T., Steffen, B. (eds.) TACAS 1996. LNCS, vol. 1055, pp. 147–166. Springer, Heidelberg (1996). https://doi.org/10.1007/3-540-61042-1_43

32. Meier, S., Schmidt, B., Cremers, C., Basin, D.: The TAMARIN prover for the symbolic analysis of security protocols. In: Sharygina, N., Veith, H. (eds.) CAV 2013. LNCS, vol. 8044, pp. 696–701. Springer, Heidelberg (2013). https://doi.org/10.1007/978-3-642-39799-8_48

33. Modesti, P.: AnBx: automatic generation and verification of security protocols implementations. In: Garcia-Alfaro, J., Kranakis, E., Bonfante, G. (eds.) FPS 2015. LNCS, vol. 9482, pp. 156–173. Springer, Cham (2015). https://doi.org/10.1007/978-3-319-30303-1_10

34. Needham, R.M., Schroeder, M.D.: Using encryption for authentication in large networks of computers. Commun. ACM **21**(12), 993–999 (1978). https://doi.org/10.1145/359657.359659

35. Nipkow, T., Paulson, L.C., Wenzel, M.: Isabelle/HOL: A Proof Assistant for Higher-Order Logic, vol. 2283. Springer, Heidelberg (2002). https://doi.org/10.1007/3-540-45949-9_5

36. Otway, D., Rees, O.: Efficient and timely mutual authentication. SIGOPS Oper. Syst. Rev. **21**(1), 8–10 (1987). https://doi.org/10.1145/24592.24594

37. Pozza, D., Sisto, R., Durante, L.: Spi2Java: Automatic cryptographic protocol java code generation from SPI calculus. In: Proceedings of the 18th International Conference on Advanced Information Networking and Application (2004). https://doi.org/10.1109/AINA.2004.1283943

38. Protzenko, J., et al.: Verified low-level programming embedded in f. Proc. ACM Program. Lang. **1**(ICFP), 17–1 (2017). https://doi.org/10.1145/3110261

39. Sprenger, C., Basin, D.: Developing security protocols by refinement. In: Proceedings of the 17th ACM Conference on Computer and Communications Security, pp. 361–374 (2010). https://doi.org/10.1145/1866307.1866349
40. Swamy, N., Weinberger, J., Schlesinger, C., Chen, J., Livshits, B.: Verifying higher-order programs with the Dijkstra monad. In: Proceedings of the 34th annual ACM SIGPLAN Conference on Programming Language Design and Implementation, PLDI 2013, pp. 387–398 (2013). https://doi.org/10.1145/2499370.2491978

How to Avoid Repetitions
in Lattice-Based Deniable
Zero-Knowledge Proofs

Xavier Arnal[1], Abraham Cano[1], Tamara Finogina[1,2](✉) ⓘ,
and Javier Herranz[1](✉) ⓘ

[1] Dept. Matemàtiques, Universitat Politècnica de Catalunya,
Barcelona, Spain
{xavier.arnal,abraham.cano,javier.herranz}@upc.edu
[2] Scytl Election Technologies, S.L.U., Barcelona, Spain
tamara.finogina@scytl.com

Abstract. Interactive zero-knowledge systems are a very important cryptographic primitive, used in many applications, especially when deniability (also known as non-transferability) is desired. In the lattice-based setting, the currently most efficient interactive zero-knowledge systems employ the technique of rejection sampling, which implies that the interaction does not always finish correctly in the first execution; the whole interaction must be re-run until abort does not happen.

While repetitions due to aborts are acceptable in theory, in some practical applications it is desirable to avoid re-runs for usability reasons. In this work we present a generic technique that departs from an interactive zero-knowledge system (that might require multiple re-runs to complete the protocol) and obtains a 3-moves zero-knowledge system (without re-runs). The transformation combines the well-known Fiat-Shamir technique with a couple of initially exchanged messages. The resulting 3-moves system enjoys honest-verifier zero-knowledge and can be easily turned into a fully deniable proof using standard techniques. We show some practical scenarios where our transformation can be beneficial and we also discuss the results of an implementation of our transformation.

1 Introduction

In some applications, it is mandatory to ensure that the result of an interaction between a prover and a verifier is non-transferable, i.e., deniable. For example, electronic voting requires ballot content correctness proofs (i.e., proof that the ballot indeed contains the option voter selected) to be non-transferable to prevent vote selling. It means no one except the voter should be able to realize that valid content correctness proof is coming from the voting device and not simulated. Similarly, a deniable authentication should produce a proof that convinces only protocol participants and no one else.

Informally deniability means that only the verifier who interacted with the prover can be convinced that some statement is true. No one else looking at

H. P. Reiser and M. Kyas (Eds.): NordSec 2022, LNCS 13700, pp. 253–269, 2022.
https://doi.org/10.1007/978-3-031-22295-5_14

the same transcript should be able to say if it comes from a real interaction or from one simulated by the verifier. At first glance, it might seem that a standard notion of zero-knowledge (ZK) definition, which requires the existence of a simulator algorithm that can produce transcripts indistinguishable from the ones produced in a real execution, suffices for achieving deniability. However, it is not always the case. For deniability, it is crucial that the verifier can run such a simulator algorithm in the real life; definitions of the ZK notion where the simulator controls a random oracle or a common reference string are thus not satisfactory.

Let us consider for instance non-interactive proofs that are ZK in the random oracle model (ROM). To simulate the transcript, one needs to have control over the hash oracle, which is impossible in real-life settings. Hence, ZK in ROM results in only theoretical deniability: any valid non-interactive proof is, without a doubt, coming from the prover.

The impossibility of achieving deniability with a one-round protocol (in ROM or CRS model) was proven already by Rafael Pass [24]. Also, he argued that two rounds are necessary and sufficient for achieving deniability in ROM. His solution for proving that some public x belongs to some language $\mathcal{L}_\mathcal{R}$ (borrowing notation from Sect. 2) was to use a two-rounds proof of the following form: in the first round, the verifier generates a commitment to a trapdoor and a non-interactive zero-knowledge proof of knowledge (NIZKPoK) of the trapdoor. In the second round, the prover verifies the received NIZKPoK and, if valid, creates an OR proof for the statement "$x \in \mathcal{L}_\mathcal{R}$ OR I know the verifier's trapdoor". We, however, claim that this solution is non-deniable. A malicious verifier can easily copy an existing commitment and corresponding NIZKPoK from some other party/execution and, therefore, engage in a protocol without knowing the trapdoor. Later such a verifier can somehow demonstrate that it could not have known the trapdoor, which makes the origin of any valid proof undeniable.

Therefore, it seems natural that, for deniability, we need a protocol with full zero-knowledge (ZK)[1] in the plain model (with no extra assumptions like a random oracle, a common reference string, a public key infrastructure, etc.). Achieving ZK in the plain model requires at least three rounds of interaction. Furthermore, existing 3-rounds ZK systems are quite theoretical and inefficient; we will thus focus on achieving efficient and 4-rounds ZK systems.

Two classical ways of doing so (and thus to obtain a deniable proof system), assuming the existence of an interactive proof system Π for proving $x \in \mathcal{L}_\mathcal{R}$, are:

(a) If Π is a 3-rounds (Sigma) protocol, where transcripts have the form (a, c, z), then add an initial round where the verifier commits to the challenge c. In round 3 now the verifier opens the commitment; the prover sends z only if the opening is correct. Soundness and ZK hold if the commitment is perfectly hiding and trapdoor.

---

[1] Honest-verifier zero-knowledge (HVZK) is not enough, since the notion of deniability is intrinsically related to a dishonest verifier who could be interested in transferring its conviction to somebody else.

(b) The verifier sends Y in the first round, where $Y = F(X)$ for some homomorphic one-way function F and input X. It also engages a Sigma protocol for proving knowledge of X, which is finished in the two next rounds. In round 4, if the Sigma protocol has been successful, the prover computes a non-interactive (via Fiat-Shamir) proof for the statement "$x \in \mathcal{L_R}$ OR I know X".

The Lattice-Based Setting. Both solutions (a) and (b) above require execution of a Sigma protocol for some language. In the lattice-based setting (the most promising one for achieving security in front of quantum computers, through the hardness of some shortest vector problems in lattices [2] such as the learning with errors (LWE) problem and the short integer solution (SIS) problem) such Sigma protocols are not trivial to construct: the security of LWE and SIS requires that the solution not only has a specific structure but also is small. Thus, a masking term has to be small, but that unavoidably leaks parts of the secret.

A solution to this problem was proposed by Lyubashevsky in [18]. He proposed the smart idea of a (possibly) aborting prover, using rejection sampling to ensure that the answer's distribution is independent of the secret. The rejection sampling allowed to ensure correctness and security and led to many fundamental cryptographic constructions: canonical identification (CID) and signatures (e.g. [18]), zero-knowledge proofs (e.g. [20]), blind signatures (e.g. **BLAZE+** [4]), and others.

The main downside of the idea is the possibility of multiple protocol repetitions that may be very undesirable in practical applications. Real people expect to interact with a system only once and always receive the (correct) result at the end. Hence, an unpredictable number of repeats due to rejection sampling makes deniable protocols unpractical.

Unfortunately, eliminating aborts in lattice-based ZK proofs is quite challenging. Behnia et al. [8] studied rejection conditions in Lyubashevsky's CID scheme and found a way to remove one of the two conditions. However, they concluded that full elimination of rejection sampling is problematic.

An alternative is to reduce the occurrence of protocol re-runs. One of the simplest methods to ensure the protocol terminates after a fixed number of repetitions $M \geq 2$ (with a high probability) is to use a large enough distribution over $\mathbb{Z}$. However, this comes at the cost of increased execution time and proof size.

Another method to decrease the occurrence of aborts is to run several protocols in parallel. Usually, parallel repetition aims to reduce the knowledge error rather than the completeness error. However, we can use it for decreasing rejects as well. Prover starts N independent instances of the protocol and sends N commitments to the verifier, replying only with the first proof that did not cause an abort. While this increases the probability of successful protocol termination, it significantly increases communication and computational complexity (by a factor of N) and does not eliminate aborts completely.

Another work by Attema et al. [5] proposes an s-out-of-t threshold parallel repetition, where the verifier accepts if s out of t of the parallel instances are accepting. Unfortunately, the completeness error is still $\geq \rho^t$, where ρ is the completeness error of a single protocol run. Therefore, achieving a negligible probability of aborts would require a substantial t and would result in an increased proof size and proving time.

An improvement over parallel repetition—a generic construction for reducing aborts in 3-moves protocols—was proposed in [4]. This construction builds on top of the idea of ℓ parallel repetitions and uses (unbalanced) binary hash trees to reduce the size of the first answer, from ℓ-commitments to a tree root.

An alternative to the aborts approach is probabilistically checkable proofs (PCPs) and interactive oracle proofs (IOPs) cleverly combined with lattice-based algebraic techniques. For example, [10] presents a zero-knowledge system for proving knowledge of Learning With Errors (LWE) pre-images, which does not involve aborts. Unfortunately, this solution is more efficient than a general lattice-based system (with aborts) only for some specific settings, for instance, when proving at the same time knowledge of a lot of LWE pre-images with the same matrix A. In other cases, the initial commitment and Merkle paths result in bigger proofs than possible alternatives, especially considering that we need several iterations to achieve negligible soundness.

All in all, the currently most efficient and compact interactive zero-knowledge systems in the lattice-based setting are those with aborts and, so far, there is no efficient way to eliminate them.

1.1 Our Contribution

In this work, we show a simple way to construct a deniable lattice-based proof system that always requires just a single execution for completeness. We depart from any multi-round interactive lattice-based zero-knowledge systems (possibly with re-runs due to the presence of aborts). We demonstrate the security and effectiveness of our construction and its applicability to a wide class of protocols. In particular, we have implemented the system that results from applying our construction to the system proposed in [11].

The general idea of the transformation is to apply the Fiat-Shamir transformation to the original system Π, combined with an initial message by the prover; the challenges of the non-interactive Fiat-Shamir version of Π will not be simply the outputs of the hash functions (as in Fiat-Shamir), but a combination (a sort of trapdoor commitment) of these outputs with the values sent by the prover in the initial message. This allows us to prove that the resulting 3-rounds protocol enjoys the honest-verifier zero-knowledge (HVZK) property.

At this point, we can use both (a) and (b) solutions depicted above: if the system Π was for proving the desired statement, then we can use (a); otherwise, if Π is for proving the knowledge of a pre-image for a lattice-based homomorphic one-way function, we can use (b).

1.2 Illustrating Our Technique

We show how to eliminate the necessity of the protocol re-runs using the lattice-based CID scheme [18] as an example (see Fig. 1). First, we briefly recall the CID scheme and then show how to apply our transformation.

Let A be a public matrix selected uniformly at random from $\mathbb{Z}_q^{n \times m}$. The prover $\mathcal{P}$ would like to prove the knowledge of a secret matrix $S \in \mathbb{Z}^{m \times n}$ with small entries such that $B = A \cdot S \pmod{q}$, where $B \in \mathbb{Z}_q^{n \times n}$ is also public. To do so, $\mathcal{P}$ samples a fresh masking vector y from χ^m, where χ is some distribution over $\mathbb{Z}$ (the discrete Gaussian over $\mathbb{Z}$ or the uniform over a small subset of $\mathbb{Z}$). Then it sends commitment $v = A \cdot y \pmod{q}$ to the verifier $\mathcal{V}$. The $\mathcal{V}$ picks a random challenge from the challenge space $\mathcal{C} = \{(c_1, \ldots, c_n) \in \mathbb{Z}^n : c_i \in \{-1, 0, 1\}, \sum_{i=1}^n |c_i| = \kappa\}$. The $\mathcal{P}$ returns response $z = y + c \cdot S$ to the challenge only if rejection sampling algorithm RejSampl(z) does not abort. The protocol is repeated by sampling a fresh y until RejSampl accepts. The verifier $\mathcal{V}$ accepts if and only if $v = A \cdot z - B \cdot c \pmod{q}$ and $||z||_p$ is smaller than a pre-defined bound B, where $p \in \{2, \infty\}$ depending on the distribution χ.

In our construction, a proof is generated non-interactively (via the Fiat-Shamir transformation) and turned back into an interactive one with the help of a very simple trapdoor commitment:

1. To prove a statement st, $\mathcal{P}$ samples a value $r \in \{0,1\}^\ell$ at random and sends it to the verifier $\mathcal{V}$.
2. $\mathcal{V}$ sends to $\mathcal{P}$ a random challenge $\gamma \in \{0,1\}^\ell$.
3. $\mathcal{P}$ runs a non-interactive version of the CID scheme (if necessary, re-running it until abort does not happen) to get a typical proof (com, e, z); but the challenge e is defined as $e = H_1(r \oplus H(st, com, \gamma))$ instead of the usual H(st, com) in the Fiat-Shamir transformation.

Figure 1 gives an example of a singe-run (without re-runs) CID scheme. Note that in case of aborting, a fresh y is sampled and the process is repeated until RejSampl(z) accepts, ensuring z is statistically indistinguishable from $e \cdot S$.

Intuitively, we see that security is inherited from the non-interactive version of the protocol. On the one hand, $\mathcal{P}$ commits to r prior to receiving the verifier's challenge γ, thus it cannot manipulate the non-interactive challenge e. Therefore the resulting proof behaves as a standard non-interactive version of the initial (interactive) protocol. On the other hand, thanks to the use of the simple trapdoor commitment, anyone can generate a simulated transcript that is indistinguishable from the real one.

In the protocol described in Fig. 1, $H : \{0,1\}^* \to \{0,1\}^\ell$ and $H_1 : \{0,1\}^\ell \to \mathcal{C}$ denote two hash functions and $\oplus$ denotes component-wise XOR operation between two strings of ℓ bits.

2 Preliminaries: (Public Coin) Interactive Proofs

Let $\mathcal{R} \subset \{0,1\}^* \times \{0,1\}^*$ be a binary relation. If a pair $(x, w) \in \mathcal{R}$, we call x an statement and w a witness for x. The relation is an NP-relation if, given (x, w), one can decide in polynomial time if $(x, w) \in \mathcal{R}$ or not. Such a relation $\mathcal{R}$ gives rise to the set of "yes"-instances defined as $\mathcal{L}_{\mathcal{R}} = \{x \in \mathcal{X} \mid \exists w \in \mathcal{W} \text{ s.t. } (x, w) \in \mathcal{R}\}$, known as the language of $\mathcal{R}$. The set of witnesses for a valid statement $x \in \mathcal{L}_{\mathcal{R}}$ is denoted as $R(x)$.

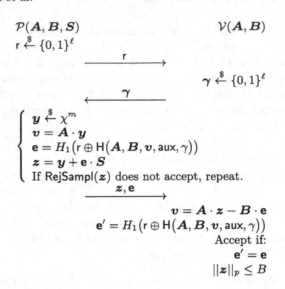

$$\mathcal{P}(\boldsymbol{A}, \boldsymbol{B}, \boldsymbol{S}) \qquad\qquad\qquad \mathcal{V}(\boldsymbol{A}, \boldsymbol{B})$$

$$r \xleftarrow{\$} \{0,1\}^{\ell}$$

$$\xrightarrow{\quad r \quad}$$

$$\gamma \xleftarrow{\$} \{0,1\}^{\ell}$$

$$\xleftarrow{\quad \gamma \quad}$$

$$\begin{cases} \boldsymbol{y} \xleftarrow{\$} \chi^m \\ \boldsymbol{v} = \boldsymbol{A} \cdot \boldsymbol{y} \\ \mathsf{e} = H_1(r \oplus \mathsf{H}(\boldsymbol{A}, \boldsymbol{B}, \boldsymbol{v}, \mathsf{aux}, \gamma)) \\ \boldsymbol{z} = \boldsymbol{y} + \mathsf{e} \cdot \boldsymbol{S} \\ \text{If RejSampl}(\boldsymbol{z}) \text{ does not accept, repeat.} \end{cases}$$

$$\xrightarrow{\quad \boldsymbol{z}, \mathsf{e} \quad}$$

$$\boldsymbol{v} = \boldsymbol{A} \cdot \boldsymbol{z} - \boldsymbol{B} \cdot \mathsf{e}$$
$$\mathsf{e}' = H_1(r \oplus \mathsf{H}(\boldsymbol{A}, \boldsymbol{B}, \boldsymbol{v}, \mathsf{aux}, \gamma))$$
$$\text{Accept if:}$$
$$\mathsf{e}' = \mathsf{e}$$
$$\|\boldsymbol{z}\|_p \le B$$

Fig. 1. Interactive CID scheme that always terminates after a single run.

Interactive Proofs. An interactive proof system Π for relation $\mathcal{R}$ is an interactive protocol between two probabilistic polynomial-time (PPT) algorithms, the prover $\mathcal{P}$ and the verifier $\mathcal{V}$. The common input of the two parties is a statement x, whereas $\mathcal{P}$ has as an additional input a witness $w \in R(x)$. We thus denote an execution of such a protocol as $\langle \mathcal{P}(y), \mathcal{V}(y)\rangle_{\Pi}$. The final output of the protocol is a bit — 1 if $\mathcal{V}$ accepts, 0 otherwise. The set of messages exchanged during the execution of Π is called an (accepting or rejecting) transcript.

We will consider in this work a specific but very common type of interactive proof systems: those where the first and last messages are sent by $\mathcal{P}$, leading to $(2\mu + 1)$ rounds of communication, for some integer $\mu \ge 1$. We will be considering *public coin* systems: all the random choices of $\mathcal{V}$ are made public during the execution of Π. This is equivalent to say that the $2i$-th message of the protocol, sent by $\mathcal{V}$ to $\mathcal{P}$, is a random element $c_i \leftarrow_R \mathcal{C}_i$, called a challenge, taken from some challenge space(s) $\mathcal{C}_i$.

The first property that must be required to such an interactive system is δ-completeness: if $(x, w) \in \mathcal{R}$ then it holds $Pr[\langle \mathcal{P}(x, w), \mathcal{V}(x)\rangle_{\Pi} = 1] = 1 - \delta$.

Zero-Knowledge. A public coin interactive protocol Π as above enjoys the *honest-verifier zero-knowledge* (HVZK) property if there exists a PPT algorithm M_{Π} such that, for any $(x, w) \in \mathcal{R}$, on input x and μ challenge values $c_1, \ldots, c_{\mu}$ with $c_i \in \mathcal{C}_i$, outputs an accepting transcript with the same distribution as the one produced by an execution of $\langle \mathcal{P}(x, w), \mathcal{V}(x)\rangle_{\Pi}$ run with a honest verifier $\mathcal{V}$ that has chosen those challenges $c_i \leftarrow_R \mathcal{C}_i$, for $i = 1, \ldots, \mu$.

A stronger notion is *full zero-knowledge* (ZK), which clearly implies deniability; it requires that, for every verifier $\mathcal{V}^*$ there exists a PPT simulator $M_{\mathcal{V}^*, \Pi}$ such that for every $(x, w) \in \mathcal{R}$ the output $\langle \mathcal{P}(x, w), \mathcal{V}^*(x)\rangle_{\Pi}$ is identically distributed to the output $M_{\mathcal{V}^*}(x)$. This property can be relaxed requiring that the outputs only be statistically or computationally indistinguishable.

(Knowledge) Soundness. A protocol Π has the ϵ-soundness property if, for any $x \notin \mathcal{L_R}$, it holds $Pr[\langle \mathcal{P}(x), \mathcal{V}(y) \rangle_\Pi = 1] \le \epsilon$.

There is a stronger version of soundness — that of knowledge soundness. A protocol Π enjoys *knowledge soundness* with knowledge error $\kappa : \mathbb{N} \to [0, 1]$ if there exist a positive polynomial $q(\cdot)$ and algorithm K, such that for every prover $\mathcal{P}^*$ and $x \in \mathcal{L_R}$, the extractor K, on input x, with black-box oracle access to $\mathcal{P}^*$ and within an expected number of steps polynomial in $|x|$, outputs a witness $w \in R(x)$ with probability at least

$$\frac{Pr[\langle \mathcal{P}(x, w), \mathcal{V}(x) \rangle_\Pi = 1] - \kappa(|x|)}{q(|x|)}$$

3   The Transformation

Let $\Pi = \langle \mathcal{P}(x, \omega), \mathcal{V}(x) \rangle_\Pi$ be a public coin $(2\mu + 1)$-rounds interactive proof system for language $\mathcal{L_R}$. We denote as a_i the message sent by $\mathcal{P}$ to $\mathcal{V}$ in round $2i - 1$, for $i = 1, \ldots, \mu$, and as z the last message sent by $\mathcal{P}$ in round $2\mu + 1$. The message sent by $\mathcal{V}$ in round $2i$ is a random challenge $c_i \in \mathcal{C}_i$, for some challenge space $\mathcal{C}_i$, for $i = 1, \ldots, \mu$.

Let us consider $1 + \mu$ hash functions: on the one hand $H : \{0, 1\}^* \to \{0, 1\}^\ell$ and on the other hand $H_i : \{0, 1\}^\ell \to \mathcal{C}_i$, for $i = 1, \ldots, \mu$.

We construct a 3-rounds interactive proof system $\Sigma = \langle \mathcal{P}(x, w), \mathcal{V}(x) \rangle_\Sigma$ for the same language $\mathcal{L_R}$, as follows.

1. For $i = 1, \ldots, \mu$, $\mathcal{P}$ chooses $r_i \in \{0, 1\}^\ell$ uniformly at random. These values $r_1, \ldots, r_\mu$ are sent to $\mathcal{V}$.
2. $\mathcal{V}$ chooses a challenge $\gamma \in \{0, 1\}^\ell$ uniformly at random and sends it to $\mathcal{P}$.
3. $\mathcal{P}$ runs an execution of the system Π by using inputs (x, ω), and playing also the role of the verifier, by defining the challenges as $c_i = H_i(r_i \oplus h_i)$, where $h_i = H(x, a_1, \ldots, a_i, c_1, \ldots, c_{i-1}, \gamma)$, for $i = 1, \ldots, \mu$. The resulting transcript $(a_1, a_2, \ldots, a_\mu, z)$ is sent by $\mathcal{P}$ to $\mathcal{V}$.

$\mathcal{V}$ accepts the interaction as valid if $(a_1, c_1, a_2, c_2, \ldots, a_\mu, c_\mu, z)$ is an accepting transcript for Π with input x, where $c_i = H_i(r_i \oplus h_i)$ and $h_i = H(x, a_1, \ldots, a_i, c_1, \ldots, c_{i-1}, \gamma)$, for $i = 1, \ldots, \mu$.

3.1   Security Analysis

The completeness property of Σ is trivially satisfied, assuming the interactive system Π enjoys completeness. In the next sections we show how the zero-knowledge and soundness properties of Π are also inherited by Σ.

Zero-Knowledge

Proposition 1. *Assuming Π enjoys the honest-verifier zero-knowledge (HVZK) property, then the new interactive system Σ also enjoys the HVZK property.*

Proof. The goal is to show that, for any $(x, w) \in \mathcal{L}_\mathcal{R}$, a simulator algorithm M_Σ can, on input x and any (honest) random challenge $\gamma \in \{0, 1\}^\ell$, produce transcripts $(r_1, \ldots, r_\mu, \gamma, a_1, \ldots, a_\mu, z)$ indistinguishable from those produced by an execution of $\langle \mathcal{P}(x, w), \mathcal{V}(x) \rangle_\Sigma$ with a honest verifier $\mathcal{V}$ which takes that γ uniformly at random in $\{0, 1\}^\ell$.

By hypothesis, there is a simulator M_Π for Π. What the simulator M_Σ does first is to choose uniformly at random μ values $v_1, \ldots, v_\mu \overset{\$}{\leftarrow} \{0, 1\}^\ell$ and to compute $c_i = H_i(v_i)$ for $i = 1, \ldots, \mu$. Then M_Π runs simulator M_Π with input x and challenges $c_1, \ldots, c_\mu$, which results in an accepting transcript $(a_1, c_1, a_2, c_2, \ldots, a_\mu, c_\mu, z)$, indistinguishable from those produced by $\langle \mathcal{P}(x, w), \mathcal{V}(x) \rangle_\Pi$. After that M_Σ computes the values $h_i = H_i(x, a_1, \ldots, a_i, c_1, \ldots, c_{i-1}, \gamma)$ and $r_i = v_i \oplus h_i$, for $i = 1, \ldots, \mu$.

It is easy to check that the transcript has the same distribution as those produced in a real execution of $\langle \mathcal{P}(x, w), \mathcal{V}(x) \rangle_\Sigma$ where γ is the challenge chosen by the honest verifier.

Assuming hash functions H_i are pseudo-random functions, the values $c_i = H_i(v_i)$ generated by M_Σ and given as inputs to M_Π are random and uniform elements in $\mathcal{C}_i$. $\qquad\square$

If we combine this 3-rounds and HVZK protocol Σ with a trapdoor and perfectly hiding commitment scheme (as scheduled in item (a) in the Introduction), we can obtain full zero-knowledge in the plain model and thus, deniability.

Alternatively, we can apply our construction to a protocol Π for proving knowledge of a pre-image X for some value $Y = F(X)$, where F is a lattice-based homomorphic one-way function. The resulting protocol Σ can then be used in the solution depicted in item (b) in the Introduction.

Soundness

Proposition 2. *Assuming Π has ϵ-soundness and if ℓ is big enough, then the new interactive system Σ has the ϵ'-soundness, in the (classical) Random Oracle Model, where $\epsilon' \leq \epsilon \cdot Q^\mu$ and Q is an upper bound on the number of hash queries that a prover of Σ can make.*

Proof. The proof of this result works in a similar way as the well-known (in its naive, non-optimized version) proof that the Fiat-Shamir transformation of a public-coin interactive system with soundness results in a secure non-interactive system: the idea is to rewind the adversary several (in our case, μ times), by fixing the randomness and the answers to the hash queries up to a specific point, and then to use the Forking Lemma [25] to ensure that, with non-negligible probability, all the instances of the adversary will lead to forgeries with the desired outputs (that have been fixed in the rewinds).

First of all, if ℓ is big enough, then the probability $2^{-\ell}$ of breaking soundness by guessing the challenge $\gamma \in \{0,1\}^{\ell}$ is negligible. In that setting, let us assume that Σ still does not have ϵ'-soundness. Thus, there exists a prover $\mathcal{P}_{\Sigma}$ that is accepted with probability $> \epsilon'$, when run with some instance $x' \notin \mathcal{L}_{\mathcal{R}}$. We are going to construct a prover $\mathcal{P}_{\Pi}$ against the soundness of Π, running thus with the same $x' \notin \mathcal{L}_{\mathcal{R}}$.

As its first instruction, $\mathcal{P}_{\Pi}$ starts running $\mathcal{P}_{\Sigma}$, which sends its first message $(r_1, \ldots, r_{\mu})$. Now $\mathcal{P}_{\Pi}$ chooses at random $\gamma \in \{0,1\}^{\ell}$ and sends it to $\mathcal{P}_{\Sigma}$. We remark that $(r_1, \ldots, r_{\mu})$ and γ are going to be fixed for all the calls that $\mathcal{P}_{\Pi}$ makes to $\mathcal{P}_{\Sigma}$. In this first call, $\mathcal{P}_{\Sigma}$ gives its final answer $(a_1^{(1)}, \ldots, a_{\mu}^{(1)}, z^{(1)})$, which is valid with probability $\geq \epsilon'$.

During this and the other executions of $\mathcal{P}_{\Sigma}$, our new prover $\mathcal{P}_{\Pi}$ has to answer the hash queries made by $\mathcal{P}_{\Sigma}$. This is done in the usual way, by keeping track of all previous queries, selecting a random output for new queries, storing the (input,output) relations in a table, etc. With overwhelming probability, a successful prover $\mathcal{P}_{\Sigma}$ will have made all the key queries $h_i \leftarrow H(x', a_1^{(1)}, \ldots, a_i^{(1)}, c_1^{(1)}, \ldots, c_{i-1}^{(1)}, \gamma)$ and $H_i(r_i + h_i)$, for $i = 1, \ldots, \mu$.

After the first execution, $\mathcal{P}_{\Pi}$ sends the value $a_1^{(1)}$ to its verifier $\mathcal{V}_{\Pi}$, which then sends a challenge c_1. With overwhelming probability, it will be the case that $c_1 \neq H_1(r_1 \oplus h_1)$. What $\mathcal{P}_{\Pi}$ does now is to rewind: it starts a new running of $\mathcal{P}_{\Sigma}$, with the same random tape and the same answers to the hash queries, up to the point where the query $H_1(r_1 \oplus h_1)$ is made; this time, the answer to this query is defined as c_1. The Forking Lemma ensures that, with non-negligible probability, this second execution of $\mathcal{P}_{\Sigma}$ will produce a valid transcript $(a_1^{(1)}, a_2^{(2)}, \ldots, a_{\mu}^{(2)}, z^{(2)})$ with the same value $a_1^{(1)}$ as in the first execution (because, with overwhelming probability, the value $a_1^{(1)}$ had been queried to hash oracle H to produce h_1, before the key query $H_1(r_1 \oplus h_1)$ was made). At this point, $\mathcal{P}_{\Pi}$ sends the value $a_2^{(2)}$ to its verifier $\mathcal{V}_{\Pi}$, which then sends a challenge c_2.

The same rewind argument is done again, with the same random tape and hash answers as in the second execution, but now defining $H_2(r_2 \oplus h_2)$ to be c_2. Again with overwhelming probability this query, which depends on h_2 which depends on c_1, must have been made after the query $H_1(r_1 \oplus h_1)$, which is again answered as c_1. With non-negligible probability, this third execution of $\mathcal{P}_{\Sigma}$ produces a valid transcript $(a_1^{(1)}, a_2^{(2)}, a_3^{(3)}, \ldots, a_{\mu}^{(3)}, z^{(3)})$.

Repeating this argument μ times, letting $\mathcal{P}_{\Pi}$ send $a_i^{(i)}$ to its verifier $\mathcal{V}_{\Pi}$ in round i, getting c_i as answer and rewinding $\mathcal{P}_{\Sigma}$ accordingly, at the end we eventually finish, after $\mu + 1$ executions of $\mathcal{P}_{\Sigma}$, with a valid transcript $(a_1^{(1)}, a_2^{(2)}, a_3^{(3)}, \ldots, a_{\mu}^{(\mu)}, z^{(\mu+1)})$ satisfying $c_i = H_i(r_i \oplus h_i)$, where $h_i = H_i(x', a_1^{(1)}, \ldots, a_i^{(i)}, c_1, \ldots, c_{i-1}, \gamma)$. Thus, our $\mathcal{P}_{\Pi}$ has convinced its verifier $\mathcal{V}_{\Pi}$ with non-negligible probability ϵ. By the iterated use of the Forking Lemma, the relation between ϵ and ϵ' is essentially $\epsilon \approx \frac{\epsilon'}{Q^{\mu}}$. $\square$

3.2 Extensions

- The same idea as in the proof for soundness can be applied to prove that knowledge soundness of Π implies knowledge soundness of Σ.
- The soundness property of Σ is obtained in the classical Random Oracle Model. If one wants to achieve soundness in the Quantum Random Oracle Model, then one can use alternative transformations to Fiat-Shamir, either generic [12,29] or specific for lattice-based systems [17], that have been proposed in the last years.
- The naive reduction in our proof for the soundness property implies a loss factor Q^μ which is exponential in the number of rounds of Π. This problem can be solved by using the results in [6], whenever the starting protocol Π enjoys $(k_1, \ldots, k_\mu)$-special soundness. We stress that most (if not all) popular interactive systems Π enjoy this property, including lattice-based ones.
- If the challenge spaces C_i of the interactive protocol Π are closed spaces for some mathematical operation (that we denote for simplicity as $+$), then a small modification to our construction is possible, basically choosing $r_i \leftarrow_R C_i$ and then defining $c_i = r_i + h_i$, where $h_i = H_i(x, a_1, \ldots, a_i, h_1, \ldots, h_{i-1}, \gamma)$, being now $H_i : \{0,1\}^* \to C_i$. This situation happens for instance when Π is the protocol in [30]: the challenge space contains integers modulo a prime p.

4 Applications

The transformation proposed in the previous section is useful in settings where a lattice-based interactive zero-knowledge protocol is mandatory (for instance, if deniability is required), or for some reason preferable to a non-interactive protocol. In such a situation, the most efficient existing protocols Π involve rejection sampling and thus aborts [11,13,14,20,21,30]. Our transformation results in a 3-rounds protocol Σ without mandatory protocol restarts, at the cost of relying on the Random Oracle Model to achieve provable security.

We give below three specific examples of situations where such interactive protocols are used. After that, we discuss other situations where our result in the previous section does not seem applicable.

4.1 Canonical Identification Schemes

Canonical Identification (CID) schemes are three round public coin protocols in which a prover (who sends the first and third messages) proves knowledge of the secret key matching a specific public key. The second message, sent by the verifier, is a random challenge.

Although these schemes are often used as building blocks to design other cryptographic protocols (in particular, signature schemes, with no interaction between the signer and the verifier), they can be used on their own: for instance, in access control systems where the user trying to get access proves to the access entity (the verifier, in this context) that he owns the secret key which matches a public key of some authorized user. If the users want their access to remain private, a solution can be to run a CID scheme, so that the transcript is non-transferable and the (possibly dishonest) access entity cannot prove to someone else that a user got access to the system. An example of the use of such non-transferable identification schemes can be found in [9].

CID schemes are one of the examples considered in the work [4] to motivate their use of trees of commitments, in order to reduce the abort probability of lattice-based interactive zero-knowledge systems. They use Lyubashevsky's identification protocol [18] (recalled in the Sect. 1.2 of this work) as an illustrative lattice-based CID scheme. Therein, the probability of aborting in a single execution of the protocol is $\approx 1 - \frac{1}{M}$, where $M = \exp\left(\frac{12}{\alpha} + \frac{1}{2\alpha^2}\right)$, being α a lattice parameter that affects the size of the standard deviation σ used to sample the underlying Gaussian distribution: $\alpha = T\alpha$.

There are basically four options[2] if one wants to be sure that the identification protocol will finish with overwhelming probability p_{sc} in three rounds of communication (that is, without forcing the verifier to send more than one message):

1. keep the typically proposed parameters for α, σ, and repeat the protocol, in parallel, at least M times. Here the choice of α will depend on the desired probability p_{sc}. The M repetitions imply that the global communication contains M vectors in the ring $(R_q)^k$;
2. run a single execution of the protocol, but with highly increased parameters α, σ so that M is very close to one;
3. keep the typical values for α, σ and apply the tree of commitments technique introduced in [4], which increases the computational complexity of the prover by a factor ℓ and the communication complexity by $\log(\ell)$ hash values, where ℓ (the number of leaves in the tree) depends on α, p_{sc};
4. apply our transformation to Lyubashevsky's CID scheme, which results in a protocol that always succeeds; the communication complexity of the protocol is almost the same as in the original CID scheme, whereas the computational cost for the prover is essentially the same as in options 1, 2, and 3 above.

Note that option 4 is the only one that ensures that the protocol will always finish successfully. The other advantage of option 4 over the three first options is, of course, its communication complexity. On the negative side, option 4 is the only one that needs the heuristic Random Oracle Model to have provable security.

Some specific values given in Sect. 3 of [4] are as follows, for $p_{sc} = 1 - 2^{-10}$: option 1 could have $\alpha = 11$ and $M \approx 3$, option 2 should have $\alpha > 2^{13.6}$ and option 3 could have $\alpha = 23$ and $\ell = 8$ or alternatively $\alpha = 12$ and $\ell = 16$.

For higher values of p_{sc}, parameters in options 1,2,3 must be increased even more. As an example, authors of [4] show that $\alpha = 42$ and $\ell = 64$ are needed for $p_{sc} = 1 - 2^{-128}$.

---

[2] We stress that the abort-free protocol in [10] is not really suitable for this setting, in terms of efficiency.

4.2   Non-transferable Signatures

In some kinds of signature schemes that have been introduced in the last decades, the validity of the signature is not universally verifiable as it happens in standard signatures. In contrast, the signer puts some limit on the user(s) who can verify a signature, and also on the capability to transfer this conviction to other users. Examples of this kind of signature schemes are designated verifier signatures, directed signatures, nominative signatures, undeniable signatures, and designated confirmer signatures.

Some of them are aggregated under the name of on-line non-transferable signatures [27]. In such schemes, the signing algorithm is run by the signer, but then there are interactive protocols, Confirm and Disavow, run by both the signer and the verifier, which confirm the verifier of the validity or invalidity of a signature. The verifier cannot convince anybody else of any of these facts. Applications of these kinds of signatures include machine-readable travel documents and identity documents like e-Passports [7,23].

The interaction between signer and verifier typically involves a 3-rounds zero-knowledge system. If one intends to design such schemes in a lattice-based setting, thus, our result in this paper can be directly used as an ingredient of such designs, so that the interaction between signer and verifier needs to be run only once, without the verifier noticing the presence of aborts and without (parallel) repetitions.

As a particular example, the first (and maybe only) secure lattice-based undeniable signature scheme is the one in [26]. The confirmation and disavowal protocols of the scheme are designed by using Stern's techniques [28]: a dishonest prover is accepted with probability $2/3$ (soundness error), which means the protocols must be run a large number of times to achieve real soundness. Our techniques, combined with some suitable and efficient lattice-based zero-knowledge system Π for the languages involved in those confirmation/disavowal protocols, would result in protocols Σ with overwhelming soundness, without repetitions due to aborts. There are many options today (see for instance [20] and references therein) to find a suitable and efficient Π for the specific lattice-based languages appearing in the confirmation/disavowal protocols of [26].

4.3   eVoting with CAI and CR Properties

Two important properties of an electronic voting system are cast-as-intended (CAI) verifiability and coercion-resistance (CR). CAI verifiability means that the voter is convinced that the option inside a ciphertext that goes to the ballot box is the one that he/she has chosen, when the ciphertext has been created by an external (possibly dishonest) voting device. Coercion-resistance is achieved if a voter has means of deceiving a coercer who tries to force the voter to act in a specific way during the voting protocol.

In scenarios where voters do not receive secret information (such as credentials) from the election authorities, it has been recently shown [15] that at least three rounds of interaction between the voter and voting device are necessary in order to achieve CAI and CR at the same time. The authors of that paper propose two generic constructions involving four rounds of communication. For instance, in one of the constructions, the interaction is essentially a combination of a commitment scheme (where the voter commits to the challenge that will be used later) and a zero-knowledge system, with honest-verifier zero-knowledge, where the voting device proves knowledge of randomness r such that $\mathsf{Enc}_{pk}(m; r) = c$, for some public parameters pk, m, c: the public key pk of the encryption scheme Enc, the plaintext m which the voting option chosen by the voter and the ciphertext c that will go to the ballot box.

If one wants to instantiate this construction with post-quantum secure tools, one can choose a lattice-based encryption scheme, for instance, one based on the hardness of the Ring Learning With Errors (RLWE) problem [22] and combine it with some of the recent efficient zero-knowledge systems for lattice-based relations [11,13,14,20,21,30]. Since the interactive versions of all these zero-knowledge systems Π involve rejection sampling and aborts, we can apply our transformation to get a 3-rounds system Σ, with honest-verifier zero-knowledge as desired, and without any repetitions. This means that the voter does not need to run many executions of the system (in parallel or not) in order to get convinced that the ciphertext contains the voting option m.

4.4 Settings Where Our Result Is Not Useful

We insist once again that the "abort problem" of zero-knowledge systems based on lattices is not an issue if these systems are to be used in the non-interactive version resulting from applying Fiat-Shamir or a similar transformation. In these cases, the party acting as the prover will eventually abort and start the process again, without the final verifier noticing. This happens in a lot of practical uses of these protocols—including standard/group/ring/attribute-based signatures.

A kind of signature that requires interaction is blind signature, where a user wants to obtain a signature by a signer on some message m, without the signer obtaining any information about the message m. Currently, in the setting of lattice-based blind signatures, the tree of commitments technique introduced in [4] to reduce the abort probability has been successfully used a couple of times, first in the same paper [4] as an improvement of the signature scheme BLAZE [3] and then in [16] to construct a provably-secure (in contrast to BLAZE and BLAZE+) but inefficient scheme which involves three rounds of communication.

A natural question is thus: can our $\Pi \to \Sigma$ transformation be applied in the setting of (lattice-based) blind signatures, as it happened with the tree of commitments technique? The answer seems to be no, as a blind signature scheme where the signer proves something using Σ appears to be very far from achieving the blindness property. In any case, a positive answer to the question would result in a blind signature scheme with at least three rounds of communication, which would not improve the state-of-the-art: recently, a couple of schemes involving only two rounds of communication have been proposed in the lattice setting [1,19].

5   Implementation

In this section we present our experimental results of the implementation of our transformation. We applied our transformation to the 5 round protocol of Bootle et al. [11], using a custom-built library for polynomial operations over $Z_q/\langle x^n + 1\rangle$, along with the RustCrypto library for computing SHA2 hashes in Rust.

The tests were performed on an Intel Core i7-10750H CPU. We have performed 1,000 tests over the protocol with and without the transformation. We have found that, when using the parameters proposed by Bootle et al. [11], the mean execution time increases from 20.6 to 21.5 s ($\sigma < 0.3$), amounting to an increase of about 5% in execution time. In Fig. 2, we can see the time distribution of the protocol over the executions with (orange) and without (blue) the transformation.

While we have obtained an expected decrease in the performance of a single run of the protocol, we have been able to avoid the need for re-runs and thus achieve an improvement over the whole testing. For completeness, Fig. 3 gives the distribution of the number of aborts produced in another 10,000 tests of the non-transformed protocol with faster parameters ($n = 16$). For instance, more than 6% of the executions required 10 repetitions or more of the protocol; this may be very undesirable in some real-life interactive protocols.

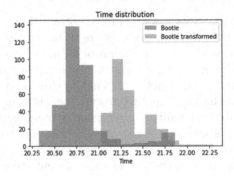

Fig. 2. Time distribution (in seconds) of the 1,000 executions of the first sampling test. (Color figure online)

6   Conclusion

This work presents a theoretical result related to the cryptographic primitive of interactive zero-knowledge systems: a transformation from any public coin $(2\mu + 1)$-rounds interactive proof system to a public coin 3-rounds proof system for the same language. This result, by itself, may seem not original nor useful at all, because the well-known Fiat-Shamir transformation can transform the same

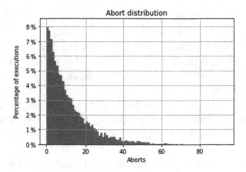

Fig. 3. Percentage of executions in the second sampling test, with 10,000 executions, that suffered i aborts, for each i in the x-axis. For instance, 1.5% of the executions had 20 repetitions with aborts.

$(2\mu+1)$-rounds interactive proof system into a non-interactive (one-round) proof system.

But in some practical settings, when proofs must be deniable, non-interactive systems are not a valid solution; in these cases, a 3-rounds solution is essentially optimal. When all this happens in the post-quantum secure setting of lattice-based cryptography, such $(2\mu+1)$-rounds interactive proof systems use to employ the rejection sampling technique, which leads to a non-negligeable number of repetitions of the protocol, before the proof is securely produced. This means that the verifier must be on-line for a while and, in case of required repetitions, choose again different random challenges. All in all, this may lead to an undesirable user-oriented experience, for instance in electronic voting applications.

The most relevant property of our transformation, in the lattice-based setting, is that possible repetitions due to rejection sampling do not affect the verifier: they are done internally by the prover, in the 3rd (and last) round of the proof system. The verifier can choose a single challenge and disconnect; the proof will be produced with 100% probability in any case.

Acknowledgements. This work is partially supported by the Spanish *Ministerio de Ciencia e Innovación (MICINN)*, under Project PID2019-109379RB-I00.

References

1. Agrawal, S., Kirshanova, E., Stehlé, D., Yadav, A.: Can round-optimal lattice-based blind signatures be practical? Cryptology ePrint Archive, Report 2021/1565 (2021). https://ia.cr/2021/1565
2. Ajtai, M.: Generating hard instances of lattice problems (extended abstract). In: Proceedings of the Twenty-Eighth Annual ACM Symposium on Theory of Computing, New York, NY, USA, pp. 99–108. Association for Computing Machinery (1996)
3. Alkeilani Alkadri, N., El Bansarkhani, R., Buchmann, J.: BLAZE: practical lattice-based blind signatures for privacy-preserving applications. In: Bonneau, J.,

Heninger, N. (eds.) FC 2020. LNCS, vol. 12059, pp. 484–502. Springer, Cham (2020). https://doi.org/10.1007/978-3-030-51280-4_26

4. Alkeilani Alkadri, N., El Bansarkhani, R., Buchmann, J.: On lattice-based interactive protocols: an approach with less or no aborts. In: Liu, J.K., Cui, H. (eds.) ACISP 2020. LNCS, vol. 12248, pp. 41–61. Springer, Cham (2020). https://doi.org/10.1007/978-3-030-55304-3_3

5. Attema, T., Fehr, S.: Parallel repetition of $(k_1, \ldots, k_\mu)$-special-sound multi-round interactive proofs. In: Dodis, Y., Shrimpton, T. (eds.) CRYPTO 2022. LNCS, vol. 13507, pp. 415–443. Springer, Cham (2022). https://doi.org/10.1007/978-3-031-15802-5_15

6. Attema, T., Fehr, S., Klooß, M.: Fiat-Shamir transformation of multi-round interactive proofs. IACR Cryptol. ePrint Arch. 1377 (2021)

7. Balli, F., Durak, F.B., Vaudenay, S.: BioID: a privacy-friendly identity document. In: Mauw, S., Conti, M. (eds.) STM 2019. LNCS, vol. 11738, pp. 53–70. Springer, Cham (2019). https://doi.org/10.1007/978-3-030-31511-5_4

8. Behnia, R., Chen, Y., Masny, D.: On removing rejection conditions in practical lattice-based signatures. In: Cheon, J.H., Tillich, J.-P. (eds.) PQCrypto 2021 2021. LNCS, vol. 12841, pp. 380–398. Springer, Cham (2021). https://doi.org/10.1007/978-3-030-81293-5_20

9. Blundo, C., Persiano, G., Sadeghi, A.-R., Visconti, I.: Improved security notions and protocols for non-transferable identification. In: Jajodia, S., Lopez, J. (eds.) ESORICS 2008. LNCS, vol. 5283, pp. 364–378. Springer, Heidelberg (2008). https://doi.org/10.1007/978-3-540-88313-5_24

10. Bootle, J., Lyubashevsky, V., Nguyen, N.K., Seiler, G.: More efficient amortization of exact zero-knowledge proofs for LWE. In: Bertino, E., Shulman, H., Waidner, M. (eds.) ESORICS 2021. LNCS, vol. 12973, pp. 608–627. Springer, Cham (2021). https://doi.org/10.1007/978-3-030-88428-4_30

11. Bootle, J., Lyubashevsky, V., Seiler, G.: Algebraic techniques for short(er) exact lattice-based zero-knowledge proofs. In: Boldyreva, A., Micciancio, D. (eds.) CRYPTO 2019. LNCS, vol. 11692, pp. 176–202. Springer, Cham (2019). https://doi.org/10.1007/978-3-030-26948-7_7

12. Don, J., Fehr, S., Majenz, C., Schaffner, C.: Security of the Fiat-Shamir transformation in the quantum random-oracle model. In: Boldyreva, A., Micciancio, D. (eds.) CRYPTO 2019. LNCS, vol. 11693, pp. 356–383. Springer, Cham (2019). https://doi.org/10.1007/978-3-030-26951-7_13

13. Esgin, M.F., Nguyen, N.K., Seiler, G.: Practical exact proofs from lattices: new techniques to exploit fully-splitting rings. In: Moriai, S., Wang, H. (eds.) ASIACRYPT 2020. LNCS, vol. 12492, pp. 259–288. Springer, Cham (2020). https://doi.org/10.1007/978-3-030-64834-3_9

14. Esgin, M.F., Steinfeld, R., Liu, J.K., Liu, D.: Lattice-based zero-knowledge proofs: new techniques for shorter and faster constructions and applications. In: Boldyreva, A., Micciancio, D. (eds.) CRYPTO 2019. LNCS, vol. 11692, pp. 115–146. Springer, Cham (2019). https://doi.org/10.1007/978-3-030-26948-7_5

15. Finogina, T., Herranz, J., Larraia, E.: How (not) to achieve both coercion resistance and cast as intended verifiability in remote eVoting. In: Conti, M., Stevens, M., Krenn, S. (eds.) CANS 2021. LNCS, vol. 13099, pp. 483–491. Springer, Cham (2021). https://doi.org/10.1007/978-3-030-92548-2_25

16. Hauck, E., Kiltz, E., Loss, J., Nguyen, N.K.: Lattice-based blind signatures, revisited. In: Micciancio, D., Ristenpart, T. (eds.) CRYPTO 2020. LNCS, vol. 12171, pp. 500–529. Springer, Cham (2020). https://doi.org/10.1007/978-3-030-56880-1_18

17. Katsumata, S.: A new simple technique to bootstrap various lattice zero-knowledge proofs to QROM secure NIZKs. In: Malkin, T., Peikert, C. (eds.) CRYPTO 2021. LNCS, vol. 12826, pp. 580–610. Springer, Cham (2021). https://doi.org/10.1007/978-3-030-84245-1_20

18. Lyubashevsky, V.: Fiat-Shamir with aborts: applications to lattice and factoring-based signatures. In: Matsui, M. (ed.) ASIACRYPT 2009. LNCS, vol. 5912, pp. 598–616. Springer, Heidelberg (2009). https://doi.org/10.1007/978-3-642-10366-7_35

19. Lyubashevsky, V., Nguyen, N.K., Plancon, M.: Efficient lattice-based blind signatures via Gaussian one-time signatures. In: Hanaoka, G., Shikata, J., Watanabe, Y. (eds.) PKC 2022. LNCS, vol. 13178, pp. 498–527. Springer, Cham (2022). https://doi.org/10.1007/978-3-030-97131-1_17

20. Lyubashevsky, V., Nguyen, N.K., Plançon, M.: Lattice-based zero-knowledge proofs and applications: shorter, simpler, and more general. In: Dodis, Y., Shrimpton, T. (eds.) CRYPTO 2022. LNCS, vol. 13508, pp. 71–101. Springer, Cham (2022). https://doi.org/10.1007/978-3-031-15979-4_3

21. Lyubashevsky, V., Nguyen, N.K., Seiler, G.: Shorter lattice-based zero-knowledge proofs via one-time commitments. In: Garay, J.A. (ed.) PKC 2021. LNCS, vol. 12710, pp. 215–241. Springer, Cham (2021). https://doi.org/10.1007/978-3-030-75245-3_9

22. Lyubashevsky, V., Peikert, C., Regev, O.: On ideal lattices and learning with errors over rings. J. ACM **60**(6), 43:1–43:35 (2013)

23. Monnerat, J., Pasini, S., Vaudenay, S.: Efficient deniable authentication for signatures. In: Abdalla, M., Pointcheval, D., Fouque, P.-A., Vergnaud, D. (eds.) ACNS 2009. LNCS, vol. 5536, pp. 272–291. Springer, Heidelberg (2009). https://doi.org/10.1007/978-3-642-01957-9_17

24. Pass, R.: On deniability in the common reference string and random oracle model. In: Boneh, D. (ed.) CRYPTO 2003. LNCS, vol. 2729, pp. 316–337. Springer, Heidelberg (2003). https://doi.org/10.1007/978-3-540-45146-4_19

25. Pointcheval, D., Stern, J.: Security arguments for digital signatures and blind signatures. J. Cryptol. **13**(3), 361–396 (2000)

26. Rawal, S., Padhye, S., He, D.: Lattice-based undeniable signature scheme. Ann. Télécommun. **77**(3–4), 119–126 (2022)

27. Schuldt, J.C.N., Matsuura, K.: On-line non-transferable signatures revisited. In: Catalano, D., Fazio, N., Gennaro, R., Nicolosi, A. (eds.) PKC 2011. LNCS, vol. 6571, pp. 369–386. Springer, Heidelberg (2011). https://doi.org/10.1007/978-3-642-19379-8_23

28. Stern, J.: A new identification scheme based on syndrome decoding. In: Stinson, D.R. (ed.) CRYPTO 1993. LNCS, vol. 773, pp. 13–21. Springer, Heidelberg (1994). https://doi.org/10.1007/3-540-48329-2_2

29. Unruh, D.: Post-quantum security of Fiat-Shamir. In: Takagi, T., Peyrin, T. (eds.) ASIACRYPT 2017. LNCS, vol. 10624, pp. 65–95. Springer, Cham (2017). https://doi.org/10.1007/978-3-319-70694-8_3

30. Yang, R., Au, M.H., Zhang, Z., Xu, Q., Yu, Z., Whyte, W.: Efficient lattice-based zero-knowledge arguments with standard soundness: construction and applications. In: Boldyreva, A., Micciancio, D. (eds.) CRYPTO 2019. LNCS, vol. 11692, pp. 147–175. Springer, Cham (2019). https://doi.org/10.1007/978-3-030-26948-7_6

Security Analysis

Obfuscation-Resilient Semantic Functionality Identification Through Program Simulation

Sebastian Schrittwieser[1]([✉])[ID], Patrick Kochberger[1,3][ID], Michael Pucher[1][ID], Caroline Lawitschka[1], Philip König[2], and Edgar R. Weippl[1,2][ID]

[1] University of Vienna, Vienna, Austria
{sebastian.schrittwieser,patrick.kochberger,michael.pucher,
caroline.lawitschka,edgar.weippl}@univie.ac.at
[2] SBA Research, Vienna, Austria
{pkoenig,eweippl}@sba-research.org
[3] St. Pölten University of Applied Sciences, St. Pölten, Austria
patrick.kochberger@fhstp.ac.at

Abstract. Figuring out whether a particular semantic functionality exists in a binary program is challenging. While pattern-matching-based detection is susceptible to syntactic changes of the code, formal equivalence proofs quickly hit complexity limitations in practice. In this paper, we present SIMID, a novel approach to semantic detection of functionality based on observation of input-output behavior of functions during simulated program execution. An evaluation with 4259 functions from 31 binary programs demonstrates that the approach has high detection accuracy across various compilers and even computing architectures (x86-64 and ARM64) as well as in the presence of state-of-the-art obfuscations such as code virtualization. Analysis complexity is low enough for practical use cases.

Keywords: Code equivalence · Binary similarity · Binary analysis · Code obfuscation

1 Introduction

Binary code similarity, i.e. the identification of a similarity of two programs in binary form is an area of intensive research in computer science [10,18]. In the past it has been addressed with a wide range of different research methodologies such as comparison of execution traces and machine learning-based matching of different artifacts such as the disassembled code, etc. However, all these approaches come with their own set of advantages and disadvantages (see Sect. 2) and in general, accuracy is far from perfect.

Similarity can exist in different areas of a binary program. Syntactic similarity results from the presence of similar sequences of instructions in two binaries. This type of similarity is used when comparing concrete implementations

H. P. Reiser and M. Kyas (Eds.): NordSec 2022, LNCS 13700, pp. 273–291, 2022.
https://doi.org/10.1007/978-3-031-22295-5_15

of programs (e.g., in plagiarism detection). It is not particularly robust to code transformations such as optimization and obfuscation because although the functionality remains the same, the concrete sequences of instructions might change significantly.

In contrast, structural similarity of programs compares graph representations of programs (e.g., control flow graph, call graph). Since these graphs are usually quite stable, the robustness against code transformations is higher.

Semantic similarity compares the functionalities of programs independent of their actual implementation. This equivalence can be identified in three different ways [10]. First, the binary code can be enriched with semantic information (e.g., type of instruction such as arithmetic or logic) and then the semantic content of the program can be derived from this sequence. A second method is to create symbolic formulas from the binary code, for which semantic similarity can then be calculated using graph distance, semantic hashing, or theorem proving. However, since in modern computing architectures a semantic description of functionality can be expressed by an infinite number of syntactic statements, a formal proof of equivalence is often not feasible in practice due to complexity issues. Third, it can be evaluated whether two programs executed with the same input parameters produce the same output while intermediate program states are completely ignored.

A sub-aspect of semantic code similarity is the identification of functionality in a program independent of its specific implementation. Thus, instead of examining two programs for similarity, the goal is to determine whether a particular semantic functionality is contained in a program. For functionalities that have deterministic input-output behavior, a promising approach to their identification is to search for their characteristic input-output relationship in the binary program. In the past, it has been shown, that this methodology works well in dynamic analysis settings, where the program is monitored during runtime or traces of its execution are recorded for offline analysis [2]. However, dynamic analysis comes with a number of shortcomings. Firstly, the appropriate execution environment must be available for each binary (computing architecture and operating system) and it must be isolated from the rest of the analysis system when analyzing software with unknown functionality (e.g., malware). Secondly, code coverage is challenging but crucial, as only functionality that is actually executed can be analyzed.

In this paper, we present a novel approach that uses the idea of identifying a deterministic algorithm based on known pairs of inputs and outputs in simulated program execution. Program simulation is architecture-agnostic and allows targeted analysis of individual functions, thus solving the coverage limitations of dynamic analysis.

In particular, the main contributions of our paper are:

- We present SIMID, a novel semantic functionality identifier based on program simulation.
- We demonstrate the robustness of our approach in the presence of different build configurations, architectures, and even state-of-the-art code obfuscations by measuring costs and resilience.

– We introduce different strategies for runtime optimization of the analysis, making real-life use cases for SIMID possible.

The remainder of this paper is structured as follows: In Sect. 2, we describe related work on binary similarity and functionality identification. Section 3 explains our approach in detail. In Sect. 4 we evaluate the effectiveness of our approach and its practicability in real-world scenarios. In Sect. 5 results are presented. Finally, Sect. 6 concludes the paper.

2   Related Work

Binary code similarity detection is researched for different motivations and concepts proposed in the literature use a large set of different methodologies. A recent survey by Haq and Caballero [10] systematically analyzes binary code similarity concepts from 70 publications based on their application areas, methodologies, implementations and how they were evaluated. In recent years, the advent of better and better machine learning techniques has greatly boosted binary similarity research. A 2022 paper by Marcelli et al. [18] comes to the conclusion, that today's machine learning-based approaches (e.g., [20,27,33]) for detecting code similarity are more accurate than simpler concepts based on fuzzy hashing (i.e. hashing algorithms that output similar hash values when given similar input data).

2.1   Semantic Binary Code Similarity

The sub-field of semantic binary code similarity research aims at finding semantic similarity between two pieces of binary code or identifying functionality independent of its concrete implementation in binary programs. In the past, various different—both static and dynamic—methodologies have been proposed.

Dynamic Approaches. Egele et al. [8] introduced *blanket-execution*, a dynamic equivalence testing primitive for matching functions in binaries that compares their side effects during execution. Wang and Wu [30] proposed in-memory fuzzing in order to gather different kinds of program behaviors. Similarity scores of behavior traces are calculated based on the longest common subsequence and used as a feature vector to train a machine learning model. Kargén and Shahmehri [14] developed another method based on dynamic analysis. Two semantically similar binaries are executed with the same input while their runtime traces are recorded. Input and output values are the principle matching features. Hu et al.'s MOCKINGBIRD [12] is a semantic-based similarity detection tool to identify functions in binaries ported across architectures. It extracts signatures consisting of system call information and conditional operations and compares them to measure similarity. Calvet et al.'s ALIGOT [2] detects cryptographic functions based on their input-output parameters. In contrast to our work, which is based on static analysis and simulation of individual function calls, ALIGOT uses traces of dynamic program execution as its foundation.

Hybrid Approaches. There also exist hybrid methods combining both static and dynamic methodologies. For example Ming et al. [19] addressed binary diffing through what they call *sliced segment equivalence checking*. With this concept, they identify differences and similarities between execution traces and compare the logic of instructions that influence observable behavior. CACOMPARE [11] by Hu et al. detects similar binary code across architectures by emulating functions to extract semantic signatures. The semantic signatures are composed of the input and output values, comparison operands, and the according condition as well as library function calls.

Static Approaches. The majority of methodologies described in the literature, as surveyed by Marcelli et al. [18], use static analysis concepts. For instance, Luo et al. [17] attempted to take on the issue of obfuscated code within automated code similarity detection by using the longest common subsequence of semantically equivalent basic blocks. The semantics of a basic block is defined through its input/output behavior, whereupon the similarity of blocks is checked based on the equivalence of the symbolic formulas of the output. A similar method by David et al. [7], finds common vulnerabilities and exposures within stripped firmware images. Their tool, FIRMUP, takes the context of the surrounding executable into consideration for their similarity analysis, using data-flow slices of basic blocks as representations for pairwise evaluation. Pewny et al. [21] lifted code to an intermediate representation and sampled concrete input values to observe the I/O behavior of basic blocks to identify binary functionality throughout different instruction sets. In contrast to our work, the authors explicitly excluded obfuscated code from their scope, as they were able to show that certain code transformations would increase false negatives. Another source that can be analyzed to gain data about vulnerabilities is security patch patterns. Xu et al. [31] introduced SPAIN, a tool that focuses on identifying patch patterns and corresponding vulnerabilities. Patches are identified through a semantic analysis of traces and patterns through a taint analysis of the patched functions. The so-gained patterns are then used to statically search for similar patches in other binary code. Identifying open-source software packages in binaries was researched by Alrabaee et al. [1]. The authors proposed an approach that includes syntactic as well as semantic analysis. A Markov model was applied to test extracted syntactical features of functions and further, a neighborhood hash graph kernel was applied in order to obtain the semantics of functions. The extracted behavior of instructions was then combined through a Bayesian network to identify a known function. To capture the complete semantics of a function, Xue et al. [32] came up with a concept based on selective inlining of relevant library and user-defined functions. The approach not only considers input and output values but also different categories such as high-level semantic features in order to improve matching throughout different architectures and compilers, as well as to improve accuracy. DISCOVRE by Eschweiler et al. [9] aims at detecting vulnerable code segments in large code bases across different operating systems, compiler optimizations, and CPU architectures. Starting with a known vulnerable binary function, similar functions containing the same vulnerability are identified based on the similarity of their control flow graphs. The tool SEMDIFF by Wang et al. [29] uses angr [26] to extract data read and written to memory. It uses these memory signatures to identify differences in two binary files even in the presence of simple transformation (e.g., inlined functionality). Qiu et al. [24] identified library functionality inside binaries by searching for subgraphs in an execution dependence graph. The well-known commercial tool BINDIFF[1] identifies differences in disassembled code of two binaries.

3 Approach

The static analysis approach of SIMID uses program simulation to observe the input-output behavior of the individual functions of a binary.

3.1 Program Simulation

Program simulation mimics the behavior of a program without the results differing from a real execution of the program. Unlike an emulator, which creates a replica of the execution environment for the program, the simulator does not execute the actual binary code of the program but runs a simulation of an abstracted version of it. More formal concepts such as abstract interpretation have also been used in the past to identify functionality in programs [6, 23]. However, due to the complexity of such approaches only limited real-world use is possible. In contrast, its lower level of abstraction makes program simulation fast enough for practical use cases (e.g., functional malware analysis). In addition, it is possible to simulate individual functions of a binary in isolation, thus mitigating the challenge of coverage that exists in dynamic analysis approaches. Thus, for SIMID program simulation represents a perfect sweet spot between formal modeling and the actual execution of a program.

Simulation Model. One major challenge when working with program simulation, however, is the quality of its underlying model of the computing architecture. Abstractions might result in discrepancies between a real execution of a program and its simulation. In our project, we built upon the binary simulation engine of angr. angr lifts binaries to Valgrind's VEX IR [25], a RISC-like intermediate language, and is able to perform simulations on the entire program or parts of it (e.g., individual functions). To model the execution environment (e.g., system calls to the operating system) as well as calls to library functions (e.g., to libc), angr uses the concept of "function summaries": many external calls are replaced by simulations (so-called *SimProcedures*) written in Python.

Program State. To be able to simulate individual functions isolated from the rest of the program, an appropriate program state must be created beforehand. angr provides different state constructors. One of them (`call_state()`) constructs a state ready to simulate a given function. This constructor must be passed the starting address of the function and its arguments.

---

[1] https://www.zynamics.com/bindiff.html.

3.2 Function Input and Output Matching

The general concept of our function identification algorithm works similar to Calvet et al.'s ALIGOT [2]. If the input-output behavior of a deterministic algorithm is known in advance, it can be identified independently of its concrete syntactic implementation in a program by comparing the input and output values of all functions during execution or simulation. While ALIGOT uses traces of dynamic program execution as its foundation, our approach is based on a simulation of individual function calls. Algorithm 1 shows the high-level concept of our functionality identification. SIMID operates at the function level. This means that we simulate each function of a program with the arguments corresponding to a known input-output pair.

Algorithm 1: Basic concept of SIMID in pseudocode.

Input: P (Program in binary representation)
Input: EIN (Expected INput)
Input: $EOUT$ (Expected OUTput)
Input: $PROTO$ (expected function PROTOtype)
Output: CF (List of candidate functions implementing the searched functionality)

```
 1  CFG ← reconstructControlFlowGraph(P)
 2  for functions in P as FUNC do
 3      CC ← reconstructCallingConvention(FUNC, CFG)
 4      if CC.PROTOTYPE ∨ CC.PROTOTYPE = PROTO then
 5          CS ← generateCallState(FUNC, EIN, PROTO)
 6          C ← createCallable(FUNC, PROTO, CS)
 7          RET ← C(EIN)
 8          if RET = EOUT then
 9              CF ← CF + FUNC
10      else
            /* wrong function prototype                              */
11          WFP ← WFP + FUNC
12  if CF is empty then
13      for functions in WFP as FUNC do
14          CS ← generateCallState(FUNC, EIN, PROTO)
15          C ← createCallable(FUNC, PROTO, CS)
16          RET ← C(EIN)
17          if RET = EOUT then
18              CF ← CF + FUNC
19  return CF
```

Function Prototype Recovery. In order to pass the input arguments correctly to the simulated execution of the function, the structure of the arguments (order and size) must match that of the function prototype of the function. For optimal analysis efficiency, only functions in the binary with a matching function prototype shall be run through simulation. However, function prototype extraction is always error-prone, as prototypes are not stored explicitly in the binary but must be derived from the function calls at the callees according to the specifications of the calling convention of the binary architecture. Thus, simulating only functions with exact matches on the function prototype will result in an unacceptable number of false negatives (i.e., functions which include the search functionality but are omitted from simulation because of an incorrect extraction of their prototype). We developed several strategies for handling inaccurate function prototypes and performed experiments to determine the most efficient one. In the most efficient strategy, SIMID tries to extract the function prototype of all functions of a binary and excludes those for which extraction fails or for which the function prototype does not match. The other functions are then simulated. If a candidate function is found, analysis for that binary is finished. If the functionality is not found, the remaining functions are simulated despite their non-matching or unextractable function prototype. This strategy prevents false negatives while keeping the analysis fast. A detailed discussion of the different analysis strategies is presented in Sect. 4. In all strategies, we disabled analysis of functions for which *SimProcedures* (see Sect. 3.1) exist as these contain reimplementations of system functionality and thus cannot host the searched functionality.

Nested Functions. SIMID does not search for functionality directly but identifies functions that have input-output behavior corresponding to the functionality. How this input-output behavior is generated is not relevant for SIMID. Thus, its methodology also works for nested functions that have split the implementation of the searched functionality into multiple functions—a concept often used in code obfuscation (e.g., *function splitting*). In our evaluation of SIMID, we observed this behavior in multiple samples (see Sect. 5).

4   Evaluation

For the evaluation of SIMID, we reimplemented the domain generation algorithm (DGA) of the Ramdo malware [22] in C and embedded it in a simple fake malware. The fake malware includes a help message, checks the system's name, decodes a hardcoded, ROT13 encrypted filename, and writes the first 1.000 domains generated by the DGA into the file.

DGAs are widely used by malware authors to make connections to their command and control servers resilient against blocking attempts. A DGA usually is a deterministic algorithm that can generate an arbitrarily large number of domain names. Periodically, a malware would pick a few of them at random and try to establish connections. Malware analysts need to reverse engineer the algorithm in order to be able to block further communication. Because of their determinism property and well-defined inputs (usually some seed) and output (domain names) DGAs are prime candidates for functionality identification methodologies. Listing 1 shows our reimplementation of the DGA in C. Basically, the algorithm (located in the `generate_domain` function) returns a 16 characters long string which has ".org" appended to create a valid domain name. The string is generated from a hardcoded seed and a counter through a combination of several mathematical operations.

```c
struct node {
    void *data;
    struct node *next;
};
typedef struct node * llist;
struct sSelf {
    long int seed;
    long int nr;
    long int generateddomains;
    char lastdomain[50];
    llist *domainhistory;
};
char * generate_domain(struct sSelf *self){
    long int s = ((2 * self->seed) * (self->nr + 1));
    long int r = ((long int) s ^ (long int) ((26 * self->seed) *
        self->nr));
    char domain[50] = "";
    for (int i = 0; i < 16; i++){
        r = (r & 4294967295);
        strcat(domain, chr(((r
        r += ((long int) r ^ (long int) ((s * pow(i,2)) * 26));
    }
    strcat(domain, ".org");
    strcpy(self->lastdomain,domain);
    self->nr += 1;
    return self->lastdomain;
}
```

Listing 1: Reimplementation of Ramdo's DGA. This code is part of the fake malware used to evaluate SIMID. The generate_domain function implements the DGA functionality. The input and output data is stored in a struct variable and the function returns a pointer to the domain name.

4.1 Samples

The source code of the fake malware is 380 LoC (lines of code) long and has a size of about 8.700 bytes. For sample generation, the source code was compiled with a total of 31 build and obfuscation configurations (see Table 1). Besides `musl-gcc` (version 12.1.1.20220730), samples were also compiled with `musl-clang` (version 14.0.6), CompCert (version 3.10), TenDRA (version 5.0/x32_64 git:abecfa3), and TinyCC (versions 0.9.27 and mob:1de025c) and obfuscated with Obfuscator LLVM [13] (version 4.0.1) and Tigress[2] [3] (version 3.1). `musl` is a general-purpose implementation of the C library. We have chosen the `musl-gcc` wrapper for comparability reasons because it is also used by the Tigress obfuscator.

Moreover, we also added four samples compiled with `gcc` for the ARM64 (AArch64) architecture. The builds generated with `gcc`, `clang`, as well as the Tigress builds were compiled for different optimization levels (O0, O1, O2, and O3) to increase the variation of the samples. Table 1 lists all build and obfuscation configurations, while Table 2 shows the identification results.

Sample Sizes. Binary sizes range from 9.5 kB (TinyCC) to 114.3 kB (CompCert). The function extraction algorithm of angr reports a total of 100 functions in the x86-64 binary representation of our fake malware compiled with `musl-gcc` at optimization level O2. The least functions were generated by TinyCC (58) and the most functions are present in the virtualization-obfuscated samples of Tigress (539). In total, the 31 binaries contain 4.259 functions (reported by angr).

For matching the starting addresses of identified functions with a ground truth, the samples were compiled with debug symbols, and function starting addresses were extracted using angr. However, those symbols were never used by SIMID at any stage for identification.

Test System. All, except the ARM runtime, evaluations and measurements were performed on a Arch Linux machine, kernel version 5.19.5 with an AMD Ryzen 9 5900X (24) @ 3.700 GHz CPU and 32006 MiB of memory. The evaluation system ran angr version 9.2.13 and Python version 3.10.6. To measure the times it took to make (compile and obfuscate) $\overline{t_m}$ and run $\overline{t_r}$ the samples we used the `hyperfine`[3] tool version 1.14.0. The analysis times t_A, t_B, t_C, t_D and t_E are reported by SIMID using the `datetime`[4] Python package. The runtime for the ARM binaries was also measured using the `hyperfine` tool version 1.14.0, but inside a QEMU Virtual Machine running Ubuntu 20.04.4 LTS aarch64 kernel version 5.15.0-46-generic using 4 CPU cores and 3908 MiB of memory on a MacBookAir10,1 (M1).

4.2   Obfuscation Techniques

For evaluating the robustness of SIMID against code obfuscations, we applied protections of Obfuscator LLVM [13] (OLLVM) and Tigress [3] to a subset of our samples. These two obfuscators are freely available and often used in academic research on software protections. OLLVM implements three obfuscations—*bogus control flow, control flow flattening* and *instruction substitution*—which we all

---

[2] https://tigress.wtf/.
[3] https://github.com/sharkdp/hyperfine.
[4] https://docs.python.org/3/library/datetime.html.

Table 1. Details about the sample. For each sample the table gives the filesize s in Byte, the increase of the file size $s \nearrow$ (compared to tinycc-latest), the mean runtime $\overline{t_r}$ and its standard deviation $\sigma(t_r)$ in ms for 15.000 runs, the mean make time $\overline{t_m}$ and its standard deviation $\sigma(t_m)$ in ms for 1.000 runs (all but compcertcc) and 100 runs (only compcertcc), and the number of functions $|F|$. † produces malformed samples (see Sect. 5.2). * measured on a separate ARM-based system. Also see Sect. 4.1.

Compiler	s	$s \nearrow$	$\overline{t_m}$	$\sigma(t_m)$	$\overline{t_r}$	$\sigma(t_r)$	$|F|$
clang-O0	16,576	175.00%	93.7	1.3	3.6	1.2	83
clang-O1	16,616	175.42%	123.0	2.1	2.4	0.8	89
clang-O2	16,656	175.84%	126.8	2.2	2.4	0.9	89
clang-O3	20,752	219.09%	131.0	2.2	2.3	0.6	88
compcertcc	114,320	1,206.93%	6,228.0	80.0	3.6	0.6	82
gcc-aarch64-O0	17,856	188.51%	39.6	0.6	0.4 *	0.1 *	68
gcc-aarch64-O1	13,760	145.27%	59.9	1.1	0.4 *	0.1 *	68
gcc-aarch64-O2	13,824	145.95%	81.6	1.0	0.4 *	0.1 *	79
gcc-aarch64-O3	13,848	146.20%	92.9	1.4	0.4 *	0.1 *	77
gcc-O0	16,632	175.59%	39.0	1.0	3.1	1.5	71
gcc-O1	16,632	175.59%	54.6	0.9	2.4	0.8	71
gcc-O2	16,672	176.01%	70.4	1.3	2.4	1.0	100
gcc-O3	16,672	176.01%	79.5	1.4	2.2	0.5	104
ollvm-b	32,544	343.58%	43.5	1.4	4.1	0.6	84
ollvm-bf	36,640	386.82%	46.9	1.1	27.1	1.2	86
ollvm-bfs	44,832	473.31%	48.1	1.7	33.4	1.7	84
ollvm-bs	32,544	343.58%	44.1	0.8	4.5	1.0	86
ollvm-f	27,528	290.63%	43.3	0.7	13.6	1.3	84
ollvm-fs	27,528	290.63%	43.2	0.4	13.0	1.1	84
ollvm-s	27,528	290.63%	41.4	0.5	3.3	1.0	83
tendra †	91,108	961.87%	96.3	1.3	3.6	0.9	75
tigress-f-O0	20,832	219.93%	145.0	1.7	35.7	1.9	70
tigress-f-O1	16,736	176.69%	167.2	1.6	20.1	1.4	174
tigress-f-O2	20,832	219.93%	189.9	1.6	22.5	1.9	264
tigress-f-O3	20,832	219.93%	189.4	1.8	22.4	1.5	264
tigress-v-O0	98,528	1,040.20%	215.7	2.3	737.9	13.3	262
tigress-v-O1	86,256	910.64%	258.7	2.4	347.7	9.9	258
tigress-v-O2	86,256	910.64%	312.9	3.9	241.7	7.9	539
tigress-v-O3	86,256	910.64%	315.9	5.4	244.4	7.9	539
tinycc-0-9-27	9,516	100.46%	15.1	0.3	2.9	0.9	96
tinycc-latest	9,472	100.00%	15.1	0.5	2.6	0.3	58
sum	1,086,584		9,451.7		1,804.9		4,259.0
min	9,472	100.00%	15.1	0.3	2.2	0.0	58.0
max	114,320	1,206.93%	6,228.0	80.0	737.9	13.3	539.0
avrg	35,051	370.05%	304.9	4.1	66.8	2.4	137.4
median	20,832	219.93%	81.6	1.4	4.1	1.1	84.0

used for sample generation. Tigress supports many protection techniques. We picked *flattening* to be able to compare results with the corresponding obfuscation of OLLVM and *virtualization* which can be considered as one of the strongest protections.

Substitution (s). Substitution replaces standard operators or instruction sequences with semantically equal but more complex ones. This protection is rather simple, but it adds variation to protected programs.

Bogus Control Flow (b). This obfuscation makes the control flow graph of a program look more complicated than it actually is. In the implementation of OLLVM the call graph is changed in such a way that before a basic block a new block is generated, which contains an opaque predicate and a conditional jump to the original basic block depending on it. An opaque predicate always evaluates to the same truth value (true or false), regardless of the input. However, this property is difficult for a static analyst to determine. Thus, although the control flow always follows the same path at the conditional jump, it does not appear to do so in the control flow graph.

Flattening (f). The control flow flattening [16] obfuscation technique reduces the depth of the control flow graph by removing the structured flow. The obfuscator generates a dispatcher code block which is responsible for selecting in which order the basic blocks are executed.

Virtualization (v). Virtualization [15] translates the code of a function into a custom bytecode and replaces the original function with a virtual machine. At runtime the virtual machine interprets the bytecode by looking up the corresponding machine code instruction and executing it. Virtualization adds significant runtime overhead to a program, as bytecode interpretation is time-consuming.

5 Results

In this section, we present the results of our evaluation of SimID with a special focus on its robustness in the presence of code obfuscations. In 1997 Collberg et al. [4,5] proposed four metrics to estimating the strength of software protections: potency, resilience, cost, and stealth. Potency describes how much more obscure an obfuscated program is for human analysts, while resilience measures the strength of a protection against automatic analysis tools. Costs quantify the performance penalty (e.g., runtime, memory usage, binary size, etc.) and stealth is a measurement for how hard it is to detect a protection. We measured the resilience and costs of the obfuscations used in our evaluation against function identification with SimID. Potency and stealth are not relevant for our evaluation as SimID is an automated tool that aims at identifying functionality and not protections.

5.1   Costs

The costs of all protections (and build configurations) are summarized in Table 1. Building samples with Tigress takes longer than with other configurations (except CompCert compiler which has a significantly longer build time than any other configuration). However, the differences are small (e.g., 145 ms for Tigress flattening compared to 126.8 ms for clang with optimization level O2). Most obfuscated samples have significant runtime costs. Samples obfuscated with substitution and bogus control flow (OLLVM) result in the lowest overhead on runtime. Virtualization extends the runtime by a factor of up to 300 compared to the default gcc O2 build configuration. When looking at the file size CompCert is again the exception that builds by far the biggest binary, virtualization increases the file size by a factor of 9–10.

5.2   Resilience

To make the runtimes of the analyses of the individual samples comparable to each other, we continued the function identification in a sample even if the searched functionality has already been already found. Overall, SimID was able to correctly identify the searched functionality in all samples in our evaluation. Thus, no obfuscation was completely resilient against SimID's functionality identification approach. However, analysis times were heavily influenced by obfuscating transformations applied to the sample binaries. We ran SimID using five different strategies for dealing with incomplete function prototype recovery (labeled A, B, C, and D in Table 2).

Prototype Recovery Strategies. Strategy A simulates each function regardless of its function prototype. With this approach, although the functionality is correctly identified for all samples, the analysis time of over 3.5 h is significantly longer than with other strategies. This overhead is primarily caused by the samples on which virtualization obfuscation was applied using Tigress. This is not surprising given how virtualization obfuscation works (see Sect. 4.2). The overhead caused by the protection, already considerable in the native execution of the program (more than 200 ms vs less than 5 ms runtime—see Table 1), adds to the slowdown in the simulation environment of SimID. Strategy B attempts to recover the prototype of each function. Functions with a non-matching prototype are not analyzed, but functions for which prototype recovery fails are run in the simulation environment. This approach results in numerous functions not being analyzed and therefore false negatives due to incorrectly recovered prototypes. Strategy C works similarly to B except that functions for which prototype recovery fails are also not analyzed. As expected, this strategy resulted in an even larger number of false negatives in our evaluation. However, the runtimes of strategies B and C are significantly shorter than those of strategy A. The combination strategies described in Sect. 3 are labeled as D and E in Table 2. The combination strategy D first uses strategy B, and only if the functionality cannot be found in a sample, all functions are simulated as a fallback (strategy A). Similarly, for strategy E, first strategy C is applied, and as a fallback (strategy A). Using combination strategy E, we were able to detect the searched functionality in all samples with only 60% of the runtime of strategy A.

Multi-function Identification. In many samples, two functions were identified by SimID to contain the searched functionality. A manual analysis of the corresponding samples showed that in some cases anger's conservative function recognition marked two addresses pointing to the same function as separate functions. Listing 2 and Listing 3 show the two different types of this behavior that we identified in our samples based on two examples. In the `clang-03` sample a `NOP` instruction is placed before the start of the `generate_domain` function. Angr marks the `NOP` and the first instruction of the actual function as starting addresses of two separate functions. As the `NOP` does not modify the state of the program, the input-output behavior of both functions is identical. In `tinycc-0-9-27` sample angr both marks the first instruction of the `generate_domain` function as well as its reference in the jump table in the PLT section of the binary as the starting addresses of two separate functions. Ignoring all functions identified in the PLT section reduced the total analysis time of our sample set by only a few minutes (total runtime of 3 h 17 m 32 s with strategy A). We decided to follow a conservative approach and include PLT section functions in SimID to avoid false negatives.

Malformed Binary. In a first analysis run, SimID was not able to identify the searched functionality in the sample compiled with TenDRA. A manual analysis showed that the DGA of this binary generated wrong domains (and thus the binary generated by TenDRA was malformed). We then adjusted the analysis to look for the domain actually generated by the DGA of the TenDRA binary. SimID was then able to correctly identify the corresponding function.

5.3   Analysis Times

Overall, it took SimID approximately 3.5 h/1.6 h/1.5 h/2.2 h/2.1 h to analyze the 31 samples with the strategies A/B/C/D/E and no termination of the search algorithm after the first identification of functionality in a binary (1.3 h with termination and strategy E). However, there are significant differences in the time required by SimID to analyze the various samples. While the vast majority of samples could be analyzed in well under two minutes, the analysis of one virtualization-protected sample required almost three-quarters of an hour with strategy A. In general, it can be observed that those samples to which the Tigress obfuscations were applied led to significantly longer analysis times, while the obfuscations on Obfuscator LLVM generated almost no additional overhead. Therefore, the samples generated with Tigress have a higher resilience at the price of higher costs. There is a strong correlation (0.94) between the number of functions in a binary and the runtime of the analysis. Correlations between the native runtime of the samples and runtime of the analysis (0.77) as well as sample size and runtime of the analysis (0.64) are weaker.

Table 2. Evaluation results for each build and obfuscation configuration. A, B, C, D, and E are the results (number of detected candidate functions) for the different strategies (see Sect. 5.2). The columns t_A, t_B, t_D, and t_E give the time it took the analysis in hours:minutes:seconds. For comparability reasons, we continued all analysis runs in this evaluation even after the searched functionality has been found in a function. † The sample generated with TenDRA is executable, but generates incorrect domain names (see Sect. 5.2). The results in the table depict the results with the new expected value.

Compiler	A	t_A	B	t_B	C	t_C	D	t_D	E	t_E
clang-O0	2	00:01:17	1	00:00:34	1	00:00:13	1	00:00:35	1	00:00:14
clang-O1	2	00:01:23	✗	00:00:25	✗	00:00:03	2	00:01:26	2	00:01:24
clang-O2	2	00:01:22	✗	00:00:26	✗	00:00:03	2	00:01:25	2	00:01:23
clang-O3	2	00:01:21	✗	00:00:26	✗	00:00:03	2	00:01:23	2	00:01:21
compcertcc	2	00:01:30	1	00:00:33	1	00:00:16	1	00:00:32	1	00:00:15
gcc-aarch64-O0	1	00:01:00	1	00:00:34	1	00:00:09	1	00:00:34	1	00:00:09
gcc-aarch64-O1	1	00:00:59	✗	00:00:33	✗	00:00:09	1	00:01:00	1	00:00:59
gcc-aarch64-O2	1	00:01:12	✗	00:00:32	✗	00:00:06	1	00:01:13	1	00:01:11
gcc-aarch64-O3	1	00:01:08	✗	00:00:32	✗	00:00:06	1	00:01:10	1	00:01:09
gcc-O0	1	00:01:01	1	00:00:35	1	00:00:13	1	00:00:35	1	00:00:13
gcc-O1	1	00:01:01	✗	00:00:32	✗	00:00:10	1	00:01:02	1	00:01:01
gcc-O2	2	00:01:35	✗	00:00:30	✗	00:00:06	2	00:01:37	2	00:01:35
gcc-O3	2	00:01:40	✗	00:00:30	✗	00:00:06	2	00:01:43	2	00:01:41
ollvm-b	2	00:01:20	1	00:00:30	1	00:00:11	1	00:00:30	1	00:00:11
ollvm-bf	2	00:01:37	1	00:00:34	1	00:00:15	1	00:00:34	1	00:00:15
ollvm-bfs	2	00:01:37	1	00:00:34	1	00:00:16	1	00:00:34	1	00:00:16
ollvm-bs	2	00:01:21	1	00:00:30	1	00:00:11	1	00:00:29	1	00:00:11
ollvm-f	2	00:01:23	1	00:00:30	1	00:00:12	1	00:00:30	1	00:00:12
ollvm-fs	2	00:01:25	1	00:00:29	1	00:00:11	1	00:00:29	1	00:00:11
ollvm-s	2	00:01:17	1	00:00:28	1	00:00:10	1	00:00:28	1	00:00:10
tendra †	2	00:01:17	✗	00:00:23	✗	00:00:04	2	00:01:19	2	00:01:19
tigress-f-O0	1	00:04:48	1	00:04:35	1	00:04:16	1	00:04:32	1	00:04:06
tigress-f-O1	1	00:06:33	✗	00:01:48	✗	00:01:27	1	00:07:01	1	00:06:52
tigress-f-O2	2	00:10:23	✗	00:01:39	✗	00:01:17	2	00:10:53	2	00:10:28
tigress-f-O3	2	00:10:34	✗	00:01:38	✗	00:01:18	2	00:10:54	2	00:10:27
tigress-v-O0	1	00:34:05	1	00:30:06	1	00:30:30	1	00:30:22	1	00:28:58
tigress-v-O1	1	00:24:23	1	00:19:53	1	00:20:33	1	00:20:41	1	00:19:41
tigress-v-O2	2	00:43:54	1	00:13:46	1	00:14:20	1	00:14:26	1	00:13:38
tigress-v-O3	2	00:43:09	1	00:13:40	1	00:13:24	1	00:14:17	1	00:13:13
tinycc-0-9-27	2	00:01:33	1	00:00:36	✗	00:00:01	1	00:00:37	2	00:01:33
tinycc-latest	1	00:00:47	1	00:00:31	1	00:00:12	1	00:00:31	1	00:00:12
31	**31**	**03:27:55**	**18**	**01:38:52**	**17**	**01:30:31**	**31**	**02:13:22**	**31**	**02:04:28**

```
1  0x000012f6      ret
2                  nop       word [rax   rax]
3  ; generate_domain (int64_t arg1, uint64_t arg_2150h);
4                  push      rbp
5  0x00001301      push      r15
6  0x00001303      push      r14
7  0x00001305      push      r13
8  0x00001307      push      r12
9  0x00001309      push      rbx
10 0x0000130a      sub       rsp, 0x2158
```

Listing 2: SimID reports the searched functionality to be present in two functions (0x12f7 and 0x1300) of the sample clang-O3. However, this behavior is a result of angr's conservative function recognition which tends to favor false positives over false negatives. Except for the NOP instruction which does nothing, the two functions are identical.

```
1  0x00400a52      ret
2  ; generate_domain (int64_t arg1);
3                  push      rbp
4  0x00400a54      mov       rbp, rsp
5  0x00400a57      sub       rsp, 0x2370
6  0x00400a5e      mov       qword [var_8h], rdi ; arg1
7  0x00400a62      mov       rax, qword [var_8h]
8  ;-- section..plt:
9  0x00401968      push      qword [0x00601e28] ; [14] -r-x section size
   ↪ 448 named .plt
10 0x0040196e      jmp       qword [0x00601e30]
11 0x00401974      add       byte [rax], al
12 0x00401976      add       byte [rax], al
13 0x004019c8      jmp       qword [strcat] ; 0x601e70
14 0x004019ce      push      8         ; 8
15 0x004019d3      jmp       section..preinit_array
16 ; fcn.004019d8 ();
17                 jmp       qword [generate_domain] ;
18 0x004019de      push      9         ; 9
19 0x004019e3      jmp       section..preinit_array
```

Listing 3: Excerpt from the disassembly of the sample tinycc-0-9-27: SimID correctly reports the generate_domain function at address 0x400A53. However, SimID additionally identifies the searched functionality in the PLT section at 0x4019D8. The explanation for this behavior is that angr identifies the reference to the generate_domain function inside the jump table located in the PLT section as a function.

5.4   Limitations

The most obvious limitation of SimID is its dependence on a specific structure of input and output values. The semantic recognition of functionality can only work if it is defined in advance how the passed function arguments of the searched functionality are processed and in which form the output is returned. This means that the approach is not robust to modifications of the function prototype. For example, adding additional arguments to the function breaks our algorithm as it renders the mapping between concrete input values and function arguments ambiguous. In addition as already discussed in Sect. 3, function prototype reconstruction is never accurate. In our approach, we rely on angr's logic for function prototype reconstruction which is very capable of at least identifying the correct number of arguments and their sizes. SimID performs a conservative matching to avoid false negatives by running function simulation if the number of arguments extracted from the function prototypes matches the expected number and all functions of a program in a second iteration if the searched functionality was not found in the first pass. For a more complex matching (e.g., based on data types) the function prototype reconstruction of angr is not precise enough. In future work, we aim at implementing more advanced function prototype approximations (such as a use-def analysis at all callees described by Veen et al. [28]) which might allow more sophisticated function prototype matching and thus increase the robustness of the approach to modification to the function prototypes.

A similar challenge is input values, which are not passed as function arguments, but are written to a specific memory location (e.g., by a function, which would run before the analyzed function in a non-simulated execution). Without executing this function in the simulation, these input values would be missing. In the future, we want to solve this challenge by observing accesses to uninitialized memory.

Another limitation is the incompleteness of the simulation. The semantic functionality identification is based on a comparison of the input-output behavior of a simulated function execution with known values. If the simulation is incomplete, it may lead to deviating output values and thus the identification may fail. In the course of our research, we have already found such deviations and extended angr's model (*SimProcedures*). However, in the evaluation, we found that the model is complete enough for handling our diverse binaries for x86-64 and ARM64. Still, edge cases can occur.

6   Conclusions

In this paper we presented SimID, an approach to semantically identify program functionality through its deterministic input-output behavior. Compared to similar approaches presented in the literature, SimID uses program simulation, which allows selectively probing individual functions for the presence of specific functionality. Our approach is robust to syntactical variations resulting from different build configurations and works even across different computing architectures. Moreover, none of the obfuscating transformations which we have applied to sample programs with Tigress and Obfuscator LLVM prevented functionality identification during evaluation. With an analysis time of around 2 h and 4 min for 31 samples containing a total of 4259 functions, the approach qualifies for real-world use cases.

Acknowledgements. This work was funded by the Austrian Science Fund (FWF) under grant I 3646-N31.

References

1. Alrabaee, S., Shirani, P., Wang, L., Debbabi, M.: FOSSIL: a resilient and efficient system for identifying FOSS functions in Malware binaries. ACM Trans. Priv. Secur. **21**, 1–34 (2018). https://doi.org/10.1145/3175492
2. Calvet, J., Fernandez, J.M., Marion, J.-Y.: Aligot: cryptographic function identification in obfuscated binary programs. In: Proceedings of the 2012 ACM Conference on Computer and Communications Security, pp. 169–182 (2012). https://doi.org/10.1145/2382196.2382217
3. Collberg, C., Martin, S., Myers, J., Nagra, J.: Distributed application tamper detection via continuous software updates. In: Proceedings of the 28th Annual Computer Security Applications Conference, ACSAC 2012, Orlando, Florida, USA, pp. 319–328. Association for Computing Machinery (2012). https://doi.org/10.1145/2420950.2420997. ISBN 9781450313124
4. Collberg, C., Thomborson, C., Low, D.: A taxonomy of obfuscating transformations. Technical report. 148. University of Auckland (1997). https://researchspace.auckland.ac.nz/handle/2292/3491
5. Collberg, C., Thomborson, C., Low, D.: Manufacturing cheap, resilient, and stealthy opaque constructs. In: Proceedings of the 25th ACM SIGPLAN-SIGACT Symposium on Principles of Programming Languages, POPL 1998, San Diego, California, USA, pp. 184–196. Association for Computing Machinery (ACM) (1998). https://doi.org/10.1145/268946.268962. ISBN 0897919793
6. Dalla Preda, M.: Code obfuscation and malware detection by abstract interpretation. Ph.D. thesis. Università degli Studi di Verona (2007). https://iris.univr.it/bitstream/11562/337972/1/main.pdf
7. David, Y., Partush, N., Yahav, E.: FirmUp: precise static detection of common vulnerabilities in firmware. In: Proceedings of the Twenty-Third International Conference on Architectural Support for Programming Languages and Operating Systems, ASPLOS 2018, Williamsburg, VA, USA, pp. 392–404. Association for Computing Machinery (ACM) (2018). https://doi.org/10.1145/3173162.3177157. ISBN 9781450349116
8. Egele, M., Woo, M., Chapman, P., Brumley, D.: Blanket execution: dynamic similarity testing for program binaries and components. In: 23rd USENIX Security Symposium (USENIX Security 2014), pp. 303–317 (2014)
9. Eschweiler, S., Yakdan, K., Gerhards-Padilla, E.: discovRE: efficient cross-architecture identification of bugs in binary code. In: NDSS, vol. 52, pp. 58–79 (2016)
10. Haq, I.U., Caballero, J.: A survey of binary code similarity. ACM Comput. Surv. **54**(3) (2021). https://doi.org/10.1145/3446371. ISSN 0360-0300

11. Hu, Y., Zhang, Y., Li, J., Gu, D.: Binary code clone detection across architectures and compiling configurations. In: 2017 IEEE/ACM 25th International Conference on Program Comprehension (ICPC). Institute of Electrical and Electronics Engineers (IEEE) (2017). https://doi.org/10.1109/ICPC.2017.22. ISBN 978-1-5386-0535-6

12. Hu, Y., Zhang, Y., Li, J., Gu, D.: Cross-architecture binary semantics understanding via similar code comparison. In: 2016 IEEE 23rd International Conference on Software Analysis, Evolution, and Reengineering (SANER), vol. 1, pp. 57–67 (2016). https://doi.org/10.1109/SANER.2016.50. ISBN 978-1-5090-1855-0

13. Junod, P., Rinaldini, J., Wehrli, J., Michielin, J.: Obfuscator-LLVM - software protection for the masses. In: Wyseur, B. (ed.) Proceedings of the IEEE/ACM 1st International Workshop on Software Protection, SPRO 2015, pp. 3–9. Institute of Electrical and Electronics Engineers (IEEE) (2015). https://doi.org/10.1109/SPRO.2015.10. ISBN 978-1-4673-7094-3

14. Kargéen, U., Shahmehri, N.: Towards robust instruction-level trace alignment of binary code. In: 2017 32nd IEEE/ACM International Conference on Automated Software Engineering (ASE), pp. 342–352. Institute of Electrical and Electronics Engineers (IEEE) (2017). https://doi.org/10.1109/ASE.2017.8115647. ISBN 978-1-5386-2684-9

15. Kochberger, P., Schrittwieser, S., Schweighofer, S., Kieseberg, P., Weippl, E.: SoK: automatic deobfuscation of virtualization-protected applications. In: Proceedings of the 16th International Conference on Availability, Reliability and Security, ARES 2016. Vienna, Austria, pp. 1–15. Association for Computing Machinery (ACM) (2021). https://doi.org/10.1145/3465481.3465772. ISBN 9781450390514

16. László, T., Kiss, Á.: Obfuscating C++ programs via control flow flattening. In: Annales Universitatis Scientiarum Budapestinensis de Rolando Eötvös Nominatae. Sectio Computatorica, vol. 30, pp. 3–19 (2009). http://compalg.inf.elte.hu/annales/computatorica/VO30.pdf

17. Luo, L., Ming, J., Wu, D., Liu, P., Zhu, S.: Semantics-based obfuscation- resilient binary code similarity comparison with applications to software and algorithm plagiarism detection. IEEE Trans. Softw. Eng. **43**(12), 1157–1177 (2017). https://doi.org/10.1109/TSE.2017.2655046. ISSN 1939-3520

18. Marcelli, A., Graziano, M., Ugarte-Pedrero, X., Fratantonio, Y., Mansouri, M., Balzarotti, D.: How machine learning is solving the binary function similarity problem. In: USENIX Security, pp. 2099–2116 (2022). https://www.usenix.org/conference/usenixsecurity22/presentation/marcelli

19. Ming, J., Xu, D., Jiang, Y., Wu, D.: BinSim: trace-based semantic binary diffing via system call sliced segment equivalence checking. In: 26th USENIX Security Symposium (USENIX Security 2017), Vancouver, BC, pp. 253–270. USENIX Association (2017). https://www.usenix.org/conference/usenixsecurity17/technical-sessions/presentation/ming. ISBN 978-1-931971-40-9

20. Peng, D., Zheng, S., Li, Y., Ke, G., He, D., Liu, T.-Y.: How could neural networks understand programs? In: Meila, M., Zhang, T. (eds.) Proceedings of the 38th International Conference on Machine Learning, vol. 139, pp. 8476–8486. Proceedings of Machine Learning Research (PMLR) (2021). https://doi.org/10.48550/arXiv.2105.04297. https://proceedings.mlr.press/v139/peng21b.html

21. Pewny, J., Garmany, B., Gawlik, R., Rossow, C., Holz, T.: Cross-architecture bug search in binary executables. In: 2015 IEEE Symposium on Security and Privacy, pp. 709–724. IEEE (2015)

22. Plohmann, D., Yakdan, K., Klatt, M., Bader, J., Gerhards-Padilla, E.: A comprehensive measurement study of domain generating malware. In: 25th USENIX Security Symposium (USENIX Security 2016), Austin, TX, pp. 263–278 (2016). https://www.usenix.org/conference/usenixsecurity16/technical-sessions/presentation/plohmann. ISBN 978-1-931971-32-4

23. Dalla Preda, M., Madou, M., De Bosschere, K., Giacobazzi, R.: Opaque predicates detection by abstract interpretation. In: Johnson, M., Vene, V. (eds.) AMAST 2006. LNCS, vol. 4019, pp. 81–95. Springer, Heidelberg (2006). https://doi.org/10.1007/11784180_9 ISBN 978-3-540-35636-3

24. Qiu, J., Su, X., Ma, P.: Library functions identification in binary code by using graph isomorphism testings. In: 2015 IEEE 22nd International Conference on Software Analysis, Evolution, and Reengineering (SANER), pp. 261–270. Institute of Electrical and Electronics Engineers (IEEE) (2015). https://doi.org/10.1109/SANER.2015.7081836

25. Shoshitaishvili, Y., Wang, R., Hauser, C., Kruegel, C., Vigna, G.: Firmalice - automatic detection of authentication bypass vulnerabilities in binary firmware (2015). https://doi.org/10.14722/NDSS.2015.23294

26. Shoshitaishvili, Y., et al.: SoK: (state of) the art of war: offensive techniques in binary analysis. In: IEEE Symposium on Security and Privacy (2016). https://doi.org/10.1109/SP.2016.17

27. Tian, D., Jia, X., Ma, R., Liu, S., Liu, W., Hu, C.: BinDeep: a deep learning approach to binary code similarity detection. Expert Syst. Appl. **168** (2021). https://doi.org/10.1016/j.eswa.2020.114348. ISSN 0957-4174

28. van der Veen, V., et al.: A tough call: mitigating advanced code-reuse attacks at the binary level. In: 2016 IEEE Symposium on Security and Privacy (SP), pp. 934–953 (2016). https://doi.org/10.1109/SP.2016.60. ISBN 978-1-5090-0824-7

29. Wang, S.-C., Liu, C.-L., Li, Y., Xu, W.-Y.: Semdiff: finding semtic differences in binary programs based on angr. In: ITM Web of Conferences, vol. 12, p. 03029. EDP Sciences (2017). https://doi.org/10.1051/itmconf/20171203029

30. Wang, S., Wu, D.: In-memory fuzzing for binary code similarity analysis. In: 2017 32nd IEEE/ACM International Conference on Automated Software Engineering (ASE), pp. 319–330. Institute of Electrical and Electronics Engineers (IEEE) (2017). https://doi.org/10.1109/ASE.2017.8115645. ISBN 978-1-5386-2684-9

31. Xu, Z., Chen, B., Chandramohan, M., Liu, Y., Song, F.: SPAIN: security patch analysis for binaries towards understanding the pain and pills. In: 2017 IEEE/ACM 39th International Conference on Software Engineering (ICSE), pp. 462–472. Institute of Electrical and Electronics Engineers (IEEE) (2017). https://doi.org/10.1109/ICSE.2017.49. ISBN 978-1-5386-3868-2

32. Xue, Y., Xu, Z., Chandramohan, M., Liu, Y.: Accurate and scalable cross-architecture cross-OS binary code search with emulation. IEEE Trans. Softw. Eng. **45**(11), 1125–1149 (2019). https://doi.org/10.1109/TSE.2018.2827379. ISSN 1939-3520

33. Yang, S., Cheng, L., Zeng, Y., Lang, Z., Zhu, H., Shi, Z.: Asteria: deep learning-based AST-encoding for cross-platform binary code similarity detection. In: 2021 51st Annual IEEE/IFIP International Conference on Dependable Systems and Networks (DSN), pp. 224–236. Institute of Electrical and Electronics Engineers (IEEE) (2021). https://doi.org/10.1109/DSN48987.2021.00036. ISBN 978-1-6654-3572-7

Malware Analysis with Symbolic Execution and Graph Kernel

Charles-Henry Bertrand Van Ouytsel(✉) and Axel Legay

INGI, ICTEAM, Université Catholique de Louvain, Place Sainte Barbe 2,
LG05.02,01, 1348 Louvain-La-Neuve, Belgium
{charles-henry.bertrand,axel.legay}@uclouvain.be

Abstract. Malware analysis techniques are divided into static and dynamic analysis. Both techniques can be bypassed by circumvention techniques such as obfuscation. In a series of works, the authors have promoted the use of symbolic executions combined with machine learning to avoid such traps. Most of those works rely on natural graph-based representations that can then be plugged into graph-based learning algorithms such as Gspan. There are two main problems with this approach. The first one is in the cost of computing the graph. Indeed, working with graphs requires one to compute and representing the entire state-space of the file under analysis. As such computation is too cumbersome, the techniques often rely on developing strategies to compute a representative subgraph of the behaviors. Unfortunately, efficient graph-building strategies remain weakly explored. The second problem is in the classification itself. Graph-based machine learning algorithms rely on comparing the biggest common structures. This sidelines small but specific parts of the malware signature. In addition, it does not allow us to work with efficient algorithms such as support vector machine. We propose a new efficient open source toolchain for machine learning-based classification. We also explore how graph-kernel techniques can be used in the process. We focus on the 1-dimensional Weisfeiler-Lehman kernel, which can capture local similarities between graphs. Our experimental results show that our approach (1) outperforms existing ones by an impressive factor, (2) is resistant to static adversarial attacks.

Keywords: Malware analysis · Symbolic execution · Malware classification

1 Introduction

According to the independent IT security institute AV-Test [5], the number of malware infections has increased significantly over the last ten years, reaching a total of 1287.32 million in 2021. With approximately 450 000 new malware every day, companies spend on average 2.4 millions dollars [1] on defenses against such malicious software. For this reason, effective and automated malware detection

ⓒ The Author(s), under exclusive license to Springer Nature Switzerland AG 2022
H. P. Reiser and M. Kyas (Eds.): NordSec 2022, LNCS 13700, pp. 292–310, 2022.
https://doi.org/10.1007/978-3-031-22295-5_16

and classification is an important requirement to guarantee system safety and user protection.

Most malware classification approaches are based on the concept of signature and signature detection. A malware signature, which is often built manually, represents the DNA of the malware [7,13,18]. Consequently, deciding whether a binary file contains a specific malware boils down to checking whether the signature of such malware is present in the binary. The simplest type of signature is the syntactic signature, i.e., signatures based on syntactic properties of the malware binaries (length, entropy, number of sections, or presence of certain strings). Alternatively, behavioral signatures are based on the malware's behavioral properties (interaction with the system and its network communications).

Different types of signature give rise to different malware classification approaches. In static malware analysis approaches, the classification boils down to detecting the presence of a given static signature directly in the binary that has been disassembled. This signature often boils down to a sequence of characters [15]. The two main advantages of this approach is that it is fast and does not require executing the malware. On the other hand, static signatures are very sensitive to obfuscation techniques that modify the binary code to change its syntactic properties [22]. An illustration of those limitations is given in [7,25] where the authors show the approach is not robust to variants of the MIRAI malware. Other static approaches use machine learning algorithms (see [34] for an illustration in the context of Android systems). Several works shows that those are not resistant to adversarial examples (e.g: [33]).

Another classification approach is that of dynamic analysis, which executes the malware and observes if its effect on the system corresponds to some behavioral signature [21,38]. This approach is based on the fact that a static obfuscation does not modify the behavior of the malware and therefore has no influence on the classification of a behavioral signature. To avoid infecting the analyst's system and to prevent the malware from spreading, the malware is commonly executed in a sandbox. Unfortunately, malware can implement sandbox detection techniques to determine whether they are being executed in a sandbox. As dynamic analysis is limited to one execution, a malware can pass detection by avoiding exhibiting malicious behavior [3]. More information on static and dynamic malware analysis can be found in the following tutorial [7].

Aware of those limitations, several authors have proposed using some exploration techniques coming from the formal verification areas. This includes symbolic execution [10,12,14], a technique that explores possible execution paths of the binary without either concretizing the values of the variables or dynamically executing the code. As the code exploration progresses, constraints on symbolic variables are built and system calls tracked. A satisfiability-modulo-theory (SMT) checker is in charge of verifying the satisfiability of the collected symbolic constraints and thus the validity of an execution path.

The advent of symbolic execution has led to the development of a new set of machine learning-based fully automatised malware classification methods. Those continue and extend the trend of applying machine learning to malware classification [20,34,35]. In particular, in [25] the authors have proposed combining symbolic execution with Gspan [37], a machine learning algorithm that allows us to detect the biggest common subgraphs between two graphs. In its training phase, the algorithm collects binary calls via symbolic analysis. Such calls are then connected in a System Call Dependency Graph (SCDG), that is a graph that abstracts the flow of information between those calls. Gspan can compute the biggest common subgraphs between malware of a given family. Those then represent the signature for the family. In its classification phase, the approach extracts the SCDG from the binary and compares it with each family's signature.

Unfortunately, the above-mentioned approach has several limitations. The first one is that it depends on the efficiency of the symbolic analysis engine. The second one is that SCDGs are built as an abstraction of the real behavior of the binary. In particular, the approach will connect two calls that have the same argument even though those calls may be from different function. Such a choice, which is motivated by efficiency reasons, may lead to a crude over-approximation of the file's behavior and hence to misclassification.

Relying on the biggest common subgraphs may exclude important but isolated calls that are specific to the malware. In addition, using graphs poses a particular challenge in the application of traditional data mining and machine learning approaches that rely on vectors. To surmount those limitations, the authors in [24] proposed using a graph kernel [23], which can be intuitively understood as a function measuring the similarity of pairs of graphs. In their work, the authors used the approach in a non-supervised process. However, such kernel can be plugged into a kernel machine, such as a support vector machine. Results in [24] show that the graph kernel outperforms Gspan in terms of accuracy. Unfortunately, the kernel used in [24] still implicitly relies on detecting the biggest commonalities between graphs. Individual important calls are out of its scope.

Our paper makes several contributions to improving symbolic analysis-based malware classification. The first contribution consists in a flexible and open source implementation of a malware analysis toolchain based on [32] (available here [6]). In addition to obtaining better performances, the flexibility of the new implementation allows us to plug in and compare various classification algorithms and symbolic execution strategies. In particular we develop and compare several efficient resource-based strategies that enable us to build compact but more informative SCDGs than those in [24,25]. The approach is able to distinguish more SCDGs and hence obtain a finer grain in both training and classification processes. Another important contribution of this paper is the comparison of the Weisfeiler-Lehman Kernel [31] with other classifiers. Such a graph kernel is capable of comparing the graph's local small structures by a ingenious relabelling of its vertices. Finally, a major contribution of the paper is a series of experimental results showing that our approach outperforms those in [25] and in [24] when being used in a supervised context. We also show that our approach outperform static approaches when facing adversarial examples.

2   On Graph Comparison for Malware Analysis

This section briefly introduces several notions related to graphs. It also outlines the limits of graph-based representation in malware analysis and advantages of graph kernels.

A graph G is defined as a pair (V, E), where V is a set of Vertices and E a set of edges such that $\{\{u, v\} \subseteq V | u \neq v\}$. The set of edges and vertices of G are given by $E(G)$ and $V(G)$, respectively. We also consider labelled graphs where a label function $l : V(G) \rightarrow \Sigma$ assigns a label from Σ to each vertex of G. We use $l(v)$ to denote the label of vertices v. A graph G' = (V', E') is a *subgraph* of G = (V, E) if $V' \subseteq V$ and $E' \subseteq E$. We are interested in applying graph comparison to extract and compare malware signatures represented by SCDGs. In particular, graph isomorphism is considered to be a powerful tool that allows us to detect structural similarities between graphs that may not be identical. Two unlabelled graphs G and H are said to be isomorphic $(G \simeq H)$ if there exists a bijection $\phi : V(G) \rightarrow V(H)$ such that $(u, v) \in E(G)$ if and only if (1) $(\phi(u), \phi(v)) \in E(H)$ (for all $u, v \in V(G)$), and (2) $l(v) = l(v')$ for each $(v, v') \in \phi$. There exists a wide range of graph similarity measures. This includes, e.g., subgraph isomorphism used to compute the largest common subgraph. Checking graph isomorphism is known to be NP. Moreover, reducing the comparison of two graphs to checking their isomorphism is known to be restrictive as it requires both graphs to have same structure. This situation is rarely encountered when comparing (classes of) malware. The situation is illustrated in Fig. 1, where two malware from the same family are considered to be different since Vertex *SetFilePointer* cannot be covered by an isomorophic relationship.

To address the problem, authors in [25] proposed an approach based on Gspan. This is a popular algorithm for frequent graph-based pattern mining. Given a set of graphs $\mathbb{G}$ and a desired support *min_supp*, Gspan (whose pseudo-code is given in Appendix A) tries to extract all subgraphs present at least in *min_supp* graphs of $\mathbb{G}$. If $\mathbb{G}$ represents a set of malware from the same family, the set of common subgraphs represents their signatures.

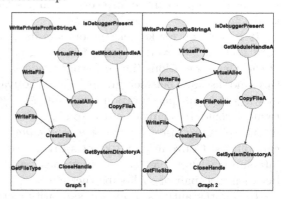

Fig. 1. Example of non-isomorphic graphs with high similarities

Unfortunately, relying on computing the biggest subgraphs may dismiss small but important connected components that do not belong to the biggest subgraphs. The situation is illustrated in Graph 3 of Fig. 2, where important calls such as *IsDebuggerPresent* may be ignored. An inefficient solution could be to extend the number of subgraphs. Unfortunately, when bigger graphs than in our example are involved, this approach will mostly favor a variant of the biggest connected component, as we will see in Sect. 4. In order to address this problem, we resort to the concept of Graph Kernels.

2.1 Graph Kernels

In machine learning, *kernel methods* are algorithms that allow us to compare different data points with a particular similarity measure. Consider a set of data points X such as $\mathbb{R}^m$ and let $k : X \times X \to \mathbb{R}$ be a function. Function k is a valid kernel on X if there exists a Hilbert space $\mathcal{H}_k$ and a feature map $\phi : X \to \mathcal{H}_k$ such that $k(x, y) = \langle \phi(x), \phi(y) \rangle$ for $x, y \in \mathcal{X}$, where $\langle \cdot, \cdot \rangle$ denotes the inner product of $\mathcal{H}_k$. It is known that ϕ exists only if k is a positive semidefinite function. A well-known kernel is the Gaussian radial basis function (RBF) kernel on $\mathbb{R}^m$, $m \in \mathbb{N}$, defined as:

$$k_{RBF}(x, y) = exp(-\frac{\|x - y\|^2}{2\sigma^2}) \tag{1}$$

with σ, the bandwidth parameter. Observe that RBF kernel gives an explicit definition of ϕ. In practice, this is not always required. Indeed, algorithms such as Support Vectors Machine (SVM) use the data X only through inner products between data points. Having the kernel value $k(x, y)$ between each data point is thus sufficient to build an SVM-based classifier. This approach is known as the *kernel trick* [16]. A Gram matrix K, is defined with respect to a finite set of point $x_1, .., x_n \in X$. Each element $K_{i,j}$ with $i, j \in \{0, .., n\}$ represents the kernel value between pairs of points $k(x_i, x_j)$. If the Gram Matrix K of Kernel k is positive semi-definite for every possible set of data points, then k is a valid kernel.

It is common for kernels to compare data points using differences between data vectors. However, the structures of graphs are invariant to permutations of their representations (i.e., ordering of edges/vertices does not influence structure and distance between graphs). This motivates the need to compare graphs in ways that are permutation invariant. Moreover, to avoid strict comparison (which would be equivalent to isomorphism), it is common to use smoother metrics of comparison, such as *convolutionnal kernels*, for better generalization capabilities. Convolutionnal kernels divide structures (i.e., graphs in our case) into substructures (e.g., edges, subgraphs, paths, etc) and then evaluate a kernel between each pair of such substructures.

In [24], the authors propose a similarity metric for malware behavior graphs based on common vertices and edges. Concretely, they define a similarity σ between two graphs G and H as:

$$\sigma(G, H) = \alpha \sigma_{vertices}(G, H) + (1 - \alpha)\sigma_{edges}(G, H) \tag{2}$$

where α is the vertice-edge factor allowing to adjust weights of vertices and edges in the similarity function (set to 0.25 in the conclusion of their work). The vertice similarity is defined as:

$$\sigma_{vertices}(G, H) = \frac{|\mathcal{V}(G) \cap \mathcal{V}(H)|}{min(\mathcal{V}(G), \mathcal{V}(H))} \tag{3}$$

and the edge similarity as:

$$\sigma_{edges}(G, H) = \frac{|\mathcal{CC}_{max}(G \cap H)|}{min(|\mathcal{CC}_{max}(G)|, |\mathcal{CC}_{max}(H)|)} \tag{4}$$

where $\mathcal{V}(G)$ are the set of vertices of G and $\mathcal{CC}_{max}(G)$ is the biggest connected component of G.

While this approach adds information related to all nodes labels compared to Gspan, it suffers from similar drawbacks than Gspan. Indeed, it focus on the biggest connected component, neglecting edges in other connected components. This problem is illustrated on Graph 4 of Fig. 2. One can see that the kernel identifies similarities between nodes of Graph 1 and Graph 2. However, it ignores important edge dependencies such as *GetModuleHandle*, *CopyFileA*, and *GetSystemDirectoryA*.

To tackle this problem, a popular approach in graph kernels is the comparison of local structure. In this approach, two vertices of different graphs are considered to be similar if they share the same labels. The two vertices are considered to be more similar if, in addition, they share similar neighborhoods (i.e., vertices with the same labels). Using this approach, Shervashidze et al. [31] introduced graph kernels based on the 1-

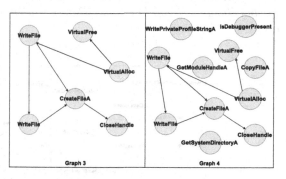

Fig. 2. Graph 3 represents the subgraph extracted with Gspan from graphs of Fig. 1. Graph 4 corresponds to the extraction with the kernel from [24]

dimensional Weisfeiler-Lehman (WL). Let G and H be graphs, and $l : V(G) \cup V(H) \rightarrow \Sigma$ be a function giving their vertices labels. By several iterations $i = 0, 1, ...,$ the 1-WL algorithm computes a new label function $l_i : \mathcal{V}(G) \cup V(H) \rightarrow \Sigma$, with each iteration allowing comparison of G and H. Let $N(v)$ be the neighborhood of a vertex $v \in G$ in $V(G)$, i.e., $N(v) = \{u \in V(G)|(v, u) \in E(G)\}$. In the first iteration, $l_0 = l$, and in subsequent iterations,

$$l_i(v) = relabel(l_{i-1}(v), sort(l_{i-1}(u)|u \in N(v))) \tag{5}$$

with $v \in V(G) \cup V(H)$, sort(S) returning a sorted tuple of S and function $relabel(p)$ maps the pair p to a unique value in Σ which is not already used in previous iterations. When the cardinality of l_i equals the cardinality of l_{i-1}, the algorithm stops. The idea of the WL sub-tree kernel is to compute the previous function for $h \geq 0$ and after each iteration i to compute a feature vector $\phi_i(G) \in \mathcal{R}^{|\Sigma_i|}$ for each graph G, where $\Sigma_i \subseteq \Sigma$ denotes the image of l_i. Each component $\phi_i(G)_{\sigma_j^i}$ counts the number of appearances of vertices labelled with $\sigma_j^i \in \Sigma_i$. The overall feature vector $\phi^{WL}(G)$ is defined as the concatenation of the feature vectors of all h iterations, i.e.,

$$\phi^{WL}(G) = (\phi^0(G)_{\sigma_1^0}, ..., \phi^0(G)_{\sigma_{|\Sigma_0|}^0}, \phi^h(G)_{\sigma_1^h}, ..., \phi^h(G)_{\sigma_{|\Sigma_h|}^h}) \qquad (6)$$

Finally, to compute similarity between two different feature vectors, we apply the following formula:

$$k_{WL}(G, G') = \sum_{\phi \in \phi^{WL}(G)} \sum_{\phi' \in \phi^{WL}(G')} \delta(\phi, \phi') \qquad (7)$$

where δ is the Dirac kernel, that is, it is 1 when its arguments are equals and 0 otherwise. The more labels the two graphs have in common, the higher this kernel value will be. Compared with Gspan and the kernel from [24], this kernel also targets similarities related to all nodes and edges of the biggest subgraph but also local similarities. This is illustrated in Fig. 3, where dependencies between *GetModuleHandle*, *CopyFileA*, and *GetSystemDirectoryA* are kept in the learning process.

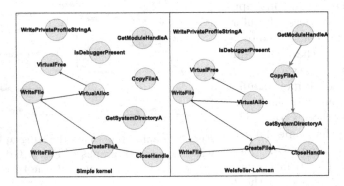

Fig. 3. The figure shows that, contrary to Simple Kernel, the Weisfeiler-Lehman kernel captures all common edges between the graphs of Fig. 1

3   Approach: Symbolic Execution + Machine Learning for Malware Analysis

We propose an open source toolchain for malware analysis that is based on machine learning and SCDGs (available here [6]). The toolchain relies on the following important components: the first component consists in collecting and labelling a series of binaries from different malware families. Then, **angr** [32], a python framework for symbolic execution, is used to execute those files. The result is used to extract a SCDG for each such binary. One of the contributions of this paper will be to improve and adapt the symbolic engine to malware analysis as well as the construction of SCDGs. Those SCDGs are then used to train machine learning algorithms. If Gspan is used, the training will result in common subgraphs to represent signatures for each family. If SVM is used, a Gram matrix between all the malware programs is created. Finally, the toolchain also contains supervised classifiers. If Gspan is used, the SCDG of the new malware is compared with those of the signature of each family and the classifier retains the one with the closest distance. If SVM is used, a Gram matrix is created between all trained malware and the new malware. This matrix is then used in the SVM classification process. A main contribution of this paper is to compare those two types of classification.

3.1   Extraction of Calls

The construction of the SCDG is based on Symbolic Execution. This approach envisages the exploration of all the possible execution paths of the binary without either concretizing the values of the variables or dynamically executing the code (i.e., the binary is analyzed statically). Instead, all the values are represented symbolically. As the code exploration progresses, constraints on symbolic variables are built and system calls tracked. A satisfiability-modulo-theory (SMT) checker is in charge of verifying the satisfiability of the collected symbolic constraints and thus the validity of an execution path. A wide range of tools and techniques have been developed for efficient symbolic execution analysis. Most of those techniques agree on the fact that symbolic execution still suffers from state-space-explosion and, consequently, only a finite set of symbolic paths can be explored in a reasonable amount of time. This is particularly the case with malware analysis where the classification process must be done with very limited resources. As the calls that form the SCDG are collected directly from those symbolic paths, the choice of which paths to follow will have an impact on the machine learning process.In a recent work, authors showed how SMT solving could impact performances [8,11,29]. In this paper, we focus on path selection strategies. The work in [25] implements a Breadth-First Search (BFS) approach, that is, at each execution step all ongoing paths are explored simultaneously. This approach leads to an important growth of states and memory usage. As we have limited resources, we propose to explore one subset of paths at a time. We prioritize states from which one can explore new assembly instruction addresses of the program. Our Custom Breadth-First Search Strategy (**CBFS-Strategy**) is presented in Algorithm 1. The algorithm begins by taking L states for exploration from the set of available states and putting them in the list R of states to explore next (line 4). It then iterates among all other available states. If it finds a state leading to an unexplored part of the code or with a shorter path of execution (line 6), it puts it in R and takes out a state with a lower priority (i.e.: state not leading to a new instruction or state with a longer depth). After going through each state, it returns R to allow angr to perform a new execution step on

R' states. In addition to **BFS-Strategy**, we also implemented a Custom Depth-First Search Strategy (**CDFS-Stategy**), which is presented in Algorithm 2 (the main difference with CBFS-Strategy being the condition to select successor state at Line 6). Observe that symbolic execution with this coverage heuristic is not new. However, the implementation and evaluation of restricted versions within a tool for malware classification are.

Algorithm 1. CBFS exploration	Algorithm 2. CDFS exploration
1: Inputs: A set of states: S	1: Inputs: A set of states: S
2: Limit of states: L	2: Limit of states: L
3: Outputs: A set of L states: R	3: Outputs: A set of L states: R
4: $R \leftarrow S[:L]$	4: $R \leftarrow S[:L]$
5: **for** *state* $s \in S$ **do**	5: **for** *state* $s \in S$ **do**
6: **if** new(s.next_ip)|{$\exists state \in$ R|s.depth $<$ state.depth & !new(state.next_ip)} **then**	6: **if** new(s.next_ip)|{$\exists state \in$ R|s.depth $>$ state.depth & !new(state.next_ip)} **then**
7: Remove state from R	7: Remove state from R
8: Add s to R	8: Add s to R
9: **Return** R	9: **Return** R

Another important challenge in symbolic execution is that of handling loops. Indeed, the condition of such loops may be symbolic. In addition, the loop may create an infinite repetitive behavior. In those situations, deciding between staying in the loop or exiting the loop remains a tricky choice that has been the subject of several works focusing on the possibilities, which include Loop-extended Symbolic Execution [26], Read-Write set [9], and bit-precise symbolic mapping [36]. As those approaches may be too time-consuming, we propose to reuse two intermediary heuristics from [25]. The first one applies to loops whose condition contains a symbolic value. Such loops may give rise to two states at each iteration: one that exits the loop for those symbolic values that exceed the condition and one that remains within the loop for other values, with this last state being used again to iterate on the loop. We chose to stop such iteration after four steps. For loops that do not contain symbolic values, since such loop may still lead to an unbounded number of behaviors, our approach consists in limiting the execution to a finite, arbitrary fixed, number of steps and then forcing the execution to exit the loop.

3.2   Creating SCDGs

Symbolic execution allows us to obtain several paths representing executions of a given binary. Our next step is to collect the sets of calls present on each such path as well as their addresses and arguments. Those are used to build the SCDG corresponding to this binary. Following [25], SCDGs are graphs where each vertex is labelled with the name of a system call; and the edges correspond to (an abstraction of) information flow between these calls. Concretely, each

SCDG is built from the symbolic representation by merging and linking calls from one or more symbolic paths. Their construction could be influenced by applying different **SCDG-Strategies**.

Consider first the creation of a graph execution from one symbolic path. We consider three types of edge. In the first one, two calls are linked if they both share an argument with identical value (i.e.: one-edge strategy). This is, for example, the case of two calls with the same file handler. The second link is established between two calls that both have an argument with the same symbolic value. An example is a symbolic file size returned by a call and passed to a second call added to another value. In addition, we consider that two calls can be linked if an argument of the first call is the calling address of the second one. This situation typically arises in dynamic loading of a library. We also label each edge with the index of the argument in both calls (return value of a call is given index 0). The three-edges strategy is called **SCDG-Strategy 1** and the one-edge strategy is called **SCDG-Strategy 2**. Our experiments shows that **SCDG-Strategy 2** loses important dependency between calls and leads to more isolated nodes in SCDGs. Indeed, this strategy suffers from two types of problem. First, symbolic values may be modified before being passed to another call. Second, some calls used by obfuscation techniques exhibit address-arguments links. A typical example is given by *GetProcAddress*, used to hide real content of the import table of PE files.

An example of an SCDG is given in Fig. 4 with **SCDG-Strategy 1** and **SCDG-Strategy 2**. The program first calls *CreateFile*, which returns a handle to the file with the specified filename. A vertex is thus constructed for *CreateFile*. Then, a call to *SetFilePointer* on the preceding file handle occurs. This leads to the creation of a new vertex (*SetFilePointer*). Since the returned argument of *CreateFile* (index 0) is the same as the first argument of *SetFilePointer* (index 1), an edge is added between them. Vertices *ReadFile* and *WriteFile* are created and linked following similar principles.

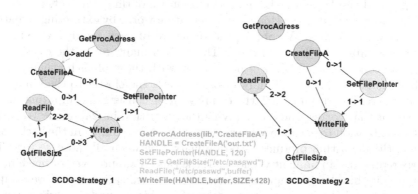

Fig. 4. Illustration of a SCDG built with **SCDG-Strategy 1** and **SCDG-Strategy 2**

There are situations where different calls in the same execution share the same API name and occur at the same instruction address but with distinct arguments. One may decide to merge the two calls into one single vertex. In this case, we conserve the set of arguments of the first call observed in the execution. This merge incurs a loss of precision but leads to a more compact SCDG representation [29]. This may be of importance when one has to train the system with a large number of different types of malware. This merging strategy is called **SCDG-Strategy 3**. Merging calls gives different advantages. First, it decreases the size of the SCDG, which may lead to better classification/detection performances. In addition, it may reduce the impact of some calls in the learning phase. An example is given with the wabot malware, which uses a hundred of calls to *WriteFile* during its execution. If not merged, those calls that are not part of the main actions of the malware will constitute an important part of the signature. This may have a negative impact on the training phase. On the other hand, there are situations where **SCDG-Strategy 3** merges calls with different goals. This situation may result in losing part of the malware behavior.

The above strategies apply to single symbolic paths only. When several symbolic paths are considered, one can decide to produce an SCDG that is composed of the disjoint union of such executions. Such a strategy is referred to as **SCDG-Strategy 5**. On the other hand, **SCDG-Strategy 4** consists in merging successive executions from different symbolic paths. **SCDG-Strategy 5** is simpler to compute, but **SCDG-Strategy 5** gives smaller graphs. According to our experimental results, **SCDG-Strategy 4** may speed up the computation time by an exponential factor for families with high symbolic execution numbers.

3.3   Creating a Classification Model and Evaluate New Samples

The toolchain uses SCDGs to train a classifier which is used to detect and classify malware. We have implemented two classifiers. One implementation is based on Gspan and follows the idea from [25]. Another one implements the graph kernel from [24] and the Weisfeiler-Lehman extension we outlined in Sect. 2.

The classifier that uses Gspan implementation works by extracting signatures from malware families. We obtain the signature of each family by computing the biggest subgraphs between the SCDG of each malware. In the classification phase, we compare the SCDG of new binary with those of each signature. The file belongs to the malware family whose graph is the closest to the binary's.

For the case of graph kernel, the training phase consists in computing the feature vector that corresponds to applying the algorithm in [24] or the Weisfeiler-Lehman extension to each malware of the family. As explained in the background section, the algorithm produces a Gram matrix between all those vectors. This matrix represents an implicit version of the kernel. A support vector machine can then exploit this implicit representation. In the classification phase, we compute a Gram matrix between the feature vector of the binary under classification and the vectors of all malware used in the training set. Observe that, contrary to the Gspan approach, graph kernel does not require us to produce an explicit and hence all-encompassing representation of the signature of each family.

4   Experimental Results

This section describes the methodology used to assess our toolchain's performance in both extracting SCDGs and classifying new binaries. Our evaluation set was composed of 1874 malware divided into 15 families plus 150 cleanware samples. The data set's exact composition is given in Table 1. In terms of origins, 64 percent of the samples were obtained thanks to a direct collaboration with Cisco. The remaining 36% were extracted from MalwareBazaar [2]. Samples were labelled using AVClass [28], a python tool to label malware samples. This tool is fed with VirusTotal reports and outputs the most likely family of each sample. To evaluate detection performance, we used 150 open source programs found online [27]. To show the relevance of approach, we also compare our classifier performance with a SVM classifier trained on Ember [4] static features. Those features are known to be representative features for existing static machine learning approach. We then demonstrate how easily it could be fooled with adversarial examples generated with framework such as MAB-malware [33].

In the rest of the section, all experiments were performed on a desktop PC with an Intel Core i7-8665U CPU (1.90 GHz × 8) and 16 GB RAM running Ubuntu 18.04.5. Our experimental results relied on our ability to extract SCDGs efficiently. In all experiments, we used a timeout of ten minutes for each SCDG. Note that 20% of the SCDGs were computed in time while 80% never computed

Table 1. Composition of the dataset

Family	#samples	Family	# samples
bancteain	91	remcosRAT	476
delf	78	sfone	32
fickerstealer	44	sillyp2p	269
gandcrab	92	simbot	126
ircbot	36	sodinokibi	75
lamer	61	sytro	115
nitol	71	wabot	134
redlinestealer	35	cleanware	150

entirely. For the case of BFS-Strategy, we used the same parameters as in [29] (loop threshold of 4, unlimited number of states to explore, z3 optimization enabled). However, for CDFS-Strategy and CBFS-Strategy we imposed a limit of 10 states that could be explored simultaneously. All metrics for multi-class classification are weighted average.

Environment Modelling. Proper environment modelling is a major challenge in developing efficient symbolic execution techniques. Indeed, when we apply symbolic execution we avoid exploring/executing API call code. Since performing such an operation would drastically increase the computation time [19]. In angr, when a call to an external library occurs, the call is hooked to a simulated procedure called *simprocedures* that will produce the symbolic outputs for the function. A simple but crude implementation of such procedure is to assume that the external function returns a symbolic value without any constraint. In such a case, *simprocedures* simply returns symbolic values covering the full range of outputs given in the specification. In practice, such a solution gives good results in 26 percent of the analyzed families. However, this solution may generate outputs that are not defined in the specification. In addition, it ignores many potential effects of the call, which include the modifications of input parameters or the number of its arguments. This may lead to incoherent executions if those parameters impact the rest of the execution (e.g.: in branch choices). We propose several improvements to fix those issues. The first one consists in restricting the ranges of outputs to those given in the specification. As an example, if the output is an integer variable that can take only four values, *simprocedures* would generate those values instead of the full range of integers. Another one concerns the case where an execution is blocked because modifications of some arguments by the external call are not performed. This happens in situations where the external call may modify some of its inputs or even some environment variables. In such case, we emulate several potential modifications with concrete values. Observe that this improvement work must be performed for each call in our dataset that causes problems. That is why, we have constituted a *simprocedures* library that is constantly enriched with experiments and calls.

We first apply Gspan to SCDGs obtained with combinations of different strategies. Signatures are obtained by sampling randomly 30% of the SCDGs of each family; those SCDGs constitute the training set. Other SCDGs are then classified to assess the quality of those signatures; those SCDGs constitute the test set. This process is repeated three times and performance is averaged.

Table 2. Results of Gspan classifier with different exploration strategies

SCDG-strategy					BFS-strategy			CBFS-strategy			CDFS-strategy		
1	2	3	4	5	Precision	Recall	F_1-score	Precision	Recall	F_1-score	Precision	Recall	F_1-score
x		x	x		0.685	0.566	0.619	0.721	0.604	0.657	0.652	0.609	0.629
x		x		x	0.623	0.552	0.585	0.674	0.568	0.616	0.61	0.587	0.5983
x		x			0.683	0.589	0.632	0.698	0.555	0.619	0.669	0.597	0.631
x				x	0.609	0.534	0.569	0.651	0.534	0.586	0.629	0.54	0.581
	x	x	x		0.684	0.651	0.667	0.736	0.655	0.693	0.693	0.639	0.664
	x	x		x	0.614	0.594	0.614	0.686	0.615	0.648	0.645	0.586	0.614
	x		x		0.679	0.587	0.629	0.623	0.465	0.532	0.68	0.597	0.636
	x			x	0.602	0.556	0.578	0.587	0.448	0.508	0.632	0.578	0.603

In Table 2, we observe that **CDFS-Strategy** generally outperforms **CBFS-Strategy** and **BFS-Strategy**. By inspecting the results, we observed that **BFS-Strategy** ran out of memory for 7 percent of the binaries, thus reducing its performance compared to **CBFS-Strategy**. While **SCDG-strategy 4** showed improvements with **SCDG-strategy 5**, it should be noted that **SCDG-strategy 5** entails significant overhead in SCDG building (up to 100 times slower) and signature size (5 times bigger on average). In general, the best performances were obtained by combining **SCDG-strategy {2, 3, 4}**. Upon inspecting best classifier in Fig. 6, we see a lot of confusion between different classes. This can be explain by plotting similarities between signatures built with Gspan, as illustrated in Fig. 5. There, different signatures share important similarities, leading to confusion between different malware families, as illustrated in Fig. 6.

This problem is directly linked to a problem exposed in Sect. 2, that is, Gspan focus on the biggest subgraph while neglecting other components.

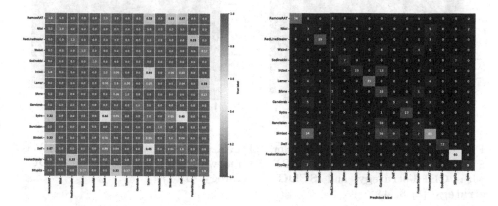

Fig. 5. Similarity matrix between signatures obtained with Gspan

Fig. 6. Confusion matrix obtained for Gspan with **CBFS-strategy** and **SCDG-strategy {2, 3, 4}**.

We now turn to applying kernel from [24]. Table 3 shows that overall performance increased compared with Gspan. Moreover, **CBFS-Strategy** and **CDFS-Strategy** outperformed both **BFS-Strategy** and **SCDG-strategy {2, 3, 4}** strategies appeared to be more efficient. However, Fig. 7 shows that several families were still indistinguishable.

Table 3. Results of SVM classifier and kernel from [24] with different exploration strategies

SCDG-strategy					BFS-strategy			CBFS-strategy			CDFS-strategy		
1	2	3	4	5	Precision	Recall	F_1-score	Precision	Recall	F_1-score	Precision	Recall	F_1-score
x		x	x		0.754	0.691	0.721	0.845	0.812	0.828	0.833	0.787	0.8093
x		x		x	0.728	0.673	0.699	0.785	0.736	0.759	0.77	0.714	0.741
x			x		0.742	0.71	0.725	0.827	0.778	0.801	0.82	0.754	0.786
x				x	0.711	0.649	0.678	0.771	0.703	0.735	0.74	0.698	0.718
	x	x	x		0.769	0.723	0.745	0.851	0.826	0.838	0.847	0.813	0.829
	x	x		x	0.738	0.645	0.688	0.813	0.752	0.781	0.802	0.738	0.768
	x		x		0.747	0.632	0.684	0.798	0.747	0.771	0.835	0.772	0.802
	x			x	0.714	0.654	0.682	0.781	0.733	0.756	0.763	0.718	0.739

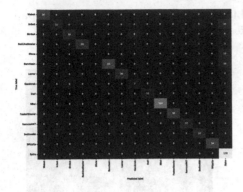
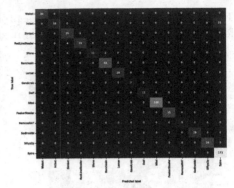

Fig. 7. Confusion matrix obtained for SVM classifier and kernel from [24] with **CBFS-strategy** and **SCDG-strategy {2, 3, 4}**

Fig. 8. Confusion matrix obtained for WL kernel with **CDFS-strategy** and **SCDG-strategy {1, 4}**.

Weisfeiler-Lehman Kernel (WL). Finally, we investigated the SVM classifier with the WL kernel. The results in Table 4 clearly outperformed the others, reaching an F_1-score of 0.929 with **CDFS-Strategy** and **SCDG-strategy {1, 3, 4}**. Families were better distinguished, as illustrated in Fig. 8. Those results confirm our supposition of Sect. 2: taking advantage of an SCDG's local structure increases the efficiency of machine learning in malware classification.

Adversarial Examples. Contrary to a static approach, our observed classifiers are resistant to adversarial examples based on static features. This is illustrated in Table 5 where we show that the MAB-malware adversarial framework [33] can easily mutated and corrupt Ember features [4] used in most of static classifiers. This fact highlights that, although offering good performance, those static classifiers are highly vulnerable and there is a need to develop new approaches.

Training Time. In general, WL kernel outperforms Gspan by a factor of 15 and Kernel in [24] by a factor of 10 000. We suspect that the overhead is due to the extensive use of pairwise graph mining in the similarity metric presented in Sect. 2. Compare to the Kernel in [24], Gspan reduces these number of computation since it first create a signature for each family before comparing those signature with the binary to classify.

These experiments permit to draw several conclusions. First, **SCDG-strategy 1** gives overall better results than **SCDG-strategy 2** with WL kernel. That is not the case for the other classifier where these information seems to lead to overfitting and **SCDG-strategy 2** should be preferred. Moreover, the impact of **SCDG-strategy 3** varies. While it improves classification for kernels that are based on the biggest common subgraph, its impact when combined with other strategies varies. Finally, while **SCDG-strategy 5** leads to a considerable overhead, it does not improve performance of any classifier. On the other hand, **SCDG-strategy 4** leads to more compact signatures, better computation times and good classification performances. Regarding exploration

Table 4. Results of SVM and WL kernel with different exploration strategies

SCDG-strategy					BFS-strategy			CBFS-strategy			CDFS-strategy		
1	2	3	4	5	Precision	Recall	F_1-score	Precision	Recall	F_1-score	Precision	Recall	F_1-score
x		x	x		0.852	0.847	0.846	0.865	0.864	0.852	0.936	0.931	**0.929**
x		x		x	0.832	0.824	0.827	0.85	0.842	0.846	0.915	0.91	0.912
x		x			0.895	0.891	0.892	0.894	0.881	0.874	0.937	0.933	**0.929**
x				x	0.847	0.836	0.841	0.86	0.851	0.855	0.918	0.911	0.914
	x	x	x		0.86	0.855	0.857	0.897	0.879	0.867	0.929	0.925	0.924
	x	x		x	0.812	0.795	0.803	0.867	0.862	0.864	0.885	0.877	0.881
	x		x		0.895	0.891	0.891	0.895	0.891	0.886	0.939	0.933	**0.929**
	x			x	0.834	0.828	0.831	0.862	0.858	0.859	0.891	0.887	0.888

Table 5. Comparison in the context of adversarial examples (mutated dataset)

Model	Initial dataset			Mutated dataset		
	Precision	Recall	F_1-score	Precision	Recall	F_1-score
Gspan	0.911	0.914	0.911	0.911	0.914	0.911
SVM kernel from [24]	0.965	0.95	0.957	0.965	0.95	0.957
SVM Weisfeiler-Lehman	0.989	0.975	0.981	0.989	0.975	0.981
SVM Ember features	0.964	0.965	0.964	0.763	0.564	0.502

strategies, **BFS-strategy** is generally outperformed by **CBFS-strategy** while **CDFS-strategy** outperforms other strategies when used with the WL graph kernel.

5 Future Work

We propose a new efficient approach for malware detection. Directions for future work includes new exploration heuristics, such as concolic executions [30] or smart sampling [17]. Another objective is to apply our kernel in a non-supervised approach like in [24]. We are also interested in implementing a distributed version of the toolchain. In this context, the federated learning paradigm should allow us to combine information from different contributors. We also plan to investigate resistance to adversarial examples based on semantical modifications of malware. In addition, we will continue to improve our toolchain with new *simprocedure* and plugin interfaces.

Acknowledgments. Charles-Henry Bertrand Van Ouytsel is an FRIA grantee of the Belgian Fund for Scientific Research (FNRS-F.R.S.). We would like to thank Cisco for their malware feed, VirusTotal for their API and the CyberExcellence project funded by the Walloon Region under convention 2110186.

A   Gspan Algorithm

The Gspan algorithm is presented hereunder in Algorithm 3. Given a dataset of graphs $\mathbb{G}$ and a desired support min_supp, Gspan tries to extract all subgraphs present at least in min_supp graphs of $\mathbb{G}$. If $\mathbb{G}$ represents a set of malware from the same family, the output set of common subgraphs $\mathbb{S}$ represents their signatures. To this purpose, Gspan defines a DFS Code of a graph G as an ordered edge sequence constructed from a DFS exploration of G. Original Gspan paper [37] defines a way to order these DFS codes, allowing to define a unique minimum DFS code for a graph G ($min(.)$ function in Algorithm 3). Given a DFS code s, c is called a child of s if it expands s with a new edge to create a valid DFS code.

Algorithm 3. Gspan algorithm
1: In: A set of graphs: $\mathbb{G}$
2: Out: A set of common subgraphs $\mathbb{S}$
3: Sort labels in $\mathbb{G}$ by their frequency
4: Remove infrequent vertices/labels
5: Relabel remaining vertices and edges
6: $\mathbb{S}^1 \leftarrow$ all frequent 1-edge graphs in $\mathbb{G}$
7: Sort $\mathbb{S}^1$ in lexicographical order
8: $\mathbb{S} \leftarrow \mathbb{S}^1$
9: **for** each edge $e \in \mathbb{S}^1$ **do**
10:     initialize s with e
11:     Subgraph_mining($\mathbb{G}$,$\mathbb{S}$, s)
12:     $\mathbb{D} \leftarrow \mathbb{D} - e$
13:     **if** $|\mathbb{G}| < min\_supp$ **then**
14:         break
15: **Return** $\mathbb{S}$

Algorithm 4. Main procedure *Subgrap_mining* of Gspan algorithm
1: **if** $s \neq min(s)$ **then**
2:     return;
3: $\mathbb{S} \leftarrow \mathbb{S} \cup \{s\}$
4: enumerates s in each graph in $\mathbb{G}$
5: and count its children;
6: **for** each c; c is a child of s **do**
7:     **if** $support(c) \geq min\_supp$ **then**
8:         $s \leftarrow c$
9:         Subgraph_mining($\mathbb{G}$, $\mathbb{S}$, s)

References

1. Eighth Annual Cost of Cybercrime Study. https://www.accenture.com/us-en/insights/security/eighth-annual-cost-cybercrime-study. Accessed 29 Oct 2021
2. MalwareBazaar by abuse.ch, fighting malware and botnets. https://bazaar.abuse.ch/. Accessed 29 Oct 2021
3. Afianian, A., Niksefat, S., Sadeghiyan, B., Baptiste, D.: Malware dynamic analysis evasion techniques: a survey. ACM Comput. Surv. (CSUR) 52(6), 1–28 (2019)
4. Anderson, H.S., Roth, P.: EMBER: an open dataset for training static PE malware machine learning models. arXiv preprint arXiv:1804.04637 (2018)
5. AV-Test: AV-Test, the independent IT-Security institute (2021). https://www.av-test.org/en/statistics/malware/
6. Bertrand Van Ouytsel, C.H., Crochet, C., Dam, K., Legay, A.: SEMA: a toolchain using Symbolic execution for malware analysis. In: 17th International Conference on Risks and Security of Internet and Systems (CRiSIS) (2022, to appear)

7. Biondi, F., Given-Wilson, T., Legay, A., Puodzius, C., Quilbeuf, J.: Tutorial: an overview of malware detection and evasion techniques. In: Margaria, T., Steffen, B. (eds.) ISoLA 2018. LNCS, vol. 11244, pp. 565–586. Springer, Cham (2018). https://doi.org/10.1007/978-3-030-03418-4_34

8. Biondi, F., Josse, S., Legay, A., Sirvent, T.: Effectiveness of synthesis in concolic deobfuscation. Comput. Secur. **70**, 500–515 (2017)

9. Boonstoppel, P., Cadar, C., Engler, D.: RWset: attacking path explosion in constraint-based test generation. In: Ramakrishnan, C.R., Rehof, J. (eds.) TACAS 2008. LNCS, vol. 4963, pp. 351–366. Springer, Heidelberg (2008). https://doi.org/10.1007/978-3-540-78800-3_27

10. Cadar, C., Ganesh, V., Sasnauskas, R., Sen, K.: Symbolic execution and constraint solving (Dagstuhl seminar 14442). Dagstuhl Rep. **4**(10), 98–114 (2014)

11. Chen, Z., et al.: Synthesize solving strategy for symbolic execution. In: Cadar, C., Zhang, X. (eds.) ISSTA, pp. 348–360. ACM (2021)

12. David, R., et al.: BINSEC/SE: a dynamic symbolic execution toolkit for binary-level analysis. In: 2016 IEEE 23rd International Conference on Software Analysis, Evolution, and Reengineering (SANER), vol. 1, pp. 653–656. IEEE (2016)

13. Faruki, P., Laxmi, V., Bharmal, A., Gaur, M.S., Ganmoor, V.: AndroSimilar: robust signature for detecting variants of android malware. J. Inf. Secur. Appl. **22**, 66–80 (2015)

14. Godefroid, P.: Test generation using symbolic execution. In: IARCS Annual Conference on Foundations of Software Technology and Theoretical Computer Science (FSTTCS 2012). Schloss Dagstuhl-Leibniz-Zentrum fuer Informatik (2012)

15. Griffin, K., Schneider, S., Hu, X., Chiueh, T.: Automatic generation of string signatures for malware detection. In: Kirda, E., Jha, S., Balzarotti, D. (eds.) RAID 2009. LNCS, vol. 5758, pp. 101–120. Springer, Heidelberg (2009). https://doi.org/10.1007/978-3-642-04342-0_6

16. Hofmann, M.: Support vector machines-kernels and the kernel trick. Notes **26**(3), 1–16 (2006)

17. Jegourel, C., Legay, A., Sedwards, S.: Importance splitting for statistical model checking rare properties. In: Sharygina, N., Veith, H. (eds.) CAV 2013. LNCS, vol. 8044, pp. 576–591. Springer, Heidelberg (2013). https://doi.org/10.1007/978-3-642-39799-8_38

18. Kirat, D., Vigna, G.: MalGene: automatic extraction of malware analysis evasion signature. In: Proceedings of the 22nd ACM SIGSAC Conference on Computer and Communications Security, pp. 769–780 (2015)

19. Lin, Y.: Symbolic execution with over-approximation. Ph.D. thesis, University of Melbourne, Parkville, Victoria, Australia (2017)

20. Macedo, H.D., Touili, T.: Mining malware specifications through static reachability analysis. In: Crampton, J., Jajodia, S., Mayes, K. (eds.) ESORICS 2013. LNCS, vol. 8134, pp. 517–535. Springer, Heidelberg (2013). https://doi.org/10.1007/978-3-642-40203-6_29

21. Massicotte, F., Couture, M., Normandin, H., Michaud, F.: A testing model for dynamic malware analysis systems. In: 2012 IEEE Fifth International Conference on Software Testing, Verification and Validation (ICST), pp. 826–833. IEEE (2012)

22. Moser, A., Kruegel, C., Kirda, E.: Limits of static analysis for malware detection. In: Twenty-Third Annual Computer Security Applications Conference (ACSAC), pp. 421–430. IEEE (2007)

23. Nikolentzos, G., Vazirgiannis, M.: Learning structural node representations using graph kernels. IEEE Trans. Knowl. Data Eng. **33**(5), 2045–2056 (2019)

24. Puodzius, C., Zendra, O., Heuser, A., Noureddine, L.: Accurate and robust malware analysis through similarity of external calls dependency graphs (ECDG). In: The 16th International Conference on Availability, Reliability and Security (ARES), pp. 1–12 (2021)
25. Said, N.B., et al.: Detection of mirai by syntactic and behavioral analysis. In: 2018 IEEE 29th International Symposium on Software Reliability Engineering (ISSRE), pp. 224–235. IEEE (2018)
26. Saxena, P., Poosankam, P., McCamant, S., Song, D.: Loop-extended symbolic execution on binary programs. In: Proceedings of the Eighteenth International Symposium on Software Testing and Analysis (ICST), pp. 225–236 (2009)
27. Sébastien, C.: Portable freeware dataset (2019)
28. Sebastián, M., Rivera, R., Kotzias, P., Caballero, J.: AVCLASS: a tool for massive malware labeling. In: Monrose, F., Dacier, M., Blanc, G., Garcia-Alfaro, J. (eds.) RAID 2016. LNCS, vol. 9854, pp. 230–253. Springer, Cham (2016). https://doi.org/10.1007/978-3-319-45719-2_11
29. Sebastio, S., et al.: Optimizing symbolic execution for malware behavior classification. Comput. Secur. **93**, 101775 (2020)
30. Sen, K.: Concolic testing: a decade later (keynote). In: Xu, H., Binder, W. (eds.) WODA@SPLASH. ACM (2015)
31. Shervashidze, N., Schweitzer, P., Van Leeuwen, E.J., Mehlhorn, K., Borgwardt, K.M.: Weisfeiler-Lehman graph kernels. J. Mach. Learn. Res. **12**(9), 2539–2561 (2011)
32. Shoshitaishvili, Y., et al.: SOK: (state of) the art of war: offensive techniques in binary analysis. In: 2016 IEEE Symposium on Security and Privacy (SP), pp. 138–157. IEEE (2016)
33. Song, W., Li, X., Afroz, S., Garg, D., Kuznetsov, D., Yin, H.: MAB-malware: a reinforcement learning framework for blackbox generation of adversarial malware. In: Proceedings of the 2022 ACM on Asia Conference on Computer and Communications Security (AsiaCCS), pp. 990–1003 (2022)
34. Taheri, R., Ghahramani, M., Javidan, R., Shojafar, M., Pooranian, Z., Conti, M.: Similarity-based android malware detection using hamming distance of static binary features. Futur. Gener. Comput. Syst. **105**, 230–247 (2020)
35. Ucci, D., Aniello, L., Baldoni, R.: Survey of machine learning techniques for malware analysis. Comput. Secur. **81**, 123–147 (2019)
36. Xu, D., Ming, J., Wu, D.: Cryptographic function detection in obfuscated binaries via bit-precise symbolic loop mapping. In: 2017 IEEE Symposium on Security and Privacy (SP), pp. 921–937 (2017)
37. Yan, X., Han, J.: gSpan: graph-based substructure pattern mining. In: 2002 IEEE International Conference on Data Mining, pp. 721–724. IEEE (2002)
38. Zhang, Z., Qi, P., Wang, W.: Dynamic malware analysis with feature engineering and feature learning. In: Proceedings of the AAAI Conference on Artificial Intelligence, pp. 1210–1217. AAAI (2020)

WearSec: Towards Automated Security Evaluation of Wireless Wearable Devices

Bernhards Blumbergs[1] , Ēriks Dobelis[1] , Pēteris Paikens[1(✉)] ,
Krišjānis Nesenbergs[2] , Kirils Solovjovs[2] , and Artis Rušiņš[2]

[1] Institute of Mathematics and Computer Science, University of Latvia,
Raina blvd. 29, Riga, Latvia
{bernhards.blumbergs,eriks.dobelis,peteris.paikens}@lumii.lv
[2] Institute of Electronics and Computer Science, 14 Dzerbenes St., Riga, Latvia
{krisjanis.nesenbergs,kirils.solovjovs,artis.rusins}@edi.lv

Abstract. Wearable devices are becoming more prevalent in the daily
life of society, ranging from smartwatches, and fitness bracelets to acces-
sories and headphones. These devices, both from their hardware manufacturing and wireless firmware development perspectives may possess
drawbacks. In recent years security researchers have uncovered a series
of vulnerabilities. In this paper we introduce the concept and describe
the key ideas towards the development of an automated security evaluation prototype for wireless wearable devices using device fingerprinting,
as well as passive and active vulnerability identification. Furthermore
we describe the technical approaches, challenges, and implementation
choices we faced while developing the first stages of the prototype for this
concept and handling full-spectrum Bluetooth analysis with software-
defined radio.

1 Introduction

In recent years there has been a steady rise in wearable device usage - from 325
million connected wearable devices in the world in 2016 to 1105 million in 2022
[23]. These devices may contain personally identifiable information about the
user, electronic health record (EHR) data [7], geolocation information, and may
be connected to private networks. Thus, such a combination may be introducing
privacy and security risks. Compromised wearable devices may reveal significant personal information, and may facilitate the execution of attacks by an
adversary leading to, for example, the breach of private network security, covert
account takeover, and performing direct or indirect targeted attacks. Common
wearable devices use wireless communication standards, such as Bluetooth Classic (BT), Bluetooth low energy (BLE), or WiFi, to communicate with other
devices. Therefore these standards, their implementation, and inherent vulnerabilities are the focus of our research [20].

© The Author(s), under exclusive license to Springer Nature Switzerland AG 2022
H. P. Reiser and M. Kyas (Eds.): NordSec 2022, LNCS 13700, pp. 311–325, 2022.
https://doi.org/10.1007/978-3-031-22295-5_17

This paper provides the following contributions:

1. automated wireless wearable device security evaluation prototype conceptual design, its specific functionality requirements, and patent description;
2. the overview of the first stage of the prototype technical implementation.

This paper is structured as follows – Sect. 2 covers the related work on wireless device fingerprinting and security assessment; Sect. 3 describes the proposed system architecture conceptual prototype considerations for performing automated security evaluation of wireless wearable devices; Sect. 4 describes the specific implementation stages, issues encountered during the first stage of the prototype implementation, and solutions to overcome these problems; Sect. 5 discusses future work related to this research.

2 Related Work

For the envisioned approach we are aiming at a dual use system which can be used for unsupervised security review of wireless devices across multiple wireless protocols, identifying them and checking for known vulnerabilities, and also as a supporting testbed for experts performing vulnerability research. For the latter, there is specific research in IoT/wearable area such as the SecuWear platform [17,18] and others using the popular Ubertooth platform [16], however it has hardware limitations preventing from capturing the full data transmitted (e.g. Bluetooth Classic Enhanced Data Rate packets, and missed packets due to channel hopping), and they focus on manual exploration of vulnerabilities as opposed to automated fuzzing.

In our proposal the first step in a potential attack against wearable devices is the detection and identification of the device, such as fingerprinting to identify either a model or a specific device; followed by scanning for known vulnerabilities and applying fuzzing approaches to identify new potential vulnerabilities.

2.1 Device Detection and Fingerprinting

Device fingerprinting [40] is a method where the target device is identified using its unique features and imperfections of its hardware components and/or higher layer features. A combination of these unintended features and possibly values derived from these features are called device fingerprints. Fingerprinting process may be split into two parts: feature extraction and classification. The focus of this section is feature extraction. Successful fingerprinting may lead to serious security risks if the identified chipset has publicly known attack vectors with available exploitation proof-of-concept (PoC) code.

Feature extraction can start from the moment when the target device is powered and starts broadcasting or responding to incoming signals. For example, there are cases when a device may be identified by its signal level ramp time while the transmitter is turning on or off (i.e., transient-based radio frequency fingerprinting) [22]. The start and stop time of the transient signal can be found using Bayesian detection, variance fractal dimension threshold detection, phase detection, mean change point detection, or permutation entropy and generalized likelihood ratio test [38]. Further analysis of transient signal frequency and phase spectrum can also be done, however, the drawback of this method is that since the transient time is short high sample rates are required for accurate analysis. This method requires capturing to be started before the device (or its transmitting circuit) is powered and activated.

The implemented wireless standard determines carrier frequencies, which shall be used by the device. Since this frequency is generated by the use of a non-ideal radio frequency (RF) circuit in the transmitter some carrier offset is expected. This offset can also be used as one item of the RF fingerprint. To achieve a reliable data transmission it is important to deal with this expected CFO (carrier frequency offset) and it is usually solved in the transmission standard itself. For example, in Bluetooth, every advertising data packet contains some bits at the beginning of transmission, which the receiver uses to estimate and correct the CFO. The longer these training sequences are, the more precise the CFO estimate can be achieved.

Devices, which have both Bluetooth and WiFi functionality often use a combo chipset to combine both of these standards. Wireless protocol bits are encoded in I and Q channels, resulting in hardware imperfections such as IQ (In-phase and quadrature component) imbalance, IQ offset, and previously mentioned CFO [14]. IQ offset is the shift from the center of the constellation diagram [37]. IQ imbalance can be split into two imperfections: amplitude error and phase error. To quantify both of these errors EVM (error vector magnitude) [28] can be calculated. IQ imbalance occurs because the carrier oscillator signal at the Q channel is never perfectly offset by 90° when compared to the I channel, also it is very hard to achieve identical gain for both I and Q channel oscillator signal. IQ offset occurs because the baseband signal has a DC component and carrier frequency signal leaking through the mixer into the baseband signal. The usage of a combined chipset means that even though Bluetooth uses a GFSK (Gaussian frequency-shift keying) modulated signal, which might be implemented without the separation of I and Q signals, it will still have IQ imperfections.

There have also been successful attempts at fingerprinting using machine learning technology for image recognition, where the used image is compiled from RF samples. For example, waterfall images, constellation diagrams, and wavelet coefficients projected onto time scale plane or multiple windowed time diagram images compiled into one [2, 24, 26].

It is possible to fingerprint devices using features, which are present at higher levels of communication. There is no need for expensive specialized hardware to perform higher-layer fingerprinting. One could use a device, such as, Ubertooth [16], various WiFi dongles, or some other commercial-off-the-shelf tools. Researchers at [6] have used freely available open-source tools to extract GATT (Generic attribute profile), which contains a UUID (Universally unique identifier) of the device, which may reveal information about the device, used protocols as defined by the Bluetooth specification [3], service classes and profiles, GATT services, and manufacturer of thhe device.

There has been related work done on using response to non-standard IEEE 802.11 frame with modified MAC header as a WiFi fingerprinting method. Different devices responded differently to frames with control flags and frame types prohibited by IEEE 802.11 standards. This method yielded good results for fingerprinting access points, but not so good for client devices [4].

Researchers in [31] propose the following network parameters to be used as IEEE 802.11 device fingerprints:

1. Transmission rate as different NICs (Network interface cards) have a different distribution of used transmission rates;
2. Frame size, which depends on the data being sent;
3. Access time of the medium, the time device waits after transmission before going idle and starting to broadcast frames;
4. Time between received frames.

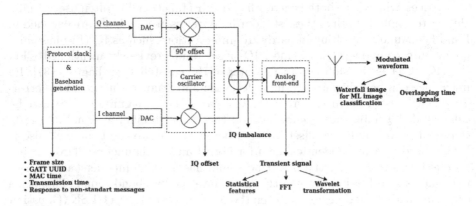

Fig. 1. Overview of extractable fingerprints

Figure 1 summarizes all of the previously described features, which may be used as fingerprints by their origin.

2.2   Vulnerability Identification

Within this project, the two main directions for vulnerability identification will be pursued:

1. known and publicly released vulnerability applicability, based on the DUT (device-under-test) passive fingerprinting and intercepted communication analysis;
2. active attempts to trigger unknown vulnerabilities by the use of *black-box* fuzz testing techniques.

To allow the identification of applicable publicly released vulnerabilities, enough details, such as, operating system and firmware build versions, have to be collected through the process of passive DUT fingerprinting. A vulnerability database assembled by researchers or available databases, such as, the well-known Exploit-DB [32], may be used to search for the best match of applicable vulnerabilities based on the extracted fingerprinting information. In cases, when existing databases do not include known vulnerabilities and related proof-of-concept code, the researchers should evaluate the database's completeness and perform its enrichment, if necessary. This approach to vulnerability identification heavily depends on two key factors: 1) implementing a set of efficient methods for device fingerprinting, and 2) developing a complete and structured database of applicable vulnerabilities. Within this research, a custom-structured database of identified and publicly released vulnerabilities related to wearable devices, their firmware, and their protocol stack implementations, will be attempted to be assembled to be used in the initial stages of the wireless DUT security assessment.

Discovery of the vulnerabilities would mostly be done through one or a combination of multiple approaches, such as, fuzz testing, reverse engineering, or source code analysis. However, in the scope of this research, only black-box fuzz testing is assessed due to having limited or no prior information related to the DUT implementation. Fuzz testing or fuzzing is a software testing technique aimed at uncovering issues, such as, coding errors and security vulnerabilities, by the use of random or malformed data to trigger an unexpected behavior [11,13]. In a nutshell, the two most commonly used fuzzing methods have been recognized [29]:

1. mutation-based (also referred to as coverage-guided or dumb fuzzing) - is aimed at introducing changes by modifying the existing values blindly (e.g., random values, bit-flips, and other binary modifications), that may keep the input valid, but trigger new or unexpected behavior. The injected test cases are derived from known good data, such as, captured Bluetooth communication frames;
2. generation-based (also referred to as behavior-based or intelligent fuzzing) - focuses on describing data and state models based upon the communication protocol specification (e.g., RFC).

The most recent relevant related work on Bluetooth fuzzing over the air is the Braktooth publication [9], detailing an approach and an engineering solution based on the modified firmware of an Espressif ESP32 development kit for instrumenting interventions in an otherwise well-behaved Bluetooth stack. There is also a similar work on Bluetooth Low Energy testing [10]. Attacks on BT (Bluetooth) and other accessory firmware are especially insidious, because in some popular configurations (e.g., iPhones) the Bluetooth chip will be powered and can be engaged in activities even when the primary device is turned off [8]. This is a relevant consideration within the risk profile of this project.

In contrast to the static vulnerability identification through DUT fingerprinting and lookup in a database of known vulnerabilities, the fuzz testing will heavily rely on three core aspects: 1) valid test case sample acquisition or their specification in accordance with the standard, 2) identification of protocol fields and their mutation strategies, and 3) required larger time-span for fuzz testing process execution and appropriate means of its orchestration to identify a likely anomaly or recover from a dead-end state. Within this research, both mutation-based and generation-based approaches may be employed, depending on the availability and openness of the wireless protocol specification. With the primary effort being set on mutation-based fuzz testing the loss of code coverage is anticipated [29]. The use of mutation-based fuzzing would permit the test case automated generation based on the captured frames during the device finger-printing process or when performing an active interrogation, while maintaining limited or no knowledge of the underlying communication protocols. This, in turn, may provide support for a wider range of wearable DUT testing, while considering a likely increased time and process context management penalties. The main goal for the initial active vulnerability identification is focused on identifying anomalous conditions, and not on in-depth assessment and zero-day vulnerability analysis for exploit development.

There has been significant work in the field of software vulnerability identification with fuzz testing technique development and tool implementations, both from academic [25], industry [12], and community [33] perspectives. The publication [21] lists and assess 32 research papers, which introduce novel fuzzing strategies and their tool implementation, however, by no means this is a conclusive list. Furthermore, it has to be noted, that the field of vulnerability assessment and fuzz testing is dynamic and constantly changing, with new projects appearing, and existing ones either being deprecated, abandoned, or reworked. To mention a few notable projects with a primary focus on mutation-based strategies – AFL (American Fuzzy Lop) [15], Boofuzz [35], Bbuzz [27], and Zzuf [5]; and with a primary focus on generation-based strategies – Peach [34] (now part of GitLab), Spike [19] (abandoned), and Defensics [39] (commercial solution).

3   Prototype Concept Description

To perform an automated security evaluation of wireless wearable devices, we introduce the key principles, define functional requirements and design an operational prototype of the technology. The anticipated design of a finalized prototype is similar to a security gate and utilizes an array of sensors, performing a variety of functional tests and assessments in a fully automated manner on devices being carried through this gate. Such a conceptual approach has been chosen to facilitate the security assessment of the wearable devices while being worn openly or being hidden by their wearer. Such an approach would permit the achievement of at least the following high-level effects: 1) assessing the security level of wearable devices worn by their user, 2) evaluation of identified vulnerabilities and their severity level, 3) prohibition of wearing and use of wearable devices at places with a certain security level, and 4) identification of hidden or clandestine wearable devices.

The core automated functionality tests and assessment of the wireless wearable devices are directed toward the following activities:

1. passive fingerprinting of wearable devices based on their radio spectrum broadcast interception. In this stage, the received broadcast data is being interpreted to identify at least the hardware chip manufacturer and its model and, if possible - the device itself, based on the transmitted data, its unique patterns, and signatures;
2. passive fingerprinting-based identification of known vulnerabilities of wearable devices. In this stage, the collected fingerprint data is queried against a database, which combines the known and publicly disclosed generic or specific vulnerabilities and their metadata for wireless wearable devices;
3. active interaction with wearable devices to validate the identified vulnerability, acquire further data for fingerprinting or perform automated tests to attempt triggering unknown vulnerabilities. In this stage, the identified vulnerabilities are further probed to validate their exploitability in case there is a publicly disclosed proof-of-concept exploit code. Secondly, active interaction evokes responses from the device, which allows for further fingerprinting. And thirdly, automated vulnerability identification and probing are done by the use of fuzz-testing approaches at the wireless protocol level.

The prototype process flow has the following blocks in a hierarchical order (Fig. 2):

1. wireless device-under-test (DUT). One or multiple commercial-off-the-shelf (COTS) wearable wireless devices under test;
2. wireless sensors with related hardware-protocol driver (HPD) modules. The prototype design includes a set of necessary hardware to cover the respective radio frequency bands used by the COTS wearable devices. This can be implemented using a chip designed for the protocols or generic SDR (software-defined radio). To enable the interaction with the DUT, related HPD integrations are required at the prototype model's operating system level (e.g., kernel modules and libraries). HPD modules are supervised by relevant wrappers to ensure the interaction with higher abstraction levels of the overall automated interaction process. It is important to note that the prototype needs to be able to gather not only data, which is relevant for normal device operation, but, also, side information (e.g. signal amplitude, frequency offset, etc.) for fingerprinting, and it needs to generate radio protocol variations, which sometimes might be outside normal bounds of the protocol specification. The wrapper permits interaction with a specific wireless sensor through the message queuing process;
3. asynchronous message queuing and management. This block allows the higher abstraction layers to inject and receive data intended for one or multiple HPDs;
4. domain-specific language (DSL) is a common API-based construct permitting to form the messages for injection or receiving data from the messaging queue. This layer permits either creation and interpretation of raw data packets or standard messages according to the wireless protocol specifications;

5. traffic recording and filtering capture all raw traffic as well as other parameters of the RF signal traversing HPD. This permits interaction with recorded wireless packet or frame data via DSL construct for purposes, such as, validation of delivered message compliance and received data interpretation for passive fingerprinting or assessing the results of fuzz-testing operations;
6. The user scripts are the top-level entity permitting the definition and conduct of activities by interacting via the DSL API. The user script may be written in any scripting or programming language allowing the JSON-based API interaction with the DSL.

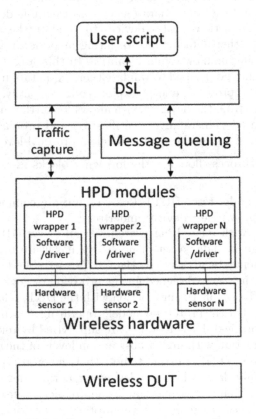

Fig. 2. Prototype concept process flow

The stages of the operational technological prototype development are addressed in the following order:

Stage 0. identification and acquisition of wearable DUTs and prototype hardware specification definition;

Stage 1. recording of the wearable device wireless communications in a broad spectrum range;

Stage 2. assessment and fingerprinting of the wireless communication patterns;
Stage 3. labeled data-set creation of recorded wireless communications for machine learning-assisted automated fingerprinting;
Stage 4. active device probing and assessment.

In this paper, the scope is kept within stage 1 of the prototype implementation, with respective implementation considerations and identified issues described in Sect. 4, while the overall high-level concept is described in submitted patent application [30].

4   Implementation Considerations

This chapter focuses on the Stage 1 implementation of the described prototype and aims to provide the attempted approaches taken, identified challenges and issues, and describe any applicable solutions.

The prototype will include both protocol-specific chips and a generic SDR mechanism. Readymade chips allow an easy way to communicate using standard protocol mechanisms without complex implementation efforts. At the same time, they are limited only to those functions that are allowed by the manufacturer and will neither allow significant deviations from the protocol nor allow the gathering of nuances of the radio signal. SDR allows any conceivable data collection and generation of any signal variations as long as we can implement those. The rest of this chapter elaborates on the choice and implementation of the SDR mechanism as readymade chip usage is relatively straightforward.

4.1   Frequency Bandwidth Consideration

To capture all the channels of Bluetooth and Bluetooth LE simultaneously a recording at an 80 MHz wide spectrum band is required. Within our tests, none of the low-cost SDR devices offered a bandwidth as wide as 80 MHz, and the use of multiple devices was considered to ensure the capture of the required bandwidth combined between the devices.

4.2   Choice of SDR Device

The first device we tested was a widely known hobbyist SDR device *HackRF One* by Great Scott Gadgets. It provides up to 20 million complex samples per second, thus we would need four such devices to record the whole 80 MHz bandwidth.

Another positive side to HackRF was previous references on using multiple hardware synchronized devices for recording (such as described on this blog: https://olegkutkov.me/tag/hackrf/ and a different method implemented in firmware [1].

Following initial tests with HackRF, we came to the conclusion that described method of hardware synchronization does not easily lead us to results. Synchronization of the HackRF devices on the firmware level was clearly described only for two devices, but we needed four. Though from the description we could guess that it is extendable to more devices, the way to do this was not obvious.

A major issue we encountered with HackRF was the differing quality of the four devices. Signal level, signal-to-noise-ratio (SNR), and other characteristics differed widely across the devices, sometimes by more than 10 dB. This introduced an inconvenience in data processing, as it was clear that for each recording the four streams have to be put through calibration routines to be convenient for analysis, and some issues (e.g. differing SNR) cannot be easily taken away even with calibration. Also, this creates a risk that our recordings might not be easily repeatable by other HackRF devices.

Of course, this is likely not something that is wrong with HackRF One device design itself, but more of different manufacturing and supply chains for each of the devices. As HackRF is an open hardware design, they are produced not only by the original manufacturer but, also, by other unlicenced manufacturers with possibly different quality assurance processes and possible variations in hardware components.

We had an option to procure other four HackRF One devices with additional emphasis on ensuring they come from the original manufacturer. This was complicated from a procurement perspective as the original manufacturer is not represented locally, and we did not have control of the procurement processes of local suppliers. Thus we made a decision to utilize existing HackRF One devices by the team for individual exploratory experiments and look for alternative SDR devices.

We identified 3 manufacturers providing devices within our budget and quality criteria:

- Ettus Research USRP B series
- Nuand BladeRF
- Lime Microsystems LimeSDR

After limited experiments with BladeRF we chose Ettus Research products due to better software support in GNU Radio, which was part of the plan for the software stack. Also, "UHD: USRP source" (the block providing integration with Ettus Research SDRs from GNU Radio) provides tagging of the data capture overruns, which turned out to be a repeating issue in our experimentation when capturing the full Bluetooth spectrum. We did not identify comparable features in competing products.

The eventually chosen hardware setup was combining two Ettus Research USRP b205mini devices with synchronized clocks, which provide 56 Msps each, covering the required 80 MHz bandwidth.

4.3   Data Capture Bandwidth Issues

The first issue we encountered during experiments was - the limited throughput of the USB connection. Initial recordings had a mismatch of data file size compared to the expected value (based on recording time and sample size in bytes).

Unfortunately, none of the software tools (GNU radio and HackRF native CLI tools) we used had an in-built capability to warn us of the issue. We concluded that data loss is due to loss in USB connection as data loss further down the processing shall be identified by the software processing stack.

The second issue was the disk writing speed. We wanted to use GNU radio for initial processing steps as it provided the convenience of visual feedback (via built-in frequency and waterfall sinks) and a library of built-in filters and other tools. The minimal data rate for raw data from the device is 2×12 bits $\times 80$ Msps, which equals 240 MBps with optimal data packing, which could match the SSD writing speed of a single drive. GNU Radio typically uses 2×32 bit floating point numbers to represent a complex data stream and saves them into the file in this format. Thus the size of the stream becomes 8 bytes $\times 80$ Msps, which equals 640 MBps. This in turn exceeded the writing speed of our commodity SSD hardware.

Theoretically, we could have used a more optimal data recording format, but this would decrease the convenience of using the default format and would require additional work on creating data packing code. Also, we knew that we cannot predict all the specific needs for the next stages, and we might need to store processed data for which converting to 2×12 bit complex numbers might lead to loss of precision, therefore it would create additional software incompatibility risks and overhead, which cannot be fully estimated at the moment. Ultimately, we chose to keep the default data format of GNU radio and to overcome disk writing speed limitations we chose a RAM-based disk for the recording process. If we would need to decrease stored sampled sizes, we can add postprocessing in the future.

Another gain of this approach was faster data processing speed as reading and writing data to/from RAM-based disk is significantly faster than commodity SSD.

The only drawback (considered minor by us) was another procurement need - additional RAM for the processing computer. Fortunately, this is a common procurement need and was easy to implement. As a result, the following workstation for data collection and analysis was acquired for data acquisition and processing:

- CPU: Intel Xeon Silver 4208 (32) @ 3.2 GHz;
- RAM: 1 TB;
- HDD: 10 TB;
- SSD: 512 GB;
- Kernel: 5.15.0-25-generic;
- OS: Ubuntu 22.04 LTS.

4.4   Interference by Surrounding Signals

As the 2.4 GHz band is full of other signals, such as, WiFi, Zigbee, and other BT devices, which are out of the scope of this research, one of the challenges in preparing a radio data stream dataset is making a clean recording without the noise. Even though the most obvious solution would be a Faraday cage, it is not sufficient, because the signals would be reflected within the cage multiple times leading to interference, thus for this purpose, it was decided that we need to design an electronic anechoic chamber environment. Such an environment insulates external transmissions as a Faraday cage but also has internal absorbers, that absorb any internal signal without reflecting it. The dimensions of such environment and absorbers must be comparable to wavelengths of interest, thus the dimensions cannot be too small. We opted for external dimensions of 1 m, that satisfy this requirement. Also, in order to reduce any leaking of external signals all data lines for conducting the experiment are optically disconnected to isolate internal and external signals of this environment. This also allows us to test malicious transmissions, which should not be allowed in public environments. Additionally, the power supply for test equipment must also be filtered in order to isolate external signals further.

The electronic anechoic chamber we are currently acquiring has the following technical properties:

- Outside dimensions: 1.0 m × 1.0 m × 1.0 m;
- Inside dimensions (from the edge of absorbers): 0.8 m × 0.8 m × 0.8 m;
- RF parameters: 100 dB attenuation from 150 kHz to 10 GHz;
- Connections: 4 optically decoupled USB 3 connectors, power sockets that supply filtered 220 V 16 A;
- Material: Stainless steel with foam pyramid absorbers.

By using an electronic anechoic chamber we are ensuring that devices under test are sources of all activity in the radio frequency spectrum, no external signals will interfere with the experiments, and also the experiments will not interfere with external signals.

4.5   Lack of Open Source, Instrumentable Low-Level Protocol Stack

A key limitation for protocol analysis and interaction (especially, using SDR) is the availability of the open-source, instrumentable low-level protocol stack. Bluetooth is a complex set of protocols, which are not described clearly thus it is not trivial to implement correct behavior. Our requirements include particular modifications to the protocol to attempt the exploitation of the protocol vulnerability, and the available implementations of lower protocol layers are all closed source compiled firmware, which will perform only standards-compliant behavior.

The key part is the ability to receive and send arbitrary, modified, or noncompliant Bluetooth frames without having to reimplement the full Bluetooth protocol functionality. The approach proposed by Braktooth [9] relies on a reverse-engineered and modified version of the existing Espressif firmware for ESP32 systems that allows it to intercept BT packets and forward them to a computer controlling logic, which may craft an appropriate BT response packet in the time that is required to respond. Other authors propose an approach that instruments and observes the firmware on a phone or computer [36], which allows more effective fuzzing but is limited to the specific chipsets used on phones and computers.

5   Conclusions and Future Work

The main conclusion from the current implementation stage is that the identified engineering challenges are not an obstacle to implementing the proposed prototype concept and this would be a usable framework for automated security evaluation of wireless wearable devices. The development of the prototype is currently a work in progress, with the key hardware and software infrastructure working as a proof of concept, but still needing development on the DSL/HPD interface part. We hope that the lessons learned from our practical experimentation will be useful for other researchers working on low-cost RF protocol analysis.

The immediate future work includes recording and publishing an RF dataset for analysis and direct experimentation with protocol fuzzing, replicating the existing experiments, and extending it to a broader set of devices, focusing specifically on wearable devices. The dataset should be open and expandable in the future in a standardized way.

Future work towards automated vulnerability discovery should focus on the following aspects:

1. identification, implementation, and validation methods and approaches for wireless wearable device fingerprinting;
2. assembly of a dedicated vulnerability database, based on known and publicly released vulnerabilities affecting wireless wearable devices;
3. evaluation, design, and validation of applicable black-box fuzz testing approaches and methods for mutation-based and generation-based strategies;
4. implementation of the fuzz testing test case generation, process management, and physical wireless wearable device state identification and recovery, with limited feedback or interaction capabilities.

Acknowledgements. This research is funded by the Latvian Council of Science, project "Automated wireless security analysis for wearable devices", project No. LZP-2020/1-0395.

References

1. Bartolucci, M., del Peral-Rosado, J.A., Estatuet-Castillo, R., Garcia-Molina, J.A., Crisci, M., Corazza, G.E.: Synchronisation of low-cost open source sdrs for navigation applications. In: 2016 8th ESA Workshop on Satellite Navigation Technologies and European Workshop on GNSS Signals and Signal Processing (NAVITEC), pp. 1–7. IEEE (2016)
2. Bertoncini, C., Rudd, K., Nousain, B., Hinders, M.: Wavelet fingerprinting of radio-frequency identification (RFID) tags. IEEE Trans. Industr. Electron. **59**(12), 4843–4850 (2011)
3. Bluetooth SIG Inc: Assigned numbers. https://www.bluetooth.com/specifications/assigned-numbers/. Accessed 26 Aug 2022
4. Bratus, S., Cornelius, C., Kotz, D., Peebles, D.: Active behavioral fingerprinting of wireless devices. In: Proceedings of the first ACM Conference on Wireless Network Security, pp. 56–61 (2008)

5. Caca Labs: zzuf - multi-purpose fuzzer. http://caca.zoy.org/wiki/zzuf. Accessed 30 Aug 2022
6. Celosia, G., Cunche, M.: Fingerprinting bluetooth-low-energy devices based on the generic attribute profile. In: Proceedings of the 2nd International ACM Workshop on Security and Privacy for the Internet-of-Things, pp. 24–31 (2019)
7. Cilliers, L.: Wearable devices in healthcare: privacy and information security issues. Health Inf. Manag. J. **49**(2-3), 150–156 (2020). https://doi.org/10.1177/1833358319851684. PMID: 31146589
8. Classen, J., Heinrich, A., Reith, R., Hollick, M.: Evil never sleeps: when wireless malware stays on after turning off iphones. In: Proceedings of the 15th ACM Conference on Security and Privacy in Wireless and Mobile Networks, pp. 146–156. WiSec '22, Association for Computing Machinery, New York, NY, USA (2022). https://doi.org/10.1145/3507657.3528547
9. Garbelini, M.E., Chattopadhyay, S., Bedi, V., Sun, S., Kurniawan, E.: Braktooth: causing havoc on bluetooth link manager (2021)
10. Garbelini, M.E., Wang, C., Chattopadhyay, S., Sumei, S., Kurniawan, E.: *SweynTooth*: unleashing mayhem over bluetooth low energy. In: 2020 USENIX Annual Technical Conference (USENIX ATC 20), pp. 911–925 (2020)
11. Garg, P.: Fuzzing: mutation vs. generation. https://resources.infosecinstitute.com/topic/fuzzing-mutation-vs-generation/. Accessed 28 Aug 2022
12. GitLab: Devsecops with gitlab. https://about.gitlab.com/solutions/dev-sec-ops/. Accessed 30 Aug 2022
13. GitLab DEVSECOPS blog: What is fuzz testing?. https://about.gitlab.com/topics/devsecops/what-is-fuzz-testing/. Accessed 28 Aug 2022
14. Givehchian, H., et al.: Evaluating physical-layer ble location tracking attacks on mobile devices. In: IEEE Symposium on Security and Privacy (SP) (2022)
15. Google: american fuzzy lop. https://github.com/google/AFL Accessed 28 Aug 2022
16. Great Scott Gadgets: Ubertooth one. https://greatscottgadgets.com/ubertoothone/. Accessed 26 Aug 2022
17. Hale, M.L., Ellis, D., Gamble, R., Waler, C., Lin, J.: Secu wear: an open source, multi-component hardware/software platform for exploring wearable security. In: 2015 IEEE International Conference on Mobile Services, pp. 97–104. IEEE (2015)
18. Hale, M.L., Lotfy, K., Gamble, R.F., Walter, C., Lin, J.: Developing a platform to evaluate and assess the security of wearable devices. Digit. Commun. Netw. **5**(3), 147–159 (2019)
19. ImmunitySec: Spike. https://www.kali.org/tools/spike/. Accessed 30 Aug 2022
20. Ken Research: Worldwide wearable devices cybersecurity market. https://www.kenresearch.com/defense-and-security/security-devices/worldwide-wearable-devices/179018-16.html. Accessed 28 Aug 2022
21. Klees, G., Ruef, A., Cooper, B., Wei, S., Hicks, M.: Evaluating fuzz testing. In: Proceedings of the 2018 ACM SIGSAC Conference on Computer and Communications Security, pp. 2123–2138. CCS'18, Association for Computing Machinery, New York, NY, USA (2018). https://doi.org/10.1145/3243734.3243804
22. Köse, M., Taşcioğlu, S., Telatar, Z.: RF fingerprinting of IoT devices based on transient energy spectrum. IEEE Access **7**, 18715–18726 (2019). https://doi.org/10.1109/ACCESS.2019.2896696
23. Laricchia, F.: Number of connected wearable devices worldwide from 2016 to 2022. https://www.statista.com/statistics/487291/global-connected-wearable-devices/. Accessed 28 Aug 2022

24. Li, B., Cetin, E.: Waveform domain deep learning approach for RF fingerprinting. In: 2021 IEEE International Symposium on Circuits and Systems (ISCAS), pp. 1–5. IEEE (2021)
25. Liang, J., Wang, M., Chen, Y., Jiang, Y., Zhang, R.: Fuzz testing in practice: obstacles and solutions. In: 2018 IEEE 25th International Conference on Software Analysis, Evolution and Reengineering (SANER), pp. 562–566 (2018). https://doi.org/10.1109/SANER.2018.8330260
26. Liu, D., Wang, M., Wang, H.: RF fingerprint recognition based on spectrum waterfall diagram. In: 2021 18th International Computer Conference on Wavelet Active Media Technology and Information Processing (ICCWAMTIP), pp. 613–616. IEEE (2021)
27. Lockout: Bbuzz: a bit-aware network protocol fuzzing and reverse engineering framework. https://github.com/lockout/Bbuzz. Accessed 28 Aug 2022
28. Mahmoud, H.A., Arslan, H.: Error vector magnitude to snr conversion for nondata-aided receivers. IEEE Trans. Wireless Commun. 8(5), 2694–2704 (2009)
29. Miller, C., Peterson, Z.N.: Analysis of mutation and generation-based fuzzing. DefCon vol. 15 (2007). https://defcon.org/images/defcon-15/dc15-presentations/Miller/Whitepaper/dc-15-miller-WP.pdf
30. Nesenbergs, K., Paikens, P., Blumbergs, B., Rusins, A., Dobelis, E.: Apparatus and method for wireless security analysis of wearable devices (2022). IV Patent application No. EPLV202200000033380
31. Neumann, C., Heen, O., Onno, S.: An empirical study of passive 802.11 device fingerprinting. In: 2012 32nd International Conference on Distributed Computing Systems Workshops, pp. 593–602. IEEE (2012)
32. Offensive Security: Exploit-DB. https://www.exploit-db.com/ Accessed 26 Aug 2022
33. OWASP: Fuzzing. https://owasp.org/www-community/Fuzzing Accessed 30 Aug 2022
34. Peach: Peach fuzzer community edition. https://peachtech.gitlab.io/peach-fuzzer-community/ Accessed 30 Aug 2022
35. Pereyda, J.: boofuzz: network protocol fuzzing for humans. https://github.com/jtpereyda/boofuzz. Accessed 30 Aug 2022
36. Ruge, J., Classen, J., Gringoli, F., Hollick, M.: Frankenstein: advanced wireless fuzzing to exploit new bluetooth escalation targets. In: 29th USENIX Security Symposium (USENIX Security 20), pp. 19–36. USENIX Association (2020). https://www.usenix.org/conference/usenixsecurity20/presentation/ruge
37. Sköld, M., Yang, J., Sunnerud, H., Karlsson, M., Oda, S., Andrekson, P.A.: Constellation diagram analysis of DPSK signal regeneration in a saturated parametric amplifier. Opt. Express 16(9), 5974–5982 (2008)
38. Soltanieh, N., Norouzi, Y., Yang, Y., Karmakar, N.C.: A review of radio frequency fingerprinting techniques. IEEE J. Radio Freq. Identif. 4(3), 222–233 (2020)
39. Synopsys: Defensics fuzz testing. https://www.synopsys.com/software-integrity/security-testing/fuzz-testing.html
40. Xu, Q., Zheng, R., Saad, W., Han, Z.: Device fingerprinting in wireless networks: challenges and opportunities. IEEE Commun. Surveys Tutorials 18(1), 94–104 (2015)

Forensics

Maraudrone's Map: An Interactive Web Application for Forensic Analysis and Visualization of DJI Drone Log Data

Tobias Latzo[1]([⊠]), Andreas Hellmich[2], Annika Knepper[2], Lukas Hardi[1],
Tim Phillip Castello-Waldow[1], Felix Freiling[2], and Andreas Attenberger[1]

[1] Central Office for Information Technology in the Security Sector (ZITiS),
Munich, Germany
`{tobias.latzo,lukas.hardi,timphillip.castellowaldow,`
`andreas.attenberger}@ZITiS.bund.de`

[2] Friedrich-Alexander-Universität Erlangen-Nürnberg (FAU), Erlangen, Germany
`{andreas.hellmich,annika.knepper,felix.freiling}@fau.de`

Abstract. Unmanned Aerial Vehicles (also known as *drones*) are an increasingly important source of forensic evidence, especially for commercial drones offered by the market leader DJI. The forensic analysis of this type of evidence, however, is still in its infancy. We present the design and implementation of an open-source tool that supports the visualization and analysis of log data acquired in the DATv3 format, which is the standard log format used by DJI. In our evaluation we not only show the usefulness of the interactive visualization of our tool, but also give an empirical overview over the log message types and other artefacts that can be used for anomaly and manipulation detection, an extensible feature also offered by our tool.

Keywords: DJI · UAV · Visualization · Log analysis · Anomaly detection

1 Introduction

Over the past years, drones have been established as widespread *Unmanned Aerial Vehicles* (UAV) that are also popular with private customers as well as enterprises. Today's drones are easy to fly, mostly used for taking photos or videos and are offered for a reasonable price. In 2021, the Chinese manufacturer *Shenzhen DJI Sciences and Technologies Ltd.* (DJI) had the biggest market share in this area [17]—despite the bigger drop of the market share in DJI's commercial drone market share. DJI is also popular with authorities and fire departments [6]. Usually, these drones are controlled via a remote control that is connected to a smartphone or tablet. The smartphone or tablet runs an app that shows a live feed from the camera and other telemetry data.

Supplementary Information The online version contains supplementary material available at https://doi.org/10.1007/978-3-031-22295-5_18.

However, the ever-increasing spread of drones can also entail security issues. In 2018, hundreds of flights at the Gatwick airport were cancelled due to reports of drone activity. Also, cheaper consumer drones have already been used for drug trafficking [15], spying [9], or for dropping fireworks [18].

When it comes to an incident and the police is able to seize a drone, it needs to be analyzed forensically. Drones often come with a flight recorder that is probably originally intended for checking warranty claims. However, there is no standard that allows authorities to analyze these logs. For example, DJI generates massive propriety log data during the flight in so called DAT files. Besides the GPS track the logs contain many other sensor data that can be relevant during a forensic investigation.

In this paper we introduce an easily extensible interactive web application that visualizes DJI drone log data. Additionally, it is also able to analyze the logs for anomalies that can help the investigator to find data of interest.

1.1   Related Work

The number of drone incidents increased [5] and so drone forensics has become a lively topic. This is documented by a recent survey by Al-Dhaqm et al. [1] who reviewed more than 30 papers in the field of drone forensics. They observed that the security of drones has become better and better but that this also makes acquisition of log files more difficult. Based on a review of existing drone forensic analysis models, the authors developed an integrated forensic model that can help digital forensic investigations of drones. The authors also assert that, while many tools for forensic analysis exist, they either are not specific to drone data or are not open-source.

A notable exception is *DRone Open source Parser* (DROP) [3], an open-source software framework implemented to parse DAT files for the DJI Phantom III. The authors also studied the log files that are generated by the corresponding mobile app and correlated these logs with the logs that are resident on the drone's non-volatile storage. They showed that the best way of acquiring the on-board logs is to remove the glued-in microSD card of the DJI Phantom III and to not turn it on since this may delete older logs. DROP, however, neither supports newer versions of the DJI log format nor does it offer visualization.

There is also some existing work in the field of anomaly detection of DJI flight records. Moon et al. [14] address the problem of whether a drone incident was caused by malfunction, crime, mistake or external forces by trying to detect drone anomalies in the flight records of a DJI Phantom 4. For this, they make use of motor current values and controller direction values. Basically it is possible to detect some abnormal flight data on the four main axes (forwards, backwards, rightwards, and leftwards), but they do not provide any software to replicate the results. Furthermore, Lieser et al. [13] utilized the *Inertial Measurement Unit* (IMU) sensor data to interact with the drone via user taps.

1.2   Contribution

In this paper, we analyze DJI's drone log messages and introduce a tool for their visualization. Our main contributions are as follows:

- We extend the *DRone Open source Parser* (DROP) [3] so it is also able to parse DATv3 log files. Our extension also offers human-readable JSON output. Since we publish the code open-source[1], the code can serve as a documentation of DJI's DATv3 format.
- We introduce *Maraudrone's Map*[2] which visualizes DJI's DATv3 log files that were parsed with DROP. Maraudrone's Map is implemented as an interactive, easily extensible web application and easy to use. It is designed to play-back a flight. The user can choose from a variety of sensor data to be displayed in interactive graphs. For transparent analysis of data provenance, there is always a link to the raw JSON messages and also a link back to the original DAT files.
- To make digital forensic investigations more efficient, Maraudrone's Map also allows to detect various anomalies. Our application can be extended by adding self-written modules for detecting anomalies.

1.3   Outline

In Sect. 2 we give some background information that is needed to understand the rest of the paper. Section 3 is about the DROP extension for DATv3. In Sect. 4 we classify and define anomalies that can be detected. Furthermore, in Sect. 5 we describe the implementation of Maraudrone's Map. In Sect. 6 we evaluate the DROP extension and Maraudrone's Map. Eventually, Sect. 7 concludes this paper.

2   Background

In this section we provide some background information about the drones we use for our experiments (see Sect. 2.1). We show the setup of the drones and describe what logging information is typically saved on them (see Sect. 2.2). Furthermore, in Sect. 2.3 we describe the *DJI Universal Markup Language* that is used for the communication.

2.1   UAV Models

We investigate three major drone models of the manufacturer DJI [8]: DJI Phantom 4 Advanced, DJI Inspire 2, and the DJI Matrice 600 Pro. We start with the widespread DJI Phantom 4 Advanced, a mid-size quadcopter (1.3 kg) designed mainly for the private and semi-professional sector. It is equipped with four rotors and can fly as fast as 72 km/h up to 30 min while carrying a 332 g camera.

---

[1] https://github.com/dumbledrone/DROP.
[2] https://github.com/dumbledrone/MaraudronesMap.

Following that, we examine the professional drone DJI Inspire 2. Since it can carry professional camera equipment as heavy as 800 g while flying for 25 min up to 94 km/h, its large size and high weight (3.44 kg), it is mainly used by film-making crews. We were able to extract the log files from the glued-in microSD card (see Fig. 1). Next we looked at the DJI Matrice 600 Pro—a large and heavy (9.5 kg) hexacopter made for industrial use with a payload capacity of 6 kg. This is achieved by six rotors, enabling the drone to fly for up to 32 min depending on the carried weight. Similarly to the DJI Inspire 2 the log files were located in a glued-in microSD card.

Fig. 1. Flight recorder module of the DJI Inspire 2 with a glued-in microSD card (top, marked in red). (Color figure online)

2.2   DJI Drone Setup

The DJI drone setups of our investigated devices are as follows (see Fig. 2). A smartphone or tablet is connected with the remote control via USB. The smartphone needs to start a specific app, i.e., *DJI Go 4* or *DJI Go* [7]. On the screen, the user can see a live video feed as well as *On-Screen Display* (OSD) information, i.e., telemetry data like the battery level, altitude, horizontal and vertical speeds, etc. Basically, the drone is controlled via the remote control. There are also (semi-)automatic flight manoeuvres possible like follow a person, circle around a point of interest or return-to-home. These usually require input via the app. It is also possible to change flight parameters like the maximum altitude via the app.

DJI drones store videos and photographs in higher quality on a microSD card that can easily be removed. Furthermore, DJI drones perform a significant amount of activity logging. The corresponding logs are stored in files which are named FLYXYZ.DAT with XYZ signifying a consecutive three digit number. All our investigated models store the log data on the internal glued-in microSD card. Figure 1 shows the flight recorder module of the DJI Inspire 2 with the attached microSD card. Although the log can often be downloaded with the computer, it is recommended to directly copy them from the microSD card. If the computer is used, the drone needs to be switched on and so older log files can be removed. The computer application additionally encrypts the logs. However, the key can be easily extracted. Furthermore, it is also possible to download the logs directly from the FTP server.

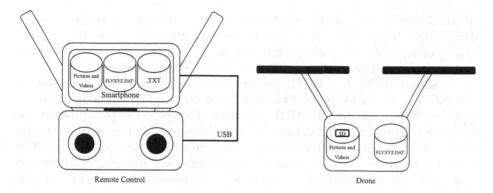

Fig. 2. Overview of a typical DJI drone setup with the relevant data including the corresponding data storage locations.

The app stores pictures and videos in lower quality. Furthermore, the app stores DAT and TXT files. However, these DAT files contain much less logging data. The TXT files can be displayed using the *DJI GO 4* app. Here the flight can be replayed while all OSD information is visible. In this paper, we focus on the DAT files of the drone.

2.3   DJI Universal Markup Language

Block	Header						Log-Info				Payload					Tail	
Description	Magic	Length	Version	CRC8	Source	Destination	Tick				Log-Message Payload					CRC16	
Offset	00	01	02	03	04	05	06	07	08	09	0A	0B	0C	0D	... FD	FE	FF
Blocksize [Byte]	6						4				0...253					2	

Fig. 3. The DUML log message format.

The *DJI Universal Markup Language* (DUML) protocol is used for the communication between onboard hardware components as well as for the communication to peripheral components. As the information in the log files (DAT files) of the UAV contains DUML messages, it was necessary for us to understand the message structure. Several tools and publications offer an overview over the structure of DUML messages [2,3,16]. Knowledge of the protocol message structure is a pre-requisite for further analysis. In the following, we describe the

DUML format that occurs in the DAT files. In its shortest form, a DUML message shows a length of 13 bytes in total. The length of the message can be extended to a maximum of 255 bytes by adding a payload of variable length. Messages containing a larger payload are split into several, single messages.

As shown in Fig. 3, a DUML message can be split into four main blocks. The message header as the first block (offset 0x00 to 0x05) contains the magic byte, which is 0x55 for all DUML messages. The second byte represents the length of the message, followed by one byte characterizing the protocol version of the message. This is followed by an error protection, derived from a CRC8 checksum. Furthermore, the header contains transport information. Hence, it consists of one byte identifying the source of the message followed by one byte as index for the destination.

The next block (offset 0x06 to 0x09) of a DUML message contains the tick number. The tick number represents the internal bus clock and is stored with each packet.

The *message type* (or *packet type*) of a DUML message is identified by the source and destination bytes (see Fig. 3). As we later show, there are some packet types that not yet understood, i.e., only a subset of around 30 packet types are analyzable. We will return to this topic in Sect. 3.

The tick block is followed by the payload of the message. Here, different parameters (for example, longitude, latitude, velocities, height, rotational speeds, voltages) are encoded and transmitted [2]. The DUML message is closed by a two bytes tail, derived from a CRC16-checksum [16].

3   DROP Extension for DATv3

Before the DJI log data can be visualized and analyzed for anomalies, it needs to be parsed. For this, we make use of the *DRone Open source Parser* (DROP) [3]. Since the original DROP is implemented to parse DATv2 log files, we extended DROP to also support DATv3. We did this by analyzing DatCon [10]. In this section, we describe the implementation of this DROP extension. Note that we focus on DROP's parsing functionality and not on the correlation of DAT and TXT files.

DROP is implemented for Python 3.4. We neither make use of any other language features nor have any other dependencies. Our implementation is tested with Python 3.10 on macOS Monterey (12.5). We used the DJI Phantom 4 Advanced (see Sect. 2.1) as a reference drone. However, the evaluation in Sect. 6 showed that we can also parse DATv3 logs of other UAVs.

3.1   Usage

The original DROP application [3] saves the result as a CSV file. Each parsed sensor value is represented as a value in a column. These values are updated when a corresponding message appears, i.e., in the CSV it is harder to find out which message updated a value. For this reason, we introduce JSON output with the -j switch. Each parsed DUML message is represented by a JSON object. Maraudrone's Map (see Sect. 5) expects DROP's JSON output.

To generate a suitable JSON file, the following command can be executed:

./DROP.py −j DAT_FILE

Table 1 shows the four new switches that we introduced to DROP. For Maraudrone's Map only the -j switch is necessary. Note that using this switch only the DUML messages that can be visualized by Maraudrone's Map (see Sect. 5) are extracted and not all messages. For deeper manual analysis, i.e., to analyze also the unknown message types, the other switches can be used (especially -a).

Table 1. DROP's new switches.

Switch	Description
-a	Create additional output files containing all unknown messages
-g	Create additional output files containing only GPS messages
-v	Include all messages in standard output file
-j	Create JSON output file instead of CSV

3.2 Parsing of Log Messages

First, we need to distinguished between DATv2 and DATv3 files. This can be done by parsing the log file's header information. Note, DATv2's header is 128 bytes in size. DATv3's header is 256 bytes in size and contains the ASCII letters DJI_LOG_V3 at offset 0xF2.

DAT files consist of multiple DUML messages (see Sect. 2.3), i.e., each messages starts with the magic value 0x55. DROP then reads successively the log messages (also referred to as packets). The packet length is defined in each DUML packet (see Fig. 3).

The payload of our analyzed DUML messages is XOR encrypted. The encryption scheme is very simple and has not changed for DJI LOG V3. The encryption key k is calculated as $k = t \bmod 256$ where t is the current *tick number* (see also Fig. 3). Each byte of the payload is xor'd with k. After decryption of the payload, it can be decoded.

Our DROP extension comprises more than 30 packet types using the -a switch. Without that switch, DROP parses 15 different packet types which are currently sufficient for the visualization in Maraudrone's Map (see Table 2).

Listing 1.1 shows an example of a gps message in the JSON format. All parsed message types can be found in the corresponding repository in modules/V3Messages.

4   Anomaly Detection

When it comes to an incident, the digital forensic investigator faces the problem of finding the reason why the incident happened. A specific manoeuvre may be

Table 2. DROP's standard packet types that are visualized in Maraudrone's Map.

#	Label	Description
1	gps	Contains the GPS coordinates
2	battery_info	Contains battery information
3	controller	Contains information of the remote control
4	usonic	Contains sensor data of the ultrasonic sensor
5	osd_general_data	Contains OSD data for the app
6	osd_home	Contains OSD data of the home point
7	rc_debug_info	Contains debug information of the remote controller
8	imu_atti	Contains sensor data of the *Inertial Measurement Unit* (IMU)
9	esc_data	Contains data of the *Electronic Speed Controller* (ESC)
10	rec_mag	Contains information of the compass
11	motorctrl	Contains PWM data of the motors
12	recordSD_logs	
13	flylog	Contain text-based log messages
14	syscfg	
15	recflylog	

caused by external forces (e.g., wind), malfunction, manipulation or intention. In this section we define and classify some anomalies that might be useful for digital forensic investigations. All anomalies we identified were determined empirically using the DJI Phantom 4 Advanced. However, we observed that this also applies to other models. Since there is a diversity of sensory data in the logs, we expect that there are many similar anomalies that can be detected.

We distinguish between *technical anomalies* (see Sect. 4.1) and *flight anomalies* (see Sect. 4.2).

```
{
    "date": 20220501,
    "time": "9:35:21",
    "longitude": 49.1038296,
    "latitude": 11.7279622,
    "altitude": 344.262,
    ...
    "messageid": 47542981,
    "pktId": 2096,
    "offset": 1015597
}
```

Listing 1.1. Example of a parsed GPS message. We have redacted the coordinates for the review.

4.1 Technical Anomalies

We identified two technical anomalies that may occur. Technical anomalies are those that are not directly related to the flight or flight control but technical artefacts.

Controller Ticks. First, the remote control sends ticks in the field `ctrl_ticks`. These ticks are numbered in ascending order starting with 0. Usually, there is no gap between those ticks. Bigger gaps may be an indicator that the communication between the UAV and the remote control was lost. Also, manipulation can be a reason.

GPS Packet Frequency. Our reference flights revealed that the log files contain about five GPS packets per second. Major deviations should also be considered more closely.

4.2 Flight Anomalies

Flight anomalies are based on actual sensor data. We identified three flight anomalies.

Battery Capacity. The battery capacity decreases steadily. This means, the battery capacity should not increase. Furthermore, there are many battery logs and gaps should not appear.

Drone Orientation. Using the internal compass, the orientation of the drone is logged frequently. This means there should not be any major fluctuations. These would be indications that there could be some problems with the compass. External forces or a crash are also possible. Furthermore, we check if the commands of the remote control match sensor values of the drone. This means, we expect that if the joystick input is more than 20%, there should be some reaction of the drone that is observable in the nearer future.

Rotor Speed. Here, we also check if the rotor speeds match the commands of the remote control. This mean acceleration, slow down, increase of altitude, or decrease of altitude. Here, we also expect a change of the rotor speeds in the nearer future if the joystick input is more than 20%. However, we get a lot of anomalies when there is movement regarding multiple axes as Moon et al. [14] also observed. Additionally, we check if one rotor is stopped while the others are rotating.

4.3 Severity of Anomalies

The anomalies we described in the previous sections were determined empirically. A detection of an anomaly does not automatically mean that something is wrong but is more meant as an indication that there could be something wrong. Usual log files also exhibit some anomalies. To help a digital forensic investigator better understand the anomaly we additionally define different severity levels (see Table 3) that quantify it.

Table 3. Severity levels of anomalies.

Level	Description
Severe	Should not appear in regular flights, have a potentially high impact on the flight
Medium	May appear in regular flights and have a potentially medium impact on the flight
Minor	Appear quite often in regular flights and have a potentially low impact on the flight

5 Maraudrone's Map

Maraudrone's Map is an easy-to-use, interactive, easy extensible, forensic, Angular-based [11] web application that visualizes DJI drone log data. The drone log data needs to be preprocessed using our DROP extension (see Sect. 3). The imported log files are stored locally in the browser's IndexedDB.

We make use of observables, i.e., every display element is implemented as an Angular component. This makes it easy to extend the application by further display components.

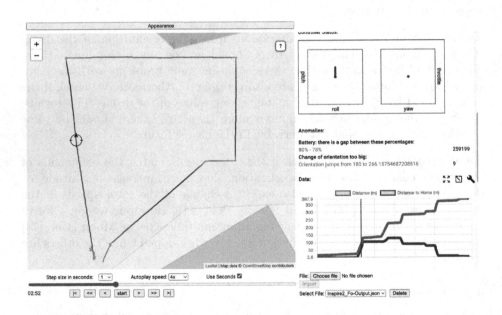

Fig. 4. Screenshot of Maraudrone's map.

Figure 4 shows a screenshot of Maraudrone's Map. The screen is divided into three components in two columns. On the upper left hand side, the map with the drone's track is shown. Below, there is a timeline of the flight including buttons to playback the flight in realtime, as a time lapse, or in slow motion respectively. The right side shows some general information about the flight as well as current telemetry data.

Map. Since for drone investigations the location is crucial, the map view takes up the largest part of the screen. It shows the drone's current position and orientation. The investigator can choose between Google Maps [12] and Open-StreetMap [4]. The user can also choose between satellite map, street map or terrain map. For easier navigation, the track of the whole flight is shown. This track can additionally be colorized indicating the flight altitude, horizontal speed, and flight time.

Timeline. The timeline and time control is located directly under the map. One can quickly navigate through time using the timeline. The `start` button starts the playback of the flight. One can choose between playback by second and message. The latter gives more fine-grained control over the playback.

Flight Information. The right side of the screen shows flight information. These consist of multiple parts. First, the *Flight Info* consists of static information about the flight including the UAV model, the date, flight time, time until takeoff, etc. This information is derived and calculated from various DUML messages. Next, the *General Info* is information about the current status of the drone including the current position, altitude above the ground, ultrasonic altitude, vertical and horizontal speeds, etc. Then, there is the *Controller Status* where the current joystick positions are shown. *Anomalies* (see Sect. 4) are displayed under the controller status. Furthermore, there is a graph view that can show arbitrary sensor data as a graph (see Fig. 5). Note that it is also possible to navigate using data points on the graph. Furthermore, the current packet can be viewed in *Raw Data*. For transparent data provenance, there is always a link back to the original log file. Eventually, the text-based messages are displayed in the *Flight Log Entries* section.

6 Evaluation

In the previous sections, we have shown how we extended DROP and how Maraudrone's Map is implemented. In this section, we evaluate these implementations using real world flight data from different drones (see Sect. 2.1).

6.1 DROP Extension

In Sect. 3 we showed how we extended DROP to be compatible with DJI's `DATv3` log files. In this section, we evaluate which and how many packet types DROP is able to parse. This gives some insights into how DJI uses logging in different drones. Furthermore, the evaluation shows how much and what data is logged.

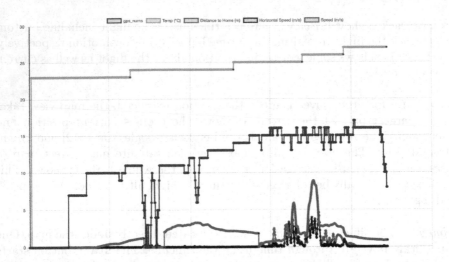

Fig. 5. Example of the graph view of Maraudrone's Map. This graph shows the battery's temperature (green), number of satellites (blue), distance to home (red), horizontal speed (black) and overall speed (purple). (Color figure online)

We start with an overview of the huge mass of DJI logging data. Table 4 shows the number of logged packets that each of the reference flights generated. It stands out that different models produce a very different number of log messages. The DJI Inspire 2 generates about 8600 messages per second while the smaller DJI Phantom 4 Advanced produces about 2100 messages per second.

Figure 6 shows the number of logged messages after tick x. The corresponding graphics for the DJI Inspire 2 and the DJI Matrice 600 Pro look quite similar and can be found in Appendix A in Fig. 9 and Fig. 10. One can see that the number of messages that are logged per second is quite stable. If there would be some bigger gaps this may be an indication of tampering (see Sect. 4).

Maraudrone's Map only needs a small subset of packet types (15) for visualization (see Sect. 3). Our DROP extension is able to parse more than 30 different packet types. However, this is still a subset of occurring packet types. Table 4 shows the number of occurring packet types by drone model. For the DJI Inspire 2, there are 115 occurring packet types while for the DJI Phantom 4 Advanced, there are 80. With our DROP extension we can parse up to about 36% of the occurring packet types. Table 5 also shows how many packets in total can be

Table 4. Known and unknown packet types by model.

Model	Duration	Total Pkt types	Known Pkt types	Unknown Pkt types
Phantom 4 Advanced	03:25	80	29 (36.25%)	51 (63.75%)
Inspire 2	08:56	115	28 (24.35%)	87 (75.65%)
Matrice 600 Pro	06:12	113	25 (22.12%)	88 (77.88%)

Table 5. Known and unknown packets by model.

Model	Duration	#Packets	#Packets/s	Known Pkts	Unknown Pkts
Phantom 4 Advanced	03:25	431k	2104/s	221k (51.44%)	209k (48.56%)
Inspire 2	08:56	4611k	8603/s	576k (12.49%)	4035k (87.51%)
Matrice 600 Pro	06:12	1442k	3877/s	496k (34.43%)	945k (65.57%)

parsed. The values in the table reveal that we can only parse about 51% of all occurring packets in the log for the DJI Phantom 4 Advanced. We can only parse about 12.5% of the log messages of the DJI Inspire 2. While these values seem to be low, DROP is nevertheless able to parse a lot of information that might be interesting for a forensic investigation.

Figure 7 shows the number of occurrences of the 15 most frequent packet types that we are able to parse with our DROP extension for the DJI Phantom 4 Advanced. It is noticeable, that there are packet types in the logs that appear exactly in the same amount, e.g., `controller` and `aircraft_condition`. Figure 7 shows four nearly perfect steps. Each stage roughly halves the number of messages in the corresponding packet types. Probably, this comes from periodic messages with different frequencies. Figure 8 shows the 15 most frequent messages that appear at all. Three definite stages are apparent. About half of these packet types cannot be parsed using DROP. The graphs of the DJI Inspire

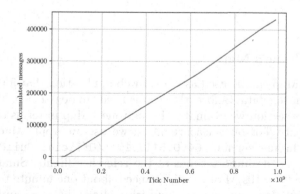

Fig. 6. Number of logged messages after tick x for the DJI Phantom 4 Advanced.

2 (see Fig. 11 and Fig. 12) and DJI Matrice 600 Pro (see Fig. 13 and Fig. 14) can be found in Appendix A.

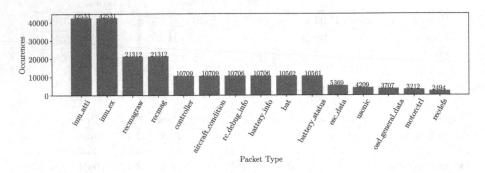

Fig. 7. Occurrences of the 15 most frequent *known* packet types for the DJI Phantom 4 Advanced.

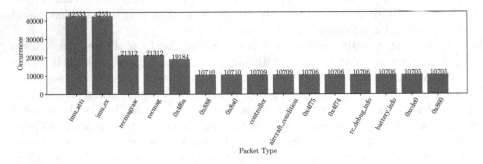

Fig. 8. Occurrences of the 15 most frequent (known and unknown) packet types for the DJI Phantom 4 Advanced.

6.2 Maraudrone's Map

Maraudrone's Map can be used as a local web application that forensically visualizes DJI drone log data. Before, the log file needs to be parsed using DROP (see Sect. 3). In this section we evaluate Maraudrone's Map in terms of performance and compatibility. For our measurements, we use an Apple MacBook Air M2 with Google Chrome Version 104.0.5112.101 (Official Build) (arm64).

Table 6 shows the import times of the reference flights. Smaller flights are imported quite fast (10s). Longer flights need about one minute to be imported. Since JavaScript does not support multithreading, the app cannot be used in the meantime. Once the flight is imported and the corresponding data is stored in the IndexedDB, loading the flight takes place immediately.

Table 6. Import times of Maraudrone's Map.

Model	Duration	#Messages	Filesize	Import time
Phantom 4 Advanced	03:25	221953	118 MiB	10s
Inspire 2	08:56	576178	287 MiB	70s
Matrice 600 Pro	06:12	496679	235 MiB	55s

Maraudrone's Map visualizes the logs for all three drones. We used the DJI Phantom 4 Advanced as a reference. During development we experienced some weird behavior of some displayed values or joystick positions. This is because DJI uses different packets for the same packet type. However, in all these cases we were able to fix it by additionally checking the packet lengths and assuming that the packet type in combination with the packet length yields distinct semantic data. Another indication of this assumption is that the same apps are used for different drones and this communication happens also via DUML.

6.3   Anomaly Detection

In Sect. 4 we identified and classified seven anomalies. In this section we want to show that the anomaly detection works as intended and discuss the anomalies that occur in our reference flights. Beside the source code, the repository of Maraudrone's Map[3] contains also some hand-crafted JSON files that trigger the anomalies as intended.

In Table 7 one can see the occurring anomalies in the reference flights. The anomalies that appear very early (i.e., the tick number in squared brackets is low) are caused by the drone's startup process. The many orientation jumps of the DJI Phantom 4 Advanced are because of *Inertial Measurement Unit* (IMU) inaccuracies.

6.4   Limitations

While the evaluation showed that DROP and Maraudrone's Map are very powerful tools, it also revealed some limitations.

Since the log files are stored in a propriety and binary format, we must rely on the result of the parser. Parsing DJI's `DAT` files is quite cumbersome and error-prone. We adapted DROP by analyzing DatCon [10]. So we also rely on the correctness of this tool. It is not guaranteed that DJI does not change the file format in newer drones and the parser produces nonsense. There are many more DUML messages that we are not able to parse but might be relevant for digital forensic investigations. The time it takes to import a JSON file is relatively long and longer flights will cause also longer import times. This might be a problem if the investigator needs to analyze many flights. Other models like the DJI

---

[3] https://github.com/dumbledrone/MaraudronesMap.

Table 7. Anomalies in the reference flights (log level: medium). Values are rounded. The value in squared brackets shows the position. By clicking the value in the app it jumps to that position.

Model	Anomalies

Phantom 4 Advanced	Time Stamps: other number than 4–6 per second:
	`[Medium] Time stamp 46870 occurred 10 times [34638]`
	Change of orientation too big:
	`[Severe] Orientation jumps from 180 to 291 [122]`
	`[Medium] Orientation jumps from 244 to 147 [160292]`
	`[Medium] Orientation jumps from 83 to 180 [160767]`
	`[Medium] Orientation jumps from 180 to 263 [160836]`

Inspire 2	Battery: there is a gap between these percentages:
	`[Medium] 80% - 78% [389054]`
	Change of orientation too big:
	`[Medium] Orientation jumps from 180 to 266 [206]`

Matrice 600 Pro	Change of orientation too big: `[Medium] Orientation jumps from 298 to 242 [260]`

Mavic 2 or the DJI Mavic Air 2 encrypt their logging data. It is also not clear if the decrypted logs use the same DUML format we can parse using DROP.

7   Conclusion and Future Work

In this paper, we introduced *Maraudrone's Map*—an interactive, easy extendible and easy-to-use web application for digital forensic investigation of DJI drone log data. For this, we extended DROP [3] to be compatible with the newer `DATv3` format. Maraudrone's Map allows to analyze DJI's `DAT` files and comes with playback functionality, visualization of many sensor data, anomaly detection, etc. To make data provenance transparent, there is always a link back to the original log file as well as the parsed message that can be viewed in human-readable JSON format.

The evaluation revealed that there are many more packet types that may also contain relevant information. Future work should parse more packet types. To reduce the risk of parsing errors, it would be beneficial to derive the packet types including the payload from existing DJI software. For better anomaly detection, it might be beneficial to make use of machine learning techniques. While it is quite easy to manipulate single log messages like the drone's positions, it might be hard to change the logs consistently. The performance of Maraudrone's Map for larger files should be enhanced. Furthermore, Maraudrone's Map should be able to visualize multiple `DAT` files at once. Then, an analyst would be able to quickly navigate to the flight of interest.

References

1. Al-Dhaqm, A., Ikuesan, R.A., Kebande, V.R., Razak, S., Ghabban, F.M.: Research challenges and opportunities in drone forensics models. Electronics **10**(13), 1519 (2021)
2. Christof, T.: DJI Wi-Fi Protocol Reverse Engineering (2021). https://epub.jku.at/obvulihs/download/pdf/6966648?originalFilename=true
3. Clark, D., Meffert, C., Baggili, I.M., Breitinger, F.: DROP (DRone Open source Parser) your drone: forensic analysis of the DJI Phantom III. Digit. Investig. **22 Supplement**, S3–S14 (2017). https://doi.org/10.1016/j.diin.2017.06.013
4. Community: OpenStreetMap (2022). https://www.openstreetmap.org/
5. Dedrone: Worldwide Drone Incidents (2022). https://www.dedrone.com/resources/incidents/all
6. DJI: Public Safety. https://enterprise.dji.com/public-safety
7. DJI: DJI Apps (2022). https://www.dji.com/downloads
8. DJI: DJI Models (2022). https://www.dji.com/products/comparison-consumer-drones
9. DroneBlogger: Spy drone halts Bayern Munich training (2020). https://dronenews.africa/spy-drone-halts-bayern-munich-training/
10. flylog.info: DatCon and CsvView. https://datfile.net/
11. Google Inc.: Angular (2022). https://angular.io
12. Google Inc.: Google Maps (2022). https://maps.google.de
13. Lieser, M., Schwanecke, U., Berdux, J.: Tactile human-quadrotor interaction: metrodrone. In: Wimmer, R., Kaltenbrunner, M., Murer, M., Wolf, K., Oakley, I. (eds.) TEI 2021: Fifteenth International Conference on Tangible, Embedded, and Embodied Interaction, Online Event/Salzburg, Austria, 14–19 February 2021, pp. 30:1–30:6. ACM (2021). https://doi.org/10.1145/3430524.3440649
14. Moon, H., Jin, E., Kwon, H., Lee, S., Gibum, K.: Digital forensic methodology for detection of abnormal flight of drones. J. Inf. Secur. Cybercrimes Res. **4**(1), 27–35 (2021)
15. Naylor, C.: BC men charged after drone flies drugs into Manitoba prison (2022). https://www.castanet.net/edition/news-story-375140-3-.htbeym
16. Original Gangsters: DUPC Packet Builder (2019). https://github.com/o-gs/dji-firmware-tools/blob/master/comm_mkdupc.py
17. Singh, I.: DroneAnalyst report reveals dramatic drop in DJI's commercial drone market share (2021). https://dronedj.com/2021/09/14/droneanalyst-dji-market-share-2021/
18. Singh, I.: California man arrested for dropping illegal fireworks from drone (2022). https://dronedj.com/2022/06/07/drone-fireworks-arrest-california/

VinciDecoder: Automatically Interpreting Provenance Graphs into Textual Forensic Reports with Application to OpenStack

Azadeh Tabiban[1]([⋈])(iD), Heyang Zhao[1], Yosr Jarraya[2], Makan Pourzandi[2](iD),
and Lingyu Wang[1](iD)

[1] CIISE, Concordia University, Montreal, QC, Canada
{a_tabiba,z_heyang,wang}@ciise.concordia.ca
[2] Ericsson Security Research, Ericsson Canada, Montreal, QC, Canada
{yosr.jarraya,makan.pourzandi}@ericsson.com

Abstract. The operational complexity and dynamicity of clouds highlight the importance of automated solutions for explaining the root cause of security incidents. Most existing works rely on human analysts to interpret provenance graphs for root causes of security incidents. However, navigating and understanding a large and complex cloud-scale provenance graph can be very challenging for human analysts. Without such an understanding, cloud providers cannot effectively address the underlying security issues causing the incidents, such as vulnerabilities or misconfigurations. In this paper, we propose VinciDecoder, an automated approach for generating natural language forensic reports based on provenance graphs. Our main observation is that the way nodes and edges compose a path in provenance graphs is similar to how words compose a sentence in natural languages. Therefore, VinciDecoder leverages a novel combination of provenance analysis, natural language translation, and machine-learning techniques to generate forensic reports. We implement VinciDecoder on an OpenStack cloud testbed, and evaluate its performance based on real-world attacks. Our user study and experimental results demonstrate the effectiveness of our approach in generating high-quality reports (e.g., up to 0.68 BLEU score for precision).

1 Introduction

With the recent worldwide surge in adopting cloud computing, there is an increasing need for explaining the root cause of security incidents in large scale cloud infrastructures [1]. Sharing detailed forensic reports about such root causes and attack techniques can raise cybersecurity awareness, and improve threat detection and attack prevention techniques [24]. However, most existing provenance-based solutions (e.g., [40,47,53]) would face a critical challenge in such a context, i.e., it would be impractical to rely on human analysts to interpret the large and complex provenance graphs produced by such solutions for a large cloud with tens of thousands of inter-connected virtual resources [35].

© The Author(s), under exclusive license to Springer Nature Switzerland AG 2022
H. P. Reiser and M. Kyas (Eds.): NordSec 2022, LNCS 13700, pp. 346–367, 2022.
https://doi.org/10.1007/978-3-031-22295-5_19

There exist rule-based techniques (e.g., [49]) for generating textual summaries of provenance graphs. However, only relying on a set of specified rules [49] would not be sufficient, as the unpredictable nature of security incidents [57] will necessitate to constantly develop new rules, which may be costly especially for large clouds. We will further illustrate such limitations through the following example.

Motivating Example. Figure 1(a) depicts a provenance graph (left), and an analyst manually performing the task of creating a human-readable report (right) based on the provenance graph. Specifically, upon receiving an alert about the leakage of network traffic, the analyst begins investigating the suspicious paths of the provenance graph (left) generated by existing tools (e.g., [54]) to manually report the root cause as shown in Fig. 1a (right) (the exploit of a vulnerability [3] by updating the *device_owner* field of a port attached to a created VM). However, such a task can be challenging to an analyst, especially as a real world cloud provenance graph may have tens of thousands of nodes and edges [47].

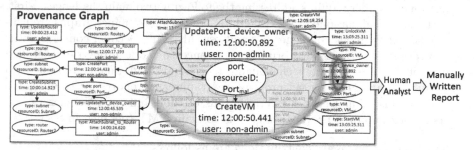

(a) Challenges of interpreting provenance graphs: excerpt of the provenance graph (left); an analyst manually creating a report based on the provenance graph (right).

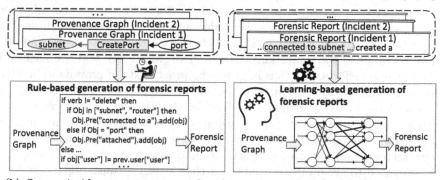

(b) Our main idea: provenance graphs of several incidents (top left); existing reports (top right); automatic generation of forensic reports (bottom left and right).

Fig. 1. Motivating example.

– **Key ideas.** Figure 1(b) shows the two main approaches adopted by our solution, namely *VinciDecoder*, for automatically interpreting provenance graphs into forensic reports. First, our rule-based approach generates customized forensic reports based on lexicons and grammar rules as illustrated in Fig. 1(b) (bottom left). Such rules are specified by the analyst according to his/her criteria (e.g., domain-knowledge) and understanding of the existing paired provenance graphs and forensic reports for similar types of future attacks. Second, for use cases where such criteria are too dynamic (e.g., new types of attacks) for a rule-based approach to handle, we also propose a learning-based approach (bottom right) which automatically learns the correspondence between pairs of provenance graphs and forensic reports using Neural Machine Translation (NMT). Specifically, similar to words (e.g., verbs and object) of a sentence, there is a dependency between nodes (e.g., operations and their affected resources) in a provenance graph, which inspires us to train a translation model by applying NMT to provenance graphs (source language) paired with human-readable reports (target language), and automatically translate future provenance graphs into a natural language interpretation using the trained model.

– **Challenges.** Although our vision for adopting NMT seems plausible, realizing VinciDecoder requires addressing the following two main challenges. First, NMT is typically applied to textual data, whereas provenance graphs are usually stored as nodes and edges. To address this, VinciDecoder converts paths of provenance graphs into primitive sentences of node properties (detailed in Sect. 3.2). Second, it is challenging to generate high quality reports with a limited number of paired provenance graphs and reports for training. To address this, VinciDecoder leverages tens of thousands of CVE entries and their corresponding provenance graphs to train NMT (detailed in Sect. 4.2).

In summary, our main contributions are as follows:

- To the best of our knowledge, VinciDecoder is the first solution for generating forensic reports based on provenance analysis results using both rule-based and learning-based techniques. By reducing the reliance on human analysts to interpret and document large and complex provenance graphs, our approach can avoid the limitations, human error, and delay that are natural to such manual efforts, and thus improve the practicality of provenance analysis in large-scale cloud environments, enable automated documentation of root causes for security incidents, and allow for more timely incident-response.

- To automatically generate reports using NMT, we design several mechanisms as follows. VinciDecoder first converts provenance graph paths into primitive sentences representing properties of nodes, and removes instance-specific information to avoid mis-translation; it then learns a translation model based on the paired primitive sentences and reports; finally, when given target paths, VinciDecoder applies the learned model to the primitive sentences representing the paths to generate the forensic report. Optionally, our rule-based approach can form forensic reports by linking the node properties extracted from the target path based on pre-specified rules.

- We implement VinciDecoder on an OpenStack-based cloud testbed, and validate its effectiveness based on real-world security incidents. Our experiments and user study show that VinciDecoder generates high-quality results (e.g., up to 0.68 BLEU score for precision) with sufficient readability for human analysts (e.g., 92% of our participants agree that understanding the attack steps is much easier using VinciDecoder's report than using provenance graphs).

The rest of this paper is organized as follows: Sect. 2 provides some background on data provenance and NMT. Section 3 details our methodology. Section 4 describes our implementation and presents the evaluation results. We discuss different aspects of our work and the related work in Sect. 5 and Sect. 6, respectively. We conclude the paper in Sect. 7.

2 Preliminaries

This section provides a background on data provenance, NMT and our assumptions.

2.1 Provenance Graph

As a powerful technique to capture the dependencies between data objects (e.g., virtual resources or operating system files) and events (e.g., management operations or system calls) in a graph representation, data provenance has been applied to clouds. We show an example of a cloud management-level provenance graph [47] in Fig. 2(a) consisting of two types of nodes: *entities* (shown as ovals) and *activities* (shown as rectangles), where entities represent virtual resources (e.g., a virtual port $Port_{mal}$), and activities represent cloud management operations (e.g., an operation $CreateVM$). Each node stores several properties such as the type of the operations/resources and the user who triggers the operations. Edges indicate the dependency between an operation and its affected resources. For example, in Fig. 2(a), the edge from $CreateVM$ to $Port_{mal}$ shows that this operation attaches $Port_{mal}$ to the created VM VM_{mal}.

2.2 Neural Machine Translation

Neural Machine Translation (NMT) [46] builds a conditional probability model, $P(Y|X)$, such that the likelihood of a target sentence Y given a source sentence X is maximized [22]. As Fig. 2(b) shows, NMT usually consists of an encoder and a decoder, which typically utilize recurrent neural networks (RNN) such as a Long Short-Term Memory (LSTM) [23]. To initialize the training, LSTM cells are assigned with random *weights*, and the encoder captures the semantics of X by encoding it into a fixed-length vector H. Then, the decoder generates the target sentence given the computed vector H. NMT computes the deviation of the generated sentence from the reference sentence Y and improves the model by optimizing the assigned weights based on other pairs of sentences. In Sect. 3.4 and 3.5, we detail how VinciDecoder leverages this mechanism to generate forensic reports.

2.3 Assumptions

We assume the accuracy of provenance analysis results provided by existing tools (e.g., [54]), such as suspicious paths capturing the attack steps or malicious

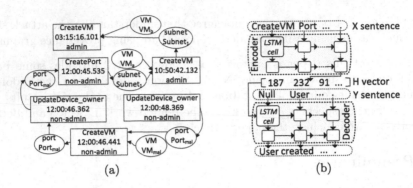

Fig. 2. An excerpt of a cloud management-level provenance graph (a); an example of NMT Encoder-Decoder model (b).

behavior. We also assume the correctness and completeness of provenance-based root cause analysis solutions (e.g., [21,54]) in identifying suspicious paths capturing the attack steps. We assume that the provenance construction tool is not compromised. Finally, similar to most other learning-based data-to-text techniques (e.g., [42]), we assume the availability of a sufficient amount of training data (i.e., paired forensic reports and suspicious paths) for training our model[1].

3   VinciDecoder

In this section, we provide an overview of VinciDecoder, detail its different modules, and describe the interaction between them.

3.1   Overview

Figure 3 shows an overview of VinciDecoder, which consists of two main phases: learning phase and automatic report generation phase. In the learning phase, VinciDecoder collects paired suspicious paths and reports for training, and then transforms suspicious paths into primitive sentences in our intermediary language (Sect. 3.2), which represents the properties of a node as a compound word, and removes the instance-specific information (Sect. 3.3). Next, it applies NMT to train a translation model profiling the correspondence between the obtained sentences and their forensic reports (Sect. 3.4). In the automatic report generation phase, VinciDecoder applies the trained translation model to generate forensic reports based on the suspicious paths of the provenance graph associated with the newly detected incident (Sect. 3.5). Optionally, VinciDecoder can generate reports using our rule-based mechanism (Sect. 3.5).

3.2   Path to Intermediary Language Translation (PILT)

NMT is typically applied to textual sentences, which renders its application to provenance graphs challenging. To address this, the PILT module converts each

---

[1] In Sect. 4.2, we discuss how we obtain more pairs of reports and paths for training.

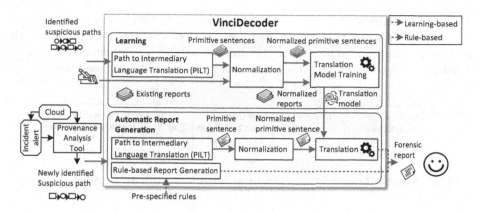

Fig. 3. Overview of VinciDecoder.

suspicious path into a primitive sentence by querying the database to sequentially scan the nodes, extract their properties, and record them as one compound word of the sentence (see Fig. 3). Algorithm 1 details the mechanism of PILT as follows: PILT extracts the properties *type* and *user* from operation nodes and appends them to the created primitive sentence (line 3–5). Moreover, it calculates the *elapsed time* between the timestamp properties stored at two consecutive operation nodes (line 6–7) and appends the calculated value with a proper post-fix (e.g., "-millisecond", "-hours", etc.) to the sentence (line 8–9). The elapsed time may be interesting for reporting the incidents where the attacker attempts to issue a large number of operations in a short period of time, e.g., to launch race condition or DoS attacks. PILT also records the *type* and the identifier of resources (line 10–13). In the next section, we detail how obtained sentences are modified and leveraged to train the translation model.

Algorithm 1 Path to Intermediary Language Translation

Input: path ← Suspicious path identified by the provenance analysis tool
Output: SenRepresentingPath
1. **foreach** node ∈ path **do**
2.   **if** isOperation(node) **then** %Appending the operation properties to sentence
3.   OperationType ← node["data"]["OperationType"]
4.   User ← node["data"]["user"]
5.   SenRepresentingPath.append("type:" + OperationType + "user:" + User)
           %Appending the approximate elapsed time between operations to sentence
6.   **if** isNotFirstNode(node) **then**
7.   ElapsedTime ← ThisOperation – PreviousOperationTime
8.   ElapsedApprox ← ElapsedTimeApproximator (ElapsedTime)
9.   SenRepresentingPath.append(ElapsedApprox)
10.   **else if** isResource(node) **then**%Appending resource properties to sentence
11.   ResourceType ← node["data"]["ResourceType"]
12.   ResourceID ← node["data"]["ID"]
13.   SenRepresentingPath.append("type:" + ResourceType + "ID:" + ResourceID)
14. **return** SenRepresentingPath

Example 1. Figure 4 shows the translation of a path (left) into a primitive sentence (right) in our intermediary language. As we can see, the properties of each node (e.g., the node representing *CreatePort* operation) are represented by a word (e.g., *"type:CreatePort,user:non-admin"*) in the obtained sentence.

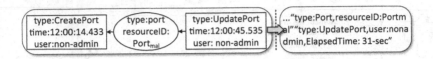

Fig. 4. Simplified example path (left) translated into a primitive sentence (right).

3.3   Normalization

To allow NMT to focus on generic words in the primitive sentences instead of application-specific ones (which may lead to mis-translation), VinciDecoder needs to remove instance-specific information from the dataset before feeding it to NMT. Specifically, the forensic reports and their corresponding primitive sentences used for training may contain values (e.g., the name/ID of resources) that are related to semantics of the specific scenarios (which NMT is not aware of). Retaining such values is known to reduce the quality of the reports generated by the trained neural translation model [43]. Therefore, VinciDecoder identifies and replaces all instance-specific values (e.g., the number preceding the string "-milliseconds"[2]) with a placeholder (i.e., \0), and the name of the applications or software platforms with the word *"platform"* based on our specified rules.

3.4   Translation Model Training

This module builds a translation model to profile the correspondence between the existing forensic reports and their associated suspicious paths. To this end, we leverage NMT [26], as it automatically captures the *context* of words and nodes (i.e., the dependencies between words in a report and nodes in a path) using embeddings. By applying NMT, VinciDecoder first projects words of a report and the words of the obtained primitive sentences (i.e., properties of nodes) into a high-dimensional numerical vector space such that words/nodes with similar contexts have closer vector representations. Next, VinciDecoder builds a translation model based on the derived vectors that optimally maps each provided forensic report to its paired primitive sentence.

Example 2. Figure 5 shows an excerpt of the training dataset composed of the primitive sentences obtained from the suspicious paths (left) and their corresponding manually created reports (right). The semantically related information on each side are illustrated with the same type of lines.

---

[2] Despite removing the numbers, the range of the elapsed time (e.g., milliseconds vs. hours) retains useful information about the incidents.

"type:CreatePort,ElapsedTime:\0-seconds,user:non-admin, ID: Portmal" "type:port,user:non-admin" "type:CreateVM, Elapsed Time:\0-seconds,user:non-admin" "type:port, user:non-admin" "type:UpdatePortDeviceOwner, Elapsed Time: \0-milliseconds" ...	A non-admin user creates a port, then creates a VM attached to that port, and immediately updates the port device_owner field so the anti-spoofing rule is bypassed due to the vulnerability exploit. ...

Fig. 5. Example paths in our intermediary language (left) and their corresponding manually written reports (right). Semantically related information are highlighted by the same type of lines.

3.5   Automatic Report Generation

Once a new security incident is detected, VinciDecoder automatically generates forensic reports based on the suspicious path identified by existing tools (e.g., [21, 54]) using our learning-based and rule-based techniques.

Learning-Based Report Generation. After building the translation model in the learning phase, VinciDecoder can be applied to generate forensic reports based on the detected suspicious path. Specifically, VinciDecoder converts the suspicious path into a primitive sentence in our intermediary language, and removes the instance-specific information by following the same techniques as mentioned in Sect. 3.2 and Sect. 3.3. Next, it applies the translation model to each normalized primitive sentence to automatically generate the corresponding forensic report. To improve the quality of generated reports, VinciDecoder also allows the analyst to conduct post-editing [28] by identifying the instance-specific information using the primitive sentences and adding them to the reports.

Rule-Based Report Generation. To ensure the applicability of our approach when there is a lack of a sufficient number of reports for training, VinciDecoder is also equipped with a rule-based mechanism, which enables translation without training data. Specifically, VinciDecoder sequentially scans nodes on each path, and extracts the following properties stored at each node: the *type* and *ID* of resources/operations, the *user* triggering an operation, and the *elapsed time* between the timestamp values stored in two consecutive operation nodes. Then, it creates an ordered list, where each item represents the properties of a node. Next, VinciDecoder generates sentences based on rules specified by the analyst, and it sequentially links the items such that the extracted user, resource, operation and elapsed time are included as the subject, object, verb and propositional phrase in generated sentences, respectively (detailed in Appendix). Finally, VinciDecoder generates an introductory and a concluding sentence to describe an overview of the incident (e.g., describing the time of the detection).

Example 3. Figure 6 shows the report related to the incident in our motivating example (Sect. 1). The report starts with explaining the number of operations in the suspicious path, continues with describing the attack steps, and concludes with indicating the ID of nodes in the suspicious paths.

By the detection time, there are 4 operations performed in 1 minute corresponding to the resource vmmal. A nonadmin user created a port named portmal on a subnet. Once done, this user modified portdeviceowner after less than a minute. (S)He also created a vm named vmmal on that port after less than a second. Then, (s)he modified that portdeviceowner after less than a second. More details can be found in the provenance graph in path [416 - 419 - 422 - 425].

Fig. 6. Automatically generated report on the incident discussed in our motivating example (Sect. 1).

4   Implementation and Evaluation

In this section, we detail the implementation of VinciDecoder and evaluate our solution.

4.1   Evaluation Using Cloud Management-Level Provenance Graphs

To evaluate VinciDecoder under different scenarios (e.g., various lengths of suspicious paths), we apply VinciDecoder to cloud management-level provenance graphs generated in our testbed cloud.

4.1.1   Implementation and Data Collection

We implement VinciDecoder in a cloud testbed based on OpenStack [8] (a popular open-source cloud platform). We note that only our PILT module (Sect. 3.2) and our rules (Appendix) are platform-specific, and the modular design of VinciDecoder makes it easily portable to other platforms or provenance models (e.g., OS-level provenance [25]). We export provenance graphs from Neo4j [7] into JSON format for processing. We leverage Open-Source Toolkit for Neural Machine Translation (ONMT) [26] (a popular tool for language translation). Similar to some other solutions (e.g., [54]), we choose the default options for embedding paths (i.e., 500 dimensional vector) as well as the batch size and the dropout rate (i.e., 64 and 0.3, respectively). We leverage the metrics in [45] to evaluate our approach. We run VinciDecoder on an Ubuntu 20.04 server equipped with 128 GB of RAM. We generate the provenance graphs through deploying and updating different types of virtual resources. Moreover, we enrich our training dataset by leveraging the rule-based mechanism (detailed in Sect. 3.5). To simulate reports authored based on various writing styles, we specify rules capturing the writing styles of our different authors.

Table 1. Statistics of our testbed datasets.

Dataset	Training								Testing	
	$D_{tr\text{-}size1}$	$D_{tr\text{-}size2}$	$D_{tr\text{-}size3}$	$D_{tr\text{-}size4}$	$D_{tr\text{-}len1}$	$D_{tr\text{-}len2}$	$D_{tr\text{-}len3}$	$D_{tr\text{-}len4}$	D_{ts1}	D_{ts2}
# of paths	2000	4000	6000	8000	2000	2000	2000	2000	2000	2000
l_{min}	4	4	4	4	4	8	12	16	4	8

Table 1 shows the statistics of our datasets. To evaluate the effect of length and number of available samples (i.e., the suspicious paths) on the performance, we conduct our experiments based on two groups of training datasets: 1) varying the number of paths: four datasets ($D_{tr-size1}$ to $D_{tr-size4}$) each consisting of a different number of paths with the same minimum length; 2) varying the length of paths: four datasets ($D_{tr-len1}$ to $D_{tr-len4}$) consisting of the same number of paths with different specified minimum lengths. We randomly select 70% and 30% of the paths from each training dataset to build and validate (used by NMT to automatically tune the hyperparameters in training [22]) the models, respectively. Our training and testing datasets are selected from disjoint parts of the provenance graph, so we can evaluate the ability of VinciDecoder in handling unseen datasets. We also evaluate our approach based on two testing datasets with paths of different minimum lengths as shown in Table 1.

4.1.2   Effectiveness Evaluation

We reproduce in our testbed eight real-world incident scenarios that involve cloud management operations, and apply VinciDecoder to generate reports based on the captured provenance graphs. Table 2 shows those scenarios and corresponding incidents. Most of those scenarios are discussed in previous works (e.g., [14,34,48,50,55]) focusing on security verification. For all cases, our generated reports capture all operations that led to the incidents. Table 3 demonstrates the effectiveness of VinciDecoder based on five scenarios. We also showcased our result for the sixth scenario in Sect. 3.5. The other two scenarios (Table 2, seventh and eighth rows) involve fewer types of operations and are thus omitted due to space limitation.

Table 2. Attack scenarios used to evaluate the effectiveness of VinciDecoder.

Index	Root cause	Incident
1	Improper authorization [55]	Port Scanning
2	Failed update of security groups [48]	Data leakage
3	Soft-rebooting migrated VM [5]	Data corruption
4	Deleting resized VM [4]	Disk utilization
5	Incorrect role assignment [50]	Data leakage
6	Race condition in update port [48]	Data leakage
7	Wrong VLAN ID [14]	Data leakage
8	Excessive VM creation on a host [34]	Disk utilization

Table 3. Reports generated by VinciDecoder for five scenarios in Table 2. The sixth scenario is showcased in Sect. 3.5.

Index	Provenance graph path	Automatically generated report
1		An admin user created a port named porta on a subnet. This admin user attached that subnet to a router after around 1 hours. A nonadmin user created a port on that subnet and on that router, previously affected by a different user. After that, (s)he created a vm named vmmal, which is associated to the alert.
2		A nonadmin user created vm named vmmal on a subnet. An admin user created a vm named vmb on that subnet. Once done, (s)he started that vm vmb. Then attached a securitygroup named SG1 on that vm. The administrator deleted securitygrouprule from that SecurityGroup after around 1 minutes.
3		An admin user livemigrated a vm named vma to a host. A nonadmin user softrebooted that vm, previously affected by a different user.
4		A nonadmin user created a vm named vma on a host. Later, (s)he resized that vm after less than a minutes. Next, (s)he deleted that vm after less than a minute.
5		An admin user created a vm, named vma on a subnet. A nonadmin user changedpassword a vm, previously affected by a different user after around 3 hours.

Example of Verifying the Captured Information Figure 7(a) shows the automatically generated report explaining the operations (i.e., the creation of a rogue port on a router created by a different user) to exploit a vulnerability [2] that led to the attack on VM_a (Table 2, first row). VinciDecoder correctly details the steps described by the manually created report shown in Fig. 7(b).

4.1.3 Performance Evaluation

We showcase the high quality of generated reports with different number and length of paths in training datasets based on well known translation metrics BLEU and ROUGE [45]. BLEU (*precision*) measures the fraction of the generated information that are relevant to the manually written reports and ROUGE

Automatically generated report: By the detection time, there are 4 operations performed in 3 hours corresponding to the alert entity of vm vmmal. An admin user created a port named porta on a subnet. This admin user attached a subnet named subnet1 on a router after around 1 hours. A nonadmin user created a port on a subnet and on a router, previously affected by a different user. After that, he created a vm named vmmal, which is associated with the alert. This node (ID: 60) might worth a closer look because this operation is performed on admin resource by nonadmin user.	**Manually written report [2]:** The l3-agent does not check tenant_id and allows tenants to plug ports into other's routers if the device_id is set to another tenants router.
	# use admin's credential
	$ source openrc admin
	# Create router as admin
	$ neutron router-create admin-router
	# use a different cloud tenant's credential
	$ source openrc non-admin
	# Create port with the router device_id
	$ neutron port-create --device-id (router-id)

(a) Automatically generated report.   (b)   Manually created report about exploiting the same vulnerability [2].

Fig. 7. Verifying the information captured by our generated report. The semantically relevant information are highlighted with the same type of line.

(*recall*) indicates the fraction of information from the reference reports that are included in automatically generated reports. As VinciDecoder proposes the first learning-based provenance translation solution, we cannot directly compare our results to existing works, while we note that scores above 0.5 are generally known to reflect high quality translations [29].

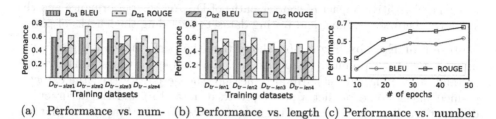

(a) Performance vs. number of training samples. (b) Performance vs. length of training samples. (c) Performance vs. number of epochs.

Fig. 8. Evaluation with cloud management-level provenance graphs.

Number of Training Samples. Figure 8(a) shows that, in most cases, there is a minor variation in the evaluated performance as the number of the training samples increases. This can be explained by the possibility that our translation models trained by larger datasets may become more biased [33] due to the frequent appearances of similar patterns of cloud management operations. To further illustrate this effect, Fig. 9 compares an excerpt of a manually written report of a path with the ones generated by VinciDecoder based on the four training datasets. As we can see, larger training datasets (e.g., $D_{tr-size4}$) cause more extra or missing information in the generated reports. We conclude that our approach remains useful even with a limited number of training samples.

Path (converted to a sentence in the intermediary language): '"type:CreateServers,user:Admin, ElapsedTime:\0-seconds" "type:port" "type:UpdatePorts,user:Admin,ElapsedTime:\0-seconds"
Manually written report: An admin user created a server attached to a port, named \0. He later updates that port after less than a minute.

$D_{tr-size1}$: An Admin user created a server named \0 attached to that port. Once done, he updated a port named\0 [missing elapsed time].	$D_{tr-size2}$: An Admin user created a server named \0 attached to that port. [not using pronoun] The Admin user modified a port named\0, after less than a minute.

$D_{tr-size3}$: [missing create server] An Admin user updated a port named \0. ~~The administrator updated a port named \0, after around \0minutes.~~
$D_{tr-size4}$: An Admin user ~~created a port named \0 connected to that subnet. Then created a port named\0 connected to that subnet. This Admin user created a port named \0 connected to that subnet after around minutes. Once done, he created a port named \0 connected to that subnet.~~ He created a server named \0 attached to that port after less than a minute. [not using pronoun] This Admin user modified a port named \0 after less than a minute. ~~Then updated a port named \0.~~

Fig. 9. Comparing reports generated by training datasets with different numbers of samples (irrelevant parts of the generated reports are crossed out).

Length of Training Samples. Figure 8(b) shows that the performance decreases when the length of paths in the training dataset increases, which may be due to the degraded performance of NMT for longer sentences [18]. The reduction is more significant for D_{ts1} due to the difference between the length of paths in this testing dataset (with minimum four nodes) and that of paths in the training datasets, $D_{tr\text{-}len3}$ and $D_{tr\text{-}len4}$ (with minimum 12 and 16 nodes). The training datasets $D_{tr\text{-}len1}$ and $D_{tr\text{-}len2}$ (with paths of minimum four and eight nodes) cause a noticeably higher performance for D_{ts1} than for D_{ts2} due to the general positive impact of shorter paths of D_{ts1} on the performance and the similarity between training and testing datasets regarding the lengths of paths.

Number of Epochs. Figure 8(c) shows that the performance is significantly improved with the number of epochs (i.e., the number of times NMT iterates through a training dataset). We also measure the perplexity (i.e., the extent a trained model could predict a newly provided data [15]) and the accuracy for different numbers of epochs and training datasets. Figure 10(a) shows that the perplexity decreases to around 1.2 after 20 epochs, and Fig. 10(b) shows that the accuracy increases to around 97% after 40 epochs. We conclude that the perplexity and accuracy of VinciDecoder improve with the number of epochs, and reach almost constant values after training over maximum 40 epochs.

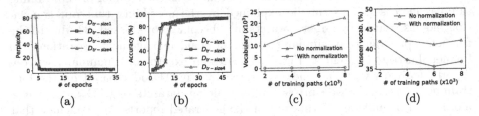

(a)   (b)   (c)   (d)

Fig. 10. (a) Perplexity (the smaller is better) and (b) accuracy at different epochs; (c) the growth of vocabulary size, and (d) the proportion of unseen words.

Out-of-Vocabulary Evaluation. Figure 10(c) shows that, without normalization (Sect. 3.3), the size of the vocabulary significantly grows with the size of the dataset, which may subsequently reduce the performance. Furthermore, Fig. 10(d) shows that, on average, the proportion of unseen words in the testing dataset (i.e., words that do not exist in the training datasets, and thus may be translated incorrectly) is around 6% less after conducting normalization. This shows that our normalization technique effectively increases the applicability of the trained models for describing new provenance graphs in testing datasets. In summary, our results demonstrate the feasibility and quality of the produced reports for datasets with different number and length of paths.

4.2 Large Scale Experiments Using CVE-Based Provenance Graphs

As our evaluation in Sect. 4.1 is limited to the data collected from our testbed, to evaluate our approach based on more realistic and larger scale datasets, we apply VinciDecoder to CVE-based provenance graphs in this section.

Data Collection. The performance of NMT may be adversely affected by the scarce available pairs of input data [19]. Therefore, to enrich our dataset, we adopt an approach similar to recent works (e.g., [13,20,44]) on extracting provenance graphs from cyber threat intelligence (CTI) reports such as vulnerability databases [6]. Similar to such solutions, we leverage a combination of rule-based and machine learning techniques (e.g., Part-of-Speech Tagging [17]) to extract different components of provenance graphs (e.g., affected systems, attackers' activities, and the impact of attacks), which allows us to generate a large number of provenance graphs paired with their CTI reports to train our translation model. To this end, we processed 60,000 CVE entries. Inspired by existing solutions (e.g., [44]), to decrease the verbosity of CVE entries and facilitate extracting provenance information, we apply a summarization technique[3] to the entries, and subsequently, extract provenance metadata. Finally, we clean the dataset by removing the entries from which the attackers' activities and impact cannot be extracted, and we obtain six datasets with the total number of 40,151 entries as shown in Table 4. We randomly select 80%, 10% and 10% of entries in each dataset for training, testing and validation, respectively.

Table 4. Statistics of our datasets prepared with CVE entries.

	D_1	D_2	D_3	D_4	D_5	D_6
Total before cleaning	30000	36000	42000	48000	54000	60000
Total after cleaning	20626	25188	28575	32333	36283	40151
Training	16600	20271	22997	26022	29201	32314
Validation	2060	2514	2852	3227	3621	4007
Testing	1966	2403	2726	3084	3461	3830

Number of Epochs. We showcase the high quality of our generated reports by first identifying the number of epochs that yields the highest performance (average BLEU and ROUGE scores) for each dataset. Figure 11(a) shows that VinciDecoder achieves higher performance with smaller datasets after a fewer number of epochs (e.g., 30 epochs for D1). This can be explained by the possibility that training on smaller datasets for a larger number of epochs would cause overfitting [38], which decreases the performance. On the other hand, the performance related to our larger datasets (D4, D5 and D6 in Fig. 11(b)) remains high for a larger number of epochs. For instance, we maximise the performance by training on our largest dataset (D6) for 100 epochs.

Number of Training Samples. We measure the performance of VinciDecoder trained with different datasets for the number of epochs that achieved the highest performance in Fig. 11(a) and 11(b) (e.g., 30 and 100 epochs for D1 and D6, respectively). Figure 11(c) shows that both the BLEU and ROUGE scores remain

---

[3] https://pypi.org/project/nlpaug/.

almost similar and above 0.68 and 0.74, respectively, for all datasets. This shows that despite the complex content and various writing styles that are natural to CVE reports, VinciDecoder performs well in generating such reports[4].

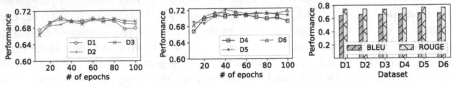

(a) Performance vs. # of epochs (smaller datasets).   (b) Performance vs. # of epochs (larger datasets).   (c) Performance vs. size of datasets.

Fig. 11. Evaluation with CVE-based provenance graphs.

4.3   User-Based Study

To evaluate the quality and usefulness of our generated reports in helping human analysts, we conduct a user study[5] based on standard practices [10], where participants have to evaluate the factual correctness and fluency of the reports generated by VinciDecoder. Our participants include eight cybersecurity researchers working in a major telecommunication organization and five graduate researchers working in cybersecurity labs of our university. Table 5 shows the percentage of participants in each group, their reported level of expertise, and the average score for all statements.

Table 5. Average quantified agreement levels for each group (scores will be explained later). PG means provenance analysis. (A), (L), and (N) signs represent advanced, little and no knowledge, respectively, as reported by the participants.

	Industry					Academia
Background (Cloud-PG)	A-A	A-L	A-N	L-L	L-N	A-L
Participants (%)	15	23	8	8	8	38
Scores (out of 5)	3.83	4.28	3.83	3.83	3	4.13

At the beginning of the study, we show an attack scenario (our motivating example in Sect. 1) to the participants. Next, we provide the participants with

---

[4] Note that while both sets of our experiments in Sect. 4.1 and 4.2 show high quality reports, directly comparing their results is not meaningful as their reports are of incomparable lengths (e.g., cloud management-level provenance graph-based reports are typically longer which has a negative effect on the performance).

[5] This study has been identified as quality assurance by Research Ethics/Office of Research of our university, which means it requires no ethics approval.

the provenance graph, the report generated by VinciDecoder, and the manually written report. Our study asks participants to evaluate their investigation with and without VinciDecoder, and accordingly express their level of agreement with the provided statements (shown in Table 6) by choosing one of the following options: *Strongly agree, Agree, Neutral, Disagree* and *Strongly disagree*. We then quantify the results by assigning an integer between one and five to each option, where five means *Strongly agree* and one means *Strongly disagree*.

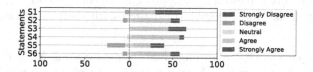

Fig. 12. Participants' agreement with statements in Table 6.

Table 6. Survey statements and scores. The agreement level of participants are converted to scores between one and five (score five represents *Strongly agree*).

	Statement	Score
S1	Understanding the attack steps using the generated text is easier than using the path	4.3
S2	The generated text is consistent with the explained attack scenario	3.92
S3	The generated text is consistent with the path regarding the relationships of operations	4.31
S4	The generated text captures all the information of the suspicious path	4
S5	The generated text is sufficiently fluent compared with the manually written report	3.46
S6	The generated text is consistent with the manually written report regarding attack steps	3.92

Figure 12 shows the distribution of participants' agreement with each statement. For most participants, understanding the attack steps is much easier using our generated report than the provenance graph (S1). According to most participants, our generated report contains no information contradicting the described attack scenario and the provenance graph (S2 and S3). Additionally, the results (S4) affirm that all the information captured by the provenance graph is reflected in our generated report. Most users find the generated report almost as fluent as the manually created one (S5), while the slightly lower fluency is expected for automatically generated reports [28]. Finally, the attack steps described by the generated report is consistent with the report created by the human analyst (S6). We show the average quantified scores in Table 5. VinciDecoder achieves scores above three among all groups despite their low level (little or no) of expertise, which confirm the benefits of VinciDecoder to users in investigating incidents.

5 Discussion

In this section, we discuss future directions and limitations of VinciDecoder.

Application to Other Models. Our approach is generic enough to support various provenance models (e.g., [25,37] and [53] for the OS and Internet of things environments, respectively) after converting paths into primitive sentences capturing both nodes and edges as words in our intermediary language. Likewise, an interesting future direction is to apply VinciDecoder to other graphical security models such as attack graphs [13] paired with their corresponding textual interpretation.

Coverage. In this work, we leverage NMT for generating forensic reports from long suspicious paths, as it is known to perform well in translating long sentences [46]. In our future work, we will further investigate the possibility of applying other translation techniques [31] that may increase the performance of VinciDecoder. Finally, our goal is to assist analysts, instead of replacing them, by allowing them to focus on more important but light-weight tasks, e.g., validating the report to ensure its legal value.

6 Related Work

Provenance-based security solutions have been extensively explored [25,40,41, 47,53]. King et al. [25] propose data provenance to investigate security incidents in operating systems. ProvDetector [54] is a provenance solution to detect anomalous programs using embedded sentences representing paths. Poirot [36] identifies attack-related subgraphs, and SteinerLog [12] detects attack campaigns across multiple hosts using alert correlation. Some of recent solutions (e.g., [37,58]) focus on increasing the interpretability of provenance graphs. ATLAS [9] adopts sequence learning to model the signature of attacks. There exist efforts adapting provenance analysis to domains other than operating systems such as the Internet of Things (IoT) (e.g., [53]) and SDN environments (e.g., [51,52]). Wu et al. [56] propose an approach explaining the absence of events. The authors in [32] and [11] propose a provenance-based investigation and access control scheme for clouds, respectively. The authors in [39], propose a solution to enhance the access control mechanism in OpenStack. Chen et. al [16] propose CLARION to capture precise provenance graphs across namespaces of different containers. Unlike our work, none of those solutions generates a human-readable description of the provenance graph, and our approach can be applied to most of those solutions to automatically translate their results into natural language reports.

Several solutions [27,30,42] have been proposed to generate human-readable descriptions based on non-linguistic information. The authors in [42] propose a solution to generate textual summaries about basketball games based on tables of information using NMT. [30] is a neural text generation solution to generate the first sentence of a Wikipedia entry based on a provided *infobox*. Finally, [27] proposes a solution that generates abstracts for scientific papers (with the BLEU score of around 0.14) based on paired titles and knowledge graphs (with 4.43 edges, on average). None of those solutions are designed for generating forensic reports based on typically larger and more complex provenance graphs that are natural to the security context or cloud scale. ProvTalk [49] proposes a rule-based approach for generating textual summaries of provenance graphs, which is generalized and complemented with a learning-based approach in VinciDecoder.

7 Conclusion

In this paper, we presented VinciDecoder, the first solution for automatically translating provenance analysis results into human-readable forensic reports using both rule-based and learning-based techniques. To this end, we first explored the characteristics of the provenance graph to represent it in an intermediary language, which can then be translated into a natural language. We showed the feasibility of our approach by implementing VinciDecoder based on an OpenStack cloud, and demonstrated the high quality of generated reports for real-world incident scenarios using both numerical (up to 0.56 and 0.68 BLEU scores for cloud management-level and CVE-based provenance graphs, respectively) and user-based evaluations. As future work, we will integrate VinciDecoder with other (e.g., OS-level) provenance analysis tools. We will also explore other translation techniques and hyperparameters (i.e., the size of embedding vectors and batch size), which may further improve the effectiveness of our approach.

Acknowledgment. We thank the anonymous reviewers for their valuable comments. This work was supported by the Natural Sciences and Engineering Research Council of Canada and Ericsson Canada under the Industrial Research Chair in SDN/NFV Security and the Canada Foundation for Innovation under JELF Project 38599.

Appendix

Algorithm 2 shows our rule-based mechanism generating reports based on the cloud management-level provenance graphs (e.g., the provenance graph in Fig. 1). To generate fluent sentences, we specify rules for indicating different subjects (line 2–5). We add resources extracted from the names of operations (e.g., a *VM* in *CreateVM*) through the template *a $resource_type named $main_resource_name* (line 7–9). We specify various rules (line 11–20) for describing other affected resources connected to an operation node. We also specify rules to record other information such as the elapsed time between operations (line 21–26). Through such rules specifically designed for each type of operations, resources, and users, VinciDecoder generates reports when there is an insufficient amount of training data for generating high quality reports.

Algorithm 2 Rule-based Report Generation

Input: path ← Suspicious path identified by the provenance analysis tool
             Middle_Sentence_Subjects = ["Next, this user", "Later, he/she", "He/She also",
             "This user then", "Once done, he/she "]
Output: Description
1. **foreach** node ∈ path **do**
2.   **if** isFirstNode(node) or isNotEqualPreviousUser(node) **then**%User of the first operation
3.   Subj_main ← Admin_NonAdmin_Specifier(userID, adminID)
4.   **else** %Other users with prior words (e.g., "Once done, he/she")
5.   Subj_main ← random_choice(Middle_Sentence_Subjects)
6.   **if** isAnOperation(node) **then**
7.   Verb, MainObject ← OperationType.split(operation)
8.   MainObject ← MainObject.setDeterminer("a")
9.   MainObject ← addAfter("with the ID " + MainObject["id"])
10.   OtherAffectedResources ← EndOfOutgoingEdges(node)
11.   **foreach** SecondaryObject ∈ OtherAffectedResources: %Choosing prior words
12.   **if** verb != "delete" **then**
13.   SecondaryObject.addBefore("on").addAfter(resource["id"])
14.   **else**
15.   SecondObject.addBefore("from a").addAfter(resource["id"])
16.   **if** previousUser(resource) != operation["user"] **then** %Update by a different user
17.   SecondaryObject.addAfter(", previously affected by a different user,")
18.   **if** isNotFirstNode(node) **then** %Range of elapsed time between operations
19.   ElapsedTime ← TimeRangeDescriptor(ThisOperation − PreviousOperationTime)
20.   **if** isAlertNode(node) **then**
21.   MainObject.addAfter(", which is associated to the alert.")
22.   sentence.setSubj(Subj_main).setVerb(Verb).setObj(MainObject) %Form sentence
23.   sentence.addAfter(SecondaryObject).addAfter(ElapsedApprox)
24.   **if** ThisOperation = PreviousOperation **then** %Emphasize the repetition
25.   sentence.addComponent("again")
26.   PathDescription.append(sentence)
27. **return** Description

References

1. Cisco AVOS. https://github.com/CiscoSystems/avos. Accessed 28 July 2022
2. CVE-2014-0056.   https://cve.mitre.org/cgi-bin/cvename.cgi?name=CVE-2014-0056/. Accessed 28 July 2022
3. CVE-2015-5240.   https://cve.mitre.org/cgi-bin/cvename.cgi?name=CVE-2015-5240. Accessed 28 July 2022
4. CVE-2016-7498. https://nvd.nist.gov/vuln/detail/CVE-2016-7498. Accessed 28 July 2022
5. CVE-2020-17376. https://bugs.launchpad.net/nova/+bug/1890501. Accessed 28 July 2022
6. CVE details. https://www.cvedetails.com/vulnerability-list/. Accessed 14 June 2022
7. Neo4j Graph Platform. https://neo4j.com/. Accessed 28 July 2022
8. OpenStack. https://www.openstack.org/. Accessed 28 July 2022
9. Alsaheel, A., et al.: ATLAS: a sequence-based learning approach for attack investigation. In: USENIX Security, pp. 3005–3022 (2021)
10. Assila, A., Ezzedine, H., et al.: Standardized usability questionnaires: features and quality focus. eJCIST **6**(1) (2016)
11. Bates, A., Mood, B., Valafar, M., Butler, K.R.B.: Towards secure provenance-based access control in cloud environments. In: CODASPY, pp. 277–284 (2013)

12. Bhattarai, B., Huang, H.: SteinerLog: prize collecting the audit logs for threat hunting on enterprise network. In: ASIA CCS, pp. 97–108 (2022)
13. Binyamini, H., Bitton, R., Inokuchi, M., Yagyu, T., Elovici, Y., Shabtai, A.: A framework for modeling cyber attack techniques from security vulnerability descriptions. In: KDD, p. 2574–2583 (2021)
14. Bleikertz, S., Vogel, C., Groß, T., Mödersheim, S.: Proactive security analysis of changes in virtualized infrastructures. In: ACSAC, pp. 51–60. ACM (2015)
15. Chen, S.F., Goodman, J.: An empirical study of smoothing techniques for language modeling. Comput. Speech Lang. **13**(4), 359–394 (1999)
16. Chen, X., Irshad, H., Chen, Y., Gehani, A., Yegneswaran, V.: CLARION: sound and clear provenance tracking for microservice deployments. In: USENIX Security, pp. 3989–4006 (2021)
17. Chiche, A., Yitagesu, B.: Part of speech tagging: a systematic review of deep learning and machine learning approaches. J. Big Data **9**(1), 1–25 (2022)
18. Cho, K., van Merriënboer, B., Bahdanau, D., Bengio, Y.: On the properties of neural machine translation: encoder-decoder approaches. In: SSST, pp. 103–111. ACL (2014)
19. Fadaee, M., Bisazza, A., Monz, C.: Data augmentation for low-resource neural machine translation. In: ACL, pp. 567–573 (2017)
20. Gao, P., et al.: Enabling efficient cyber threat hunting with cyber threat intelligence. In: ICDE, pp. 193–204. IEEE (2021)
21. Hassan, W.U., Aguse, L., Aguse, N., Bates, A., Moyer, T.: Towards scalable cluster auditing through grammatical inference over provenance graphs. In: NDSS (2018)
22. He, D., Lu, H., Xia, Y., Qin, T., Wang, L., Liu, T.Y.: Decoding with value networks for neural machine translation. Adv. Neural Inf. Process. Syst. **30**, 177–186 (2017)
23. Hochreiter, S., Schmidhuber, J.: Long short-term memory. Neural Comput. **9**(8), 1735–1780 (1997)
24. Johnson, C., Badger, L., Waltermire, D., Snyder, J., Skorupka, C., et al.: Guide to cyber threat information sharing. NIST Spec. Publ. **800**, 150 (2016)
25. King, S.T., Chen, P.M.: Backtracking intrusions. In: SOSP, pp. 223–236 (2003)
26. Klein, G., Kim, Y., Deng, Y., Senellart, J., Rush, A.: OpenNMT: open-source toolkit for neural machine translation. In: Proceedings of ACL, System Demonstrations, pp. 67–72. ACL (2017)
27. Koncel-Kedziorski, R., Bekal, D., Luan, Y., Lapata, M., Hajishirzi, H.: Text generation from knowledge graphs with graph transformers. In: NAACL (2019)
28. Läubli, S., Sennrich, R., Volk, M.: Has machine translation achieved human parity? A case for document-level evaluation. In: EMNLP, pp. 4791–4796. ACL (2018)
29. Lavie, A.: Evaluating the output of machine translation systems. AMTA Tutor. **86** (2010)
30. Lebret, R., Grangier, D., Auli, M.: Neural text generation from structured data with application to the biography domain. In: EMNLP, pp. 1203–1213. ACL (2016)
31. Lopez, A.: Statistical machine translation. ACM Comput. Surv. (CSUR) **40**(3), 1–49 (2008)
32. Lu, R., Lin, X., Liang, X., Shen, X.S.: Secure provenance: the essential of bread and butter of data forensics in cloud computing. In: ASIA CCS, pp. 282–292 (2010)
33. L'Heureux, A., Grolinger, K., Elyamany, H.F., Capretz, M.A.M.: Machine learning with big data: challenges and approaches. IEEE Access **5**, 7776–7797 (2017). https://doi.org/10.1109/ACCESS.2017.2696365
34. Madi, T., et al.: QuantiC: distance metrics for evaluating multi-tenancy threats in public cloud. In: CloudCom, pp. 163–170. IEEE (2018)

35. Miao, H., Deshpande, A.: Understanding data science lifecycle provenance via graph segmentation and summarization. In: ICDE, pp. 1710–1713. IEEE (2019)
36. Milajerdi, S.M., Eshete, B., Gjomemo, R., Venkatakrishnan, V.: POIROT: aligning attack behavior with kernel audit records for cyber threat hunting. In: CCS, pp. 1795–1812 (2019)
37. Milajerdi, S.M., Gjomemo, R., Eshete, B., Sekar, R., Venkatakrishnan, V.N.: HOLMES: real-time APT detection through correlation of suspicious information flows. In: IEEE S&P, pp. 1137–1152 (2019)
38. Mitchell, T.M.: Machine Learning. McGraw-Hill, New York (1997)
39. Nguyen, D., Park, J., Sandhu, R.: Adopting provenance-based access control in openstack cloud IaaS. In: Au, M.H., Carminati, B., Kuo, C.-C.J. (eds.) NSS 2014. LNCS, vol. 8792, pp. 15–27. Springer, Cham (2014). https://doi.org/10.1007/978-3-319-11698-3_2
40. Pasquier, T., et al.: Practical whole-system provenance capture. In: SoCC, pp. 405–418 (2017)
41. Pasquier, T., et al.: Runtime analysis of whole-system provenance. In: CCS, pp. 1601–1616. ACM (2018)
42. Puduppully, R., Dong, L., Lapata, M.: Data-to-text generation with content selection and planning. In: AAAI, vol. 33, pp. 6908–6915 (2019)
43. Santana, M.A.B., Ricca, F., Cuteri, B.: Reducing the impact of out of vocabulary words in the translation of natural language questions into SPARQL queries. arXiv preprint arXiv:2111.03000 (2021)
44. Satvat, K., Gjomemo, R., Venkatakrishnan, V.: EXTRACTOR: extracting attack behavior from threat reports. In: EuroS&P, pp. 598–615. IEEE (2021)
45. Sharma, S., El Asri, L., Schulz, H., Zumer, J.: Relevance of unsupervised metrics in task-oriented dialogue for evaluating natural language generation. CoRR abs/1706.09799 (2017)
46. Sutskever, I., Vinyals, O., Le, Q.V.: Sequence to sequence learning with neural networks. Adv. Neural Inf. Process. Syst. **2**, 3104–3112 (2014)
47. Tabiban, A., Jarraya, Y., Zhang, M., Pourzandi, M., Wang, L., Debbabi, M.: Catching falling dominoes: cloud management-level provenance analysis with application to OpenStack. In: CNS, pp. 1–9. IEEE (2020)
48. Tabiban, A., Majumdar, S., Wang, L., Debbabi, M.: PERMON: An Openstack middleware for runtime security policy enforcement in clouds. In: CNS, pp. 1–7. IEEE (2018)
49. Tabiban, A., Zhao, H., Jarraya, Y., Pourzandi, M., Zhang, M., Wang, L.: ProvTalk: towards interpretable multi-level provenance analysis in networking functions virtualization (NFV). In: NDSS (2022)
50. Thirunavukkarasu, S.L., et al.: Modeling NFV deployment to identify the cross-level inconsistency vulnerabilities. In: CloudCom, pp. 167–174. IEEE (2019)
51. Ujcich, B.E., et al.: Cross-app poisoning in software-defined networking. In: CCS, pp. 648–663 (2018)
52. Wang, H., Yang, G., Chinprutthiwong, P., Xu, L., Zhang, Y., Gu, G.: Towards fine-grained network security forensics and diagnosis in the SDN era. In: CCS, pp. 3–16. ACM (2018)
53. Wang, Q., Hassan, W.U., Bates, A., Gunter, C.: Fear and logging in the internet of things. In: NDSS (2018)
54. Wang, Q., et al.: You are what you do: hunting stealthy malware via data provenance analysis. In: NDSS (2020)
55. Wang, Y., et al.: TenantGuard: scalable runtime verification of cloud-wide VM-level network isolation. In: NDSS (2017)

56. Wu, Y., Zhao, M., Haeberlen, A., Zhou, W., Loo, B.T.: Diagnosing missing events in distributed systems with negative provenance. In: ACM SIGCOMM, pp. 383–394 (2014)
57. Yusif, S., Hafeez-Baig, A.: A conceptual model for cybersecurity governance. J. Appl. Secur. Res. **16**(4), 490–513 (2021)
58. Zeng, J., Chua, Z.L., Chen, Y., Ji, K., Liang, Z., Mao, J.: WATSON: abstracting behaviors from audit logs via aggregation of contextual semantics. In: NDSS (2021)

Actionable Cyber Threat Intelligence
for Automated Incident Response

Cristoffer Leite[1,2]([✉])([iD]), Jerry den Hartog[1], Daniel Ricardo dos Santos[2],
and Elisa Costante[2]

[1] Eindhoven University of Technology, 5612 AZ Eindhoven, The Netherlands
{c.leite.da.silva,j.d.hartog}@tue.nl
[2] Forescout Technologies, 5612 AB Eindhoven, The Netherlands

Abstract. Applying Cyber Threat Intelligence for active cyber defence, while potentially very beneficial, is currently limited to predominantly manual use. In this paper, we propose an automated approach for using Cyber Threat Intelligence during incident response by gathering Tactics, Techniques and Procedures available on intelligence reports, mapping them to network incidents, and then using this map to create attack patterns for specific threats. We consider our method actionable because it provides the operator with contextualised Cyber Threat Intelligence related to observed network incidents in the form of a ranked list of potential related threats, all based on patterns matched with the incidents. We evaluate our approach with publicly available samples of different malware families. Our analysis of the results shows that our method can reliably match network incidents with intelligence reports and relate them to these threats. The approach allows increasing the automation of its use, thus addressing one of the major limiting factors of effective use of suitable Cyber Threat Intelligence.

1   Introduction

In our ever more digital and online society, it is essential for organizations to properly protect themselves against cyber threats. Organisations under attack need to be well-informed to respond quickly and appropriately. Related information, so called Cyber Threat Intelligence (CTI), includes analysed knowledge about capabilities, infrastructure, methods, and victims of cyber threat actors. As such, this information has the potential to help organizations to better perform threat detection, incident response, threat hunting, and risk management as well as to make strategic decisions to protect themselves. However, current methods of linking incidents with CTI reports are not sufficiently actionable; they require a lot of effort of the operator.

Threat Intelligence can generally be divided in different groups based on their level of detail and long-term use, including Technical and Tactical [1]. Examples of Technical CTI include Indicator of Compromise (IoC) such as hashes of infected files, known malicious IP addresses and domain names. For detection,

© The Author(s), under exclusive license to Springer Nature Switzerland AG 2022
H. P. Reiser and M. Kyas (Eds.): NordSec 2022, LNCS 13700, pp. 368–385, 2022.
https://doi.org/10.1007/978-3-031-22295-5_20

Technical CTI is easy to use: IoCs can be matched with network traffic or endpoint information in real-time to generate alerts that indicate a network intrusion is taking place. However, this relies on aspects that are easy for attackers to change, for example by simply recompiling a malware with slightly different code or acquiring new infrastructure. This limits how helpful such CTI use is for the detection of more sophisticated or long-term attacks.

Tactical intelligence describes not just isolated IoCs but also the Tactics, Techniques and Procedures (TTPs) used by adversaries. TTPs are useful for incident response because they are harder for an attacker to change than IoCs. The problem with Tactical intelligence is that, although there are plenty initiatives for standardisation and usage of CTI, there currently is no easy, automatic way to incorporate its use in threat detection systems. This results in a lack of automated Tactical CTI use on incident response [2–4]; most incident response teams use this CTI manually if at all.

Aiming to make incident response more actionable, we investigate the following research question: **RQ:** Can the incident processing flow of an analyst be automated by employing CTI? Refining our scope leads us to the following sub questions: **SQ1:** Can related CTI provide valuable context for alerts, making them more actionable? **SQ2:** Can available CTI be matched with behavior observed in the network automatically?

To answer these questions we present a solution that automates most of the process of matching available CTI with observed network events. We build intelligence patterns for threats by gathering relevant CTI reports and mapping their included Tactics, Techniques and Procedures (TTPs) to network observable events. In addition to automation, this allow work to be done as soon as a threat becomes known, rather then when under attack. We evaluate the approach on samples of different families of malware/ransomware [5] and several open source CTI feeds and find that our approach is capable of building patterns that capture the families with high accuracy and thus provide context to network incidents based on intelligence reports.

Our core contributions include automating an important step in the response by matching CTI to network incidents. We demonstrate that it is feasible to accurately distinguish between malware families with simple patterns extracted from CTI information. By making high-level CTI more actionable we also increase its value creating an added incentive to create and share it.

The remainder of this paper is organised as follows. Section 2 introduces how Cyber Threat Intelligence is currently used, state-of-the-art in actionability and automation for CTI and analyses the gap that still remains. Section 3 presents our methodology and its core components. Section 4 describes our implementation, validation experiments and the experimental results. Finally, Sect. 5 highlights our conclusions and future work directions.

2   Background and Related Work

In this section we sketch how CTI is currently used in network intrusion detection, also defining some related terminology, and then review related work.

2.1 Current Situation

Figure 1 shows an example setup of a Network Intrusion Detection System (NIDS) generating alerts[1] about incidents for analysis while using some form of CTI. Blacklists are usually implemented by sub modules of the NIDS, while the event correlation could also be implemented externally by either a Security Information and Event Management (SIEM), which mostly generates alerts by agregating and correlating events, or a Security Orchestration, Automation and Response (SOAR), which does that but also includes response capabilities.

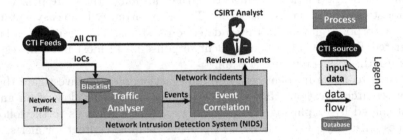

Fig. 1. A diagram of a simple NIDS solution

To identify attacks based on incidents provided by the NIDS, a Cyber Security Incident Response Team (CSIRT) usually resorts to CTI available on a Threat Intelligence Platform (TIP) or in specific intelligence feeds. CTI is usually aggregated in the form of reports related to a threat or a campaign. A report may also contain other reports. While doing a Threat Intelligence and Attack Path Analysis, for example, it is necessary to acquire information about 'observables' from a TIP to see if they match known IoCs [4].

Observables are features of events monitored in a network. When an atomic observable, like an IP address or payload hash, is potentially linked to security breaches, it is called an Indicator of Compromise (IoC). IoCs are thus low-level, non-contextual CTI that allow incident response to be executed in an (semi-)automated manner, e.g. through blacklisting, which also holds as a valid approach even during surges of data to analyse. But for high-level CTI, such as that providing tactical and operational attack information, analysts manually review events in network incidents and compare them with reports from CTI feeds. This manual approach is typical for active defence using high-level CTI [2].

The more contextual information provided by these high-level CTI is needed in the majority of the cases to properly analyse incidents. The manual process to acquire required intelligence becomes a problem especially when attack campaigns flood the NIDS with information, creating surges of data to be analysed. Some automation is needed, or at least the ability to perform as much of the manual work a-priori rather than having to wait for an attack to occur. This

---

[1] We use 'alerts' as a general term, and when more specific we use 'events' for basic alerts and network 'incidents' for the alerts after correlation.

would improve the capability of responding to threats, and allow the CSIRT to better act on the intelligence received. Automating its application on incident response would make use of CTI more actionable [3].

2.2 Related Work

Most of the recent work on CTI focuses on managing IoCs [6], gathering unstructured Open-Source CTI (OSCTI) to extract Indicators [7], Tactics, Techniques and Procedures from them [8,9], with a broad usage of Natural Language Processing (NLP) for these cases [8,10], and assessing the quality of OSCTI [11–14] or the formats used by them [15]. Some focus on generating CTI from network events for specialised use case scenarios [16], and improving visualisation of CTI.

There is a broad acceptance that there is a need for more semi-automated or actionable forms of consuming Cyber Threat Intelligence during incident response [2–4] and that automation would add great value to it [13,14]. Actionability in this context is the capability of reacting during network incidents while using the knowledge provided by CTI. In this context, J. Liu et al. [17] propose a trigger mechanism to create an actionable CTI discovery system. It focuses on portraying the relationship between IoCs and campaign stages to generate actionable CTI from intelligence reports by using NLP.

For implementation of actionable CTI on defense, Amthor et al. [18] propose the integration of the information from intelligence platforms into Security-Policy-Controlled Systems (SPCS). With two approaches to integrate detection and response scenarios: A direct integration with intelligence obtained is received and processed directly by security-critical systems, and an indirect one where it is integrated to the security tools used by the organisation. The work by Serketzis et al. [19] combines a preparation step with application of CTI to improve the usage of IoCs on Incident Response. It focus on revealing patterns of malicious activities by correlating IoCs from multiple malware instances to CTI reports.

A few different approaches aim to automate the use of CTI by linking it to TTPs or further matching attacker behaviour. Legoy et al. [20] automate the extraction of TTPs from cyber threat reports using ATT&CK. Similarly, Husari et al. [21] use NLP and Information retrieval (IR) for text mining to extract threat actions based on semantic relations, constructing attack patterns with TTPs and kill chain phases. On the work by Li et al. [22], they extract structured attack behavior graphs from CTI reports to identify the applied techniques, aggregating these reports into behavioural graphs of techniques. Another close method is the service provided by Hybrid Analysis [23]. They execute a malware sample in a sandboxed environment, generate a list of processes executions and then correlate these with host-based TTPs in a simple list.

2.3 Gap Analysis

To achieve CTI-based network protection one needs to: (1) a-prioi perform threat analysis based on available CTI and (2) map relevant threats (TTPs) found to detectable network incidents. Then at runtime, (3) matching incidents to the threats and their related CTI enables use of this CTI in (4) incident response.

Many solutions exist to create and share CTI, but as noted above, automation of its use is limited. In the related work above we limit our scope by considering our goal of automation of the incident processing flow. A considerable amount of the presented works prioritise generating better formats, analysing existing ones or suggesting new capabilities to sharing platforms to allow using CTI with response mechanisms. A small number actually tries to use available CTI in a more automated way, but even those do not focus on applying it to incident response. For the papers and tools we consider most relevant, Table 1 shows which of the four steps listed they contribute to. For example, Hybrid Anaylsis [23] considers TTP map and CTI match though in an offline host-based setting, while the graphs of Li et al. [22] help in automating threat mapping. Yet a clear gap where mapping TTPs gathered from matched CTI or from Threat Analysis assessments does not overlap with the application of them in incident response.

Table 1. Gap analysis of current approaches for automated and actionable CTI

	Threat analysis automation	TTP map	CTI match	Incident response automation
Zhu et al. [9]	✓	–	✓	–
Legoy et al. [20]	✓	✓	–	–
Husari et al. [21]	✓	✓	–	–
Li et al. [22]	✓	✓	–	–
Hybrid analysis [23]	–	✓	–	✓

From the discussion above and to the best of our knowledge, there is not any work that suggests a methodology to increase the automation and the actionability of available CTI on incident response by linking known attacker behaviour from reports to network incidents.

3   Methodology

In this section, we describe our solution for adding automation and actionability to the use of high-level CTI in network intrusion detection and incident response. As depicted in Fig. 2, we introduce an Intelligence Pattern Orchestrator (IPO) that will enrich network incidents with related high-level CTI. This directly provides the analyst with contextual information for those incidents. Related incidents matching the same pattern can also be grouped to help further reduce the workload.

The information flow of the IPO detailed in Fig. 3 is divided into four main steps that cover pattern creation and their use. Creation of patterns is triggered by threats and reliable related indicators becoming known. These indicators can, for example, come directly from sandboxed samples of a threat or from a TIP where initial related CTI is found.

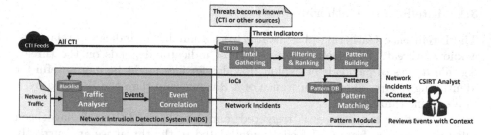

Fig. 2. Intelligence Pattern Orchestrator for actionable CTI on network events

The first step is the **Intelligence Gathering**, in which the indicators are matched with available CTI. Next in the **CTI Filtering and Ranking** phase low-level CTI is filtered out and provided to the NIDS for blacklisting as in the current situation (Fig. 1). High-level CTI are ranked based on their usefulness for network intrusion detection. All sufficiently high scoring CTI reports can be used to build patterns, but optionally the ranking can be presented to an analyst for manual adjustments and exclusion of certain CTI reports. In the following **Pattern Building** step, the CTI is matched with TTPs from MITRE ATT&CK and mapped into network detectable events. We combine these events into a pattern, which is stored along with related information.

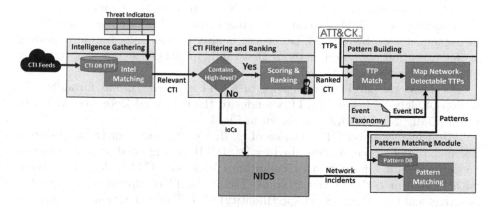

Fig. 3. The information flow of our solution

The created patterns are used in the final step, **Pattern Matching**, triggered by the detection of new incidents. These new incidents are compared with the stored patterns and matching incidents are enriched with the related information from the pattern.

3.1   Intelligence Gathering

The Intelligence Gathering phase starts from a number of indicators related to a known threat. The relevance of a type of indicator depends on the threat, e.g. file hashes of payloads or exploit downloader files might be more useful for identifying reports about an instance of a Ransomware than the IPs used by it in a specific campaign.

At the time the process is triggered, our data base (TIP) will have been filled with reports from CTI feeds, some related to the threat we are currently considering. With an initial list of indicators related to a threat, we select all CTI reports in the our database that include at least one of the indicators on the initial list (r_0). If these reports include additional indicators, we add these to our list and iterate this process until no new reports are added. This results in r_R the least fixed point of $r_R = r_0 \cup \{r_t \in TIP \mid flat(r_R) \cap flat(r_t) \neq \emptyset\}$ with $flat(r) = \{c \in r\} \cup \bigcup_{r' \in R} flat(r')$ the report flattened to a set of CTI.

3.2   CTI Filtering and Ranking

Amongst the Relevant CTI (r_R) we need to find those reports that are most useful for building patterns in the orchestrator. To that end, we first filter out reports that only contain low-level CTI. The IoCs included in these reports are provided to the NIDS (for addition to blacklists as in existing solutions) as shown in Fig. 3. But these reports are not used when building patterns as they do not include behavioural information. Next, we rank the remaining ones on their usefulness for linking to and providing contextual information for network incidents detected by a NIDS, i.e. on the quality of their information regarding attack execution plans and methods that can help identify an ongoing attack by observing the network.

To define the level of intelligence of a CTI c ($level(c)$), and formalize the notion of high- vs low-level CTI, we refer to the expanded Detection Maturity Level (DML) Model [24,25] as shown in Fig. 4.

We define low-level CTI as those of DML 1 or 2, equivalent to the group of Technical intelligence, as described by [1]. (DML 0 is ignored as it is does not contain relevant information by definition.) High-level CTI is defined as those with DML 3 or higher, which includes Tactical (TTPs), Operational (Attacker Strategy and Goals) and Strategic (Identity) CTI. This separation also matches with the different perspectives of CTI described by the authors on [15], where IoCs are artifacts, TTPs describe the attacker behaviour, and the higher levels indicate the response.

For reports, we define their level based on the highest level of CTI included in the report ($level(r) = max_{c \in flat(r)} level(c)$), so a report is low-level if it only contains low-level CTI and high-level if it contains at least one high-level CTI.

Not all high-level information is useful for network-based detection. If related to network detectable events, Tactical (TTPs) CTI might be useful to capture the attacker's behaviour detectable by a NIDS. Operational (Goals and Strategy) and Strategic (Identity) CTI on the other hand can be useful for the analist in

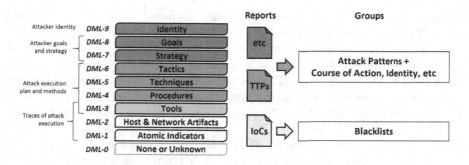

Fig. 4. Filtering CTI with the Detection Maturity Level Model [25]

planning a response. We thus need to find which TTPs are *network-mappable*, i.e. related to network detectable events.

As TTPs are typically expressed in term of the MITRE ATT&CK framework [20–23], we use that framework to find which TTPs are network-mappable, as described in more detail in Subsect. 4.1. We assume that the robustness of that framework allows an adequate coverage of up-to-date TTPs. In this section we simply assume that we have a subset *NM* of all CTI that are network mappable TTP entries in the MITRE ATT&CK matrix.

The initial ranking score assigned to reports is how many network-mappable TTPs they contain, $rank(r) = \#\{c \in flat(r) \mid c \in NM\}$. In principle, any report with a sufficiently high score can be used to build patterns. However, after the automated ranking, security analysts can manually check the list of reports related to an attack and adjust the rank accordingly, thus adapting which reports will be used in the pattern building. This (optional) review step is included because one of the problems with OSCTI is the quality of its reports in regards to coverage and inter-report conciseness [11–14].

By the end of this step, the output is a ranked list of reports r_F that include network-mappable CTI which will be used for the creation of the attack patterns. The next step will be the translation of r_F into the pattern itself. Note that the actual scores are only relevant for presentation to and evaluation by the analyst in the review step. For the Pattern Building, it only matters whether reports are included or not; $r_F = \{r \in r_R \mid rank(r) > threshold\}$.

3.3   Pattern Building

Having found TTPs that might indicate a specific threat and can be detected on the network, we need to relate them to alerts that a NIDS might produce. In order to achieve that, events in the network were ordered in a taxonomy based on their types and event types were mapped to related TTPs. With that relation in place, patterns are formed from event types related to the TTPs in r_F.

An *event type* describes a network behaviour possibly related to a threat. The list of event types we consider comes from the NIDS we use in the implementation and is the result of an aggregation of many threat data resources, including

Industrial Control Systems Cyber Emergency Response Team (ICS-CERT) and NIST National Vulnerability Database (NVD). Event types are arranged in a taxonomy tree that indicates first the event source (alerts or logs), then its variations per additional level, with a short representation by an event type ID. For example, the event type ID *alert_ops_net_unscon* is an Unstable Connection network issue that falls in the operational category of alert events, while *alert_ops_net_netmis* would be a Network Misconfiguration in the same category.

To create the link between TTPs and events, we assume the event types used by the NIDS are mapped to ATT&CK, i.e. we have a mapping *N2A* from event types to sets of TTPs in *NM*. For the NIDS we use a (partial) mapping of event types was created using the four lower stages of the framework for adversarial threat hunting described by Gunter et al. [26]. Gunter's framework gives the notion of observables as being the result of a step in the attack, and being related to TTPs. To link event types to TTPs, we thus look if the type is related to these observable which belong to a TTP.

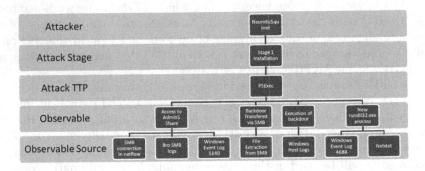

Fig. 5. Gunter's framework for adversarial threat hunting with PSExec from [26]

A NIDS could monitor possible sources of observables to detect them as network events (of a certain type). Figure 5 taken from [26] shows an example where threat hunting for PSExec (a tool used to run processes remotely using any user's credentials) gives related observables and sources that can be linked to TTPs in the higher stages. As such it provides the information needed to create the required mapping.

In our implementation, the NIDS itself is the Observable Source, and the types of events detected by it are the Observables. The TTPs are directly linkable to ATT&CK. From our analysis, each event type can be mapped to one or two Techniques on ATT&CK, e.g. a security alert related to FTP CMD buffer overflow attempt is mappable to both Network Denial Of Service (T1498) and Exploitation of Remote Services (T1210)[2].

The pattern $p = \{type \mid N2A(type) \cap flat(r_F) \neq \emptyset\}$ consist of the set of event types that are linked to some TTP in r_F. We add meta data including at least a

---

[2] https://attack.mitre.org/techniques/enterprise/.

time interval $p.T$ and the related CTI reports $p.CTI = r_R$. The analysts needs to decide the time window, possibly supported by heuristics based on the type of attack, whereas although attacks are usually short-timed [27], well-applied stealth can prolong their lifespan [28]. Other meta data can also be added such as a name, description, level of severity, etc. These optional fields can be gathered from any relevant CTI with DML 7 to 9, even if that report is not ranked for inclusion in the (detection part of the) pattern.

```
{
    "name": "Chain of Malicious Activities",
    "description": "Alerts generated by Malicious Act",
    "events": [
        alert_sec_event_type1
        alert_sec_event_type2
    ],
    "regex":[
        "[ab]"
    ],
    "base_severity": "HIGH",
    "time_window_size": "day",
    "category": "SECURITY"
}
```

Fig. 6. An example of a pattern with meta data in JSON format

Figure 6 shows an example of a pattern in JSON format (without CTI links). The event IDs are represented in a regex by a letter according to the order that they appear in the array of event types, i.e. the letter a in the example refers to *alert_sec_event_type1*. Any pattern built is added to a database of patterns for use by the Pattern Matching.

3.4 Pattern Matching

At run time, with a database of patterns in place, we aim to match patterns to incidents provided by the NIDS as shown in Fig. 2. We model incidents as non-empty sets of events. Different NIDS may represent an event e differently, but we assume they have at least: a timestamp ($e.time$), a set of involved hosts ($e.hosts$) and a type ($e.type$) as defined in the previous section. For a set of events I we then define its time: $I.time = max\{e.time \mid e \in I\}$, involved hosts $I.hosts = \cup_{e \in I} e.hosts$, and types $I.type = \{e.type \mid e \in I\}$.

To define the notion of a matching pattern we consider a pattern p, an incident I_n and a timeline of past incidents $I_1, \ldots, I_{n-1}$. For involved hosts we define related events as those involving that host within the pattern time interval; $E_h = \{e \in I_1 \cup \ldots \cup I_n \mid e.time >= i.time - p.T, h \in e.hosts\}$ and we say that such a set is a candidate set if it contains at least two different types of events from p, or if E contains only events of one type which is in p; $\#(p \cap E_h.type) >= 2 \vee E_h.type \subset p$. We say p is candidate pattern for I_n if: $\exists h \in I_n.hosts : E_h$ is a candidate set.

For candidate patterns, we define a level of coverage through *Pattern Predominance* (P), which is the percentage of all related events that have an event type from p i.e. $P(p, I_n) = max_{h \in I_n.hosts}\#\{e \in E_h \mid e.type \in p\}/\#E_h$. A pattern is considered to match if the pattern predominance is higher than some predetermined threshold which can be set according to the needs of the analyst.

This definition of match captures a heuristically determined trade-off between detection rate and false positives. It considers that for the same threat (family) many of the events are expected to of types known to belong to that threat, as captured by the requirement on Pattern Predominance. It also considers that the same event type might occur in different types of attacks. As such one of several event types from the incidents occurring in the pattern is insufficient to claim a match. However, this being the only type in the incident or, even better, having multiple shared types, provides a much stronger indication.

Any matched pattern p is added to a list (sorted by Pattern Predominance) of matches for the incident. The related meta data, such as related CTI ($p.CTI$), thus provides context to the incident.

With this methodology, an analyst or a CSIRT can use the CTI reports related to the matched patterns in a semi-automated manner for incident response. Next section evaluates this approach by implementing it and testing the creation of patterns on sandboxed scenarios.

4   Implementation and Evaluation

This section details the implementation of the methodology described in Sect. 3, with explanations about the experimental setup and results obtained.

4.1   Implementation

We detail below the formats and TIPs chosen as source for information, as well as the thresholds set for minimum compatibility of patterns.

Intelligence Gathering

TIP. Several public CTI feeds are available, like AlienVault, VirusTotal, Malware Traffic Analysis and Hybrid Analysis. There are also open-source platforms, such as MISP and OpenCTI for implementing a TIP and optionally offering its own combined info as a new feed. We run an OpenCTI instance to collect CTI reports from the four feeds mentioned above. We select OpenCTI as it has a slight focus on more contextualised information for indicators and is capable of linking them to related threats and also to their primary source (a report, a MISP event, etc.). OpenCTI is also able to consume MISP generated feeds.

Internal CTI Format. In our implementation, we use reports in the Structured Threat Information Expression (STIX) 2.1 format for its versatility in exchanging CTI and also because it is a widely adopted standard [15, 29]. In STIX we represent CTI as structured objects called STIX Domain Object (SDO)s and reports as containers called STIX Bundles.

Intel Matching. We match which reports (expressed as STIX bundles) include given threat indicators (also expressed in STIX) to get all the SDOs related to those samples.

Pattern Building

TTP Match. In this step, information about the TTPs is requested using the MITRE API and then added to the report. This is done for all network-mappable TTPs.

Mapping Events to TTPs. The NIDS can only operate network-based events, which makes it compatible with only a subset of MITRE ATT&CK. We use MITRE's diagram of techniques and their linked data sources [30] to filter the interesting ones for a NIDS. A total of 1.267 event types from the NIDS we use were mapped to network mappable techniques from both MITRE ICS and Enterprise. For each event type, only a single TTP or the two most relevant ones were assigned. As a result, only some of the mappable TTPs have related event types. Figure 7 shows a list of network mappable MITRE techniques from their Enterprise framework and a highlight for the ones mapped.

Initial Access	Persistence	Privilege Escalation	Defense Evasion	Credential Access	Discovery	Lateral Movement	Command and Control	Exfiltration	Impact
6 items	6 items	3 items	10 items	5 items	4 items	5 items	20 items*	4 items	4 items
Drive-by Compromise	Account Manipulation	Exploitation for Privilege Escalation	Connection Proxy	Account Manipulation	Network Service Scanning	Exploitation of Remote Services	Commonly Used Port	Data Transfer Size Limits	Data Destruction
Hardware Additions	Browser Extensions	Valid Accounts	DCShadow	Brute Force	Network Share Discovery	Internal Spearphishing	Connection Proxy	Exfiltration Over Alternative Protocol	Endpoint Denial of Service
Spearphishing Attachment	Port Knocking	Web Shell	File Deletion	Forced Authentication	Network Sniffing	Remote Desktop Protocol	Custom Command and Control Protocol	Exfiltration Over Command and Control Channel	Network Denial of Service
Spearphishing Link	Redundant Access		Install Root Certificate	LLMNR/NBT NS Poisoning and Relay	Remote System Discovery	Remote File Copy	...	Scheduled Transfer	Transmitted Data Manipulation
Spearphishing via Service	Valid Accounts		Obfuscated Files or Information	Network Sniffing		Remote Services	Remote File Copy		
Valid Accounts	Web Shell		Port Knocking				Standard Application Layer Protocol		
			Redundant Access				Standard Cryptographic Protocol		
			Template Injection				Standard Non Application Layer Protocol		
			Valid Accounts				Uncommonly Used Port		
			Web Service				Web Service		

Fig. 7. Network detectable techniques from MITRE with the ones used in blue (Color figure online)

Pattern Matching Module

Pattern Matching. The threshold for pattern predominance, used to determine pattern compatibility in pattern matching (see Subsect. 3.4), is set to 0.5 based our empirical experimentation. Thus patterns with at least 50% of predominance ($P \geq 0.5$) are considered as being matched with high confidence during the pattern analysis, and medium confidence if there is only one event type match with $t = 1$. Note that low-confidence approximates, i.e. candidate patterns with low predominance ($P < 0.5$), can be suggested for analysts if needed (clearly marked with as being low-confidence).

4.2   Experimental Setup

Dataset. For our experiments, we use a dataset consisting of 27 sand-boxed samples of ransomware from 4 different families: Cerber, Crysis, REvil/Sodinokibi and WannaCry [5], with a total of 78.5 GB in PCAPs. Each sample refers to an instance of a ransomware from one of the families. These PCAPS represent the network traffic and the I/O operations executed by these malwares while encrypting a network shared directory.

In selecting these samples we considered: malware and more specifically ransomware are a growing threat with industry-wide *impact*, malware families with a considerable number of samples in an *open dataset* with good adoption allow proper reproducible validation, and *related OSCTI data* must be available.

From the reports matched with these malware families, 74.13% included some TTPs, with 25.86% having only one. 15.51% had explicit information about malware instances. Files were the most common indicator, whereas email addresses the most rare ones. All the reports contained some observables which belong to DML 1–2, and only 8.76% had any CTI level 7–8.

Evaluation Metrics. In the tests, we want to verify if a pattern made out of a CTI report is strong enough to define and match a sample from a malware family rather than a single instance, and if it is unique enough to differentiate malware families. To evaluate the suitability of our methodology, we then want to check if the patterns: (1) Match same-family samples with a high score. (2) Do not match different families or match with a low enough score.

Mapping Malwares to Patterns. We divide our malware families in two groups: One is the group of sample with indicators that point to reports with higher level of CTI available, which will be then used to generate the initial patterns. Based on observations about the available CTI related to them, we selected Cerber and Sodinokibi/REvil as the sources for the attack patterns as part of the first group. And the second group consists of all samples that will be used for the validation, including the ones used to create the patterns themselves.

Figure 8 shows the process of mapping the samples from Cerber to related CTI and extracting network mappable TTPs from them. Sodinokibi/REvil followed a similar flow. To create actionable information out of reports related to

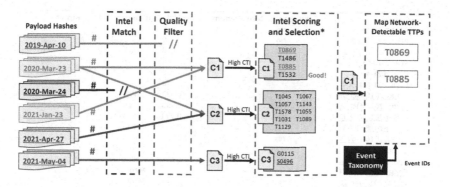

Fig. 8. Mapping Cerber samples to related high-level network-detectable CTI

these malwares, we use as a starting point a list of hashes related to the malware payloads from each sample. It is possible to match which reports as STIX bundles include these payloads to get the SDOs related to those samples. These reports are then filtered based on the level of CTI they have, and then ranked based on two scores: The percentage of related payload hashes they include from that initial list, and the amount of contextual CTI on these reports. In the case of similar reports, they can be grouped based on their related SDOs.

In our case, we decided to use the hashes from the samples themselves as the starting point to search for related CTI in a way of validating if the patterns can detect related samples, but as stated before, there is also the possibility of extracting this information from other sources, such as the reports themselves.

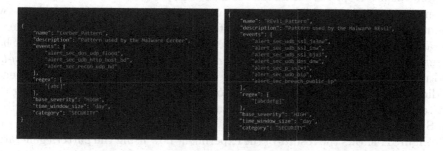

Fig. 9. Final patterns generated for cerber and REvil

Using the first group, we generated patterns for the malware families and then added them to our database. Figure 9 shows the resulting patterns. We replay the samples from that malware family in a network monitored by the NIDS, which sends the events to the pattern module for scoring and validation. After that, we run the same experiment again using the samples from all other families as a validation step. Next section shows the results of our experiments.

Dataset	Candidate Pattern	Predominance (ε/#)	Confidence	Final Result
REvil-2019-Apr-10	No	0	-	No
REvil-2020-Jan-23	No	0	-	No
REvil-2020-Mar-23	No	0.012	-	No
REvil-2020-Mar-24	No	0	-	No
REvil-2021-Apr-27	No	0	-	No
REvil-2021-May-04		0		
Cerber-2016-Oct-03	Yes	0.988	High	MATCH
Cerber-2016-Oct-04	Yes	0.995	High	MATCH
Cerber-2016-Oct-12	Yes	0.993	High	MATCH
Cerber-2016-Oct-31	Yes	0.994	High	MATCH
Cerber-2016-Nov-28	Yes	0.995	High	MATCH
Cerber-2016-Dec-11	Yes	1	Medium	MATCH
Cerber-2016-Dec-22	Yes	0.995	High	MATCH
Cerber-2017-Jan-04	Yes	1	Medium	MATCH
Cerber-2017-Jan-20	Yes	1	Medium	MATCH
Cerber-2017-Jan-24	Yes	0.995	High	MATCH
Cerber-2017-Feb-06	Yes	0.995	High	MATCH
Crysis-2016-Dec-19	No	0	-	No
Crysis-2017-Jan-01	No	0	-	No
Crysis-2018-Nov-19	No	0	-	No
Crysis-2018-Dec-27	No	0	-	No
Crysis-2020-Jun-18	No	0	-	No
Crysis-2020-Aug-20	No	0	-	No
Crysis-2020-Aug-23	No	0	-	No
WannaCry-2017-May-16	No	0	-	No
WannaCry-2021-Aug-09	No	0	-	No
WannaCry-2021-May-04	No	0	-	No

Fig. 10. Final results for detection with Cerber

4.3   Results

Figure 10 shows the results using the pattern generated for Cerber. Out of the eleven samples from Cerber instances, all of them matched with the pattern, we define eight of them as high confidence matches, because they have at least two events types matching and $t \geq 0.5$, and the remaining two as medium confidence because there is only one event type match, but $t = 1$. At the same time, there has been no match with other malware samples. One sample, *REvil-2021-May-04*, did not have any anomalous events detected by our NIDS, and by consequence it did not appear as anomalous on our observations. We ran our tests using the patterns presented and analysed the results from the main experiment described on Subsect. 4.2.

Figure 11 shows the results of the experiment now using the pattern generated for REvil. With the exception of the same sample as mentioned above, all the others matched the pattern created with high confidence. As mentioned before, the sample that did not match was not detected as anomalous. This may be due to the map presented on Fig. 7 not being broad enough to include events related to its incidents. In this test, there has been also one erroneous match with a sample from the WannaCry ransomware family. All the other samples did not match with the REvil pattern.

The detection achieved a False Negative Rate of 5.88% when considering the REvil sample with no events detected as incidents by the NIDS. At the same

Dataset	Candidate Pattern	Predominance (ε/#)	Confidence	Final Result
REvil-2019-Apr-10	Yes	0.625	High	MATCH
REvil-2020-Jan-23	Yes	0.972	High	MATCH
REvil-2020-Mar-23	Yes	0.662	High	MATCH
REvil-2020-Mar-24	Yes	0.699	High	MATCH
REvil-2021-Apr-27	Yes	0.585	High	MATCH
REvil-2021-May-04		0		
Cerber-2016-Oct-03	No	0.006	-	No
Cerber-2016-Oct-04	No	0	-	No
Cerber-2016-Oct-12	No	0	-	No
Cerber-2016-Oct-31	No	0	-	No
Cerber-2016-Nov-28	No	0	-	No
Cerber-2016-Dec-11	No	0	-	No
Cerber-2016-Dec-22	No	0	-	No
Cerber-2017-Jan-04	No	0	-	No
Cerber-2017-Jan-20	No	0	-	No
Cerber-2017-Jan-24	No	0	-	No
Cerber-2017-Feb-06	No	0	-	No
Crysis-2016-Dec-19	No	0	-	No
Crysis-2017-Jan-01	No	0	-	No
Crysis-2018-Nov-19	Yes	0.074	Low	No
Crysis-2018-Dec-27	No	0	-	No
Crysis-2020-Jun-18	No	0.500	-	No
Crysis-2020-Aug-20	No	0.035	-	No
Crysis-2020-Aug-23	No	0.250	-	No
WannaCry-2017-May-16	Yes	0.162	Low	No
WannaCry-2021-Aug-09	Yes	0.705	High	MATCH
WannaCry-2021-May-04	No	0.333	-	No

Fig. 11. Final results for detection on REvil

time, the detection achieved a False Positive Rate of 2.77%. The results give a Detection Rate of 94.11% with an accuracy of 96.22%.

5 Conclusion

The work proposed in this paper aims to increase the actionability of using CTI on incident response by automatically relating incidents to relevant CTI. Our methodology helps to define a structured way of consuming available CTI by linking them to known threats and their expected behaviour. It enables the use of the gathered intelligence by matching its attack patterns with network events related to incidents.

The evaluation shows that it is possible to correlate CTI with observed behavior with good precision, positively answering the sub questions SQ1 and SQ2. Considering the main research question we have to note a significant limitation we encountered; the scarcity of quality high-level OSCTI. This reduces the scope of our evaluation and the ability to fully answer RQ. However, having shown linking CTI and network behavior can be automated we both increase the value of such CTI, creating an incentive to generate and share it, as well as open an avenue to reducing the effort needed to produce CTI. As future work, we plan to use our results to generate CTI reports out of the network incidents. We also plan to create an advanced version of our patterns that include event chains to analyse ordered multi-host incidents.

References

1. Chismon, D., Ruks, M.: Threat intelligence: collecting, analysing, evaluating. MWR InfoSecurity **3**(2), 36–42 (2015)
2. Schlette, D.: Cyber threat intelligence. In: Jajodia, S., Samarati, P., Yung, M. (eds.) Encyclopedia of Cryptography, Security and Privacy, pp. 1–3. Springer, Heidelberg (2021). https://doi.org/10.1007/978-3-642-27739-9_1716-1
3. Nespoli, P., Papamartzivanos, D., Mármol, F.G., Kambourakis, G.: Optimal countermeasures selection against cyber attacks: a comprehensive survey on reaction frameworks. IEEE Commun. Surv. Tutor. **20**(2), 1361–1396 (2017)
4. Groenewegen, A., Janssen, J.S.: TheHive project: the maturity of an open-source security incident response platform (2021)
5. Berrueta, E., Morato, D., Magaña, E., Izal, M.: Open repository for the evaluation of ransomware detection tools. IEEE Access **8**, 65658–65669 (2020)
6. Gao, Y., Xiaoyong, L.I., Hao, P.E.N.G., Fang, B., Yu, P.: HinCTI: a cyber threat intelligence modeling and identification system based on heterogeneous information network. In: IEEE Transactions on Knowledge and Data Engineering, p. 1 (2020)
7. Liao, X., Yuan, K., Wang, X., Li, Z., Xing, L., Beyah, R.: Acing the IOC game: toward automatic discovery and analysis of open-source cyber threat intelligence. In: Proceedings of the 2016 ACM SIGSAC Conference on Computer and Communications Security (CCS 2016). Association for Computing Machinery, New York, pp. 755–766 (2016). https://doi.org/10.1145/2976749.2978315
8. Gao, P., et al.: Enabling efficient cyber threat hunting with cyber threat intelligence. In: 2021 IEEE 37th International Conference on Data Engineering (ICDE), pp. 193–204 (2021). ISSN: 2375-026X
9. Zhu, Z., Dumitras, T.: ChainSmith: automatically learning the semantics of malicious campaigns by mining threat intelligence reports. In: 2018 IEEE European Symposium on Security and Privacy (EuroS&P), pp. 458–472. IEEE (2018)
10. Afzaliseresht, N., Miao, Y., Michalska, S., Liu, Q., Wang, H.: From logs to stories: human-centred data mining for cyber threat intelligence. IEEE Access **8**, 19089–19099 (2020)
11. Tundis, Andrea, Ruppert, Samuel, Mühlhäuser, Max: On the automated assessment of open-source cyber threat intelligence sources. In: Krzhizhanovskaya, V.V., et al. (eds.) ICCS 2020. LNCS, vol. 12138, pp. 453–467. Springer, Cham (2020). https://doi.org/10.1007/978-3-030-50417-5_34
12. Noor, U., Anwar, Z., Altmann, J., Rashid, Z.: Customer-oriented ranking of cyber threat intelligence service providers. Electron. Commer. Res. Appl. **41**, 100976 (2020)
13. Brown, R., Lee, R.M.: 2021 SANS Cyber Threat Intelligence (CTI) Survey, p. 19 (2021)
14. Berndt, Anzel, Ophoff, Jacques: Exploring the value of a cyber threat intelligence function in an organization. In: Drevin, Lynette, Von Solms, Suné, Theocharidou, Marianthi (eds.) WISE 2020. IAICT, vol. 579, pp. 96–109. Springer, Cham (2020). https://doi.org/10.1007/978-3-030-59291-2_7
15. Schlette, D., Caselli, M., Pernul, G.: A comparative study on cyber threat intelligence: the security incident response perspective. IEEE Commun. Surv. Tutor. **23**(4), 2525–2556 (2021)
16. Gong, S., Lee, C.: Cyber threat intelligence framework for incident response in an energy cloud platform. Electronics **10**(3), 239 (2021)

17. Liu, J., et al.: TriCTI: an actionable cyber threat intelligence discovery system via trigger-enhanced neural network. Cybersecurity **5**(1), 8 (2022). https://doi.org/10. 1186/s42400-022-00110-3
18. Amthor, P., Fischer, D., Kühnhauser, W.E., Stelzer, D.: Automated cyber threat sensing and responding: integrating threat intelligence into security-policy-controlled systems. In: Proceedings of the 14th International Conference on Availability, Reliability and Security, pp. 1–10 (2019). https://doi.org/10.1145/3339252. 3340509
19. Serketzis, N., Katos, V., Ilioudis, C., Baltatzis, D., Pangalos, G.: Improving forensic triage efficiency through cyber threat intelligence. Future Internet **11**(7), 162 (2019)
20. Legoy, V., Caselli, M., Seifert, C., Peter, A.: Automated retrieval of ATT&CK tactics and techniques for cyber threat reports. arXiv preprint arXiv:2004.14322 (2020)
21. Husari, G., Al-Shaer, E., Ahmed, M., Chu, B., Niu, X.: TTPDrill: automatic and accurate extraction of threat actions from unstructured text of CTI sources. In: Proceedings of the 33rd Annual Computer Security Applications Conference, pp. 103–115 (2017)
22. Li, Z., Zeng, J., Chen, Y., Liang, Z.: AttacKG: constructing technique knowledge graph from cyber threat intelligence reports. In: Atluri, V., Di Pietro, R., Jensen, C.D., Meng, W. (eds) Computer Security – ESORICS 2022. LNCS, vol. 13554, pp. 589–609. Springer, Cham (2022). https://doi.org/10.1007/978-3-031-17140-6_29
23. Hybrid Analysis: https://www.hybrid-analysis.com/
24. Stillions, R.: The DML model (2014). http://ryanstillions.blogspot.com/2014/04/ the-dml-model_21.html
25. Bromander, S., Jøsang, A., Eian, M.: Semantic cyberthreat modelling. In: STIDS, pp. 74–78 (2016)
26. Gunter, D.: Hunting with rigor: quantifying the breadth, depth and threat intelligence coverage of a threat hunt in industrial control system environments, p. 21 (2018)
27. Cole, E.: Advanced Persistent Threat: Understanding the Danger and How to Protect Your Organization. Newnes, London (2012)
28. Ghafir, I., Prenosil, V.: Advanced persistent threat attack detection: an overview. Int. J. Adv. Comput. Netw. Secur. **4**(4), 5054 (2014)
29. Sauerwein, C., Fischer, D., Rubsamen, M., Rosenberger, G., Stelzer, D., Breu, R.: From threat data to actionable intelligence: an exploratory analysis of the intelligence cycle implementation in cyber threat intelligence sharing platforms. In: The 16th International Conference on Availability, Reliability and Security, pp. 1–9 (2021). https://doi.org/10.1145/3465481.3470048
30. MITRE: MITRE ATT&CK techniques mapped to data sources. Tech. Rep. (2019). http://attack.mitre.org/docs/attack_roadmap_2019.pdf

Author Index

Printed in the United States
by Baker & Taylor Publisher Services